ATROCITY, PUNISHMENT, AND INTERNATIONAL LAW

In *Atrocity, Punishment, and International Law*, Mark Drumbl rethinks how perpetrators of atrocity crimes should be punished. After first reviewing the sentencing practices of courts and tribunals that censure genocide, crimes against humanity, and war crimes, he concludes that these practices fall short of the goals that international criminal law ascribes to punishment, in particular retribution and deterrence. This raises the question whether international prosecutorial and correctional preferences are as effective as we hope. Drumbl argues that the pursuit of accountability for extraordinary atrocity crimes should not uncritically adopt the methods and assumptions of ordinary liberal criminal law. He calls for fresh thinking to confront the collective nature of mass atrocity and the disturbing reality that individual membership in group-based killings is often not maladaptive or deviant behavior but, rather, adaptive or conformist behavior. This book deploys a bold, and adventurously pluralist, interpretation of classical notions of cosmopolitanism to advance the frame of international criminal law to a broader construction of atrocity law and a more meaningful understanding of justice. Drumbl concludes by offering concrete reforms. He urges contextual responses to atrocity that welcome bottom-up perspectives, including restorative, reparative, and reintegrative traditions that may differ from the adversarial Western criminal trial.

Mark A. Drumbl is the Class of 1975 Alumni Professor at the School of Law, Washington and Lee University, where he also serves as Director of the Transnational Law Institute. He has held visiting appointments at Oxford University (University College), Trinity College Dublin, Vanderbilt University, and the University of Ottawa. In 2005, his academic work received the Association of American Law Schools Scholarly Papers Prize and, in 2003, the International Association of Penal Law (U.S. Section) Best Article Prize. He studied at McGill University (B.A., M.A.), Institut d'études politiques, University of Toronto (LL.B.), and Columbia University (LL.M., J.S.D.). When he was a graduate student at Columbia Law School in 1998, his work on Rwanda received the Gitelson/Meyerowitz Human Rights Prize. In 2001, another of his publications on Rwanda was heralded as "exemplary" in its treatment of "the possibilities of the coexistence of victims and survivors within the same society after the event" in the *Times Literary Supplement*.

Dr. Drumbl has lectured and published extensively on international law, human rights, and criminal justice. He has worked in the Rwandan prisons and as defense counsel in Rwanda's genocide trials. He has been an expert on international law in litigation in the U.S. federal courts, has taught in a variety of places – including Pakistan and Brazil – and, from 1994 to 1995, served as judicial clerk to a justice of the Supreme Court of Canada. Drumbl's legal practice experience also includes representation of the Canadian Chief-of-Defense Staff with regard to the Royal Commission investigating military wrongdoing in the United Nations Somalia Mission. He is a frequent media commentator.

Atrocity, Punishment, and International Law

MARK A. DRUMBL

Class of 1975 Alumni Professor
Director, Transnational Law Institute
School of Law, Washington and Lee University

CAMBRIDGE
UNIVERSITY PRESS

CAMBRIDGE UNIVERSITY PRESS
Cambridge, New York, Melbourne, Madrid, Cape Town, Singapore,
São Paulo, Delhi, Dubai, Tokyo, Mexico City

Cambridge University Press
The Edinburgh Building, Cambridge CB2 8RU, UK

Published in the United States of America by Cambridge University Press, New York

www.cambridge.org
Information on this title: www.cambridge.org/9780521691383

First published 2007

A catalogue record for this publication is available from the British Library

Library of Congress Cataloging in Publication Data
Drumbl, Mark A.
Atrocity, punishment, and international law / Mark A. Drumbl.
p. cm.
Includes bibliographical references and index.
isbn-13: 978-0-521-87089-4 (hardback)
isbn-10: 0-521-87089-5 (hardback)
isbn-13: 978-0-521-69138-3 (pbk.)
isbn-10: 0-521-69138-9 (pbk.)
1. Crimes against humanity. 2. Atrocities. 3. Criminal liability (International law)
4. International criminal courts. 5. Criminal justice, Administration of. I. Title.
k5301.d78 2007
345.0235 – dc22 2006035762

ISBN 978-0-521-87089-4 Hardback
ISBN 978-0-521-69138-3 Paperback

Dedicated to Victims, and Survivors, of Humanity's Inhumanity

Contents

Preface and Acknowledgments

How do we, and how should we, punish someone who commits genocide, crimes against humanity, or discrimination-based war crimes? These questions – the former descriptive, the latter normative – are the focus of this book.

These questions have received much less attention than they deserve. Although international criminal law has gone a long way to convict individuals for perpetrating atrocity, it has traversed far less creative ground in terms of conceptualizing how to sanction them. Scholars, too, have been remiss. Surprisingly little work has been undertaken that explores how and why criminal justice institutions punish atrocity crimes and whether the sentences levied by these institutions actually attain the proffered rationales. Furthermore, there is little empirical work that assesses whether what international tribunals doctrinally say they are doing actually has a consistent and predictable effect on the quantum of sentence.

In this book, I hope to respond to these lacunae and, through this endeavor, make three contributions.

First, to present data regarding how and why local, national, and international institutions punish genocide, crimes against humanity, and war crimes. Although I include information from many atrocities, the focus centers on three in particular: Rwanda, the former Yugoslavia, and World War II/the Holocaust. My methodology involves a review of positive law instruments, sentences, and sentencing jurisprudence. This part of the book (Chapters 3 and 4) is supplemented with extensive citations. This research serves important compilation and reference purposes for practitioners and scholars and, thereby, responds to the gap in the literature regarding data on sentencing and evaluative review thereof.

Second, to explore whether extant methods of sentencing actually attain the affirmed objectives of punishment. In Chapter 6, the heart of the book, I conclude that there is an overall shortfall, although certain rationales are better served than others.

Third, to move the dialogue from diagnosis to remedy. I argue that the punishment of extraordinary international crimes should not uncritically adopt the methods and assumptions of ordinary liberal criminal law that currently underpin international courts and tribunals and seep into national institutions (even those outside of liberal traditions). Extraordinary international crimes simply are not the same as ordinary common crimes. Consequently, criminal law designed for common criminals is inherently limited as a response to mass atrocity and as a device to promote justice in its aftermath. We need to think hard about transcending existing procedural and institutional frameworks. A sustained process of critique and renewal may provide international criminal punishment with its own conceptual and philosophical foundations, instead of its current grounding on borrowed stilts.

The architects of international criminal law have done much to establish and mainstream institutions such as the International Criminal Court. This is a great accomplishment. But we cannot become complacent now that these institutions have been edified. A proliferation of adversarial and individualized criminal law does not inevitably lead to enhanced effectiveness in sanctioning or deterring atrocity. Criminal trials should never become a substitute for more preventative action on the part of the international community to combat atrocity. Nor is it productive for the turn to trials to inhibit grassroots solutions that reach beyond the criminal law or, even, formal law generally.

Insofar as I am deeply concerned with improving the project of international criminal law, this book displays a reconstructive ambition. My goal is to locate a principled middle ground between, on the one hand, the most relentless skeptics of universal law as a response to mass atrocity and, on the other hand, the most relentless proponents who often remain distrustful of bottom-up initiatives in postconflict societies. If successful, my arguments could inspire short-term reforms to existing institutions and a longer-term reconstitution of the field. I chart some proposals.

Within this process of reconstitution, it is important to emphasize contributions from nonlawyers, in particular anthropologists, mental health professionals, criminologists, social workers, political scientists, and public policymakers. I think the arguments of this book will be of interest to them, and I hope they feel welcome in debates among international lawyers that pertain to complex questions of justice.

The roots of this academic project trace back to my work in 1998 in the Rwandan genocide prisons. Along the way, many colleagues provided invaluable comments, feedback, and ideas on this manuscript at various stages of drafting – from the inchoate to the nearly finished. I thank each of you. It would be impossible to list everyone who played a part. But here is an attempt, in no particular order: Rick Kirgis, Ken Gallant, Roger Clark, Diane Marie Amann, Chris Blakesley, Chandra Lekha Sriram, Erin Daly, Penny Andrews, Allison Marston Danner, Scott Sundby, Ellen Podgor, Laura Dickinson, Holger Rohne, Laurel Fletcher, Darryl Brown, Tai-Heng Chen, Louise Halper, Paul Roberts, Donal Coffey, Cyrus Tata, Michael Fowler, Rosemary Byrne, Ralph Henham, David Zaring, Brad Wendel, Dorothy Brown, and Linda Malone.

A number of individuals deserve special thanks. Bert Westbrook and Kevin Jon Heller came along near the end of the writing process. Their encouragement, insight, and careful reads of the manuscript helped sustain my energy. Chris Gosnell gave me tremendous perspective. Larry May, who has introduced me to much of the rich philosophical literature on international criminal justice, offered wonderful advice and suggestions. I also would like to acknowledge the commentary from three anonymous reviewers at Cambridge University Press, whose input at a much earlier stage in the drafting process helped frame the debates.

My wife Michelle read every chapter. Her unwavering support, love, and patience, which guided every step taken through this project, continue to brighten each of my days. My parents deserve credit for many things, not the least of which is teaching me to finish a thought before beginning a new one.

Kira Horstmeyer, Washington and Lee Law Class of 2007, provided invaluable assistance with editing and cite checking. I also thank my former students Matt Earle, Erica Richards, and Sara Sakagami for their research work; Helen Hartt for library assistance; and Diane Cochran for administrative help. The editors at Cambridge University Press were a pleasure to work with.

This project grew enormously as a result of feedback from commentators at presentations made at the following universities: Vanderbilt, St. Andrews, Nottingham-Trent, Trinity College Dublin, Maryland, Washington and Lee, Nottingham, Texas, Washington University in St. Louis, Ohio State, NUI – Galway, Georgia, Case Western, and Wilfrid Laurier. Parts of the project also were presented at meetings of the American Society of International Law, International Studies Association, Law and Philosophy Association, Association of American Law Schools, and Law and Society Association. I am grateful to participants in those meetings for their insights.

I wrote much of this book from a lovely office with a thoughtful view at University College, Oxford University, where I was appointed Visiting Fellow for Michaelmas Term 2005. I extend my warmest gratitude to Univ for hosting me. I also thank the Institute for International Integration Studies at Trinity College Dublin, where I served a very productive stint as a Visiting Scholar in May 2006. My greatest appreciation, however, goes to my home institution, Washington and Lee University, School of Law, for unflaggingly and unfailingly supporting this research agenda from its inception, including through the grant of sabbatical leave and resource support through the Frances Lewis Law Center. I owe a great professional and personal debt to Dean David Partlett for his friendship and encouragement.

Select parts of this book contain material that draws from, adapts, or is significantly reworked from my article, "Collective Violence and Individual Punishment: The Criminality of Mass Atrocity," which appeared in *Northwestern University Law Review*, Vol. 99, No. 2, 539 (Winter 2005). This article has been used by special permission of Northwestern University School of Law, *Northwestern University Law Review*. Adaptation reflects the evolution of my thinking, events on the ground, and the results of new research. I was deeply honored when this article was selected as one of two co-winners of the 2005 Scholarly Papers Competition of the Association of American Law Schools.

Select portions of Chapter 4, Part (i) draw from, update, and adapt material that originally appeared as a published lecture in the *Ohio Northern University Law Review*, Vol. 31, 41 (2005), for which the *Ohio Northern University Law Review* grants permission to reuse. Cover photo © James Nachtwey/VII.

This book incorporates material and data on sentencing gathered up to May 2006, inclusive, unless otherwise indicated. Any errors or omissions in the text are entirely my own.

List of Abbreviations

DRC	Democratic Republic of the Congo
FRY	Federal Republic of Yugoslavia
ICC	International Criminal Court
ICJ	International Court of Justice
ICTR	International Criminal Tribunal for Rwanda
ICTY	International Criminal Tribunal for the Former Yugoslavia
IHT	Iraqi High Tribunal
IMT	International Military Tribunal (at Nuremberg)
JCE	Joint criminal enterprise
OSCE	Organization for Security and Cooperation in Europe
RPF	Rwandan Patriotic Front
SCSL	Special Court for Sierra Leone
SFRY	Socialist Federative Republic of Yugoslavia
Special Panels	East Timor Special Panels
UNAMIR	United Nations Assistance Mission in Rwanda

ATROCITY, PUNISHMENT, AND INTERNATIONAL LAW

CHAPTER 1

Extraordinary Crime and Ordinary Punishment:
An Overview

Beginning on April 8, 1994, Tutsi escapees – hunted and terrified – fled to the Catholic church in Nyange, a rural parish in western Rwanda. They sought shelter from attacks incited by Hutu extremists. The attackers were determined to eliminate the Tutsi as an ethnic group and killed individual Tutsi as a means to this end.

The Nyange church soon filled with over two thousand huddled Tutsi, many of whom were wounded. These Tutsi initially thought the church, as a house of God, would be a refuge. In fact, they had been encouraged to hide there by parish priests. The priests, however, decided to demolish the church. Accordingly, workers were engaged to operate a mechanical digger.

On April 16, 1994, a worker named Anastase Nkinamubanzi bulldozed the church with the Tutsi crammed inside. The roof crashed down. A few Tutsi survived the razing of the church. Nearly one-third of the local Hutu population assembled to finish them off. They did so with machetes, spears, and sticks.

Four years later, a Rwandan court prosecuted six individuals on charges of genocide and crimes against humanity for the Nyange church massacre.[1] Nkinamubanzi was among the accused. From the case report, we learn that he was born in 1962, was a bachelor, and worked as a heavy equipment driver.[2] Nkinamubanzi had no assets. He had no prior criminal record. The case report also sets out, through the sterility of legal prose, the evidence underpinning the accusations that he mechanically leveled a church with two thousand Tutsi trapped inside. After demolishing the church, Nkinamubanzi calmly asked the priests for the promised compensation for the public service he had provided.[3]

The court found Nkinamubanzi guilty of most of the charges brought against him, including genocide. Upon conviction, he was sentenced to life imprisonment. Although Nkinamubanzi admitted he bulldozed the church bursting with escapees, the court did not formally accept his guilty plea, the details of which it found inexact. Still, the court was influenced by his request for forgiveness. It considered that request as a mitigating factor. Two other defendants, who were church leaders, received the death penalty at trial; these sentences have not been carried out.

1

As for the Nyange church, over a decade later "all that is left of the massacre site are heaps of earth and concrete."[4] And, as for Nkinamubanzi, media accounts indicate that – stricken with tuberculosis – he is serving his sentence in a Rwandan prison.[5]

Many ordinary people in Rwanda were like – or, at least, a little like – Nkinamubanzi; many others are like him in many other places, countries, and continents; moreover, many more have the potential to become like him in the future. Ordinary people often are responsible for killing large numbers of their fellow citizens, whether by their own hands, by helping the hands of others, or by encouraging the handiwork. Some revel in the killings.[6] Others simply play along nervously, grimacing while they administer the deathblows or fidgeting while they distribute a list of targeted victims. Many simply think they are doing their patriotic duty and fulfilling their civic obligation, which they satisfy with pride, *Pflicht*, composure, and the quiet support of the general population. They are the exemplars of Hannah Arendt's "banality of evil."[7] That said, those leaders who give the orders to kill or in whose name the killings are undertaken also promote banality. After all, it is they who normalize violence and make it a way of life. Acting as what Amartya Sen describes as "proficient artisans of terror,"[8] these leaders ensconce atrocity as civic duty and, thereby, become conflict entrepreneurs.

So, what exactly do we do with individuals, leading a group or acting on its behalf, who murder tens, hundreds, thousands – or more – fellow members of humanity *because of* their membership in a different group? Should we subject these killers to the process of law? If so, what kind of law? What punishment is appropriate? What about the collective forces that provide the killers with a support network and social validation? Should we sanction those, too? If so, how?

This book addresses the reasons that extant criminal justice institutions – sited domestically as well as internationally – give for punishing perpetrators of mass violence and also investigates whether the sentences levied by these institutions support these penological rationales. Little scholarship has been undertaken in this area. In fact, whereas sophisticated work explores the substantive crimes,[9] the formation of institutions and their independence,[10] and the impact of prosecuting these crimes on collective reconciliation and political transition,[11] only isolated – and often conclusory – analysis exists concerning what institutions say they are accomplishing by punishing and, most importantly, whether the punishments issued actually attain the goals they are ascribed. Leading treatises on international criminal law devote limited space to punishment and sentencing.[12] The project that follows begins to address this lacuna in the scholarly literature. With this analysis as a base, the project then pushes in a normative direction by inquiring how offenders should be punished and how extant punishment schemes might be enhanced. In this first chapter, I provide an overview of the arguments advanced in this book.

(I) EXTRAORDINARY CRIME

The liberation of the concentration camps at the end of the Second World War uncorked a torrent of emotions. For the survivors, these emotions scaled a wide spectrum. Primo Levi and Viktor Frankl poignantly recorded how survivors experienced relief, fear, and loneliness while engaged in a painful search for meaning and the relevance of their survival.[13] For the liberating soldiers, there was repulsion and shock; for the returning Axis combatants, shame, denial, and disappointment.

The Allied rulers divided about what to do with the Nazi leaders. U.K. Prime Minister Churchill sought their quick dispatch, including by extrajudicial execution, owing to the fact that their guilt was so evident that there was no need for judicial process to establish it.[14] The Soviet Union's Stalin sought similar ends, but following short show trials. U.S. President Truman, encouraged by Secretary of War Stimson, envisioned careful trials to narrate to all the value of law and the depth of the defendants' culpability.

This latter view prevailed, leading not only to the Nuremberg trials, but also to the genesis of an influential paradigm. This paradigm cast Nazi crimes as extraordinary in their nature and, thereby, understood them not only as crimes against the victims in the camps or the helpless citizens in the invaded countries, but also as crimes in which everyone everywhere was a victim.[15] This understanding gave two distinct groups a forum to express outrage: the international community and the actual individual survivors. The fact that these groups are not necessarily allied foreshadows the complicated, yet largely undeveloped, victimology of mass atrocity.

Arendt explored Nazi crimes and their relationship with totalitarianism. She initially described these crimes as they occurred within the context of the Holocaust as "radical evil," borrowing a phrase that had been coined much earlier by Immanuel Kant.[16] In subsequent work, Arendt recast the evil as "extreme" or "thought-defying," preferring such descriptions to "radical" owing to the evolution of her thinking regarding the thoughtlessness and banality of the violence.[17]

International lawmakers did not believe that extreme evil lay beyond the reach of the law. They felt that law could recognize extreme evil and sanction it as a breach of universal norms. The area of law believed to be best suited for the condemnation of extreme evil was the criminal law. And, in fact, the criminal law has gained ascendancy as the dominant regulatory mechanism for extreme evil. This ascendancy began with Nuremberg and has, in the years since, gained currency and become consolidated.

In terms of substantive categorization, however, extreme evil was no ordinary crime. After all, Arendt herself noted that extreme evil "explode[d] the limits of the law."[18] This did not mean that this evil was incapable of condemnation through law, but that the law had to catch up to it. In this regard, international lawmakers categorized acts of extreme evil as qualitatively different than ordinary common crimes insofar as their nature was much more serious.[19] These acts seeped into the realm of *extraordinary international criminality*. And the perpetrator of extraordinary international crimes has become cast, rhetorically as well as legally, as an *enemy of all humankind*.[20] I use both of these phrases in this book given that they reflect dominant understandings of the wrongdoing and wrongdoers. Those acts of atrocity characterized as extraordinary international crimes include crimes against humanity (an appellation that neatly embodies our shared victimization), genocide, and war crimes.[21]

The definitions of these crimes have evolved over time to become quite complex. Stripped to the essentials, though, crimes against humanity include a number of violent acts "when committed as part of a widespread or systematic attack directed against any civilian population, with knowledge of the attack."[22] Genocide is defined to include a number of acts (including killing and causing serious bodily or mental harm) committed with intent to destroy, in whole or in part, a national, ethnical, racial, or religious group, as such.[23] The special intent of genocide distinguishes it from crimes against humanity. War crimes represent the behavior that falls outside of the ordinary scope of activities undertaken by soldiers during armed conflict.[24] Whereas killing the enemy is part of a soldier's ordinary activity, torture, inhumane treatment, or willful murder of civilians is not. Launching attacks that are disproportionate, that fail to discriminate between military and civilian targets, or that are not necessary to secure a military advantage also can constitute war crimes.

At the very core of the extraordinariness of atrocity crimes is conduct – planned, systematized, and organized – that targets large numbers of individuals based on their actual or perceived membership in a particular group that has become selected as a target on discriminatory grounds.[25] In these situations, group members become indistinguishable from, and substitutable for, each other. The individual becomes brutalized because of group characteristics. The attack is not just against individuals, but against the group, and thereby becomes something more heinous than the aggregation of each individual murder. Moreover, the discriminatory targeting of a group is often effected in the name of the persecutor's own group. Accordingly, the interplay between individual action and group membership is central to extraordinary international criminality. This interplay engenders thorny questions of responsibility and punishment. Crimes motivated by this discriminatory animus are deeply influenced by notions of group superiority and inferiority, which, in turn, propel collective action.

To recap: international lawmakers believe that extreme evil is cognizable by substantive criminal law. Because extreme evil is so egregious, however, only special substantive categories of criminality (in some cases newly defined, named, or created) could capture it. These categories include genocide, crimes against humanity, and war crimes.

Defining the crimes, though, is only one step in the enforcement process. It would also be necessary to establish procedures, institutions, and sanctions through which perpetrators of atrocity could be brought to account. Procedures, institutions, and sanctions have emerged.[26] International criminal justice largely is operationalized through criminal tribunals. Courtrooms have gained ascendancy as the forum to censure extreme evil. Accountability determinations proceed through adversarial third-party adjudication, conducted in judicialized settings, and premised on a construction of the individual as the central unit of action.[27] A number of select guilty individuals squarely are to be blamed for systemic levels of group violence. At Nuremberg, some of the guilty were hung. Today, punishment predominantly takes the form of incarceration in accordance with the classic penitentiary model, where convicts are isolated and sequestered. The enemy of humankind is punished no differently than a car thief, armed robber, or felony murderer in those places that adhere to this model domestically.

The ascendancy of the criminal trial, courtroom, and jailhouse as the preferred modalities to promote justice for atrocity is not random. Rather, it is moored in a particular worldview that derives from the intersection of two influential philosophical currents. The first of these currents is legalism; the second is liberalism.

To follow Judith Shklar, legalism is the view that "moral relationships [...] consist of duties and rights determined by rules."[28] When it comes to atrocity, however, the application of legalism becomes narrower. It does so in two ways. One is disciplinary. The turn is not to law generally to promote justice in the aftermath of terribly complex political violence but, rather, most enthusiastically to the criminal law. I argue that the preference for criminalization has prompted a shortfall with regard to the consideration and deployment of other legal, regulatory, and transformative mechanisms in the quest for justice.[29] The second narrowing is sociocultural. The kind of legalism, voiced through the criminal law, which has become operative is one that embodies core elements of liberalism, including, as Laurel Fletcher notes, the tendency to "locate the individual as the central unit of analysis for purposes of sanctioning violations."[30] Liberalism originates in and underpins the legal structures of Western societies. Accordingly, when it comes to atrocity, the justice narrative is deeply associated with liberal legalism rooted in the ordinary procedure and sanction of the criminal law of Western states. Although I share Fletcher's definition of liberal legalism as "refer[ing] to the legal principles and values that privilege individual autonomy, individuate responsibility, and are reflected in the criminal law of common law legal systems,"[31] I would add that these values also are shared by civil law legal systems suggesting, at a deeper level, the difficulty in deracinating them from Western social and legal thought.[32] The ascendancy of these modalities of justice thereby represents the ascendancy of specific forms of procedure and sanction, which often become applied to societies where such forms are neither innate nor indigenous.

In this book, at times I turn to phrases such as *liberal legalist* or *Western legalist* to describe the dominant method of determining responsibility and allocating punishment in the wake of atrocity. At times, I also turn to the phrase *ordinary criminal law and process* as shorthand for the domestic law and process regulating common crime in liberal states. I recognize the complex philosophical debates on liberalism generally. This book is not a treatise on liberalism. Nor is it a broadside thereof. Nor is it a critique of Western philosophical traditions generally. Many of the philosophical approaches I find compelling, for example, cosmopolitanism, pluralism, and democratic theory, associate with liberal Western traditions. My goal is not to assess the merits of liberalism as a broad, and often abstractly defined, philosophical worldview. Rather, my goal is much more modest. I intend to investigate the effectiveness of criminal trials and punishment, as presently conducted internationally and nationally, as responses to atrocity. I also investigate the effects that the embrace of criminal prosecution and punishment has on other potential approaches to regulate, sanction, and prevent atrocity. Neither legalism nor liberalism can be fully disentangled from these investigations insofar as they both animate the preference for prosecution and punishment as presently constituted.

(II) ORDINARY PROCESS AND PUNISHMENT

A paradox emerges. International lawmakers have demarcated normative differences between extraordinary crimes against the world community and ordinary common crimes. However, despite the proclaimed extraordinary nature of atrocity crime, its modality of punishment, theory of sentencing, and process of determining guilt or innocence, each remain disappointingly, although perhaps reassuringly, ordinary – so long as ordinariness is measured by the content of modern Western legal systems.

At the international level, there has been a proliferation of new legal institutions to adjudge mass violence. These institutions have become legitimated as appropriate conduits to dispense justice and inflict punishment.[33] A number of justifications are evoked in this regard. One is deontological, namely that the crimes are so egregious that they victimize all of us and, hence, must be condemned internationally; it would be unjust for a particular state's courts to "confiscate" these crimes.[34] Other justifications are pragmatic. Extraordinary international crimes often trigger security concerns, threaten regional stability, affect the viability of groups, and induce cross-border refugee movements. In a very real sense, these crimes therefore implicate what Larry May calls an "international interest."[35] International institutions also derive legitimacy because, in the wake of atrocity, national institutions may be annihilated, corrupt, politicized, biased, or too insecure. Accordingly, but for the creation of an international institution, in many instances no justice would be effected.

That said, international institutions have not acquired a monopoly on the accountability business. Far from it. In fact, most of this business actually is carried out by national and local institutions, which are or increasingly look like Western criminal courts, and which rely on jurisdictional bases such as territoriality, nationality, or universality.[36] International institutions serve as tremendously important trendsetters for their national and local counterparts.[37] Therefore, the distinctions between international and national institutions are far from watertight.[38]

Newly created international institutions include the International Criminal Court (ICC, 2002),[39] ad hoc tribunals for Rwanda (International Criminal Tribunal for Rwanda, ICTR, 1994)[40] and the former Yugoslavia (International Criminal Tribunal for the Former Yugoslavia, ICTY, 1993),[41] the Special Court for Sierra Leone (SCSL, 2000),[42] and a variety of hybrid panels or chambers. Hybrid institutions divide judicial responsibilities between the United Nations, or its entities, and the concerned state.[43] Strictly speaking, they are, therefore, internationalized legal institutions instead of purely international legal institutions; that said, in the interest of simplicity, I consider them under the rubric of international institutions. A hybrid model currently operates in Kosovo;[44] one has ceased operations in East Timor;[45] another is emerging in Cambodia.[46]

There is considerable homogeneity among these international institutions. All of them largely incorporate ordinary methods of prosecution and punishment dominant in liberal states. This incorporation is noted but does not raise many eyebrows within the community of international criminal law scholars, including among its most distinguished members.[47] Within this process of incorporation, international criminal courts and tribunals have – to varying degrees *inter se* – technically harmonized aspects of Anglo-American common law procedure with tenets of the Continental civil law tradition.[48] However, this harmonization is far from a genuine amalgam that accommodates the sociolegal traditions of disempowered victims of mass violence – largely from non-Western audiences – who already lack a voice in international relations.[49] Although these traditions are not incommensurable with Western systems, and share points of commonality, they differ in important ways, including when it comes to rationales for and modalities of punishment. In short, international criminal law largely borrows the penological rationales of Western domestic criminal law.

These international institutions also borrow from the operation of human rights frameworks in dominant states, in particular due process rights accorded to criminal defendants. International criminal procedure accords great importance to the need to "pay particular respect to due process"[50] in order to avoid, in Justice Jackson's famous admonition, "pass[ing] [. . .] defendants a poisoned chalice."[51] For ICTY President Meron, "[t]here can be no cutting corners" when it comes to due process else the tribunal ceases to be credible to the public.[52] Due process rights, which apply to persons accused of common crimes in liberal states, now inure to the benefit of persons accused of extraordinary international crimes often committed far away from these states. Among legal scholars, there is little, if any, questioning of the suitability of this transplant. A *contrario*, it is often a cause for celebration. I believe that the reality on the ground is more complex and that it is problematic for international institutions to assume that formulaic reliance upon due process standards alone leads to legitimacy and credibility, particularly among populations transitioning from conflict. I do not deny the relevance of due process in preserving the humanity of those who prosecute and in serving as an example for the rule of law. I have elsewhere underscored the importance of both of these phenomena.[53] I merely suggest that justice is not a recipe; and due process is not a magic ingredient.

This replication of the process, sanction, and rationales of ordinary criminal law is reassuring to some, insofar as the familiar often is comfortable. But this replication also is vexing, in that the perpetrator of mass atrocity fundamentally differs from the perpetrator of ordinary crime. The fulcrum of this difference is that, whereas ordinary crime tends to be deviant in the times and places it is committed, the extraordinary acts of individual criminality that collectively lead to mass atrocity are not so deviant in the times and places where they are committed. Assuredly, as I explore in Chapter 2, this is not the case for *all* incidents of atrocity. However, as atrocity becomes more widescale in nature, and more popular, it becomes more difficult to construct participation therein as deviant. Insofar as international criminal law claims a regulatory interest in the most serious crimes of international concern, it concerns itself with the kind of violence that is most difficult to reconcile with deviance theory. Although widespread acts of extraordinary international criminality transgress *jus cogens* norms, they often support a social norm that is much closer to home.[54] In such cases, participation in atrocity becomes a product of conformity and collective action, not delinquency and individual pathology. This latter reality, which I initially came to appreciate experientially through my work with detainees in Rwanda,[55] brings to light complex and discomfiting issues of human agency. Although this deep complicity cascade does not diminish the brutality or exculpate the aggressor, it does problematize certain tropes central to international criminal law such as bystander exoneration, individual autonomy, and the avoidance of collective sanction. The complicity cascade also involves the misfeasance or nonfeasance of foreign governments and international organizations during times of atrocity, thereby imperiling the moral legitimacy of pronouncements of wrongdoing by foreign and international judges elected by and representing these putatively neutral governments and organizations. What is more, many extraordinary international criminals, who engaged in acts of unfathomable barbarity, are able to conform easily and live unobtrusively for the remainder of their lives as normal citizens. The examples of Nazis who fled Germany following World War II to take up residence elsewhere in Europe or the Americas stand out. This ability to fit in suggests something curious, and deeply disquieting, about atrocity perpetrators: namely, their lack of subsequent delinquency or recidivism and their easy integration into a new set of social norms.

Chapter 2 examines distinctions between the perpetrator of mass atrocity and the perpetrator of ordinary common crime. In this regard, Chapter 2 considers perspectives that contend that distinctions between the extraordinary and ordinary criminal are not so apparent and, in fact, may be quite blurred. In particular, I give careful consideration to: (1) certain ordinary common crimes that share collective characteristics; and (2) sophisticated new research on individual participation in civil war that suggests that not all participants are motivated by political goals, but that some are motivated by private goals in a manner that resembles the behavior of the common criminal. Ultimately, I conclude that there remains a materially significant difference between the perpetrator of discrimination-based atrocity and the ordinary common criminal such that the application of punishment designed for the latter to the former is ill fitting and, what is more, that this ill fit accounts for a number of the penological shortfalls of the project of international criminal law. This finding does not eviscerate the usefulness of accumulated knowledge regarding the common criminal in terms of how we consider punishing the extraordinary international criminal. Rather, it suggests that we need to transcend this knowledge instead of relying heavily upon it. Moreover, thinking hard about the perpetrator of atrocity could help us better understand the ordinary common criminal and the extent to which extant punishment schemes for common criminals (already subject to considerable criticism) can better attain their own penological objectives.

Chapter 2 also explores tensions within ordinary criminal law between individualism as a first principle[56] and the reality that ordinary criminal law exceptionally turns to notions of vicarious liability and collective responsibility that, *prima facie*, run contrary to the ethos of individual agency.[57] Paradoxically, however, even though international criminal law responds to conduct that is much *more* collective in nature than that faced by ordinary criminal law, it evokes a *similar* rhetorical archetype of individual agency.[58] This leads to deep tension and doctrinal tautness.

Despite the fact that the suitability of ordinary criminal process for collective acts of atrocity cannot be assumed, and is in fact problematic, newly created punishing institutions benefit from significant levels of enthusiasm. The turn to criminal trials to promote justice for atrocity has acquired striking support among scholars and policymakers. Payam Akhavan and Jan Klabbers are right to observe that many legal scholars ascribe lofty transformative potential to atrocity trials.[59] There is a sense that conducting more criminal trials in more places afflicted by atrocity will lead to more justice, so long as those trials conform to due process standards. Optimism regarding the potential of international criminal tribunals also echoes, albeit with greater circumspection, in other scholarly communities ranging from historians to moral philosophers.[60]

Legal practitioners, too, share this enthusiasm.[61] International human rights activists also are enthusiastic partisans and, according to William Schabas, thereby have "adjusted [their] historic predisposition for the rights of the defense and the protection of prisoners to a more prosecution-based orientation."[62] Political actors, such as states and international organizations (for example, the United Nations) – along with nongovernmental organizations and development financiers – stand behind international criminal tribunals. Even while opposing the ICC and shrinking the role of criminal law in the "war on terror," the U.S. government elsewhere propounds legalist prosecution, punishment, and incarceration for individual perpetrators of mass atrocity. The United States has supported temporary international criminal tribunals from Nuremberg in 1945 to the ICTR and ICTY today, and atrocity prosecutions in general, as exemplified by the Saddam Hussein trial.[63] Many of the substantive international crimes (and principles of individual penal responsibility) punishable by the Iraqi High Tribunal (whose Statute was drafted with considerable U.S. assistance) track those of the Rome Statute of the ICC. U.S. opposition to the ICC does not focus on the appropriateness of its methods, but, rather, on the independence of the institution and the prospect that U.S. soldiers, officials, or top leaders might become its targets.[64]

In short, faith on the part of so many activists, scholars, states, and policy-makers in the potential of prosecution and incarceration has spawned one of the more extensive waves of institution-building in modern international relations. I believe the time has come to pause and reexamine this faith, even if just for a moment. I argue that prosecution and incarceration is not always the best way to promote accountability in all afflicted places and spaces. In fact, my interviews of perpetrators and survivors in Rwanda and experiences with victims of internecine violence in Afghanistan suggest that the structural simplicity pursued by the prevailing paradigm of prosecution and incarceration squeezes out the complexity and dissensus central to meaningful processes of justice and reconciliation.[65]

To be sure, some constituencies (for example, international relations theo-rists of the realist school) express considerable reserve regarding the merits of international criminal law and its institutional operationalization. According to the realist conception, law should do no more than promote cooperation when states find this to be in their best interests. Law certainly should not redistribute power. Nor should it attempt to impose moral limits on politics. For realists such as Carl Schmitt, such an imposition only makes politics crueler.[66] Other realists, for example, George Kennan, criticize the "legalistic approach to international affairs" because this approach "ignores in general the international significance of political problems and the deeper sources of international instability."[67] Eric Posner, John Yoo, and Jack Goldsmith currently import this view into the legal academy under the auspices of rational choice theory.[68] Other scholars, in turn, have compellingly demonstrated weaknesses that inhere in this importation.[69]

There is middle ground, which I hope to cultivate, between the proponents and the naysayers. This middle ground recognizes – but does not romanticize – the potential of atrocity trials; it also recognizes the limits to the criminal law's ability to rationalize complex social phenomena. One of my goals is to offer a critical perspective rooted in criminology, victimology, and especially penology that supports the universal goal of accountability for extraordinary international criminals and the denunciation of their universal crimes of group discrimina-tion, but which expresses concern that dominant procedural and institutional methodologies fall short in terms of legitimacy and effectiveness.[70] I believe this critique is central to developing a sophisticated understanding of social con-trol at the global level for those who breach the global trust. Furthermore, I hope to look beyond the criminal law to consider the role that law generally, as well as other regulatory initiatives, can play in promoting justice following atrocity. In this regard, I hope to pursue an encouraging but tempered search for law's potential. The search for this potential begins with a review of the exist-ing accomplishments of international criminal law in sentencing extraordinary international criminals.

(III) PUNISHMENT IN INTERNATIONAL
AND NATIONAL INSTITUTIONS

Chapter 3 reviews the positive law of international criminal tribunals, their jurisprudence on sentencing, and the quantum of sentences that have been awarded. This review modestly responds to the paucity of evaluative research regarding the sentencing practices of international tribunals. In contemporary international practice, sanction effectively is limited to imprisonment, with the majority of extraordinary international criminals receiving fixed terms. There is no sentencing tariff. Although able to do so, as of the time of my data compilation (May 2006), the ICTY has not issued a life sentence.[71] The East Timor Special Panels (Special Panels) were not empowered to issue a life sentence. At the ICTY, among term sentences finalized by May 2006, the mean term was 14.3 years and the median term 12 years. The length of fixed terms of imprisonment is palpably lower at the Special Panels, where the mean sentence for extraordinary international crimes is 9.9 years and the median sentence 8 years. The ICTR sentences more severely. It routinely awards life sentences. Slightly less than half of all ICTR convicts receive life sentences; the remainder receive much longer fixed terms of imprisonment than at the ICTY.[72]

In the case of the ICTY and Special Panels, several convicts already have been granted early release after serving two-thirds of their sentence. This development is not factored into the mean and median calculations but certainly affects *ex post* the severity of sanction initially awarded. Early release has not yet occurred at the ICTR.

A more exacting review of the judgments and data suggests that international criminal tribunals are developing more sophisticated approaches to determining sentence. A typology of aggravating and mitigating factors has emerged. However, despite these steps toward greater standardization, the sentencing practice of international institutions remains confusing, disparate, inconsistent, and erratic; it gives rise to distributive inequities. The sanction imposed on extraordinary international criminals largely remains little more than an afterthought to the closure purportedly obtained by the conviction. Ultimately, relegating punishment to the status of an afterthought demeans its value and meaning.

In the area of punishment and sentencing, international tribunals very closely borrow the rationalities of ordinary domestic criminal law – in particular, retribution and general deterrence – without effectively appreciating the fundamental differences between perpetrators of extraordinary international crimes such as mass atrocity and perpetrators of ordinary domestic crimes in ordinary times. Whereas retribution is backward-looking, in that it punishes the criminal to the extent of the criminal's desert, deterrence theories are forward-looking and consequential in that they punish so that the convict, or others in the case of general deterrence, will be dissuaded by fear of punishment from offending or reoffending. Expressivism is a tertiary goal that surfaces in the international jurisprudence. Expressivist theories extol the messaging value of punishment to affirm respect for law, reinforce a moral consensus, narrate history, and educate the public. Expressivism punishes to strengthen faith in rule of law among the public, as opposed to punishing because the perpetrator deserves it or because potential perpetrators will be deterred by fear of it. Other aspirations for punishment sporadically emerge in the jurisprudence, although these are subaltern. These other aspirations, to which reference is neither patterned nor consistent, include reconciliation, reintegration, and rehabilitation.[73]

The wave of institution-building in the international legal order has influenced national and local legal orders as well. Many of these have elected to proscribe extraordinary international crimes. A particularly fertile area of comparative analysis is the study of those areas in which atrocity has become judicialized transsystemically at multiple levels through multiple institutions. I consider these multivalent sites of judicialization with regard to three atrocities: the 1994 Rwandan genocide, ethnic cleansing in the Balkans throughout the 1990s, and the Nazi Holocaust. In Chapter 4, I review the activities of national and local legal institutions sharing contacts with these three atrocities. I devote considerable attention to Rwanda because of my legal work there, the broad implementation of neotraditional *gacaca* dispute resolution, and the issuance of a large number of sentences by the domestic court system.

The data on punishment and sentencing reveal greater diversity in terms of the type of sanction at the national and local levels (which includes community service, incarceration, lustration, the death penalty, and compensation) than that available internationally. Moreover, with specific regard to incarceration, national and local institutions sentence perpetrators to a broader range of terms than their international counterparts. However, when it comes to penology, national and local institutions for the most part parrot the goal of retribution (and, secondarily, general deterrence), even where this goal may not be indigenous. Aggravating and mitigating factors track those of the ordinary criminal law of dominant states quite closely.

My review of national and local jurisdictions suggests the ebb and flow of powerful currents of legal transplant.[74] Legal processes operative in dominant national legal systems can technically meld (for example, civil law and common law methodologies), then migrate into the international order and there crystallize into the normalized methods of international law. These transplants then come full circle through their subsequent return and superimposition upon multiple legal systems at the national and local levels, including diverse disempowered systems, through vertical applications of authority. One funnel for these applications is the primacy of certain international legal institutions, such as the ICTY and ICTR, over domestic institutions. Both the ICTR and ICTY are to wind down their trial operations by the end of this decade. However, this goal only becomes attainable should the ICTR and ICTY flex their power to refer cases to national courts. The referral process prompts national legal topographies to absorb internationalized liberal modalities of criminal process and punishment as preferred responses to mass atrocity. Furthermore, although the ICC is to be complementary to national initiatives,[75] I examine – through the vehicle of two self-referrals the ICC has received (from Uganda and the Democratic Republic of the Congo) – how it also exerts conformist pressures on national and, in particular, local accountability mechanisms.

Although national institutions still punish with a broader qualitative variety of sanction and, in cases of incarceration, a broader quantitative range of length of imprisonment, I predict, as the modalities of international tribunals continue to enter national legal frameworks through referrals, complementarity, and other conduits,[76] that both the variety of sanction and range of sentences available within national frameworks increasingly will shrink. In terms of imprisonment, for example, I foresee that national institutions will raise minimum sentences – and embed duties to prosecute that might disfavor alternate modalities of accountability – while lowering maximum sentences and, in addition, eliminating the death penalty. In particular, conformist pressures are placed on local approaches, such as restorative methodologies. The situation of traditional dispute resolution – *gacaca* – in Rwanda is a telling example. Although the ICC offers potential for greater inclusiveness, which I consider, as a whole international criminal law remains distant from restorative and reintegrative methodologies, both in theory as well as in practice, which I argue weakens its effectiveness and meaning in many places directly afflicted by atrocity.

Ironically, this transplant from the international to the national may in fact be welcomed by many state actors. Particularly in transitional contexts, not all of which match the idealized path to greater democratization, state actors often crave and seek out the consolidation of power occasioned by punitive criminal law frameworks instead of the more free-ranging and authority-diffusing modalities of justice that percolate bottom-up from local constituencies. In this vein, international modalities can inform center-periphery relationships in transitional societies in a way that consolidates centralized state authority.

When aggregated, these various pressure points squeeze out local approaches to justice, most notably those that eschew the methods and modalities dominant internationally. These pressure points are proving to be of great relevance to the structure of punishment modalities for extraordinary international criminals although they have little to do with theoretical or applied determinations regarding the actual nature of extraordinary international crime. The effect of these legal migrations is a homogenization of process. This homogenized process may convey limited meaning to perpetrators, victims, or bystanders. In particular, victimological research indicates that individualized criminal trials often do not correspond to victim preferences when pursued as the dominant response, and certainly not when pursued exclusively.

In this analysis, I take as a baseline that there is little advantage in venerating the local or that which otherwise differs from dominant discourse simply to promote pluralistic difference as an end in itself. Local punishment schemes, in particular of a communitarian nature, may be prone to manipulation, abuse, or arbitrary application. Moreover, many national legal orders are corrupt, unreliable,

and illegitimate; in many postconflict societies, the industrialization of mass violence often arose as a matter of conforming to the law. International input can
ameliorate the output of national and local institutions. History boasts of many
examples of international or foreign injection of values and constitutive documents that, in turn, helped lay the foundations for peaceful and free societies to
emerge from the ruins of war and authoritarianism (for example, constitutional
arrangements in both Germany and Japan). The migration and transplant of
human rights documents can improve the lives of disempowered communities
that, hitherto, may have been excluded from decision making through application of discriminatory norms. That said, history also boasts of many examples of
failed impositions, imperial projects, and cultural manipulation. In the end, just
as it is irresponsible to sentimentally venerate the local *qua* local, it is equally
irresponsible to venerate a process simply because it has become globalized and
thereby assume its legitimacy, effectiveness, and credibility.

In the case of international criminal law, it may be that the transplanted
nature of institutionally inflicted punishment is effective precisely because it
is transplanted. In Chapter 5, I examine this contention. Ultimately, the cultural specificity of the implicated traditions gives me reason for pause, especially
because the operation of international criminal tribunals largely takes place outside of the West. The implementation of international criminal law therefore
risks a democratic deficit by excluding local values and personalities, which is
somewhat ironic because the excluded local often represents the precise population that was most traumatized by the criminality. Victims and survivors have
greater access to the ICC than to other international criminal tribunals. The
ICC offers opportunities for representatives of afflicted populations to share their
views and concerns, even at the investigatory stage. However, these opportunities, which I explore further in Chapter 5, are modest; moreover, they already
have been subject to contestation and tension among prosecutors, victims, and
judges.[77]

In contemporary cases, the application of the modalities of international
criminal law has externalized justice from the communities directly ravaged
by atrocity. Until these modalities become adapted to demonstrate greater
sensitivity to and inclusiveness of the local, phenomena of externalized justice shall continue. Although international criminal justice institutions concern themselves with a small number of defendants who share the greatest
responsibility for an atrocity, these institutions deeply influence the fabric of
national and local legal orders that may aspire to hold accountable a vastly
larger group of lower-level offenders. In the end, it seems that some of the
shortcomings of law and development movements – such as exclusion of local
involvement, top-down law reform, the imposition of alien legal process, and
the devaluing of indigenous customs – reappear in the implementation of international criminal law. Although local practices at times admittedly are problematic, international lawyers should think hard about how to accommodate their
potential.

(IV) DECONSTRUCTION: THE DISCONNECT BETWEEN ASPIRATIONS OF PUNISHMENT AND REALITIES OF SENTENCE

Chapter 6 explores the three central theoretical justifications – retribution, deterrence, and expressivism – that have been proffered for punishing perpetrators of atrocity at various jurisdictional levels. I observe disconnects between the effects of sentencing and retributive and deterrent aspirations. Expressivism, too, faces operational challenges – but presents a more viable penological justification.

Although retributive theory has many shades, these share in common the precept that the criminal deserves punishment proportionate to the gravity of the offense.[78] Those institutions that punish extraordinary international crimes place retribution very high on the list of the goals of punishment. The question, then, follows: do the sentences issued to perpetrators of extraordinary international crimes attain the self-avowed retributive goals? Can an architect, or tool, of mass atrocity ever receive just deserts?

The data presented in Chapters 3 and 4 reveal that, at both the national and international levels, punishment for multiple international crimes is generally not more severe than what national jurisdictions award for a single serious ordinary crime. Some positive law instruments at the national level provide that punishment for extraordinary international crimes could be more severe than for ordinary serious common crimes, but this is not the case in positive law instruments in other national legal orders. What is more, the practice of courts that actually punish offenders for extraordinary international crimes indicates that, for the most part, punishment for multiple international crimes ranges from as severe to less severe than for a single serious common crime. This is in part due to the reality that the massive nature of atrocity cannot be reflected in retributive punishment owing to human rights standards, which cabin the range of sanction.[79] In particular, these standards limit the amount of pain that institutions can inflict upon convicts.

At the international level, there are inconsistencies in terms of the quantum of punishment meted out to similarly situated offenders *within* institutions and also *among* institutions. These inconsistencies arise from the broad discretion that is accorded to international judges and the lack of a sentencing heuristic.[80] At the national level, there is, in the aggregate, a wider variety of sanction and, in cases of incarceration, a wider range of quantum of sentence. The wider variety and range of sanction, which give rise to considerable unpredictability in sentencing, arise from a number of sources. Included among these are political concerns that can weaken the ability of domestic prosecutors to bring charges in transitional situations that, as Mark Osiel documents,[81] often involve amnesties. Although these political concerns may satisfy other potential goals, such as reconciliation, peace, and the promotion of democratic legitimacy, they operate in tension with retribution. At the other end of the spectrum, certain national institutions sentence more harshly than international institutions (and even order the death penalty), offer conditions of imprisonment that are more onerous, permit more limited access to conditional release, or sanction simultaneously through diverse areas of law (for example, civil damages awards, although these are largely uncollected). The fact that national institutions may punish offenders more harshly than international institutions also is problematic for the retributivist insofar as international institutions tend to assert jurisdiction over the leaders and planners of atrocity who, according to conventional wisdom, are more responsible and, hence, ostensibly more deserving of harsher punishment. Although there are situations where the stigmatizing value of punishment by international criminal tribunals is greater than that of national institutions, and might outweigh the reduced pain of a shorter and more comfortable prison term, research surveys reveal that there are other situations where there is no perception of enhanced stigma.[82]

A further challenge to the retributive value of punishment at both the national and international levels is the avid procedural incorporation of plea bargains in cases of extraordinary international crime. Plea bargains involve the prosecutor and defendant negotiating an agreement in which the defendant self-convicts. In some cases, the prosecutor agrees to drop certain charges as part of the exchange (this is called charge bargaining). It is generally the case that the court or tribunal with jurisdiction will have to approve the plea agreement. The court or tribunal generally is under no obligation to adhere to the negotiated sentencing range. Independent curial review thereby provides some oversight, but also injects uncertainty. Regardless of the specific form of the plea bargain, these exchanges disconnect punishment from desert or gravity and often render it contingent on what the convict knows and who else the convict is willing to implicate. Paradoxically, plea bargaining is generally available for extraordinary international crimes at all levels of judicialization, even though in many national jurisdictions it is not possible for serious cases of ordinary crime. The fact that plea bargains are readily available for atrocity crimes, but not available in many jurisdictions for serious ordinary crimes, weakens the purportedly enhanced retributive value of punishing atrocity crimes. To be sure, there are many reasons that favor plea bargaining for atrocity crimes. However, plea bargains intersect tensely with retributive aspirations.

Deterrence is perhaps even more problematic than retribution as a goal for the sentencing of extraordinary international criminals. Although there is some scattered reference to the merits of specific deterrence in the transsystemic jurisprudence,[83] general deterrence largely remains the focus. General deterrence posits that if one person is punished, this punishment will reduce the likelihood that another person in that same place or somewhere else will offend in the future. Deterrence therefore punishes because of its social engineering function.

To this end, it makes sense to consider empirical evidence whether potential extraordinary international criminals would be deterred by the punishment of others following criminal trials. There are scattered anecdotal reports of deterrence.[84] However, no systematized or conclusive evidence of discernible deterrent effect has yet been proffered. In any event, any anecdotal research must take into account the reality that atrocity has continued to occur in places following the creation of criminal tribunals to punish perpetrators. It is true that we simply cannot know how much worse atrocity would have been, or how much more atrocity would have occurred, in the absence of judicial institutions. We can have faith and hope that deterrence works. Chapter 6 explores two challenges to this faith. The first is the reality that there is a very low – albeit, happily, growing – probability that perpetrators actually will be taken into the custody of authorities that pursue accountability. The second is the assumption of perpetrator rationality, or at least a certain degree of rationality, amid the cataclysm of mass atrocity and the furious propaganda that precedes it. Rationality is central to deterrence theory insofar as this theory assumes that perpetrators make some kind of cost-benefit analysis and thereby control their behavior. The work of anthropologists and the research of journalists in conflict zones, both of which I examine, suggests a much more nuanced picture of human agency.

Expressivism is the third rationale for punishment that emerges jurisprudentially in cases of extraordinary international crime. It occupies a less influential place than retribution or deterrence. Diane Marie Amann notes that expressivist theories look at the messaging effect of trials, verdict, and punishment.[85] Expressivists maintain that punishment affirms the value of law, strengthens social solidarity, and incubates a moral consensus among the public.[86] For expressivists, trials and punishment also serve powerful pedagogical roles. Trials narrate events – publicly – and then impose punishment on the guilty in a manner that can shame and stigmatize.[87] The result is an intensely dramaturgical process that tells a story. The performance aspect is particularly elevated for leaders and propagandists of atrocity – public figures known to many and before whom many have trembled. But performativity also can arise through prosecution of the small fry, insofar as atrocity involves many local narratives. In some cases, the expressive value of storytelling is enhanced when it takes the form of judicial pronouncement, which is cloaked in a mantle of authority, and occurs through rules of evidence, which can intone an aura of reliable impartiality. Consequently, although it seems a reach for liberal legalist punishment to exact retribution or deter individuals from killing in cataclysmic times by instilling a fear of getting caught, punishment bears greater promise to educate future generations about the effects of extreme evil and edify a moral consensus that repudiates discrimination-based violence and those who peddle in it. To this end, I believe expressivism has greater viability than deterrence or retribution as a basis for a penology of extraordinary international crime. Assuredly, the expressive value of the punishment of extraordinary international criminals will be strengthened to the extent that this value can be distinguished from that of punishing ordinary common criminals.

That said, the expressive goals of punishment are fragile. Their attainment is jeopardized by the selectivity and formalism of legal process. The historical narrative can become crimped by recourse, animated by managerial concerns, to prosecutorial strategizing and plea bargaining (in particular, charge bargaining). Gaps between international criminal process and expectations of local populations, in particular non-Western populations, may trigger an external-ization of justice, thereby diminishing the prophylactic value of verdict and punishment. In certain contexts, restorative methodologies anchored in local expectations serve as clearer conduits for the elaboration of the truth.

In conclusion, liberal prosecutorial and correctional modalities make very modest gains in terms of actualizing retributive and deterrent goals; they do somewhat better at actualizing expressive goals. In the aggregate, though, these modalities trigger a palpable disconnect. This disconnect, which operates at the level of international institutions as well as at the level of conformist domestic institutions, suggests that the preference for incarceration following what liberal international lawyers deem to be a procedurally acceptable trial on the whole falls short of its penological objectives. This may be because those objectives are too ambitious. It may also be because the criminal law, standing alone, simply is not enough nor can ever be enough.

(v) ... AND RECONSTITUTION

But what then? And where now? In Chapter 7, I begin this conversation by proposing two synergistic reforms to wean the pursuit of accountability for per-petrators of extreme evil from a selective, and ill-fitting, liberal criminal law model.

The first reform is *vertical*. I propose to recalibrate the application of author-ity among extant criminal justice institutions at multiple regulatory sites (the international, national, and local). Currently, as Chapter 5 explores, these appli-cations of authority radiate downward from the international. Instead, I propose reform to better welcome bottom-up approaches to procedure and sanction. Insofar as local and national accountability mechanisms are potentially abu-sive, corrupt, illegitimate, and susceptible to machination, there is a need for gatekeeping. Accordingly, I propose that *in situ* justice modalities be accorded a presumption of *deference*, but that this presumption be *qualified*. I outline six important criteria to qualify the presumption in favor of deference and, thereby, fulfill this gatekeeping function. I apply these criteria to three case studies: Afghanistan (customary mechanisms to sanction human rights abuses), Iraq (the Iraqi High Tribunal's prosecution of Ba'ath leaders), and the Sudan (proceedings of the Sudanese government to respond to atrocity in Darfur). Furthermore, I distinguish qualified deference from complementarity and also from doctrines such as subsidiarity and margin of appreciation.

The second reform is *horizontal*. Here, I propose a diversification in which the hold of the criminal law paradigm on the accountability process yields through a two-step process: initially, to integrate approaches to accountability offered by law generally (such as judicialized civil sanctions or group-based public ser-vice) and, subsequently, to involve quasilegal or fully extralegal accountability mechanisms such as truth commissions, legislative reparations, public inquiries, transparency, and the politics of commemoration. I hope to develop coordinated application of modalities of sanction that more closely track the peculiarities of collective violence. The goal of horizontal reform is to advance *from law to justice*: initially, by moving international criminal law to a capacious law of atrocity and, ultimately, to an enterprise that constructively incorporates extra-judicial initiatives. If operationalized, these reforms raise the possibility that a larger number of individuals could become implicated in the justice process, thereby inviting a broader conversation regarding the viability of collective responsibility for collective criminality. Chapter 7 considers this difficult and controversial issue – in theory as well as in practice – through the lens of the litigation that Bosnia and Herzegovina has initiated against Serbia and Montenegro (now Serbia)[88] before the International Court of Justice.

These vertical and horizontal reforms can operate conjunctively to promote a pluralistic implementation of accountability for mass atrocity that moves beyond ordinary criminal law designed by Western states for common criminals.

One implication of these reforms is that sanction might look different and assume different calibrations in each case of atrocity. In other words, the process of justice might look different in Sierra Leone than it does in Cambodia, and the process of justice in Cambodia might differ from that in Kosovo. This may lead to some messiness in terms of the pursuit of justice; it may also create a need for international lawyers to become more familiar with comparative methodologies, particularly from the developing world. In short, I envision a penology that gains its independence through an embrace of procedural diversity. Is such a position tenable in light of my understanding of discrimination-based atrocity as universal extreme evil?

Although I accept that a case can be made for the universality of the wrong-doing (and the universality of holding wrongdoers accountable), I do not accept that a case can be made for the universality, and certainly not for the exclusivity, of extant modalities of international criminal law as *the* method to secure these universal accountability goals. It is crucial to separate the substantive goals at hand, namely the condemnation of extreme evil, from the process regarding *how* this condemnation is to be operationalized and the institutions *where* this process occurs. In Chapter 7, I defend the proposition that certain substantive universals, such as accountability for extreme evil, can be attainable through diverse procedural mechanisms. In this regard, I draw from *cosmopolitan theory*. Cosmopolitanism has come to the fore in discussions over multiculturalism in domestic political and educational institutions. It has informed global debates over the distribution of resources. Its application to international criminal law, however, is less settled – albeit deeply promising.

Cosmopolitans, from the ancient Stoics and Cynics to their contemporary counterparts, share the belief that all human beings belong to a single moral community. Cosmopolitans differ, however, regarding the values intrinsic to this shared community. Some cosmopolitans argue that there is a very thick set of shared values and that this set should expand; whereas other cosmopolitans claim a thin set and are more agnostic regarding the question whether the content of this thin set should expand. One important issue for cosmopolitans is the place of local, patriotic, and national affiliations in human identity. All cosmopolitans acknowledge the existence of these affiliations, although contemporary cosmopolitans engage with them with particular vivacity. I consider the approaches of a broad array of cosmopolitans – ranging from the Stoics and Cynics to contemporary writers such as Martha Nussbaum, David Hollinger, David Held, Kok-Chor Tan, Kwame Anthony Appiah, and Paul Schiff Berman – to the place of local affiliations. Overall, I conclude that these cosmopolitans welcome multiple affiliations and overlapping associations. There are certain transnational commonalities intrinsic to human existence, but other aspects of the human condition remain best expressed and understood at the local level by the individual among his or her fellow citizens and neighbors.

Insofar as the model I propose recognizes the universality of our shared membership in a moral community that condemns great evil and entitles victims thereof – in particular those most directly affected – to accountability, it aligns with cosmopolitanism's basic precept. On the other hand, the model adopts cosmopolitanism's acceptance of the richness of local identifications, particularly when this richness helps promote justice. The notion of diverse procedure for universal wrongdoing thereby fits within a cosmopolitan theory of law, although it certainly tends toward the pluralist end of the continuum. My model, therefore, is one of "*cosmopolitan pluralism.*"[89]

Admittedly, there is an intrinsic tension within cosmopolitan pluralism in terms of mediating the universal and particular. However, it is *because* of this tension that cosmopolitan pluralism seems particularly well suited as a framework for emergent fields, such as international criminal law, that must fulfill difficult balancing acts between global governance and local legitimacy. Cosmopolitan pluralism justifies a position that holds that, although genocide and discrimination-based crimes against humanity are universal evils, they can be coherently sanctioned in diverse manners that might instantiate themselves differently in light of the distinctive social geographies of various atrocities. One advantage of cosmopolitan pluralist reforms is that they recognize that each occurrence of discrimination-based atrocity is somewhat different and, instead of flattening difference through application of one-size-fits-all process, endeavor to fine-tune process without undermining the expressive value of sanctioning universal wrongdoing.

Consequently, cosmopolitan pluralism does not demand the development of a singular vision of punishment for extraordinary international criminals that becomes universally applicable to all extraordinary international criminals everywhere. Assuredly, the differences between the perpetrator of ordinary common crime and the extraordinary international criminal suggest the limitations that inhere in transposing from our experiences with the former to develop a penology for the latter. Recognizing these limitations is important, insofar as it can push us toward a reconstructive direction. Such a transposition becomes particularly problematic when it derives from a circumscribed set of experiences with ordinary criminals – namely the experiences of liberal criminal law – which then become mapped onto culturally diverse contexts. This does not mean, however, that domestic law has nothing to offer in terms of regulating atrocity. Rather, until the voices of afflicted populations are more clearly heard, channeled through bottom-up perspectives, and loosened from the primacy or complementarity of internationalist visions, we simply do not know exactly what values pertaining to the punishment of enemies of humankind – if any – truly are shared among us all. Herein lie the conversational beginnings of the formulation of a *sui generis* penology for mass violence.

In sum, extraordinary international crimes are characterized, to varying degrees, by their connived collective elements. Downplaying this characteristic inhibits the emergence of effective penological and criminological goals. It seems that international lawyers have drained the collective nature of the crimes (even though they simultaneously pronounce their extraordinariness) so as to fit them within comforting procedural frameworks. A more challenging, albeit highly productive, task would be to discuss methodologies that recognize that the crimes are extraordinary precisely *because* of their collective tendencies. One approach to this task is to pursue an accretion of various layers of accountability, instead of the reductionism inherent in boiling accountability down to simple liberal criminal law terminologies. Insofar as cosmopolitan pluralism welcomes this horizontal accretion, it permits the extraordinary international criminal to be treated independently, and not as an adjunct to the common criminal.

There is some room for adversarial criminal trials within the justice matrix. The value of trials, though, best flourishes when trials constitute *a* means to justice, not *the* means to justice. Consequently, I posit that the value of prosecutions, for example those undertaken by the ICC, will increase if the ICC operates as one of many entities pursuing accountability in a diverse system where power is diffused polycentrically. If alternate, and overlapping, remedies were to become normalized and practically accessible, the political pressures for criminal convictions ironically would diminish.

Whereas Chapter 7 considers longer-term reconstitution of the field of international criminal justice engendered by cosmopolitan pluralism, Chapter 8 offers short-term reforms to extant international criminal law institutions. By proposing short-term reforms I assume the hard-won place of the ICC, and other tribunals, within the international sociolegal order; I also assume that these institutions are capable of evolution. Over time, it is through a process of building upon past experiences through a series of imperfect reforms and halting advances that the project of international criminal justice will advance. In this regard, an important step is to resist the allure of parsimonious solutions to terribly complex phenomena of communal violence and human agency. The complexities of regulating atrocity and promoting justice in its aftermath underscore that no single reform is curative.

(VI) CONCLUSION

International criminal law has come a very long way since Nuremberg. Its rapid expansion is all the more remarkable considering that, in the arc of human history, the six decades since Nuremberg amount to little more than the blink of an eye. The institutions implementing international criminal law are the product of considerable effort, relentless persistence, and great inspiration. These institutions would not have arisen but for the incredible energy, passion, and commitment of international lawyers and human rights activists. In short order, these institutions have become mainstreamed as elements of postconflict transition. The ICC now is a permanent fixture in global affairs. The mainstreaming of these institutions, however, gives rise to nettlesome questions pertaining to effectiveness. The time has come for international criminal law as a discipline to move beyond nascence and to welcome a second, and even more challenging, stage: that of reappraisal, maturation, and self-improvement. I intend this book to form part of this second-generation dialogue.

CHAPTER 2

Conformity and Deviance

History teaches that there is something novel in pursuing justice – instead of vengeance – in the aftermath of atrocity. This is a new endeavor. It is bold, fresh, exciting, at times anxious, and certainly lacking in experience. International criminal lawyers have stepped into this experiential void.

One way for the architects of international criminal process, most of whom are Western or Western-trained, to assuage anxiety is to turn to that which is familiar to them: namely, domestic criminal and human rights frameworks in liberal states. Even though experiences with these frameworks are not easily transferable to mass atrocity,[1] it is somehow easier to replay preexisting doctrinal frameworks rather than develop new ones. The fact that atrocity prosecutions are reactive to cataclysmic events – sometimes expediently so – makes them even more prone to claim a quick-fix identity.[2]

It thus becomes understandable why the structure, rules, and methodologies of the process and punishment of extraordinary international criminality largely constitute a transplant of the structure, rules, and methodologies of ordinary criminal process and punishment in those states that dominate the international order. Assuredly, the transplant is not a perfectly repotted plant. Certain adaptations have taken place along the way. Some of these, for example regarding the laws of evidence, arose in part in response to the difficulties in convicting individuals for group crimes.[3] Yet, as I explore in this chapter, these adaptations are narrow, programmatic, and at times embarrassing to the institutions that promulgate them. Other adaptations include often hasty incorporation of notions of transitional justice that, at times, can be at cross-purposes with the clarity of criminal law. However, all things considered, "[b]ecause of the power of the United States, along with other Western countries, in the international debate about prosecution of human rights atrocities, the criminal justice analogy used in that debate largely relies on Western assumptions about ordinary crime."[4]

This inclination toward borrowing from the familiar additionally is motored by a perception that borrowing can fulfill an important legitimizing function. Influential scholars such as Hersch Lauterpacht thought that the more international law resembled domestic law, the more it would look familiar and like a complete legal system and the less it would look like politics.[5] From Lauterpacht's viewpoint, there was no principled reason to differentiate between the national and the international. To the extent to which failing to differentiate legitimated international law by making it more law-like, so much the better.

Even though the resemblance between international and domestic legal process initially may have served as a legitimizing factor, once contemporary international criminal tribunals actually began to judicialize atrocity in the Balkans, East Timor, and Rwanda, this resemblance turned into somewhat of a liability. Although ordinary criminal process and our experience with common criminals certainly can teach us something about mass atrocity, this base of preexisting knowledge does not have all the answers. The complex sources of atrocity, the multitudes of victims and perpetrators, and the organic nature of responsibility challenge traditional process and institutions.[6]

Otto Triffterer, a leading architect of extant international criminal law, "poses the question of the transferability of criminal law concepts to the international sphere, but avoids giving an answer by turning the question around: 'Why not?'"[7] With great respect, this response is too facile. Considerable difficulties mar the transplantation of domestic criminal law to the international context. These difficulties transcend the standard, and at times tired, arguments according to which it is difficult to analogize from the domestic order to the international because the latter lacks a constabulary, legislature, and enforcement agencies.

Difficulties are especially evident when it comes to contrasting the focal point of the judicial process, namely the accused.[8] To be sure, extraordinary international crimes violate *jus cogens* norms and, thereby, are universally condemnable. That said, whereas for the most part individual participation in ordinary crime deviates from generally accepted social norms in the place and time where the crime is committed, extraordinary crime has an organic and group component that makes individual participation therein not so self-evidently deviant. Participation is often a matter of obeying official authority, not transgressing it.

Ordinary criminal law operates in a continuous national or local context to manage routine violations of law; extraordinary international criminal law operates in a dynamically discontinuous context of collective crisis and recovery. Although it is convenient to think of genocidal killers as common criminals, there is reason to question the usefulness of this analogy. A paradigm of individualized culpability may well be suitable for deviant isolated crime, although some criminologists challenge this premise. This same paradigm, however, is all the more ill fitting for crimes committed by collectivities, states, and organizations.[9] Group crimes can be the aggregate of the participation of all involved individuals; they, however, also can constitute a sum that exceeds the parts. In this chapter, I explore whether there is reason to doubt the assumption that the extraordinary international criminal should be subject to processes and punishments developed for ordinary common criminals. I do so through a review of the actors on the stage of atrocity: perpetrators, bystanders, beneficiaries, and victims.

(1) PERPETRATORS AND BENEFICIARIES

Perpetrators of mass atrocity are not a uniform group. They can be divided into three broad categories. First, at the apex, are conflict entrepreneurs: namely, those individuals who exacerbate discriminatory divisions, which they then commandeer. Among their goals is to acquire and retain political power. Second are those leaders who, while exercising authority over others and often ordering killings, themselves remain subject to authority and, accordingly, are ordered into ordering others. Authority, after all, is situational. The third category includes the actual killers, most of whom are ordinary folks. This category is often very large in number. It is in this third group that Anastase Nkinamubanzi, the bulldozer driver whose story opens this book, belonged. Of course, the distinctions among these groups are not watertight.[10]

A much larger group also bears responsibility for atrocity even though its members are not, strictly speaking, perpetrators. This group comprises bystanders: those multitudes who comply with the violence, who acquiesce in it, or who idle while it unfolds around them. In many cases, these bystanders benefit ideologically and politically from the atrocity. Atrocity actualizes their self-worth through group pride. They feel part of a grand social project without bloodying their own hands. These individuals also gain from atrocity in a more craven, materialistic way. They may, for example, opportunistically move into a suddenly vacant apartment, double the size of their farm, or get a promotion at work. One way to describe this subset of bystanders is as beneficiaries. Not all bystanders are beneficiaries, but many are.

These groups represent descending levels of moral blameworthiness for atrocity. In other words, conflict entrepreneurs are the most culpable according to standards adopted by traditional criminal law, namely intentionality of action. They are followed by other leaders and killers, then by those who assist atrocity, those who benefit from it, and lastly those who draw their blinds and look away. Nearly all bystanders, even benefiting bystanders, fall outside of what international criminal law defines as "guilt." They are not subjects or objects of the trial, a process to which they once again are bystanders and, as I eventually argue, benefiting bystanders insofar as the trial confers upon them the status of collective innocence.

Richard Goldstone – reflecting a widely held position – posits that leaders and those in superior positions in the chain of command are, owing to their positive governance obligations, more deserving of prosecution and weightier punishment for their involvement in mass atrocity.[11] This position has been internalized by international lawmakers. Accordingly, prosecutorial efforts have tilted toward defendants in higher-ranking positions. That said, this tilt certainly has not immunized rank-and-file killers from prosecution in international criminal tribunals.[12] For example, nearly all of the prosecutions that took place at the

East Timor Special Panels involved low-level, and often poorly educated, offenders. Furthermore, the ICTY's early convictions involved Dražen Erdemović, a lowly soldier of the Bosnian Serb army, and Duško Tadić, an essentially indistinguishable thug.

The stated prosecutorial focus on influential defendants squares with the reality that certain leaders who act as conflict entrepreneurs create the social norms that trap others as captive participants. These entrepreneurs strategically normalize hatred that initially may have been deviant and isolated. As such, sanctioning their behavior may conform to a criminology and penology that censures deviance. However, international criminal tribunals have not staked out a consistent penological position when it comes to sentencing leaders as opposed to subordinates. In fact, an ICTY Trial Chamber noted that the case law "does not evidence a discernible pattern of . . . imposing sentences on subordinates that differ greatly from those imposed on their superiors."[3]

Independent of the problem of inconsistency within international criminal law institutions, Goldstone's argument – however reasonable – fails to address a central concern. Atrocity would not reach truly epidemic levels but for the vigorous participation of the masses. For many mid-level officials and rank-and-file killers, participating in atrocity is not deviant behavior. Even less deviant is the complicity and acquiescence of the bystander. This complicity and acquiescence falls outside of the criminal law paradigm but constitutes an essential prerequisite in order for violence to become truly massive in scale. Part of the riddle of purposively responding to mass atrocity, and preventing it, is to assess how law can implicate the complicit and acquiescent masses who are responsible even if not formally guilty.

To be sure, not all atrocities, or atrocity perpetrators, fit the same psychosocial profile. There are cases in which human rights abuses are perpetrated top-down, through occasional and targeted covert state operations, such as in Chile. In these cases, leaders plausibly could be punished for deviant behavior because they themselves recognized that what they were doing was wrong and that is why they covered it up.[14] In Pinochet's Chile, torture by the DINA agency was done in isolated basements. The victims of Operation Condor were furtively thrown out of helicopters. Death flights in Argentina, which targeted political opponents of the military government, similarly resulted in secretive deaths in the depths of the sea.[15] Alternately, megalomaniacal leaders can encourage and reward violence initiated through party or military bureaucracies that involve broad networks of agents, informants, and sycophants. This apparently was the case in Saddam Hussein's Iraq.[16] But there are other cases where conflict entrepreneurs exhorted violence and, in response, substantial numbers of average people ordinarily disconnected from the political process eagerly butchered other human beings, in full view of the public, with the acquiescence or complicity of many of their fellow citizens. It is this third typology of violence that is most prone to metastasize into epidemics of atrocity, although the first two typologies also can reach widescale levels. The discriminatory nature of the violence often directly correlates with the zeal of public participation therein.

Rwanda presents a compelling case study of this third typology of violence. The Rwandan genocide disturbingly demonstrates David Luban's perception that "getting people to murder and torment their neighbors is not hard; in some ways, it turns out to be ridiculously easy."[17] Luis Salas writes that "[t]he manner in which [Rwandans] were killed, and the pleasure that attackers derived from inflicting the greatest pain, is shocking to even the most experienced investigators."[18] The Rwandan genocide was characterized by broad-based involvement and popular support.[19] It was not spontaneous, but was planned. Conflict entrepreneurs (such as media officials) and the Rwandan political and military leadership primed a Hutu population ready to kill. The killings were not secret. Rather, they "were committed publicly in full view of the population."[20] The preexisting normative structure was suspended and replaced with the normalization of ethnic elimination.[21] The act of killing required individual action, but this same act doubled as an expression of collective agency. To speak of individual *mens rea* among the rank-and-file in such contexts is a bit fanciful.[22] It is unclear whether participants acted out of the kind of free will that H.L.A. Hart would determine indispensable to the allocation of criminal guilt.[23] Throughout Rwanda, neighbors killed neighbors they had known since childhood and with whom they previously had lived in harmony. Familiarity between victim and victimizer is not a characteristic unique to Rwanda. A similar situation arose in East Timor, where "the majority of perpetrators came from the same village as the victims ... attack[ing] persons whom they had known since they were children, had attended school with [...]."[24]

Nor does Rwanda stand alone in its narration of broad public complicity and the zeal of the killers as phenomena that counter the deviance of the violence. For example, Iris Chang in *The Rape of Nanking* cites eyewitness evidence that many Japanese soldiers so enjoyed the murder and sexual terror they inflicted on hundreds of thousands of Chinese civilians in 1937, that they made a sport out of it through contests.[25] In Sierra Leone, many perpetrators were ordinary children, often – but not always – kidnapped and drugged, who began killing and maiming in the most grotesque fashion amid the company of their new families of killers. Violence in the former Yugoslavia also implicated broad levels of responsibility. The Bosnian Serb government – normally taciturn when it comes to discussing Serb ethnic cleansing campaigns – has recognized the collectivization of violence. In October 2005 it identified over 19,000 soldiers operating in the region during the Srebrenica massacre, in which 7,000 Bosnian Muslim men and boys were isolated within a UN safe zone and slaughtered.[26] This list was compiled to provide "a fuller picture of how the crimes were perpetrated."[27] Although individual participants in ethnic violence may satisfy a variety of goals, including greed and settling scores with neighbors, what characterizes the greatest evils is the actualization of goals of ethnic advancement and elimination of the other.

Peter French writes that extraordinary international criminals tend to exemplify an Aristotelian conception of wickedness.[28] Aristotle, French notes, conceived of wickedness that is perpetrated by persons who do not believe that what they are doing is wrong or immoral.[29] French contrasts this conception with what he identifies as a Christian conception of wickedness, which is "preferential" in the sense that the perpetrator knows that the act is morally wrong but still undertakes it.[30] Referencing the Balkans atrocities, French concludes that "media accounts of the average Balkan war criminals reflect an Aristotelian rather than the Christian conception of wickedness."[31] In fact, "[t]he reports make it appear that the perpetrators did what they did believing (albeit perversely) that it was the right thing to do."[32] The more the violence is linked with group-based characteristics, the more perpetrators seem to exemplify an Aristotelian conception of wickedness rather than a Christian conception; and the easier it becomes to kill rather than break away from the dominant group of killers.

For Daniel Jonah Goldhagen, Nazi Germany constitutes a similar example.[33] According to Goldhagen, ordinary Germans – fueled by eliminationist anti-Semitism and believing in large numbers that the Jews "ought to die" – became willing executioners.[34] Germans participated in the Holocaust because "they thought [...] the annihilation of the Jews was socially desirable, and that the Jews were a particularly inferior form of subhumans. They simply thought they were doing the right thing."[35] This made it possible for a radical government to implement a radical plan. Insofar as it was only in Germany that virulent anti-Semitism was combined with a radical government and sufficient military might, the Holocaust "could have been produced only by Germany."[36]

The Goldhagen thesis has generated considerable controversy. It has led to a more fractious debate than have reports of the collectivization of violence in Rwanda, the Balkans, or East Timor. Much of this controversy arises from perceptions that Goldhagen ascribes a cultural basis to the Holocaust.[37] Although these perceptions are not entirely accurate, in his subsequent foreword to the German language edition of *Hitler's Willing Executioners*, Goldhagen goes out of his way to confirm that, although the Holocaust only could have happened in Germany, this was not because of any immutable or eternal German national character.[38] He "reject[s] categorically" (not to mention somewhat defensively) the notion that essential psychological dispositions of the Germans produced the Holocaust.[39]

As I see it, rooting atrocity in culture implies that certain nationalities or ethnicities have characteristics that could immunize them from succumbing to atrocity. Because atrocity has occurred in multiple locations on multiple continents, and because all human beings have the capacity to commit brutal acts, the reality is that atrocity is not so much a cultural phenomenon as it is one tied to humanity at large. That said, there are such things as cultures of hatred and cultures of violence. People can be acculturated or socialized into eliminationism, even though atrocity cannot be explained away by culture or national character. There is a difference between culture and acculturation into hatred. I believe the process of acculturation into hatred can arise within any culture, although it may invoke culturally specific signifiers in that process. What is more, cultures of hatred can give way to cultures of peace or, at least, recognition of the horrors of hate. Goldhagen points out how this transformation has occurred in Germany over the past half-century. Were it not for the possibility of lancing cultures of hate, any consequentialist rationalization of punishment would be entirely doomed at the starting gate.

Also contributing to the controversy that dogs Goldhagen's work is his discussion regarding what exactly to do with those individuals caught up in the Nazi collectivization of violence. Goldhagen writes that these "enormous" numbers of Germans are "criminal."[40] He invokes the notion of guilt, which he applies to these individuals; he locates their guilt very traditionally in their individual actions. However, perhaps in response to the public reaction to his work, Goldhagen goes out of his way to say that he (once again) "reject[s] categorically" the notion of collective guilt, which he defines as guilt "merely by dint of [. . .] membership in a collectivity."[41]

My sense is that, were Goldhagen to operate within a model of liability that transcended liberal criminal law as the tool with which to assess wrongdoing, and instead were to contemplate an accountability model that permitted more fine-grained distinctions and polycentric remedies, then perhaps his argument would be less intimidating to many readers. Moreover, he may feel less of a need to beat a hasty retreat by trouncing the notion of collective guilt, a trouncing that seems misplaced given the focus of his research project on the complicity of the German public and how it stood primed to eliminate European Jewry. This retreat is distracting insofar as Goldhagen is right to note the deeply collective aspects of mass atrocity, its industrial nature, and the challenge this reality presents for accountability and prevention. Now that they face their own mortality, more evidence arises from the "millions of low-level functionaries who did the daily, dirty work of genocide" during the Holocaust.[42] This evidence confirms the organic nature of the violence, how its tentacles gripped deeply into the social fabric, and how average people "slipped, bit by bit, into evil."[43] After long shifts in the forced labor camps, the brutalizing guards would dance the night away and romance lovers under the stars – just like any other working person enjoying downtime from the job before once again reporting dutifully for work the next morning.

(II) CONFORMITY, TRANSGRESSION, AND THE GROUP

Drawing from their fieldwork in Bosnia, legal scholars Laurel Fletcher and Harvey Weinstein identify a "communal engagement with mass violence" that, in their estimation, criminal trials leave unaddressed.[44] They propose that individuals may not always have control over their actions in the context of collective events, particularly cataclysmic events.[45] Participants may be captives of social norms; at a minimum, they certainly are captivated by those norms. The breadth of these norms could be such that the violence itself, as Arendt provocatively noted, becomes nothing more than banal in the time and place where it is committed.[46] Paradoxically, persons with a weakened sense of individual autonomy and independence commit crimes that are normatively deemed more serious than ordinary domestic crimes.[47] This seems to fly in the face of the criminology of ordinary crime that international criminal law adopts as a self-rationalization, insofar as culpability in ordinary crime derives from the extent of the perpetrator's voluntary independent participation therein. These contradictions might well explain why, despite the rhetoric, actual punishments levied out for extraordinary international crimes are of comparable severity to (and often are more lenient than) those used to sanction serious ordinary crime in national legal systems. I further explore this phenomenon in Chapter 6.

Perpetrators of extraordinary international crimes generally belong to a collective that shares a mythology of ethnic, national, racial, or religious superiority, perhaps even infallibility.[48] Psychologists such as Gustav Le Bon and Sigmund Freud, as well as theologians like Reinhold Niebuhr, have suggested the "regression inherent in group behavior"; they have noted the effects of the group on individual personality, including how group association fragments conscience and facilitates emotion over judgment.[49] What is more, group dynamics may well diffuse responsibility, obscure individual decisionmaking, and suppress dissent. Psychologist James Waller, in his impressive work *Becoming Evil: How Ordinary People Commit Genocide and Mass Killing*, flatly remarks that "the most outstanding common characteristic of perpetrators of extraordinary evil is their normality, not their abnormality."[50] Those who commit extraordinary international crimes may be the ones conforming to social norms whereas those who refuse to commit the crimes choose to act transgressively.

Nor can these perpetrators generally be diagnosed as psychotic. Admittedly, some are.[51] However, other than certain notoriously sadistic offenders, the evidence does not suggest that most atrocity perpetrators are insane, demented, or ill. Waller surmises that there

> is no reason to expect that the distribution of [antisocial personality disorder] among perpetrators of genocide is any greater than that of the general population; there are actually very good reasons to expect that the distribution is *less* than that of the general population. [...] Even if we were to broaden our search for psychopathology beyond [antisocial personality disorder], it is doubtful that rates of abnormality among perpetrators run any higher than what we find among the general population.[52]

Douglas Kelley, a psychiatrist dispatched to the Nuremberg proceedings, did not find evidence of psychiatric disturbance among the defendants.[53] Waller notes that "none of the experts wished to go on record as stating that, according to psychological test data, many of the Nazis may actually have been normal or even well-adjusted."[54] Even though it would make it easier for the rest of humanity to distance itself from the perpetrators by proving how insane, or deviant, they were, they really were neither. Ironically, in Nazi Germany an effort was made to weed out sadists and psychopaths from even the most extreme killing personnel – for example the *Einsatzgruppen* – insofar as it was felt that such persons "would not be as efficient, effective, and dependable as killers [...]."[55]

Psychologists have studied individual obedience to violent orders. The findings from these studies are varied. Among these studies, however, Stanley Milgram's are the best known.[56] These studies involved individual interactions between teachers and a mock learner where teachers believed they were administering electric shock to the learner, even to levels described as "severe" or "XXX," when the learner failed to give the correct answers to the questions posed. Milgram's work suggests that ordinary people are quite willing to inflict harm, even serious harm, on strangers if instructed by an authority figure (in Milgram's initial test, about two-thirds of all subjects did so). Many of Milgram's subjects continued to comply even though they exhibited great consternation and nervousness at the choices they faced. To be sure, it can be difficult to extrapolate from Milgram's survey to the actual behavior of individuals in contexts where perpetrators know and can see for themselves that they are inflicting pain and killing people. Milgram's subjects, despite the cries (and eventual silence) from those given shocks for their wrong answers, were assured that no permanent physical damage would result from the shocks. The learner sat in a different room than the teachers. Subject and object were separated.

Despite these limitations, though, Milgram's experiments do ground his writing on what he labeled the "agentic state."[57] In this state, persons are drained of their personal responsibility in the sense that they become agents of the duty expected of them by authority figures. Amid the structural factors that precede mass atrocity, those individuals who resist assimilation into an agentic state are often deviant. What is more, insofar as individualized international criminal law often targets only a handful of high-profile or particularly sadistic offenders, it fails to deter the formation of an agentic state. Those who simply obey their industrial duty in the killing fields run little risk of ever being caught by the criminal trial model, yet at the time reap the benefits of membership in and social promotion within the favored group.

Although Milgram's writing on the substitute agentic state could be used to justify the exoneration of individual responsibility in situations of collective violence, this is not my intention. Nor is my purpose to venture into the world of evolutionary psychology, where certain experts – perplexed by the observation that "no other species shows the degree of premeditated mass killings of its own species that humans have shown over the centuries" – suggest that humans are simply wired to adapt to group expectations, even terribly violent ones, in order to survive.[58] Nor do I wish to enter a debate on whether collective pressures eviscerate moral choice and free will, and instead substitute determinism. Rather, I make more modest use of Milgram's findings to argue that collectivization, diffusion, and conformity whittle down the scope of individual choice and, accordingly, create group phenomena that intersect brusquely with legal systems based on the primacy of individual agency. One response might be for the law to respond collectively. Looking at responses through a collective lens might recognize the automaticity of mass atrocity. Arendt hinted at the monochrome created by totalitarianism and noted that totalitarianism makes human beings superfluous, which "happens as soon as all unpredictability – which, in human beings, is the equivalent of spontaneity – is eliminated."[59]

In sum, I contend that the perpetrator of mass atrocity is qualitatively different than the perpetrator of ordinary crime. Of course, the two are not fully shorn of any similarities. However, their differences are material, suggesting the need to judiciously contemplate a novel schematic of punishment for the extraordinary international criminal. Extraordinary international crime often flows from organic groupthink in the times and places where it is committed, making individual participation therein less deviant and, in fact, more of a matter of conforming to a social norm.[60] This deep complicity cascade does not diminish the brutality or exculpate the aggressor. But it imperils certain assumptions about bystander innocence and the salutary role of the international community; squeezes out histories of colonialism and exploitation; and assuages the many by blaming the few. The deep complicity cascade plays a much more dynamic role in the commission of mass atrocity than it does in isolated, ordinary common crimes. Ignoring or denying the uniqueness of the criminality of mass atrocity stunts the development of effective methods to promote accountability for mass criminals.

At this point, two challenges to this thesis present themselves. These pull in different directions, but share in common the precept that the lines between the extraordinary and the ordinary are blurred.

The first challenge posits that a number of ordinary domestic crimes share certain of the collective characteristics I ascribe to extraordinary international crimes. This overlap suggests that, in some instances, the distinction between ordinary crime punishable under domestic law and extraordinary crime punishable under international law is not clear cut. For example, domestic crime such as gang activity, drug offenses, hate crimes, certain white-collar crimes, and organized crime may arise from adhesion to a certain code or norm within a particular community. These may be intensely social crimes, deeply collaborative at the subgroup level. Accordingly, so goes the critique, it would be far too absolutist to posit that deviance theory serves as a basis to ground *all* criminal sanction in ordinary domestic contexts.

In response, I would agree that there is a subset of ordinary common crime where the deviant nature of individual involvement in the criminality is not self-evident. Within this subset, there is an unequivocal need for criminological and penological research that recognizes the influence of the group as a social agent and the structural nature of criminogenic conditions. Collaterally, international lawyers concerned about mass atrocity can learn from their domestic counterparts concerned with gang activity and hate crimes. However, the existence of this subset does not impugn my position that ordinary common crime and extraordinary international crime can be differentiated along an axis of deviance. Violent acts such as murder, torture, infliction of physical harm, and sexual assault deviate materially more from social norms operative in ordinary times in ordinary places than they do from social norms in places afflicted by the breakdown and remobilization that are conditions precedent to mass atrocity. The breakdown and remobilization are much more transformative than anything experienced even within violent subcultures of ordinary polities. Whereas the state punishes infractions of ordinary criminal law, in situations of mass atrocity the entire apparatus of the state urges the violence and can even go so far as to sanction nonparticipation. A society in the throes of mass atrocity, particularly discrimination-based atrocity, is often one in which the law says that killing members of the "other" group is legal, whereas killing a member of your own group is not (unless that member opposes the eliminationist policies).

Although deviance is a fuzzy concept,[61] theorists basically define it as "banned or controlled behaviour which is likely to attract punishment or disapproval."[62] Deviants "tend to make their lives rather more hazardous and problematic."[63] They demonstrate a "real strain toward concealment."[64] Yet those who participate in truly mass killing engage in an activity that is not banned and which may even be public. Those who refuse to participate are the ones who generally make their lives more hazardous and problematic.

In the prelude to and implementation of mass atrocity, group leaders distribute weapons, build industrial extermination facilities, feed and house murderers, and, in some cases, provide them sexual slaves. All of this is done in order to facilitate the targeting of victims simply based on their immutable characteristics, not any threat the victims actually pose as individuals to the group, to its control of territory, or to its status. In those few areas of ordinary domestic criminality where individual deviance is obfuscated by group ordering, such as certain gang activity, this simply does not rise to the level of conforming to the dictates of a criminal state. Even if gang-related delinquency amounted to what Albert Cohen calls a "'way of life' in [...] inner urban neighbourhoods,"[65] this lifestyle is defined in opposition to the mainstream. Travis Hirschi found that, for control theorists, delinquent acts "result when an individual's bond to society is weak or broken."[66] The killer in contexts of mass atrocity, on the other hand, often exhibits a very strong bond with both state and society. It is the delinquent in cases of mass atrocity who dissociates from the group. As David Downes and Paul Rock note, the ideal-type portrait of the nondelinquent includes being imbued with a strong belief in the need to obey rules, not deviate from them.[67] In the cauldron of atrocity, it is Holmes' good person and the Hartian official, both of whom internalize the value of positivist state law, who conform to the societal expectation of extirpation.

The second challenge is somewhat obverse to the first. This challenge posits that extraordinary international crimes really are not that extraordinary; in fact, they are not aberrational but, rather, are sufficiently commonplace throughout history so as to become ordinary. *Arguendo*, it is perfectly reasonable to subject them to the processes and modalities of ordinary common crime.

I have three responses to this second challenge. First, even if one were to accept the underlying criminality as ordinary, the reality is that the ordinary process and punishment currently invoked by legal institutions is highly selective. The personnel and modalities of international criminal tribunals, and the

national institutions they influence, implement liberal criminal law to postconflict (and, at times, conflict) societies for which this law often is exogenous.
Second, irrespective of whether the underlying criminality is characterized as
ordinary or extraordinary, the punishment of group-based atrocity crimes through
extant sanctioning modalities fails to satisfy penological aspirations. Third, and
more foundationally, it does not seem tenable to posit that occurrences of mass
atrocity are as commonplace as occurrences of, say, armed robbery or arson
to claim the insurance money. Mass atrocity that implicates an "international
interest," to borrow from Larry May's characterization of international criminality, is far from routine.[68] Discrimination-based violence, such as genocide
and persecution as a crime against humanity, that results in the mobilization of
entire societies into the killing of masses of people just because of their membership in another group is not a matter of course. Participation in an atrocity
after it has begun may be a matter of conforming to a social norm, and hence
be prosaic, but creating an atrocity that eliminates or cleanses a group based on
discriminatory grounds is not an ordinary everyday occurrence.

This third response can be unpacked further. I underscore the importance of
not falling into the trap that equates campaigns of genocide and crimes against
humanity with war. Even if war were ordinary, this does not mean that genocide
or crimes against humanity are as well. Both are quite distinct from war. As the
Rwandan experience instructs, genocide and war are separate initiatives with
separate goals. The Holocaust is not the same as Nazi aggression. Moreover,
unlike campaigns of genocide or ethnic cleansing, under international law war
exceptionally can be lawful.

Moreover, genocide and crimes against humanity differ in important regards
even from those acts that amount to unlawful conduct in war, namely war crimes
(violations of the *jus in bello*) or the unlawful waging of war (violations of the *jus
ad bellum* that lead to the crime of aggression).[69] The distinction between war
crimes, on the one hand, and crimes against humanity and genocide, on the
other, is reflected in the Rome Statute's designation of the latter two as manifestly
illegal but not the former. This distinction is further reflected in the fact that
the Rome Statute accords states the option of a seven-year opt-out period to the
ICC's jurisdiction over war crimes,[70] but not to genocide and crimes against
humanity. The crime of aggression is not yet defined in the Rome Statute and,
hence, cannot be prosecuted.

Stathis Kalyvas has found that many participants in a historical range of civil
wars in places as diverse as the United States, England, Lebanon, Afghanistan,
and Liberia were motivated by materialism, greed, and avarice.[71] The wrongdoing inflicted by these participants, some of which rises to the level of war
crimes, therefore is not inspired by ideological public motives such as the promotion of group identity but, rather, by private motives as pithy as thievery.
Conduct within the framework of nonideological civil war that Kalyvas notes is
animated by self-interested materialism targets victims not as indistinguishable
members of a group but, rather, because of their individual wealth, standing,
prior conduct, and assets. Although I do not believe that even the most privately

motivated thief in the chaos of civil war can be paralleled to the most privately motivated thief in a stable polity, one inference that arises from Kalyvas' research is that ordinary criminal modalities may be appropriate to capture individuals who commit war crimes when acting upon materialistic motivations, especially when doing so through individual action independent from the group.

That said, the inference does not extend to foot soldiers of atrocity, motivated by ideological and political goals, who turn to horrific violence to further the collective good of the group of which they are so proud. Of course, some participants in eliminationist genocide are encouraged by prospects for lucre and material gain or simply to settle personal vendettas; other participants are inspired by a medley of private and public motives. However, material motivations exert much greater influence on routine civil war participants than on actors in ethnic eliminationism for whom ideology constitutes the catalytic motivator. It is important, as I alluded to in Chapter 1, to differentiate discrimination-based crimes from other serious violations of international criminal law. Lessons from ordinary criminal law appear of least value when it comes to punishing participants in ideologically motivated discriminatory violence designed to bleach society of the "other." These crimes are often state crimes, instead of crimes committed against the state.[72]

Substantive proof of the guilt of genocide or crimes against humanity requires more than just proof of the *actus reus* of the violent act. In the case of genocide, guilt requires demonstration of the intent to wipe out a group in whole or in part. It is this goal – eliminationism or purification – that is extraordinary in its nature and bespeaks the manifest illegality at hand. Moreover, for persecution as a crime against humanity there also is a discriminatory animus; for all crimes against humanity there is the requirement to prove the systematic or widespread nature of the offense. This requires proof of a level of planning and organization that is found in few, if any, ordinary crimes. Also extraordinary is the broad network of collateral support that the perpetrators of these crimes enjoy, which simply does not apply to ordinary domestic crime. Ordinary people may become *génocidaires*, to be sure, but only under extraordinary circumstances.

(iii) POSTTRAUMATIC LIBERALISM DISORDER

My argument thus far is that collective violence cannot be rigorously analyzed without considering the effects of the collective on the individual. That said, this collective aspect creates considerable discomfort. It interfaces queasily with liberal legalism. This discomfort is manifested in international criminal law's eschewing of collective guilt and, even, collective responsibility; as well as its solemn preference for the guilt of a few individuals. International criminal law replaces the traditional subject of international law, the state, with a nontraditional subject, the individual, notwithstanding the fact that the abject criminality of mass violence often is committed at the behest of or in furtherance of the state.[73] As I introduced in Chapter 1, international criminal law thereby gloms onto what George Fletcher calls the "liberal idea that the only true units of

action in the world are individuals, not groups."[74] Cherie Booth echoes this
conventional wisdom:

> [P]roceedings before the ICC have the potential of countering the attribution
> of collective responsibility for acts committed by individuals. [Eminent South
> African jurist] Richard Goldstone put it well when commenting on the emo-
> tive photographs of the accused in the dock at Nuremberg. He said that "one
> sees a group of criminals. One does not see a group of representatives of the
> German people – the people who produced Goethe or Heine or Beethoven."[75]

The reality, however, is that the people who produced Goethe, Heine, and
Beethoven also produced Goebbels, Himmler, and Mengele. If Goldstone is
to credit the entire German people for producing artistic geniuses, why should
that same population be spared responsibility for producing mass criminals?
The logic of collective exoneration is somewhat frail. Although it is politically
or managerially expedient to insist that responsibility for mass atrocity not be
widely shared, this is not a realistic or accurate appraisal of the reality of atrocity on the ground. When an ICTY Trial Chamber held in the *Momir Nikolić*
sentencing decision that "by holding *individuals* responsible for the crimes committed, it was hoped [...] that the guilt of the few would not be shifted to the
innocent," it played to a wishful construction of atrocity rather than the bitter
reality of atrocity.[76] After all, mass violence involves the guilt of many, not a
few, and the responsibility of many more. In the end, the law is overambitious
by claiming such a transformative role, but then underambitious by involving
only a handful of characters. Philip Allot aptly remarks: "Feeble old men and
their seedy subordinates shuffle into the court-room, shrunken figures bearing
no physical relationship to the physical scale of suffering [...]."[77]

Fletcher and Weinstein maintain that the "liberal idea" elides its own effects.
Most important among these is that "individualized guilt may contribute to
a myth of collective innocence."[78] Fletcher and Weinstein's research ties into
psychoanalytic literature. It dovetails with the work of Karl Jaspers.[79] Jaspers
discusses a number of levels of guilt, including the criminal, the moral, and
the metaphysical.[80] The criminally guilty are those who gave orders or executed
crimes.[81] Moral guilt – a nonjuridical category – covers those who "conveniently
closed their eyes to events, or permitted themselves to be intoxicated, seduced or
bought with personal advantages, or who obeyed from fear."[82] The metaphysically guilty are those who fail to do whatever they can to prevent the commission
of the crime.

Trials do not involve what Jaspers identifies as the morally or metaphysically
guilty. Nor should they. It is doubtful that individual criminal punishment ought
to attach to all morally and metaphysically guilty individuals. However, this does
not mean that these individuals are blameless, or that they ought to be considered
as blameless, or that they are entitled to the law's intervening in a manner that
pronounces their innocence. That said, Fletcher and Weinstein found that "in
periods of collective violence, the focus on individual crimes has been used
by many to claim collective innocence."[83] Claims of collective innocence are
facilitated by "the conventional operation of legalism as an ideology," which

excludes bystanders from liability and fails to provide any "organized mechanism for [them] to confront and acknowledge the ways in which their inaction or passive participation contributed to the atrocities conducted in their name."[84] As Robert Meister notes, the "individuating project[,] a necessary component of criminal prosecutions[,]" neglects the world of bystanders and the reality that "[p]olitics, after all, is not merely about what people *do*, but also about what they support, wish, and condone [...]."[85] Without these wishes, this support, and all the condonation, the violence never would become truly massive and deeply rooted.

My concern is not a programmatic one that pertains to legal defense strategies. Accordingly, I am not making an argument for *ex post facto* or *nullum crimen sine proevia lege* defenses. The question of retroactivity – namely, whether persons can be convicted of acts that were perfectly legal under national laws in place at the time – has been elegantly addressed elsewhere.[86] My purpose here is not to breathe life into exculpations such as following orders, duress, or the "similarity of evil"[87] with a view to facilitating the acquittal of individual defendants. Wickedness remains wickedness, whether Aristotelian in nature or not. Victims of great wickedness deserve accountability; future generations are entitled to legal and policy responses that are purposive. Nonetheless, actually understanding something about the participants – whether perpetrators, bystanders, or beneficiaries – is a necessary step to grasp the scourge and, hence, to mitigate its effects and emphasize the deontological nature of the wrongdoing. A similar purpose is served by exploring the impact and logic of prevailing punishment frameworks – instead of taking these for granted – with a view to improving them, even if improvement entails their revision.

One attraction of extant international criminal process is that, when all is said and done, it manages to hold certain select individuals responsible. In this regard, it insists on individual responsibility within the opacity of collective anonymity. Occasionally, it can even ferret out distant acolytes who do not kill but supply the killers with the weapons necessary to elevate atrocity to massive levels.[88] Despite these accolades, however, the implementation of international criminal law is characterized by the fact that it fails to hold accountable the full array of people who individually are responsible for the collectivization of atrocity. In this sense, it skims the surface of the dynamic and diverse sources of mass atrocity. Assuredly, each responsible individual is not, and hence ought not to be found, criminally culpable. However, when the turn to criminal prosecutions squeezes out other mechanisms, whether legal or extralegal, which can instantiate a much broader rendition of responsibility, the entire justice matrix is compromised. International criminal culpability is too crude a device to assimilate and measure the small things many people do that make the larger things fewer people do truly pandemic. This crudeness suggests that the orthodoxy of the predicate of avoiding collective responsibility could be rethought and broader "ecological" approaches to the violence acknowledged.[89]

Assuredly, ordinary criminal law and process, even in those polities most apparently grounded in a theory of individual agency (e.g., the United States), are not wholly exclusive of notions of vicarious liability and collective responsibility.

American examples of the penetration of such notions include racketeering and anticorruption legislation, corporate crimes, certain instances of felony murder, and conspiracy. Other areas of law that regulate human activity also hold people responsible for the wrongdoing of others. These areas do not do so criminally, but through other manifestations of responsibility such as tortious liability or withholding of administrative privileges. Some areas of law, such as the law of agency, are entirely devoted to testing the limits of the vicariousness of responsibility. In all cases, but certainly in the case of criminal guilt, Mark Osiel notes that these departures from principles of individual responsibility remain quite controversial.[90] This controversy reveals – as I have argued elsewhere – the influence of individualism as the first principle of ordinary liberal criminal law.[91]

It is peculiar, then, that international criminal law, in procedurally transplanting from the domestic, also apparently essentializes ordinary criminal law by – at least rhetorically – caricaturizing its individualist elements into a Weberian ideal-type. The rhetoric of international criminal process insists, as the Nuremberg Tribunal intoned, that extraordinary international crimes are the crimes of men.[92] Insofar as international criminal law responds to conduct that is much more collective in nature than that faced by ordinary criminal law, the fact that it evokes a similar rhetorical archetype of individual agency suggests the broader nature of international criminal law's rhetorical preoccupation with individual culpability. International criminal tribunals vigorously assert a preoccupation to avoid collective guilt[93] and view this avoidance as promoting socially transformative goals in a manner that transcends the conventional wisdom of ordinary criminal law. As Norman Cigar and Paul Williams observe, "[t]he need to establish individual responsibility in order to avoid conclusions of collective guilt has been highlighted by both the United Nations Secretary-General and the [ICTY] Chief Prosecutor."[94] Furthermore, international criminal tribunals ardently underscore the need to "pay particular respect to due process."[95] For ICTY President Meron, "[t]here can be no cutting corners" when it comes to due process else the tribunal ceases to be credible to the public.[96] In cases where corners are found to have been cut, international judges are quite willing to reduce the sentence issued against the defendant.[97] No empirical evidence is cited for the proposition that the public (in particular, members of afflicted communities) actually invest such importance in these due process rights, especially those of the accused, although these rights support other important goals. In the main, defendants accused of extraordinary international crimes before international tribunals have access to more due process than the large majority of defendants worldwide accused of routine common crimes before national institutions.

The emphasis international criminal tribunals place upon individual agency meshes awkwardly with the connived nature of group crimes. The emphasis on individualism raises the stakes, insofar as departures that international criminal tribunals *practically* have to make from principles of individual responsibility become greater in controversy than the departures made by ordinary criminal courts. These departures, which contemplate some level of group dynamic, are seemingly necessary at the level of extraordinary international criminality given the collective nature of the violence and the acute pressure collective harms inflict on legal systems geared to ferreting out individual wrongdoing. The need for these departures arises from several sources: political pressures to obtain convictions; the forensic challenges presented by mass graves; difficulties in securing testimony and retaining its probativeness in the face of cross-examination; the complex sequencing of administrative directives that order massacre; the fact that elements of an overall crime can be committed by many different people without any person undertaking each element of the offense; the diffusion of responsibility in situations of disorder; and the need to protect the rights of victims and witnesses. Simply put, it is taxing to shoehorn collective agency into the framework of individual guilt. The application of modern laws of evidence to the context of mass violence for which they were not initially designed can be problematic. The need for institutions of international criminal law to innovate in light of these demands suggests that these institutions are capable of some independent criminological development (although evidence has not come to light of independent penological or sentencing practice).

Practical examples of departures from classical understandings of individual agency include liability theories of joint criminal enterprise (better known by its acronym JCE),[98] command responsibility,[99] and aiding and abetting.[100] The independent crime of conspiracy to commit genocide or aggressive war presents another example.[101] As the ICTY Appeals Chamber intoned when it canonically developed JCE in the *Tadić* judgment, personal culpability is the foundation of criminal responsibility but, at the same time, liability can be established through common design in situations where systems are disordered and it is difficult to determine personal culpability. National courts prosecuting extraordinary international criminality also have turned to vicarious liability theories. One example is the culpability theory of *association de malfaiteurs* (group of criminals) in Rwanda, whose application has engendered tension in the jurisprudence.[102] Another is the U.S. Supreme Court's affirmation – with some stinging dissent – of the conviction of Japanese General Yamashita for the illicit activities of troops under his command in the Philippines.

These occasional departures, however, are not treated as natural. They generate considerable controversy.[103] This controversy (reflected in, for example, the ridicule some observers exhibit toward JCE, which is demeaned as standing for "just convict everyone") is exaggeratedly heated insofar as punishing three people jointly for, say, the murder of thousands still seems nearly as artificially reductionist as punishing only one person. In truth, the level of group dynamic contemplated by international criminal tribunals is extremely modest. The level of controversy triggered by these modest departures from orthodoxies of individual agency indicates the strength of individual agency as an ordering principle.

These controversies, however, have become sufficiently poignant to prompt international judges to rein in the scope of vicarious liability and reaffirm the importance of subjective individual responsibility. Judges have done so even where the result is to modify doctrine such that a conviction at trial becomes an acquittal on appeal. For example, in July 2004, the ICTY Appeals Chamber reversed sixteen of the nineteen convictions previously entered by an ICTY Trial Chamber against Bosnian Croat military officer Tihomir Blaškić for ordering crimes against humanity and war crimes against Muslim civilians and, also, for failing as a commander to prevent the commission of those crimes.[104] The Appeals Chamber emphasized the need for the ICTY Prosecutor to prove subjective awareness or, at a minimum, recklessness on the part of the accused in order to secure a conviction based on command responsibility or ordering.[105] In another case, *Prosecutor v. Brđanin*, an ICTY Trial Chamber held JCE to be an inappropriate mode of liability when the case has an extraordinarily broad nature and the accused is physically and structurally remote from the commission of the crimes.[106]

Judicial discomfort with vicarious liability certainly is not limited to contemporary settings. The criminalization of organizations that had occurred at Nuremberg and was adhered to in subsequent proceedings also engendered controversy. This constitutes yet another example of the tensions inherent in international criminal law's impetus to criminalize collective wrongdoing through the vehicle of individual guilt. The International Military Tribunal at Nuremberg (IMT) remained insistent that "[. . .] criminal guilt is personal, and that mass punishment should be avoided."[107] Concerns over collective guilt were in part channeled to sentence, with the emergence of an IMT recommendation that the sentence for membership in a criminal organization not exceed that of the DeNazification Law (which set a maximum of ten years), in marked contradiction to the discretion given to judges.[108] Concerns over collective guilt also were in part channeled to the elucidation of standards that limited criminalization only to certain members of the declared criminal organization so that the "guilt of all or any [. . .] members remains on the traditional ground of 'personal' guilt."[109] Thus, the criminalization of organizational membership at Nuremberg was not operationalized in a manner that strayed too far from individualized guilt, thereby assuaging concerns over the derogation this would pose to liberal legalism. Furthermore, in some of the subsequent proceedings, the United States Military Tribunal placed the burden of proof in tests of personal guilt on the prosecution, instead of on the defense as was presupposed, once again citing liberal legalist concerns.[110]

In the end, international judges incorporate vicarious elements in order to render convictions, but then express great concern that criminalization ought not to be based on vicarious liability. However, the controversy with regard to JCE is not whether members of the enterprise bear some *responsibility* for atrocity but, rather, whether they are *culpable*. Therefore, an expanded accountability paradigm that implicated broader levels of group responsibility through mechanisms outside the criminal law – for which I advocate in Chapter 7 – ironically might relieve exogenous pressures on the criminal law to convict and, thereby, assuage the need to cultivate vicarious culpability theories. Yet, the internationalized accountability paradigm resists meaningful reform that would capture responsible groups. It prefers instead to stick with often fictionalized notions of individual agency, although it nervously permits the occasional compromised departure therefrom (such as through JCE).

Why did the legal fiction of individual agency and its concomitant, collective innocence, emerge? Possible motivations range from the well-intentioned to the self-serving, and include: the assuaging search for simplicity; a good faith belief that individualized guilt simply is the most effective and practical response to mass crimes; and the absolution of the acquiescent and nonfeasant through the condemnation, to borrow from Makau Mutua, of a few savages.[111] Absolving the many might be more conducive to the grand project of social healing. Such absolution may have currency as a necessary chit in the process of peace. After all, it is doubtful that beneficiaries would give up their preferred status without private property rights to protect their ill-begotten gains. Implicating too many individuals might threaten peace and, as such, the fiction of collective innocence could serve important political purposes. Externalizing the monstrosity of the atrocity on a few savages protects the humanity of the complicit masses. When the aggressor group retains its humanity, however fictional, it may simply be easier for a postconflict society to forgive, forget, and move on.

On the other hand, survey evidence from victims reveals discomfort with the selectivity of indictments and skepticism of the benefits of collective exoneration. Such evidence, which I present in the next section, demonstrates that victims prefer a broad range of fine-grained sanctions, textured according to the context of each postconflict society, that fall in between the reductionist outputs of international criminal law, namely guilt or absolution.

(IV) VICTIMS

Victims are the vilified prey stalked by the perpetrators of mass atrocity. They are targeted *en masse* based on discriminatory grounds. Once the discrimination takes root, it initially leads to the social deaths of the victims. Social death means ostracizing and dehumanizing the victim group. Its members get pushed like rubbish to the edges of society and subjected, often by law, to the dominion of the aggressor group. Degrading epithets such as cockroaches, maggots, vermin, excrement, dogs, and merchandise are used to refer to members of the "other" group. It is much easier to kill that which already has been deformed by social death. The following example, summarized by James Waller, is telling:

> A story in the *New York Times* that appeared on the last day of 1994 describes an incident in which a Bosnian Serb, armed with an automatic weapon, knocked on the door of a Muslim neighbor and ordered her outside. The Muslim woman proclaimed, "Visovic, you know me, you know my husband . . . How can you do this to me?" Visovic replied: "That time is over. I no longer know you." Whereupon he ordered her to crawl along the street as he kicked her repeatedly.[112]

Similarly, in one of the initial Rwandan *gacaca* sessions, one official commented:

> *Celui qui tuait ne voyait pas qu'il tuait un homme, il croyait tuer un animal suite aux leçons données par les autorités d'alors.*[113]

Victims are not selected because of individual fault, but because of their actual or perceived membership in a despised group.[114] For example, the Khmer Rouge murdered the Cambodian professional classes just because they were professionals who were believed to present a group threat to the veneration of peasant life. No attempt was made to select victims based on verifiable individual threats they posed to individual members of the aggressor group. The degree of collectivization (whether among aggressors, bystanders, or victims) will differ in each case of mass atrocity, but it is always present.

Some victims survive the ordeal. They embark on the road of recovery from the physical injuries they sustained, the emotional trauma from months or years of hiding, and the loss of their loved ones. These persons, as is the case for all of us, have preferences for how the future should be ordered. They also have opinions on what should happen to their oppressors. What are these?

Some empirical research exists on victim preferences regarding modalities of accountability and punishment. One comprehensive study was recently concluded by three researchers (Ernesto Kiza, Corene Rathgeber, and Holger-C. Rohne) affiliated with the Max Planck Institute in Germany.[115] The researchers interviewed over one thousand victims in eleven postconflict or conflict regions.[116] The interviewees had been subject to war victimization, which includes, but is not limited to, extraordinary international crimes.[117]

The researchers determined that, overall, victims are favorably disposed to trials conducted under international law[118] – which augurs well for adversarial international criminal justice initiatives[119] – although there was considerable unevenness to this support among regions.[120] The research does not elaborate on the provenance of international criminal process as derivative of dominant national methodologies, nor its subsequent expatriation back to diverse national levels. Respondents expressed lurking support for domestic law (across the board, 44 percent of respondents indicated that prosecutions should be based on domestic law); and also support for religious principles.[121] Overall, 49 percent of the participants responded that an international court should be responsible for prosecution whereas 28 percent opted for a domestic solution and 25 percent for a mixed domestic–foreign solution.[122] Here, too, the researchers found enormous regional variation.

Overall, in terms of sanction, 42 percent of victims supported imprisonment and 39 percent payment of money to the victims.[123] Once again, researchers found wide regional variation (for example, only 10 percent of Afghans said that perpetrators should be imprisoned). In certain of the eleven regions, monetary sanctions garnered more favorable responses than imprisonment (Afghanistan, Bosnia, Croatia, Congo, and the Philippines).[124] A different study independently initiated by different researchers (limited to Bosnia and Rwanda) similarly found preferences for various modalities of sanction, along with "expansive" ideas about punishment that involved "all wrongdoers – the big fish as well as the local small fry."[125]

One key result from the research of Kiza, Rathgeber, and Rohne is that victims and survivors tended to see responses in an integrated, and not mutually exclusive or singular, fashion. Perhaps in anticipation of this possibility, the researchers permitted interviewees to allocate favorable responses to more than one category of process or sanction. In many cases, victims expressed preferences for prosecutions based both on domestic and international law, and for sanctions also to be mutually inclusive. The fact that, overall, victims expressed strong support for reparations and restitutionary forms of justice does not augur well for criminal justice, at least as practiced by the ad hoc tribunals, and suggests that methodologies that incorporate such remedies (such as those operative in Rwanda's national legal order and, incipiently, the ICC's Trust Fund for Victims) should be pursued in earnest. More to the point is the conclusion that the research supports the merit of multiple, heterogeneous, integrative approaches to both the process of accountability and to sanction.[126] The research does not support those looking for simple solutions and singular preferences for one modality instead of another. In fact, the central conclusion supported by the research is that victims prefer pluralistic solutions and understand accountability to proceed sedimentarily, meaning that international criminal law's push for prosecution and incarceration, which may lead to operational exclusivity given scarcity of resources, may not be particularly effective.

The statistics on what victims view as the main purposes of taking action against offenders are fascinating. Sixty-nine percent said that establishing the truth about what happened is a main purpose – in fact, this is the most frequently identified purpose.[127] A further 25 percent answered that enabling people to live together was a main purpose; the same percentage indicated that taking revenge on the perpetrators was a main purpose (again, the researchers permitted multiple responses by victim interviewees).[128] A fruitful avenue of subsequent research would be to contrast these results with those of victims of crimes committed ordinarily in peacetime through deviant criminal behavior. A relevant question is whether the latter group of victims is as concerned with "telling the truth" about what happened or about living together. If not, then this additionally suggests the existence of (and need for) an independent victimology of mass atrocity; it would also provide a further justification for the philosophical concern that borrowing from the national to ground process and punishment for extraordinary international crimes is ill fitting, as is the migration of these newly minted international methodologies back into the sphere of the diversely domestic, for example through the incentive structure established by complementarity and referrals.

Although the value of Kiza, Rathgeber, and Rohne's research toward developing a victimology of mass atrocity is high, it remains subject to certain limitations. A number of methodological and practical inquiries arise.

One question is whether the interviewed population understood "international courts" and a "permanent international judiciary"[129] as something they would have any control over or participation in, or whether – in accordance with views of the violence as crimes against all of humanity – this would be a process controlled by ethnically neutral or nationally neutral foreigners (i.e., the reality of the ICTR or ICTY, and a definite prospect for ICC prosecutions). Based on my work in Rwanda, I would express skepticism that local populations would avidly support the use of international methods that actively disempowered them. On a related note, a report issued in 2005 by the Afghan Independent Human Rights Commission found a level of victimization of nearly 70 percent in the general population and a desire for approaches to justice controlled by the Afghan people and rooted in Afghan traditions, although supported by the international community.[130]

Second, public surveys, while extremely informative, generally reveal the reality that different people in the same community tend to want different things. Accordingly, it can be tenuous to generalize from surveys to truly useful operational principles, although when such surveys reveal a deep preference for polycentrism they present a challenge for the *de jure* or *de facto* primacy of prosecution and incarceration.

Third, Kiza, Rathgeber, and Rohne's research does not inquire of victims what they believe should be the purpose of punishing offenders (whether that punishment takes the form of execution, incarceration, or monetary payments). An interesting research question therefore is left unaddressed.

Finally, the border between victims and victimizers is not always firm, but is at times porous. In episodic bouts of mass atrocity, victims may in fact become victimizers; persecuted individuals or groups may in turn persecute their persecutors or innocent third parties.[131] The dual status of such individuals simultaneously presents therapeutic and punitive dilemmas.

Regardless of these limitations, victimological research is tremendously important. We need to learn much more about victims. This will prove difficult to the extent that international criminal law remains focused on the defendant's guilt or innocence, instead of integrating the victim, the harms he or she suffered, and the myriad elements that nefariously conspired to inflict those harms. Although the ICC positively takes steps in this direction (which I introduce in Chapter 3),[132] unless victim integration initiatives are taken seriously the place of victims in the justice project, as well as the experiences they have to offer, will remain marginal and untapped.

(v) CONCLUSION: LAW ON BORROWED STILTS

The international community is prosecuting extraordinary international crimes without first having developed a thorough criminology of mass violence, a suitable penology for perpetrators, or a thoughtful victimology for those aggrieved.

The disconnect between the aspirations of legal institutions and the realities of their work is specifically evident when it comes to penological rationales and sanctioning practices. As I elaborate in greater detail in Chapter 3, the dominant internationalized discourse simply assumes that isolated incarceration – at times of leaders, but not always – is an appropriate punishment in the wake of mass suffering and murder. This assumption is so ingrained that there was a dearth of substantive debate on the subject of sentencing at the Rome Conference that led to the ICC. The only exceptions were a heated discussion of the legality under international law of the death penalty and, in earlier preparatory sessions, differences over establishing minimum sentences for certain offenses.[133] I do not believe, however, that the one-size-fits-all suitability of distant incarceration and isolation of perpetrators from the roiled society should be taken as axiomatic.

CHAPTER 3

Punishment of International Crimes in International Criminal Tribunals

Contemporary international criminal tribunals – such as the ICTR, ICTY, and ICC – have inherited little penological guidance from their watershed predecessors, the Nuremberg and Tokyo Tribunals. Assuredly, Nuremberg and Tokyo were momentous occasions in terms of the prosecution of extraordinary international crimes, the establishment of liability theories, and the discrediting of certain defenses. These two international tribunals, however, were far from groundbreaking in terms of conceptualizing a sentencing policy. Although retribution and deterrence played an important role,[1] these goals were not operationalized in a sentencing heuristic.

Article 27 of the Nuremberg Charter gave judges "the right to impose...on conviction...death or such other punishment as shall be determined...to be just."[2] The sentencing provision of the Charter of the Tokyo Tribunal read the same. Accordingly, judges had nearly absolute discretion in the sentencing process. Jurisprudentially, the Nuremberg and Tokyo Tribunals did not elucidate sentencing guidelines; discussion of sentencing issues and rationales largely was perfunctory, especially in comparison to the thorough discussion of questions of legal liability. Neither tribunal had a veritable sentencing phase (either distinct or joined to the proceedings). The perception of sentence as an afterthought, instead of a vivid *situs* of analysis, permeated even the most thoughtful compilers of World War II atrocity prosecutions at the international and national levels. For example, in approximately two hundred pages of thorough summary that constitutes the final volume of the *Law Reports of Trials of War Criminals*, only three pages are devoted to punishment.[3] This may simply reflect the fact that these fifteen volumes are intended to report on legally relevant cases and, given the inattention accorded sentencing, there was little of legal relevance to report on.

Judges at Nuremberg and Tokyo expended scarce effort in identifying aggravating factors, which often were implied within the criminal conduct itself. Discussion of mitigating factors received more attention. Although (as was the case with Reichsmarschall Hermann Göring) judges often came rather quickly to the seemingly self-evident conclusion that there was "nothing to be said in mitigation,"[4] for certain defendants certain facts were accepted as mitigating. In fact, some of the factors contemporary international criminal justice institutions avail themselves of to reduce sentence trace back to the Nuremberg proceedings. Facts considered in mitigation at Nuremberg included: not being a dominant organizational figure, evidence of abiding by the laws of war, following orders, and opposing certain official policies.[5] These facts often were discussed co-extensively with the determination of liability on specific charges, so it remains unclear whether they were contemplated as being in mitigation of the sentence or in mitigation of the accused's degree of responsibility or, even, of guilt with regard to specific charges. Conflation of factors pointing to criminal liability and factors pointing to the aggravation or mitigation of sentence remains a troublesome area of international penology, although contemporary justice institutions, in particular the ICTY, have made an effort to disentangle these factors in the name not only of theoretical clarity, but also fairness to the accused.

The Nuremberg prosecutions involved major war criminals whose crimes could not be assigned a specific geographic location. The Nuremberg Tribunal (officially called the International Military Tribunal, or IMT) was authorized to prosecute crimes against the peace, war crimes, and crimes against humanity.[6] Crimes against humanity only were prosecutable to the extent that they were associated with one of the two other crimes, thereby requiring a nexus between them and armed conflict initiated by Germany (consequently, these proceedings focused on Nazi aggression). I consider the IMT to be an international court created by a multilateral treaty, although it certainly was not a global court.[7] The IMT sentences were pronounced on October 1, 1946 (the day after the IMT delivered its judgment), coinciding with Yom Kippur, the sacred Day of Atonement in Judaism. Twelve death sentences (by hanging) were issued. Göring, one of the defendants sentenced to death, ingested cyanide the night before his scheduled execution. Three individuals received life imprisonment and another four received fixed terms (two to twenty years, one to fifteen, one to ten). Three defendants were acquitted. Two individuals were not prosecuted even though scheduled for prosecution: one committed suicide before the trial began and the other was too ill to be prosecuted. Martin Bormann, chief aide to Hitler, was tried *in absentia*. A number of organizations were declared to be criminal: for example, the SS, Gestapo, and Nazi Leadership corps.

Twelve further rounds also occurred at Nuremberg. These were referred to as the "subsequent proceedings." These proceedings, constituted under Allied Control Council Law No. 10[8] and Military Government Ordinance No. 7, took place in front of American judges assembled in United States Military Tribunals. Although "organized and conducted on behalf of the United States under General Telford Taylor,"[9] the subsequent proceedings were deemed by reporters of the time to be international proceedings,[10] were explicitly constituted as such,[11] and were found by judges to be "based upon international authority and [to] retain international characteristics."[12] The subsequent proceedings involved members of criminal organizations (such as the SS and Gestapo), officials, notorious killers (e.g., *Einsatzgruppen*), industrialists, doctors, and jurists. These proceedings, taken as a whole, implicated 177 individuals. Although some defendants were acquitted, most were convicted.

Limited discussion of sentencing rationales occurred in the subsequent proceedings. In some cases the sentences were issued the same day the verdicts were
read. To give a flavor of the sentences: in the *Einsatzgruppen* trial (September
1947 to April 1948, the ninth subsequent proceeding), twenty-four individuals
were accused. Among those sentenced, fourteen were sentenced to death, two
to life, three to twenty years, one to fifteen, and two to ten years.[13] Twelve of the
death sentences later were commuted to a variety of lesser sentences ranging
from life imprisonment to fixed terms of imprisonment. The severity of sentences issued to those convicted in other rounds of the "subsequent proceedings"
ranged from comparable to the *Einsatzgruppen* defendants to more lenient. For
example, in the joint trials of industrialists, sentences imposed ranged from 1.5
to 8 years (*I.G. Farben* trial) and from just under 3 years to 12 years plus forfeiture
of property[14] (*Krupp* trial). The case reports are silent with regard to factors to
differentiate the punishment inflicted on the various individuals convicted in
the industrialists' trials.

In the *Justice* trial (February–December 1947), fifteen former jurists were
prosecuted.[15] Six were acquitted and released. Nine were convicted and sentenced: three to ten years, one to five years, one to seven years, and four to life
imprisonment. Defendants for whom there was no evidence warranting mitigation received life imprisonment; but so, too, did others for whom no discussion
was had regarding the existence or nonexistence of mitigating factors. In fact,
among all the convicted defendants, it is only in the case of one, Lautz (Chief
Public Prosecutor at the People's Court in Berlin), that the report reveals that
the military tribunal referred to mitigation of punishment: it cited Lautz's non-
activity in Nazi Party matters and his resistance to efforts by Party officials to
influence his conduct (although he was found to have yielded to Hitler's influence and guidance).[16] Lautz received ten years' imprisonment, more than others
for whom no discussion of mitigation appears in the case report.

In the *Hostages* trial, the military tribunal issued a rare discussion in which it
opined generally that the degree of mitigation depends on many factors, including the nature of the crime, the age and experience of the person, the motives
for the criminal act, the circumstances under which the crime was committed, and provocation.[17] As with IMT practice, this discussion evinces a conflation of factors pertaining to culpability and mitigation, in particular when it
came to including "the failure of the nations of the world to deal specifically
with the problem of hostages and reprisals by convention, treaty, or otherwise
[. . . which . . .] mitigates to some extent the seriousness of the offense."[18] In the
Flick trial, the Tribunal delved into "incidents" in the lives of two of the convicted defendants, "some of which involved strange contradictions," including
interceding to protect certain Jewish friends and saving survivors on a sunk ship,
to mitigate sentences to seven and five years.[19]

To be sure, the international proceedings at Nuremberg were but one sliver
of the judicialization of World War II atrocities in Europe. The vast majority
of proceedings occurred at the national level – in national courts or in military

commissions – or by instrumentalities of the occupying powers throughout Germany (for example, U.S., U.K., and Soviet military courts) and other states. Some proceedings operated prior to the trials at Nuremberg; some coincided with Nuremberg; and many occurred thereafter, in some cases initiated in ordinary courts well over half a century after Nuremberg. These proceedings are not international proceedings and, therefore, I consider their approaches to sentencing in Chapter 4, which surveys the activities of national and local legal institutions in punishing extraordinary international criminals. To foreshadow a bit, however, sentences by military instrumentalities initially gravitated more toward the death penalty than in the Nuremberg proceedings. What is more, many of these death sentences were quickly carried out, especially in regard to former concentration camp officials appearing before military courts (for whom death sentences seemed to be the norm). Some of these cases edified important substantive principles of international criminal law – for example, the *Dachau* case's development of common design[20] – but not penology. Sentences of national courts, in particular German courts, were somewhat more lenient, albeit not so in all cases (e.g., the Israeli Supreme Court's 1962 judgment upholding Adolf Eichmann's death sentence). Amnesty laws were passed in a number of national jurisdictions. Even at the level of military instrumentalities, over time there emerged pressure to parole most of those convicted.[21]

The Tokyo Tribunal officially was called the International Military Tribunal for the Far East. Its jurisdiction was based on the Tokyo Charter. Judges from eleven different countries sat on the Tribunal. This Tribunal indicted twenty-eight individuals in proceedings that began in 1946 and ended in 1948. These individuals ("Class A" criminals) mostly were military and political leaders. Of these, seven were sentenced to death, including General Tojo, Japan's Prime Minister during much of World War II, who was hanged in 1948. Sixteen others were sentenced to life in prison and two to fixed terms of confinement. Two died of natural causes before trial; another had a nervous breakdown and was removed. No acquittals were rendered. Over time, though, many of the convicts were pardoned. For example, of the sixteen individuals given life sentences, three died in prison while the remaining thirteen were paroled in the 1950s. Three convicts assumed senior government posts after their release, which suggests that their convictions did not materially discredit them among the Japanese public. Considerable doubts have been expressed regarding the quality of the proceedings, their accordance with due process, and their impartiality.[22] These doubts have cast a shadow over the Tokyo Tribunal, making its work less iconic than Nuremberg's. This shadow, in turn, attests to the connection between due process and the credibility of adversarial criminal prosecutions.

The Tokyo Tribunal was reticent when it came to discussing sentence. One defendant whose sentence was mitigated was Mamoru Shigemitsu, the former Japanese Foreign Minister, who was found not to be involved in the formulation of the war conspiracy. By the time he acceded to his ministerial post, the Tribunal noted that the machinery of war crimes and war of aggression already had been established. Shigemitsu received a seven-year sentence. Moreover, he was paroled in 1950 and subsequently served in the Japanese cabinet.

Many trials of Japanese accused of extraordinary international crimes were held separately at the national level in the United States, the United Kingdom, and other states, including throughout the Pacific arena; these trials also took place in the form of military courts-martial, some of which were conducted by the Dutch.

In sum, this formula of discretion exercised within a strict reliance on traditional modes of punishment reserved for ordinary common criminals that began at Nuremberg and Tokyo largely persists in contemporary institutions. The exercise of discretion affects the severity but not the form of punishment, which, insofar as the death sentence has been eliminated in international criminal law institutions, now effectively has become limited to incarceration. *De jure* certain contemporary international criminal justice institutions can award restitutionary remedies, but they have not yet done so in practice. Assuredly, at both Nuremberg and Tokyo different defendants did receive different sentences. The judges thereby exercised their discretion to vary the punishment according to the individual defendant. They did so, however, without providing a framework or heuristic to account for the exercise of discretion, although they did develop a rudimentary typology of facts in mitigation that continues to inform international criminal penality to this date. Let us now turn to the work of contemporary institutions.

(I) POSITIVE LAW FRAMEWORKS OF CONTEMPORARY INSTITUTIONS

For the most part, the textual bases for punishment provided by the positive law instruments of the ICTR and ICTY are thin, albeit not as thin as those of the Nuremberg or Tokyo Tribunals. The constitutive documents of the Special Court for Sierra Leone, the Extraordinary Chambers in the Courts of Cambodia, and hybrid entities in East Timor and Kosovo also are laconic when it comes to sentencing. The positive law of the ICC is richer. Those institutions that have actually punished offenders – in particular, the ICTY, ICTR, and East Timor Special Panels – have addressed sentencing in their jurisprudence. In this regard, they have improved the quality of the discussion from Nuremberg and Tokyo.

The ICTY and ICTR Trial Chambers impose sentences and penalties following the conviction of the accused. Sentences of the ICTY and ICTR Trial Chambers can be appealed to the Appeals Chamber. The Appeals Chamber will "correct" sentences of the Trial Chambers if there is proof of discernible error in the quantification of sentence or if convictions are overturned or added.[23] In such situations, the Appeals Chamber may determine its own sentence.[24] In practice, the Appeals Chamber has been quite active in revising sentences.

In the Trial Chambers, punishment initially was delivered after a separate sentencing hearing. This bifurcated structure has given way to a preference to issue sentence immediately following judgment.[25] This approach resonates with civil law traditions, in which sentencing is addressed by counsel in closing arguments and pronounced during the guilty verdict. That said, there is provision for a separate sentencing hearing if the accused has entered a guilty plea.[26] At this hearing, the parties may submit any relevant information that may assist the Trial Chambers in determining an appropriate sentence. The ICC and the Special Court for Sierra Leone appear to favor a separate sentencing hearing in all situations.[27]

Article 24(1) of the ICTY Statute limits penalties to imprisonment and stipulates that, in the determination of the terms of imprisonment, the ICTY shall have recourse to the general practice regarding prison sentences in the courts of the former Yugoslavia. Article 23(1) of the ICTR Statute reads identically, except that it refers to the courts of Rwanda instead of the courts of the former Yugoslavia. The ICTR has interpreted this provision modestly, concluding that it does not imply an obligation to conform to the relevant national practice.[28] The ICTY's approach is similar. What is more, the ICTY takes a dim view whether changes in domestic law should inure to the benefit of the accused (the principle of *lex mitior*). The ICTY Appeals Chamber held in the *Dragan Nikolić* case that "[a]llowing the principle of *lex mitior* to be applied to sentences of the International Tribunal on the basis of changes in the laws of the former Yugoslavia would mean that the States of the former Yugoslavia have the power to undermine the sentencing discretion of the International Tribunal's judges."[29]

No provision is made for a minimum sentence. The only statutory guidance the ICTY and ICTR receive in formulating sentence is to take into account "the gravity of the offence and the individual circumstances of the convicted person."[30] The ICTR and ICTY Rules of Procedure and Evidence supplement these very broad sentencing provisions. The Rules stipulate that an individual may be incarcerated for a term up to life. Therefore, ICTR and ICTY judges have the power to impose any sentence ranging from one-day imprisonment to life imprisonment for any crime over which the tribunal has jurisdiction.

The Rules do require that the Trial Chambers take into account mitigating and aggravating circumstances in determining sentences. With one exception (substantial cooperation by the offender), the Rules do not illustrate mitigating or aggravating circumstances. In cases where an accused is convicted of multiple charges, the ICTY Rules give the Trial Chambers the option to impose either a single sentence reflecting the totality of the criminal conduct or a sentence in respect of each conviction with a declaration regarding whether these sentences are to be served consecutively or concurrently.[31] In terms of the type of information to consider in fashioning a sentence suitable for a particular offender, ICTY and ICTR judges have "unfettered discretion to evaluate the facts and attendant circumstances."[32]

The ICC can sentence an offender to up to thirty years' imprisonment, with a possibility of "life imprisonment when justified by the extreme gravity of the crime and the individual circumstances of the convicted person."[33] The ICC's positive law – namely, the Rome Statute and the ICC Rules of Procedure and Evidence – jointly provide more guidance regarding sentencing than the positive law of the ad hoc tribunals, although the basic schema is similar.[34] In particular, the ICC Rules of Procedure and Evidence list aggravating and mitigating factors.[35] These replicate many of the factors developed by international judges in the jurisprudence of the ICTY, ICTR, and East Timor Special Panels that, in turn, themselves largely mirror the factors that animate sentencing of ordinary domestic criminals for ordinary domestic crimes. These factors include the nature of the harm caused, degree of intent, personal characteristics and prior criminal record of the convicted person, any demonstrated cooperation and compensation to victims, vulnerability of victims, particular cruelty, and the mental capacity of the convict. No ordering principle is provided as to the relative weight to attribute to any of these factors. "[O]ne or more aggravating circumstances" may justify the imposition of life imprisonment.[36] Nor does the ICC's positive law provide any explicit guidance as to the weight to accord to a factor in sentencing when that same factor already may have been considered in establishing the mental element of the substantive offense.[37] This is an aspect of international sentencing that has remained murky since Nuremberg's tendency to treat aggravating factors as implicit in the offense. Consequently, despite the relative richness of the positive law, at the ICC the quantification of sentence in individual cases still effectively is left to the exercise of judicial discretion in a manner similar to the ICTY and ICTR. It remains unclear what role, if any, national sentencing practice in the afflicted jurisdiction would play when the ICC affixes sentence. Nor does the ICC's positive law provide much guidance regarding the purposes of sentencing.[38] The preamble to the Rome Statute vaguely refers to deterrence, retribution, and expressivism, but does not suggest how these could be operationalized in the application of punishment.

The positive law of the Sierra Leone Special Court resembles that of the ICTR, although there are no life sentences and juvenile offenders (between fifteen and eighteen years of age) are treated with considerable clemency.[39] This clemency is oriented toward rehabilitation of juvenile offenders and constitutes a penological goal in its own right. However, despite considerable discussion during the formation of the Special Court regarding the prosecution and punishment of child soldiers, no indictments have been brought against minors. The Special Court is required to consult ICTR sentencing practices.[40] The generalized treatment of aggravating and mitigating circumstances is similar.[41]

The agreements between the UN and Cambodia regarding Extraordinary Chambers in the Courts of Cambodia are virtually silent on penalty and the determination of sentence although, taken together, they provide a minimum sentence of five years' imprisonment and a maximum sentence of life imprisonment (with the possibility of combining this with seizure of personal and real property acquired by criminal conduct, which is to be returned to the state).[42] The Kosovo hybrid panels do not receive independent guidance for sentencing international crimes beyond that provided by applicable ordinary criminal law, including a newly promulgated code in Kosovo.

The East Timor Special Panels could punish through a fixed term of imprisonment, capped at twenty-five years for a single crime.[43] Special Panel judges received a mandate very similar to those of the ICTY, ICTR, and ICC: namely to take into account the gravity of the offense and the individual circumstances of the convicted person in fashioning a sentence.[44] Another similarity to the ad hocs was that the Special Panels were to have recourse to the general practice regarding prison sentences in the courts of East Timor and under international tribunals.[45] The costs of the proceedings can be assessed against guilty defendants. As is the case with other international criminal law institutions, plea bargains were permitted.[46]

In addition to imprisonment, the positive law of international criminal justice institutions suggests the pursuit of accountability through restitution (the return of illegally obtained property), forfeiture, and fines.[47] These forms of accountability operate on a subaltern basis to punishment by imprisonment.[48] Restitution has not been awarded in the sentences of the ICTY or ICTR.[49] The ICC might prove to be more welcoming of reparative and restitutionary approaches insofar as it is joined by a Trust Fund for Victims.[50] The ICC can make reparative orders against the convict or through the Fund, for which regulations have been developed. The Fund is to be capitalized by compensation orders entered against convicts and also by voluntary grants from organizations and governments. As of April 2006, the Fund has received over 1.3 million Euros in grants. If properly supported, Fund would represent a highly desirable addition to international postconflict legal interventions. That said, it remains far too early to assess whether the Fund represents a meaningful commitment on the part of international criminal law to restorative methodologies. In the past, there has been no such commitment, either theoretically or practically. Although the East Timor Special Panels envisioned the creation of a fund for similar purposes, this never was realized.[51]

Contemporary international criminal tribunals permit sentences to be pardoned or commuted and early release to be granted.[52] This aspect of the work of these institutions remains particularly understudied. By way of example, persons convicted by the Special Panels have the right to be released from prison after two-thirds of the sentence has been served as long as they have behaved well while in custody and the release will not threaten public safety and security.[53] The ICTY and ICTR share the same formal process for early release. This process directly involves the ordinary criminal law of the state in which the convict serves the sentence. ICTY convicts are imprisoned in Germany, Austria, Spain, Italy, Denmark, Finland, Norway, the United Kingdom, Sweden, and France; several ICTR convicts are incarcerated in Mali, while Benin, Swaziland, France, Italy, and Sweden each have signed agreements with the ICTR indicating a willingness to enforce sentences. In a case where the convict is eligible for pardon or commutation of sentence pursuant to the applicable law of the state in which the convict is incarcerated, the state in question is to notify the relevant ad hoc tribunal accordingly.

By and large, the ordinary domestic law of these states (in particular where ICTY convicts currently are imprisoned) permit eligibility for early release after service of two-thirds of the sentence.[54] Once eligibility under national law arises, the detaining state can apply to the ICTY or ICTR President, as the case may be, for the convict's early release. The President (a judge who essentially occupies the role of chief judge) shall decide the matter, after consultation with others (including other international judges), on the basis of the interests of justice and general principles of law. There is no appeal from the President's decision. This decision-making discretion is contoured by points of reference enumerated in the Rules of the ICTY and ICTR and, additionally in the case of the ICTY, a practice direction.[55] Criteria to take into account in deciding early release include: the gravity of the crime or crimes for which the prisoner was convicted, the treatment of similarly situated prisoners, the prisoner's demonstration of rehabilitation, as well as any substantial cooperation by the prisoner with the ICTY Prosecutor. The ICTY Practice Direction also mentions as factors the behavior of the convict during the period of incarceration, conditions of incarceration, and the results of psychiatric or psychological examinations.

The ICTR has not yet granted early release. It may begin to do so should ICTR convicts serve sentence in states whose ordinary domestic criminal law contemplates early release (Mali's does not guarantee such a benefit).[56] The ICTY has granted early release quite actively, although it has not granted every application.[57] Anto Furundžija is one convict for whom early release has been granted. Furundžija had been charged with war crimes arising out of his interrogation of a civilian and a soldier, and his presence while both were being beaten and the civilian was raped. He was convicted in 1998 of co-perpetrating torture and of aiding and abetting outrages upon personal dignity, including rape, and sentenced to ten years' imprisonment. President Judge Meron based his decision to release Furundžija early, in August 2004, on a number of key pieces of evidence. These included: (1) the contents of a confidential memorandum from the ICTY Registry; (2) "a letter from the Minister of Justice of Finland and [...] report from the Chief Officer of the Kylmäkoski prison, where Mr. Furundžija served the majority of his sentence, [... informing ...] that Mr. Furundžija has behaved impeccably during his imprisonment; has been employed both inside and outside the prison; has been very cooperative in his relationship with the prison staff; and has maintained exceptional discipline and correct behaviour"; (3) a psychological assessment, prepared by the Finnish prison authorities, noting no impediment to Furundžija's release; and (4) an internal memorandum concerning Furundžija's cooperation with the Office of the Prosecutor.[58] Applying this evidence to the law, Judge Meron granted release based on his findings that "as reported by the Finnish authorities, Mr. Furundžija has accepted the judgement he received as fair and has expressed remorse for the suffering of victims";

that he "is resolved to be reintegrated into society, exhibited good behaviour in detention, and has a strong attachment to his family"; that the evidence "establishes the strong likelihood that Mr. Furundžija will successfully reintegrate himself into the community upon release"; and that "Mr. Furundžija's case is no less appropriate for a grant of early release than that of other prisoners previously granted early release."[59] Early release was granted in this case notwithstanding the report of the Office of the Prosecutor that Furundžija has not cooperated with it.

Although the prospect of early release may be anticipated at the time the sentence initially is fixed, ICTY judges have ruled that this prospect should not factor into the determination of the length of the sentence.[60] In other words, it is improper to increase the length of sentence to absorb the possibility of early release.

(II) SENTENCING PRACTICE

As of May 2006, the ICTR and ICTY, when taken together, have issued nearly eighty convictions. Some of these remain subject to appeal. In the discussion that follows, I refer to sentences that remain subject to appeal as "unfinalized sentences" and those sentences upon which the Appeals Chamber has rendered judgment or which the convict elected not to appeal as "finalized sentences."

The East Timor Special Panels had convicted eighty-four individuals (arising out of fifty-five trials) before ceasing operations (after funding ran out) on May 20, 2005.[61] This total represents only one-quarter of all individuals indicted for serious crimes pertaining to atrocity in East Timor in 1999. Those who bear primary responsibility for this violence have yet to be held to account. Throughout their short-lived operation, the Special Panels were hobbled by weak resources, including a lack of proper translation/interpretation and research expertise; personal Internet access for the judges only became available in late 2001.[62] At the time of writing in 2006, over a year after the Special Panels had shut down, conflict – reportedly fueled by animosity between those who sympathized with Indonesian rule and those who did not – persists in East Timor. To this end, the work of the Special Panels has not lanced the boil of violence – if such an ambitious goal ever were possible through recourse to the criminal law. The East Timorese government has expressed reluctance to empanel new courts or tribunals, although it has been more supportive of truth commissions and public inquiries.

Jurisprudentially, the work of the ad hocs has been influential. The Special Panels incorporated ICTY and ICTR jurisprudence.[63] It is quite likely that the jurisprudence of the ad hocs shall guide the ICC and other institutions, such as the Special Court for Sierra Leone and the Extraordinary Chambers in the Courts of Cambodia, when these institutions begin to issue sentences. The Kosovo hybrid panels also have issued a number of sentences: there is, however, considerable reticence on the part of the judges – even the international judges – in Kosovo to refer to the work of other international criminal justice institutions.[64]

At the ICTR, of the twenty-four individuals who have been convicted at the time of writing (unfinalized sentences), eleven have been sentenced to life imprisonment (in certain cases, to multiple life sentences). The remaining thirteen individuals have been sentenced to the following fixed terms: one to forty-five years, two to thirty-five years, one to thirty years, one to twenty-seven years, three to twenty-five years, two to fifteen years, and the remaining three to terms ranging from six to twelve years.[65] The ICTR Appeals Chamber had reduced one life sentence to a fixed term of forty-five years because of, *inter alia*, its *proprio motu* finding of serious violations of the defendant's fundamental rights during his arrest and detention.[66] In another case, that of Laurent Semanza, the Appeals Chamber increased a sentence from twenty-five to thirty-five years.[67] Nearly all of the ICTR's convictions are for genocide or crimes against humanity. There have been very few convictions for war crimes. Of those ICTR defendants who have received fixed term sentences, including those finalized on appeal and those not yet finalized, the mean sentence is 23.5 years and the median sentence is 25 years. However, as of May 2006, a number of heavy term sentences remain subject to appeal, along with four life sentences. This is why the mean and median finalized term sentences are lower. The ICTR has acquitted three defendants. One problem that has arisen is that some acquitted individuals, who are Rwandan citizens, remain in detention insofar as no country is willing to admit them into their territory. A similar situation may arise for convicts who eventually are released once they have served their sentence.

As of May 2006, the ICTY has issued forty-nine final sentences; an additional five sentences remain in the appeals process.[68] As of this juncture, all have been term sentences (the one life sentence that had been issued was reduced on appeal to a forty-year term).[69] The ICTY's finalized sentences range from 2.5 to 40 years. Among the finalized sentences, the mean sentence is 14.3 years and the median sentence is 12 years. Among all sentences, the mean is 14.75 years and the median is 13 years. The average length of sentences is slightly lower in 2006 than it had been in 2002, when the mean ICTY term sentence was fifteen years and the median term sentence sixteen years.[70] A number of lengthy sentences issued by the ICTY Trial Chambers have been reduced on appeal: the life sentence to Dr. Stakić; and forty-six years to General Krstić and forty-five years to General Blaškić, which were reduced to thirty-five and nine years, respectively.[71] In 2006, the Appeals Chamber reduced another heavy term sentence – twenty-seven years to Momir Nikolić following a plea bargain – to twenty years when it found that the Trial Chamber had committed a number of errors. On the other hand, the Appeals Chamber affirmed Dario Kordić's sentence of twenty-five years despite allowing certain grounds of his appeal. As of the time of writing, the heaviest sentence that remains under appeal is Radoslav Brđanin's thirty-two-year term.

TABLE 3.1. *Ad hoc tribunals – all sentences (including those subject to appeal as of May 2006)*

	No. of sentences	Life imp. (%)	Term sentence (%)	Mean term	Median term
ICTR	24	11 (45.8%)	13 (54.2%)	23.5 yrs.	25 yrs.
ICTY	54	0	54	14.75 yrs.	13 yrs.

As Tables 3.1 and 3.2 indicate, there is a considerable disparity between ICTY and ICTR sentencing practices. Even if all of the ICTR's life sentences are taken out, and comparison is made only between term sentences, the ICTR sentences considerably more harshly. In Chapter 6, I explore whether the difference between ICTY and ICTR sentencing can be accounted for on a principled basis. I consider three potential, and mutually inclusive, explanations for this differential judicial behavior: incorporation of national law, the sheer gravity of atrocity in Rwanda, and that a much larger proportion of ICTR convictions have been for genocide.

Disparity between ICTY and ICTR sentences grows when account is taken of one important limitation to the data as reported earlier. The data do not reflect the ICTY's practice of early release. Given that approximately 15 percent of ICTY convicts have thus far benefited from early release,[72] and that the law-in-practice of the ICTY is to grant such release after service of two-thirds of the sentence, the data summarizing length of incarceration at the ICTY could be reduced accordingly.

Table 3.3 presents the sentencing practice of the East Timor Special Panels.[73] Although I report eighty-four individuals convicted, the Special Panels actually issued eighty-five convictions. One individual, Gilberto Fernandes, was convicted on two separate occasions for two different crimes.[74] Because the Special Panels had jurisdiction over serious ordinary crimes as well as extraordinary international crimes, Table 3.3 separates the punishments reported for serious ordinary crimes (i.e., murder under the Indonesian Penal Code) from crimes explicitly identified in the case reports as extraordinary international crimes (mostly crimes against humanity). Sixty of the eighty-five convictions were for extraordinary international crimes. In some cases, particularly judgments stemming from indictments issued in the first year of the Special Panels' operation, convictions were entered for serious ordinary murder in situations

TABLE 3.2. *Ad hoc tribunals – finalized sentences (as of May 2006)*

	No. of sentences	Life imp. (%)	Term sentence (%)	Mean term	Median term
ICTR	16	7 (43.75%)	9 (56.25%)	20.9 yrs.	15 yrs.
ICTY	49	0	49	14.3 yrs.	12 yrs.

TABLE 3.3. *East Timor Special Panels*

	No. of sentences	Mean term	Median term
Ordinary Serious Crimes	25	6.3 yrs.	5 yrs.
Extraordinary International Crimes	60	9.9 yrs.	8 yrs.

where the factual context involved the kind of violence (i.e., apparently committed as part of a widespread or systematic attack on a civilian population) that could ostensibly qualify as extraordinary international criminality. In subsequent years, certain other indictments were amended to proceed on the basis of crimes against humanity. Convictions stemming from indictments issued as of 2003 overwhelmingly were for extraordinary international crimes.

The Special Panels issued a broad range of terms of imprisonment: from 11 months to 15 years for ordinary crimes and from 2 to 33 $\frac{1}{3}$ years for extraordinary international crimes. The Special Panels' enabling instruments precluded them from awarding a life sentence. Mean and median sentences issued by the Special Panels for international crimes are 9.9 and 8 years, respectively. The sentences of the Special Panels, which in early years of operation were compatible with those of the ICTY (if not slightly longer), progressively dipped well below ICTY levels. Paradoxically, as indictments increasingly began to charge extraordinary international crimes, sentences grew shorter. This decrease in length of sentence was in large part due to the frequent plea bargaining of extraordinary international crimes, even though it is unclear whether defendants who self-convicted actually were motivated by the prospect of reduced terms of imprisonment. Also, sentences tended to be reduced on appeal.

The length of Special Panel sentences becomes even shorter when the effects of conditional release and Presidential Decrees are considered. I did not include these in the data set. As with the ICTY, the Special Panels permit a convict to be conditionally released following service of two-thirds of the sentence and satisfaction of other criteria. Approximately 10 percent of all convicts have, at the time of writing, benefited from conditional release. Unlike with the ICTY, the Special Panels also permit sentence reduction by virtue of Presidential Decree. Approximately 10 percent of convicts benefited from Presidential Decrees issued on May 20, 2005 (the final day of the Special Panels' operation). Reductions ranged from 9 months to over 8 years (the three longest cumulative sentences issued by the Special Panels, namely 33 $\frac{1}{3}$ years, were reduced by Presidential Decree to 25 years).

Judges, in particular those sitting on the ICTY and ICTR, have, as the ICTR Trial Chamber held in *Prosecutor v. Rutaganda,* "unfettered discretion"[75] to sentence. Although they are limited by the positive law instruments with regard to the type of punishment they can issue (imprisonment and restitution, although the latter does not figure at all in the law-in-practice of the ICTY or ICTR), judges have been willing to utilize their "unfettered discretion to go beyond the circumstances stated in the Statute and Rules to ensure justice in matters of sentencing."[76] This self-delegation of authority has led, perhaps inexorably, to an erratic quantification of sentence. There are no formalized sentencing guidelines, whether mandatory or advisory, for international judges who sentence extraordinary international criminals. In fact, the ICTY Appeals Chamber has emphasized the inappropriateness of setting down a definitive list of sentencing guidelines.[77] Furthermore, the practice of fairly active appellate intervention leads to additional discretion and unpredictability in the operation of the ICTY, ICTR, and Special Panels. Trial judges have initial discretion to fix sentences and, then, their appellate counterparts often revisit determinations made at trial in a manner that is not clearly cabined or explicated. Insofar as there is no regular practice of count-by-count sentencing (instead, an overall sentence often is given), in the event an Appeals Chamber overturns certain convictions the process of determining exactly what the effect of those quashed convictions is on the revised sentence becomes nebulous.

International judges are comfortable with their discretionary powers to fix sentence within the traditional mode of incarceration notwithstanding the concomitant lack of consistency in sentencing. In *Delalić* (*Čelebići*), the ICTY Appeals Chamber nodded approvingly to the "considerable amount of discretion" to fashion a sentence, commenting that this discretion stems from the "over-riding obligation to individualise a penalty to fit the individual circumstances of the accused and the gravity of the crime."[78] Insofar as genocide, crimes against humanity, and war crimes can be committed "in a multitude of ways," another advantage to this "almost limitless" discretion is that punishment can be individualized to "vastly differing levels of culpability."[79] Recognition of judicial discretion in the fixing of sentences remains a firm point of reference in the jurisprudence of both the ICTY and ICTR.[80]

In the end, although individualizing the penalty certainly is desirable, the benefits thereof dissipate when there is no coherent framework in which to predictably consider the factors germane to, or the goals of, sentencing.

(III) PENOLOGICAL JUSTIFICATION AND IMPLEMENTATION: THE JURISPRUDENCE

Although they are not formally bound by *stare decisis*, judges – in particular at the ICTY and ICTR – do refer to prior judgments (of their tribunal as well as others, including national courts). For the most part, these references pertain to points of law and factors to consider in sentencing. The references do not pertain to the determination of the actual sentence. In fact, precedential guidance that may flow from previous sentences issued by the ICTY and ICTR is "very limited" and not a "proper avenue to challenge a Trial Chambers' finding in exercising its discretion to impose a sentence."[81] The ICTR Appeals Chamber held – in its 2005 judgment in *Prosecutor v. Semanza* – that "comparisons [to other cases] may be of limited value given that each case has its own particular circumstances [. . .][.] Ultimately, the decision as to the length of sentence is a discretionary one, turning on the circumstances of the case."[82] Judges demonstrate little willingness to engage in meaningful comparative analysis even of similarly situated extraordinary international criminals in determining the length of imprisonment. For example, the ICTY Appeals Chamber intoned in *Prosecutor v. Babić* that, even if a comparison were feasible owing to the substantial similarity between two cases, there only would be grounds to intervene if the two sentences were so out of reasonable proportion "so as to suggest capriciousness or excessiveness."[83] In *Prosecutor v. Stakić*, the ICTY Appeals Chamber went so far as so hold that comparisons with other cases "were inappropriate as the . . . case was of a 'unique' nature."[84] Although the upshot of this legal methodology is suppleness, which may inure to the benefit of a relatively new area of law, it also risks a slapdash approach geared to obtaining a desired result in each individual case instead of a predictable and independent sentencing heuristic.

Despite their considerable discretion, international criminal judges do refer to important theoretical principles in meting out sentences. These points of reference emanate largely from ordinary criminal law and include garden-variety rationales for punishment such as deterrence and retribution; but also expressivism, which can take on somewhat innovative meaning.[85] The structure provided by theoretical principles helps explain why international criminal tribunals punish more severely in some cases and less so in others. Insofar as the positive law documents essentially are silent as to the penological purpose of the sentences imposed, much of this structure has emerged from the jurisprudence of the sentencing institutions. While the jurisprudence provides some direction, however, it also is internally contradictory in terms of the goals of sentencing, leading to a lack of predictability or coherence regarding the actual quantum of sentence imposed in individual cases. Moreover, as I explore in Chapter 6, regardless of operational incoherence, retribution and deterrence are very difficult to operationalize in the context of mass atrocity through the tools of punishment currently available.

a. Why Punish?

Retribution and general deterrence are the two most prominent punishment rationales in international criminal law.[86] Whereas retribution had been a major motivating factor at Nuremberg,[87] the general deterrence motivation has acquired some traction in contemporary institutions.[88] However, considerable indeterminacy and confusion persist. The ad hoc tribunals vacillate when it comes to prioritizing the weight to accord to retribution and deterrence in sentencing. For example, over the past five years the ICTY has issued judgments that cite retribution and general deterrence as "equally important,"[89] judgments that cite retribution as the "primary objective" and deterrence as a "further hope," warning deterrence "should not be given undue prominence,"[90] and judgments that flatly state "deterrence is probably the most important factor in the assessment of appropriate sentences."[91] A survey of all the cases of the ad hoc tribunals over time, though, reveals a preference for retributive motivations, especially when it comes to the aggravating and mitigating factors the tribunals consider in fixing sentence.[92] The case law of the East Timor Special Panels demonstrates a similar stated preference.[93]

Although there are many divergent schools of retributivism, what all retributivists generally share is the understanding that the infliction of punishment rectifies the moral balance insofar as punishment is what the perpetrator deserves. Punishment, therefore, is to be proportionate to the nature and extent of the crime.[94] Although retribution is the most prominently cited rationale, it is also one with which the international tribunals express the most nervousness. These jitters come from concerns that punishment may be perceived as equating revenge. Accordingly, the ICTY Appeals Chamber has emphasized that "retribution should not be misunderstood as a way of expressing revenge or vengeance."[95] Judges assume the undesirability of revenge as a response to extraordinary international criminality and predicate this assumption on the belief that quashing revenge is a step in breaking the cycle of violence, maintaining the dignity of those who inflict punishment, and the civilized nature of the punishing institution.

The ICTY's fear of looking vengeful has induced it, on occasion, to push retribution in a new and contemplative direction, in which retribution is constructed as the "expression of condemnation and outrage of the international community."[96] This understanding of retribution, which remains an outlier position, diverges from the dominant narrative of retribution at the international tribunals. Interestingly, this understanding moves retribution in the direction of expressivism, which is a third, and currently subordinate, justification for punishment. The expressivist punishes to strengthen faith in rule of law among the general public, as opposed to punishing simply because the perpetrator deserves it or will be deterred by it. From an expressivist perspective, punishment proactively embeds the normative value of law within the community.[97] Expressivism also transcends retribution and deterrence in claiming as a central goal to build historical narratives and educate the public about these narratives.

General deterrence considers that the purpose of prosecuting and punishing those who commit mass atrocity is to dissuade others from doing so in the future. Specific deterrence implies that punishing the offender will deter that offender from reoffending in the future. Initially, international criminal tribunals ascribed scarce importance to specific deterrence.[98] This skepticism has thawed in more recent jurisprudence, particularly at the ICTY.[99] However, when the activity of international criminal justice institutions is taken as a whole, the focus of deterrence remains oriented to general deterrence. In the case of East Timor, the general deterrence concerns are vivid. In *Prosecutor v. Beno*, judges noted that "there is an additional requirement for deterrence because just across a hard-to-guard border live hundreds of recalcitrant ex-militia men with the capability of once again destabilizing this country by means of murder."[100]

From a deterrence perspective, punishment is inflicted not because the offender deserves it, but because of the consequentialist effect of punishment in reducing recidivism. There are other consequentialist rationales. These include rehabilitation, whose place within the practice of international sentencing remains marginal (although, again, subject to palpably inconsistent treatment among judgments and even within the same judgment).[101] Insofar as child soldiers are concerned, rehabilitation is given considerable currency in the positive law of the Special Court for Sierra Leone, although, gauging by the indictments thus far issued, it does not appear that it will figure much in the jurisprudence of the institution when it begins to hand out sentences. Consequentialist rationales also include incapacitation.[102] Although it is self-evident that, by isolating hatemongers and inhibiting their dissemination of vitriol, international criminal law may minimize conflict, incapacitation is generally not proffered as a central goal of punishment.

Reconciliation and peace were identified by the Security Council as major purposes of the ICTY and ICTR. Judges, however, have not ascribed them much influence. Assuredly, reconciliation and peace as consequential aspirations do surface as penological goals in some of the judgments of the ad hoc tribunals, in particular more recent judgments, but efforts to operationalize them in the allocation of sentence remain incoherent. The 2005 *Babić* decision by the ICTY Appeals Chamber is illustrative.[103] Babić was the former Prime Minister in the breakaway Krajina Serb republic after Croatia had declared independence in 1991. He pled guilty to a single count of persecutions as a crime against humanity. The Trial Chamber sentenced him to thirteen years' imprisonment. Babić appealed his sentence. The Appeals Chamber found the Trial Chamber had erred by giving insufficient weight to his efforts in post hoc peace negotiations. However, citing retributive concerns, the Appeals Chamber then refused to reduce the sentence issued by the Trial Chamber in spite of the error.[104] Babić committed suicide in 2006. In dissent, Judge Mumba would have reduced the sentence.[105] She noted that overturning the weight the Trial Chamber gave to Babić's contributions to the restoration of peace but then refusing to operationalize these contributions in the actual quantification of sentence implies – seemingly incorrectly – their negligible value. I would extend the analysis beyond this particular defendant. The influence of peace and reconciliation as goals of punishing extraordinary international criminals is unpredictable, perhaps because it is such an ambitious goal. I say unpredictable insofar as another high-profile plea-bargained defendant had received operational discount in the quantum of sentence for her post hoc peace-making efforts.[106]

Although their constitutive instruments mention restorative objectives, and the ICC has taken affirmative steps in this regard, in their practice international criminal tribunals still remain distant from victim-centered restorative modalities that may correspond more closely to the expectations of local populations in the places where atrocity has been and incipiently is being judicialized, including by the ICC in Uganda and the Democratic Republic of Congo.[107] The rationales on which international criminal tribunals primarily ground their punishment, namely retribution and deterrence, resonate more deeply within dominant criminal justice systems than in systems, in particular local systems, in which atrocity is becoming internationally judicialized. To be sure, nuggets of retributivism and deterrence exist in virtually all criminal justice systems (whether secular or religious; national or local; formal or informal). And nuggets of restorative objectives are found in virtually all criminal justice systems. But the role that restoration plays in dominant justice systems is less than what it plays in the justice systems of weaker states, where there remain vibrantly powerful local and customary methods of dispute resolution in which restorative goals and methods often occupy a primary place. I examine these methods in Chapters 4 and 5.

Many bottom-up transitional justice movements invoke sanctions such as apologies, shaming, sharing the truth, lustration, and reparations; and often are willing to procure these by offering amnesties to perpetrators.[108] This is the case even though such modalities are often at odds with, and largely squeezed out by, the operation of the international criminal law paradigm. International criminal law responds poorly to the preferences of local populations when such preferences conflict with its normative worldview. This leaves local populations with little recourse but to articulate these preferences outside of and at times in resistance to top-down internationalist pressures and, thereby, expend considerable resources and effort at a particularly vulnerable time in mediating with international legal regimes. To be sure, given the frequency of truth commissions and nonjudicialized approaches to postconflict justice, local populations do experience some success in this process of mediation, but this also invites a much deeper inquiry whether and how more inclusive internationalist structures can be edified to channel these energies more constructively. Although there are times when the international community declaratively can recognize the role such initiatives might play, for example in its 2005 referral of the Darfur situation to the ICC, these initiatives are at most given a role of adjunct or additional complement to the fixture of liberal procedural legalism.[109]

b. What Factors to Consider in Punishing?

At the ad hoc tribunals, determinations of what can constitute aggravating or mitigating factors – as well as the weight to attach to these – lie within the discretion of the Trial Chamber.[110] Retributive concerns dominate the factors international criminal law institutions view as aggravating or mitigating in the imposition of sentence. This is particularly the case with aggravating factors. These factors mostly attach to the extent of the wrongdoer's culpability, blameworthiness, immorality, and desert. In fact, when counsel for one defendant urged the ICTY Appeals Chamber to reconsider a Trial Chamber sentence based on a "trend in international law" away from retribution, the Appeals Chamber sharply disagreed.[111] The Appeals Chamber found this "alleged" trend to be unsubstantiated and instead underscored the importance of retribution as a general sentencing factor.[112]

Although the positive law of the ad hoc tribunals provides only one illustration of a mitigating or aggravating circumstance,[113] the jurisprudence develops many more. The following aggravating circumstances arise in the jurisprudence:

- the gravity and egregiousness of the crimes, identified as the primary consideration in imposing sentence;[114]
- the breadth of the crimes (e.g., numbers of victims)[115] and the suffering inflicted;[116]
- the youth of the victims[117] or their general vulnerability;[118]
- the nature of the perpetrator's involvement (active role, principal perpetrator, or secondary/indirect involvement);[119]
- premeditation and discriminatory intent;[120]
- position as a superior, in particular abuse of that position;[121] and
- behavior of the accused during trial.[122]

In order to affect sentence, aggravating factors must be proven beyond a reasonable doubt.[123] The ICTY has stated that an aggravating factor only can increase the sentence if that factor did not form an element of the actual offense.[124] For example, when discriminatory intent forms part of the requisite elements for proof of the crimes charged, it will not be considered separately as an aggravating factor in sentencing. The ICTY has taken a similar approach to command responsibility, holding that a defendant convicted based on command responsibility cannot receive aggravated punishment merely because he held a superior position, but only if he abused the superior position.[125]

Mitigating factors, which require proof only on a balance of probabilities,[126] include:

- whether and when the accused pled guilty;[127]
- substantial cooperation on the part of the offender;[128]
- remorse;[129]
- the youth,[130] advanced age,[131] and other personal circumstances of the offender (including whether married and with children);[132]
- the extent to which the offender was subject to duress, orders, or coercion;[133]
- the "good character" of the offender;[134]
- the chaos of constant armed conflict;[135]
- that the offender did not have a previous criminal record for ordinary common crimes;[136] and
- human rights violations suffered by the offender during pre-trial or trial proceedings.[137]

On the subject of plea bargains, the overall practice of international institutions is to sentence defendants who plead guilty to a shorter term of imprisonment than they would have received were they to be convicted following a trial. That said, as I explore further in Chapter 6, the actual discount rate that attaches to plea bargains is difficult to measure and, in fact, fluctuates markedly among defendants even when sentenced by the same institution. This creates considerable indeterminacy. In the aggregate, however, pleading guilty is a relevant, albeit controversial, mitigating factor.

Although the ad hoc tribunals began their operations by viewing plea bargains with disfavor, this approach has changed over time.[138] Rule amendments eventually were adopted that permitted plea bargaining.[139] Plea bargaining first proliferated at the ICTY, in part due to the willingness of ICTY defendants to barter for a reduced sentence.[140] In response to this heady recourse to plea bargaining, however, ICTY judges began to express the need for some caution in approving plea bargains and, in some cases, exercised a greater level of independent curial review over bargains concluded between defendants and the Office of the Prosecution.[141] Rulings by the ICTY Trial Chambers (some of which have been affirmed on appeal) in a small number of cases to impose a sentence longer than the range contemplated in the plea agreements have had somewhat of a chilling effect on plea bargaining practice.

There have been fewer plea agreements at the ICTR. The ICC permits proceedings on an admission of guilt.[142] It is reasonable to expect that ICC judges will treat an admission of guilt as a mitigating factor. The Special Panels affirmed a large number of plea bargains, particularly as the institution became defunded and its mandate wound down. In some cases the Special Panels sentenced perpetrators who self-convicted to very modest terms, including under five years for crimes against humanity.

In addition to pleading guilty,[143] the Special Panels claimed similar aggravating and mitigating factors than the ICTR and ICTY in the exercise of their discretion to punish. A review of the Special Panels' jurisprudence reveals considerable attention paid to gravity,[144] vulnerability of victims,[145] superior responsibility,[146] and political context[147] as aggravating factors; and, as mitigating factors, remorse,[148] personal/family circumstance,[149] and position as a subordinate/coercive environment.[150] In the case of the Special Panels, sentencing guidelines from more than one national justice system influenced, but certainly did not structure, the work of judges in punishing international crimes.[151] The Special Panels refer to traditional indigenous principles in sentencing, such as *adat* (taking responsibility/paying respect to authority) and, in this sense, take important steps toward the development of more autonomous, and theoretically composite, approaches to punishment pertinent for East Timor.[152]

By and large, the aggravating and mitigating factors considered by international tribunals in punishing international crimes resemble those used by domestic courts of dominant states when they sentence perpetrators of ordinary common crime. Many of these factors emerge in the international jurisprudence because international judges engage in comparative legal analysis of these dominant systems whose tenets they then incorporate. The only factor that stands out in exception is the discounting of a sentence owing to the chaos that may ensue from endemic armed conflict or coercive environments.[153] For the ad hoc tribunals, however, this is "not a decisive factor"[154] and was in fact explicitly condemned by the ICTY Appeals Chamber in the *Blaškić* decision.[155] The Special

Panels have been somewhat more reflective regarding the limitations of human agency in contexts of collective violence.[156] However, this factor remains an outlier in the actual quantification of sentence. The Special Panels, which had dual jurisdiction, did not differentiate among the criteria used or the theory of punishment espoused when it came to sentencing ordinary crimes or sentencing international crimes. They turned to the same aggravating and mitigating factors for both sets of crimes.

(IV) CONCLUSION

Positive law instruments permit incarceration and restitution as punishments for extraordinary international criminals, but thus far the law-in-practice of contemporary international institutions has been limited to incarcerating along the ordinary lines of the penitentiary model. Although the practice of the ICTR, ICTY, and East Timor Special Panels suggests that retributive motivations retain the greatest currency, a palpable level of indeterminacy remains with regard to *why* international criminal institutions punish individual offenders. Judges still remain unsure, and often divided, about the purpose of the punishments they mete out.

The vagueness of the positive law frameworks enables judges to access a wide range of evidence in determining sentence. Judges have injected some order into this process by developing a typology of aggravating and mitigating factors as variables. Although international judges have come a long way since Nuremberg and Tokyo, they have not developed a cogent framework or heuristic to standardize the weight to attribute to each of the many pieces of evidence available for consideration in the typology of aggravating or mitigating factors. International criminal sentencing practice remains "open-ended."[157] Recourse to aggravating and mitigating factors, and the weight to attribute thereto, is avowedly discretionary. This leads to indeterminacy at a second level, namely *how much* imprisonment is levied out to individual convicts. This indeterminacy endures notwithstanding the emergence of a fledgling jurisprudence that might help systematize sentencing. Although individualized sentencing has many benefits, these become jeopardized when no rubric exists to ensure consistent and proportionate application of standard criteria among individual defendants. The erratic sentencing practice could also affect the coherence[158] and legitimacy of the punishing institutions, which, in turn, may undermine confidence in their rationality and even, as H.L.A. Hart warned, bring the law into contempt.[159] Although different societies may sentence differently – and this diversity is to be welcomed – once a punishing regime has been established for an atrocity, it is important that, regardless of its theory or modality, it works in a principled and predictable manner in how it treats individual defendants.

Punishment serves a very important role in providing subtle and fine-grained assessments of individual responsibility. Criminal liability as delineated by a forced choice between acquittal or conviction offers little more than crude binary reductionism. Sentence, however, can serve to refract that reductionism.

Therefore, it becomes all the more important that sentence be effected coherently as well as thoughtfully. In the case of extant international criminal tribunals, a gap emerges between the avowed goals of sentencing and the actual outputs of the sentencing process. In the end, the abundance of discretion feeds this gap.

CHAPTER 4

Punishment of International Crimes in National and Local Criminal Justice Institutions

National and local criminal justice institutions play a key role in sanctioning extraordinary international criminals. These institutions in fact undertake the bulk of the work. International institutions are designed to prosecute individuals alleged to bear the greatest responsibility for atrocity and, therefore, are intended to focus on leaders and organizers although, in practice, they do prosecute lower-level offenders (as was routinely the case in East Timor). For the most part, though, lower-level offenders – many of whom, like the Rwandan bulldozer driver Anastase Nkinamubanzi, killed many innocents in grisly fashion – remain in the hands of national and local institutions.

The scholarly literature on how domestic courts punish international crimes when they exercise national, territorial, or universal jurisdiction is limited. This is a notable lacuna insofar as the ICC formally defers to national courts as the front line of prosecution and punishment through the doctrine of complementarity. Moreover, the completion strategies of the ICTY and ICTR activate the referral of cases to national institutions (in the states of the former Yugoslavia or Rwanda, or the courts of any state). These referrals preserve the primacy of the ad hoc tribunals over national institutions, but lead to the reality that cases will be (and already are) processed at the national level.

Overall, and to varying degrees *inter se*, national and local criminal justice institutions tend to gloss over the conceptual differences between ordinary domestic crimes, on the one hand, and extraordinary international crimes, on the other. Overwhelmingly, national frameworks in many states punish extraordinary international criminals through the same methods as ordinary common criminals – principally imprisonment – within a system designed for ordinary common criminals. They punish largely, though not entirely, for the same reasons; aggravating and mitigating factors tend to track those of select ordinary criminal law.

Survey research demonstrates that certain domestic frameworks, particularly those in European and common law countries, do punish extraordinary international criminals more harshly than ordinary domestic criminals insofar as they contemplate an increased term of imprisonment for extraordinary international crimes.[1] This phenomenon could suggest that the gravity of extraordinary international crimes is viewed as greater and that what is required to articulate this enhanced gravity – and, thereby, retributive goals – is a formulaic adjustment upward in terms of the number of years a convict serves. That said, actually adding to sentence and requiring the convict to serve these additional years is not possible in many places, insofar as, in the words of an ICTY Trial Chamber, "in most countries a single act of murder attracts life imprisonment or the death penalty, as either an optional or mandatory sanction."[2] It therefore becomes difficult to make the extraordinary international criminal, who may be responsible for the deaths of hundreds while pursuing eliminationist ends, actually spend more time in jail than the ordinary criminal who murders one person for profit, out of anger, or inadvertently in the course of committing a felony.

In any event, statutory treatment that permits longer sentences for extraordinary international crimes often emerges in countries that never have prosecuted a single individual for such crimes. When the *practice* of states that actually have prosecuted atrocity crimes is taken into account, the picture becomes considerably more nuanced and kaleidoscopic. A deep review of the jurisprudence from such states reveals a textured composition: there are several stated penological goals that, in addition to retribution, include deterrence, reconciliation, and restoration. Principled attainment of these goals is obscured by virtue of a pronounced level of discretion in sentencing. For example, in terms of underscoring the gravity of the offense, there is no predictable pattern within these jurisdictions of punishing a similar physical act (e.g., murder or rape) more severely when committed in situations of conflict or genocide than when committed in ordinary times. In Rwanda, for example, certain punishments for extraordinary international criminals are in fact lower than what would attach to offenders in ordinary times; furthermore, confessing and pleading guilty to an extraordinary international crime will trigger a significant sentencing discount that is unavailable for ordinary crimes. In the states of the former Yugoslavia, judges do not consistently sentence more severely for wrongdoing committed as war crimes than committed ordinarily. Most jurisdictions prosecuting World War II atrocity simply transplanted the punishments ordinarily available for common criminals to perpetrators of atrocity, although there are examples where punishments for atrocity crimes were explicitly made harsher than those available for common criminals.

Looking beyond, national prosecutors steering political transition may face a particularly unique set of circumstances in determining whether or not to exercise their discretion to prosecute, thereby leaving offenders unpunished for what might be perceived as a greater overall good. Many states have awarded amnesties to extraordinary international criminals that they would never award to ordinary common criminals.[3] In South Africa, for instance, political crimes were open to amnesty, whereas ordinary crimes were not.[4] Thus, individuals animated by political motives were treated more leniently than those inspired by private motives. In prosecutions following World War II, many Holocaust perpetrators were treated lightly by the courts and pardoned as early as several years after conviction, while others were quickly executed.

Although national institutions have not developed a special penology for extraordinary international crime, and have not fared much better in theorizing the criminality of mass atrocity, they do engage in some methodological creativity and, in some instances, turn to a broader diversity of sanction than international tribunals. On occasion, national and local justice institutions cultivate approaches to punishment that diverge from international norms. These approaches may more accurately reflect sociolegal norms of the places most immediately afflicted by mass atrocity. They also may prompt concerns regarding communitarian punishment and the quality of justice.

However, the range of domestic initiatives that diverge from international norms is circumscribed by the pressures that international institutions, even though they focus on a narrow band of perpetrators, exert over their national and local counterparts. This gives rise, as I explore in greater detail in this and the following chapter, to *legal transplants* from the international to the national, many of which are welcomed by state actors to manage the influence of local communities and curtail the diffusion of authority. These transplants have a homogenizing effect on the kind of sanction visited upon atrocity perpetrators. In the end, local communities, often deeply afflicted by atrocity, have been hemmed in by these exogenous pressures when they endeavor to develop approaches to punishing perpetrators that depart from liberal international modalities.

Regarding research methodology: it would be overwhelming to review every case by a national court or local institution that concerned conduct that might be classified as an extraordinary international crime. Domestic institutions have been called upon in many different contexts to retrospectively redress civil violence or sanction abuses by military personnel. Examples include, but are far from limited to: Greece, Argentina, Bolivia, Chile, Peru, Guatemala, Haiti, United States,[5] Germany (following reunification), many Eastern European countries (with regard to crimes committed under Stalin [for example, in Latvian courts] or more recently under Communist rule), Burundi, Ethiopia, Indonesia, Afghanistan, and Sri Lanka.[6]

For the purpose of the analysis at hand, I propose that a fruitful avenue of research is to explore the activities of national and local institutions in punishing extraordinary international crimes that these institutions themselves define as such *and* that also have been or are being prosecuted at the international level. I select in this regard three atrocities: the 1994 Rwandan genocide, ethnic cleansing and genocide in the Balkans throughout the 1990s, and the Nazi Holocaust (although I also include some discussion of Japanese and German war crimes against combatants and civilians). In this chapter, I comparatively review the activities of national and local legal institutions sharing contacts with these three atrocities. Each of these three case studies evidences the kind of discriminatorily motivated violence that runs to the heart of international criminal law's proscriptions.[7] Therefore, centering the analysis on these three case studies harmonizes the discussion with my focus, as set out in Chapter 1, on ideologically and politically motivated violence; it also permits comparative assessments between the international sphere and national/local spheres. The purpose of this analysis is to qualitatively document sentencing practices, see tendencies, and sketch rationales. In some places assailed by atrocity – for example, Afghanistan, Kosovo, and Rwanda – law at the state level differs from law as practiced traditionally at the local level, especially in matters of procedure. The study of local process is a complex undertaking. Given the paucity of research on local modalities of punishment for perpetrators of great evil, however, I am hopeful that even the cursory overview this chapter provides will advance the discussion and signal other important work that remains to be done.

Among these three case studies, I devote the most attention to Rwanda. I am motivated in this regard by my own experiences in the country as well as the large number of sentences that Rwandan institutions have issued. Although the quality of scholarly analysis of accountability initiatives in Rwanda has grown, much work remains to be done insofar as these initiatives still remain understudied. By way of example, Mark Osiel – one of the most insightful and influential authors on issues of international criminal justice – downplays the Rwandan experience, which does not mesh with his theoretical modeling of postconflict prosecutorial strategies.[8]

(I) RWANDA

Between April and July 1994, anywhere from 500,000 to 800,000 people were massacred in genocidal pogroms in Rwanda.[9] This is a staggering amount of death in a country with a total population of about eight million. Many of the killings were unspeakably brutal. They were in no way depersonalized through technology: a study conducted by the Rwandan government concluded that nearly 38 percent of victims were killed by machete, 16.8 percent by club, and 14.8 percent by firearm; other means of murder included grenades, swords, knives, drowning, sticks, rocks, and bare-handed assault.[10]

The perpetrators of the violence were members of the majority Hutu ethnic group, radicalized by an extremist Hutu government. The overwhelming majority of victims were members of the minority Tutsi group. The Hutu comprise approximately 85 percent of Rwanda's population, the Tutsi 14 percent. The genocide was quelled when a Tutsi army (the Rwandan Patriotic Army, RPA),[11] based in neighboring Uganda, ousted the genocidal Hutu government and seized power. The political wing of this Tutsi group, the Rwandan Patriotic Front (RPF), currently retains a firm grip on power in Rwanda.

The judicialization of atrocity in Rwanda proceeds through three sets of institutions:

(1) the ICTR, established by the Security Council and sited in Arusha, Tanzania;

(2) domestic courts, overwhelmingly in Rwanda but also in a handful of foreign jurisdictions, including Belgium; and

(3) a modified form of *gacaca* (traditional dispute resolution), adapted for genocide-related crimes and standardized through centralized national legislation.

The Organic Law on Gacaca Jurisdictions, which first took effect in 2001 and has been subsequently amended (including important amendments in 2004), creates *gacaca* courts to hear genocide-related charges. In Rwanda, the term "Organic Law" refers to laws that rank higher in normativity than ordinary laws, and are secondary only to the Constitution. Another Organic Law, from 1996, organizes criminal proceedings for genocide or crimes against humanity and offenses committed in connection thereto, initially in Specialized Chambers within the conventional national and military courts.[12] These proceedings also invoke Rwandan general criminal and constitutional law, as well as substantive international criminal law as codified in treaties, and thereby reflect an inter-penetration of various sources of law, both general and specific. The Specialized Chambers were formally abolished by the 2001 Organic Law, which formally repealed the 1996 Organic Law, but specified that the 1996 Organic Law remains applicable to all cases forwarded to the Specialized Chambers that now are to be handled by the national courts. Genocide trials have continued in the national court system, although their number has tapered off.[13] By mid-2002, 7,181 prosecutions had occurred in the Specialized Chambers; by 2003 the overall figure in the national courts rose to "slightly more than 8,000";[14] and, by 2005, approximately 10,000 prosecutions had occurred. Although this is a substantial number of trials – "better than the record of many European countries following the Second World War"[15] – it only involves a small portion of the total detainee population.

Thus far, the ICTR has arrested seventy-two individuals. The Rwandan government had initially requested the creation of an international tribunal, but then cast its Security Council vote against the ICTR. The Rwandan government objected *inter alia* to the siting of the ICTR outside Rwanda, its limited temporal jurisdiction, the absence of Rwandans on its staff, and its inability to issue a death sentence. That said, in practice the Rwandan government generally, though certainly not routinely, cooperates with the ICTR. Attitudes of the Rwandan population toward the ICTR range from disinterested to skeptical.

The International Committee of the Red Cross estimates that 89,000 individuals remain detained in Rwanda on genocide-related charges.[16] The figure formerly was higher insofar as over 36,000 other individuals had been slated for parole (provisional release) in recent years owing to lack of evidence, age, infirmity, or illness; the majority of these individuals, however, were paroled because they had confessed to involvement in the genocide.[17] Many of these parolees have undertaken to participate in *gacaca*, an undertaking on which their parole remains contingent. Many parolees have committed to attending reeducation camps where they receive government-sponsored instruction on justice and reconciliation.

Eventually, the Rwandan government intends for all but those who remain accused of the most serious offenses to be prosecuted through *gacaca*. In late 2005, the *gacaca* Secretariat announced its intention to establish a new national court to try individuals accused of the most serious offenses (estimated at up to ten thousand persons). So, once again, the Rwandan justice system is subject to profound structural reform and reconstitution. The jurisprudence of the Specialized Chambers and ongoing verdicts of conventional courts would provide some guidance to *gacaca* judges regarding finer points of liability and sanction and, thereby, likely would inform the work of this new national court. In my estimation, *gacaca*, which portended to be a significant departure from retributivism and a turn towards restoration, has been underemployed in this regard owing to pressures it has faced to reflect the ideal-type adversarial criminal trial and to serve state, as opposed to local, interests.

a. *National Courts in Rwanda, Including Specialized Chambers*

The 1996 Organic Law creates four categories of culpability. These are: (a) Category 1 (planners, organizers, those in positions of authority, notorious murderers [with zeal or excessive malice], and sexual torturers); (b) Category 2 (perpetrators of intentional homicide or serious bodily assault causing death); (c) Category 3 (perpetrators of other serious assaults); and (d) Category 4 (perpetrators of property offenses).

Article 14 of the Organic Law deals with punishment. It links the severity of punishment, as well as its form, to the gravity of the offense as represented ordinally by the category of culpability.[18] In some cases, the linkage is to a fixed sentence, while in others it is to a permissible range of sentence. The discretion of judges in fixing sentence is thereby fettered, unlike at the ICTR where judges are accorded broad discretion regarding the length of sentence to be imposed (although the nature of punishment at the ICTR is limited to imprisonment and restitution).[19] The Organic Law does not contemplate early release. The Organic Law's explicit linkage of penalty to type of offense provides a level of predictability in sentence, which is important to the credibility of the punishing framework although, as is the case with fixed sentences in any jurisdiction, might lead to inequities in individual cases. Article 14 stipulates that punishments are those listed in the Rwandan Penal Code, which applies to ordinary criminal offenses, except for:

- Category 1 offenses, which are punishable by death;
- Category 2 offenses, for which death is replaced with life imprisonment; and
- Category 4 offenses shall only give rise to civil damages determined by agreement between the parties, failing which rules related to criminal proceedings shall apply although any sentence issued is to be suspended.

The case law provides examples of Category 4 offenders sentenced to jail time.[20] Given that many Category 4 defendants have been detained for several years by the time they eventually face trial, even if they were sentenced to jail time their likely fate would be release for time already served.

The language of the Organic Law leaves Category 3 offenders subject to the ordinary sentences provided by ordinary Rwandan criminal law for serious assault. Judges have considerable scope for discretion in sentencing Category 3 offenders insofar as the sentence ranges are relatively broad. Punishments normally imposed by the Rwandan Penal Code for conduct that could constitute a Category 3 offense include, but are not limited to:

- Penal Code article 318: violent attacks (one month to one year);
- Penal Code article 319: violent attacks causing an illness or inability to work (two months to two years; six months to three years if committed with premeditation);
- Penal Code article 320: violent attacks causing, *inter alia*, serious mutilation or incurable illness (two to five years; five to ten years if premeditation is found).[21]

Although death sentences can be awarded to Category 1 offenders – and courts continue to issue them – no executions have occurred since 1998. Why have Rwandan authorities apparently abandoned the death penalty in practice? Arguably, Rwanda has decided that this particularly retributive sanction no longer promotes the goals of genocide prosecutions. Other reasons, which I also believe to be influential, include the international community's condemnation of the death penalty, the skepticism of transnational nongovernmental and donor organizations, and the ICTR's position that it will not transfer any cases to the domestic Rwandan authorities where the accused could face the death penalty. On this latter note, a similar dynamic emerges with regard to Sierra Leone: "[i]f the death penalty were not prohibited at the [Sierra Leone] Special Court, it would be next to impossible to secure funding from European and certain other major donors."[22]

The Organic Law encourages defendants to confess their guilt. It creates a scheme that incentivizes confessions and guilty pleas. Many defendants have availed themselves of this scheme, although not as many as authorities initially had hoped. In order for a confession and guilty plea to be valid, the Organic Law (articles 5 and 6) requires that it be made before trial, describe in detail all the offenses and victims, provide information regarding other involved individuals, include an apology, and contain an explicit plea offer. A plea that fails to comport with these requirements, or which the prosecutor deems is inaccurate, will be rejected.[23] Insofar as there is no explicit process of negotiation, the practice of plea bargaining in Rwanda differs from that at the ICTY or ICTR, where defendants may plead guilty to a single umbrella charge or to a subset of charges and international prosecutors, in turn, may drop other charges. Also, unlike at the ad hoc international tribunals, the statutory framework heavily regulates the effects of the confession and guilty plea on sentence.

If the court accepts a guilty plea, then Organic Law articles 15 and 16 govern. These base the extent of the sentence reduction on *when* the accused confesses and for *which* crime the accused pleads guilty. For example: under article 15, if the guilty plea is entered *before* charges are filed, then for a Category 2 offender the punishment – ordinarily life imprisonment – is reduced to a sentence of between seven and eleven years, to be fixed by the court. This is a major reduction. A Category 3 offender who properly pleads guilty before charges are filed is sentenced to one-third of the jail time that the court normally would impose.

The goal here clearly is to encourage those who believe they have committed a genocide-related offense to come forth on a voluntary basis before they officially become suspects. In one case, *Ministère Public v. Bugirimfura et al.*, one defendant pled guilty completely and sincerely to genocide (Category 2) before charges were brought and received a sentence of ten years; four other defendants went to trial, after which they were found guilty of genocide (Category 2), and were sentenced to life imprisonment.[24] In this case, the plea bargain stated the facts, the names of the victims, denounced collaborators, announced regrets, and mentioned that the defendant was sorry. The court dipped below the prosecutor's recommendation of twelve years in its issuance of a ten-year sentence. The court is not bound to follow the prosecutor's recommendation regarding sentence on a guilty plea and has the power to accept a guilty plea that the prosecutor has rejected.[25]

Article 16 establishes punishment for guilty pleas entered *after* charges have been filed. Here, the sentence for an offender pleading guilty to a Category 2 crime is to be fixed by the court within a range of twelve to fifteen years; for a Category 3 offender the sentence is one-half the term that would normally be imposed. In *Ministère Public v. Bizuru et al.*, a joint trial involving a similar set of factual circumstances, those defendants who pled guilty to a Category 2 offense before charges were brought were sentenced to eleven years, whereas another defendant who pled to a Category 2 offense after charges were brought was sentenced to fifteen years.[26]

Defendants who confess and plead guilty to a Category 1 offense are ineligible for the sentence reductions found in articles 15 and 16. There is an exception for individuals who are not on an official list of Category 1 suspects maintained by the prosecution. If individuals come forth, confess, and plead guilty to what is a Category 1 offense, they shall be reclassified as Category 2 offenders.[27]

Although the guilty pleas are heavily regulated by statute, they have spawned a considerable amount of interpretive jurisprudence, particularly with regard to factors that courts consider in specifying sentence within the ranges established by the Organic Law. A skeletal typology of aggravating and mitigating factors has thereby emerged. Another topic of concern to judges is what to do with the incomplete, irregular, or unacceptable plea: in other words, a plea that does not conform to the Organic Law's requirements regarding form, content, timeliness, or truth. In some cases, examined next, courts will give these some weight in mitigating sentence.

Article 17 of the Organic Law permits the court to punish by stripping the convict of certain civic rights. This can be permanent (*dégradation civique perpétuelle et totale* [sometimes referred to as *défintive*]) or limited either in scope or temporal duration (*dégradation civique limitée*). The Organic Law again links the severity of the *dégradation civique* to the offense for which the defendant is convicted. A review of the jurisprudence reveals that many convictions for genocide-related offenses are accompanied by an order for *dégradation civique*. This supplemental sanction can calibrate the retributive value of punishment by creating proportionality in sentence for more egregious crimes, for example through the determination whether or not to make the *dégradation civique* temporary or permanent within the same category of offenses. *Dégradation civique* is a form of shunning and stigma insofar as the perpetrator is hindered from reintegrating back into the community. In this regard, *dégradation civique* is at odds with rehabilitative, reintegrative, or reconciliatory purposes of punishment. Examples of those civic rights or privileges stripped through *dégradation civique* include: the right to vote; other political rights (such as to be a candidate); to serve as an expert or witness in trials or to be deposed judicially other than for the giving of simple facts;[28] the right to carry arms; to serve in the armed forces; to be police officers; and to teach in any educational institution.[29] The restrictions on admissibility and weight of a convict's subsequent testimony do limit the use of such testimony for the purpose of inculpating others and this explains, at least in part, why – unlike the practice at the ICTY – there is limited recourse to bargaining away charges in exchange for procuring an individual's testimony against others. The Conseil de Guerre, which adjudicates military officers accused of offenses related to genocide or crimes against humanity, also can punish by expelling convicts from the armed forces (*dégradation militaire* or *exclusion de l'armée*).[30]

In a December 2002 report, Amnesty International compiled statistics regarding a total of 7,181 persons judged for genocide-related crimes in Rwanda since 1997.[31] Amnesty International found that 9.5 percent of defendants were sentenced to capital punishment, 27.1 percent to life imprisonment, 40.5 percent to fixed prison terms, and 19.1 percent were acquitted. In a 2000 Report to the United Nations, Special Representative Michel Moussalli stated that 2,406 persons had been tried by the genocide courts of whom 14.4 percent were sentenced to death, 30.3 percent to life imprisonment, 34 percent to terms between one and twenty years, and 19 percent acquitted.[32] Longitudinally, the Amnesty International study demonstrates the following trends: decline in capital sentences from 30 percent of perpetrators in 1997 to 3.4 percent in 2002 – with steady annual decreases; decline in life imprisonment from 32.4 percent of perpetrators in 1997 to 20.5 percent in 2002; and increase in fixed prison terms from 27.7 percent of perpetrators in 1997 to 47.2 percent in 2002.[33] These trends arise from a number of factors, including that the initial trials focused on the more notorious killers and that, with the passage of time, increased recourse was made to guilty pleas (including in recent years with a view to entering the *gacaca* system). The acquittal rate in 2002 was nearly three times that in 1997.

The Amnesty International statistics, however comprehensive, do not illustrate the factors the domestic genocide courts consider in sentencing that transcend the guidelines provided by the Organic Law. The statistics are silent as to how the Rwandan genocide courts exercise their limited discretion with regard to punishing Category 2 and 3 offenders. Nor do they reveal the ways in which the Rwandan courts at times mold the statutory framework to suit unusual circumstances; or how, through the language, tone, and texture of their judgments, they give voice to certain penological goals in a manner that transcends the quantification of sentence or involves legal sanction from outside the criminal law (e.g., civil damages awards).

Accordingly, I conducted a qualitative review of the published judgments (in French) of the Rwandan genocide courts. The database of judgments I reviewed is that compiled and maintained by Avocats sans frontières (ASF), which they publish in bound volumes and maintain online.[34] These judgments comprise a wide sample from across Rwanda; however, insofar as ASF publishes only the more sophisticated judgments, this sample is not fully representative of what transpires in many Rwandan courts but, rather, is representative of those judgments that address questions of fact and law in a manner that carries interpretive value. In the cases I reviewed, when aggregated, defendants received the following sentences (largely consonant with the Amnesty International findings): 15 percent death, 30 percent life imprisonment, and 55 percent fixed terms. Among the fixed terms, I calculated the median term to be 11 years, and the mean term 15.25 years. Courts issued orders against nearly all convicted defendants for restitution/compensation based on collateral private lawsuits (*parties civiles*) filed by the victims and/or surviving family members. In the event of conviction, courts also issued orders for legal fees to be assessed against the defendant for the cost of the criminal proceedings in the event of conviction.[35] These orders are often made under threat of the forced seizure of all of the defendants' real and personal property in the event of inability to pay (which is commonly the case). In one case, the court issued a fine.[36]

These judgments are the product of a court system that has grown in sophistication since it began hearing cases, initially somewhat haphazardly, in the aftermath of genocidal devastation. Moreover, dating from well before the genocide, the history of Rwandan courts is one of corruption and partiality. To this end, the current state of the Rwandan judiciary is more reliable and competent than it likely ever has been. That said, although the judgments in the database go into great depth regarding the proof of the crimes, they remain very cursory as to sentencing. There are no separate sentencing hearings. The general practice is for the court to issue a sentence with no explanation.[37] This is not unusual, insofar as those institutions that prosecute extraordinary international criminals generally accord punishment a markedly lower level of attention than they accord questions of culpability. Nevertheless, a deep reading of the published Rwandan cases does permit the delineation of certain trends with regard to why the courts, in particular the Specialized Chambers, punish more or less severely in individual cases, especially when an exercise of discretion is involved. That said, there is surprisingly limited discussion of the purposes of punishment and how sentence can promote these various purposes. Engagement with penological theory is essentially nonexistent.

The articles of the Organic Law say nothing specific about the goals of punishment; the preamble provides only vague and generic references. One of the unofficial commentaries to the Organic Law identifies the following as penological purposes: punish the guilty (which, although unarticulated, seems to be a retributive goal), serve as a dissuasive example, protect the people, and rehabilitate the accused.[38] Reconciliation is a goal of the confession and guilty plea process, although it is unclear whether the operation of the process is effective at attaining this goal.[39] The ordinary Rwandan Penal Code also is reticent regarding the principles of punishment.[40]

Insofar as the sentences established by the 1996 Organic Law are, by statute, directly calibrated to a hierarchy of offenses ordinally ranked in light of the gravity of the crime, the primary purpose of punishment arguably is retribution. For the retributivist, after all, the severity of punishment is to be proportionate to the gravity of the offense. The retributive purpose is protected through the Organic Law's explicit removal of judicial discretion to depart from the statutorily prescribed range of sentence for each offense. Comments by Rwandan government officials and prosecutors – along with academic observers – also suggest the importance of retribution.[41] There are, however, a number of interesting wrinkles to the apparent importance of retribution. One wrinkle is that the Rwandan courts, in the judgments I reviewed, do not explicitly note the salience of retribution or explicitly apply retributive values to the specific context of genocide. A second wrinkle is one of internal consistency. The punishment for certain offenses under article 14 that would fall in Categories 2 and 4 is less onerous than the punishments ordinarily available under the Rwandan Penal Code.[42] For example, the Rwandan Penal Code provides capital punishment for certain premeditated murders and felony murders that would, in the language of the Organic Law, fall within Category 2 offenses for which life imprisonment is the sentence. Certain property damage offenses, such as arson, are punished by long terms of imprisonment under the ordinary Penal Code but much more lightly under the Organic Law. This reality intersects oddly with the retributive aims of the Organic Law and reveals that punishment in collective violence has other goals.

The domestic Rwandan courts have identified factors they consider in quantifying sentence in individual cases, especially with regard to mitigating factors. A number of mitigating factors (*circonstances atténuantes*) emerge from articles 82 and 83 of the Rwandan Penal Code. However, courts make no effort to explain why these factors, intended for common criminals committing ordinary deviant crimes, are appropriate for perpetrators of great evil in the context of collective cataclysm.

Aggravating factors, as had been the case at Nuremberg, often are assumed from the grisly nature of the conduct. What is more, in the Rwandan context they already are implied in the severity of sanction insofar as the factors that go to identifying liability for a Category 1 offense (such as senior position, zeal, organizing, notoriousness, and particular brutality [*méchanceté excessive*]) correspond to those factors to which judges pursuing retribution could be expected to turn in order to award sentence within an entirely discretionary sentencing structure. In one case, an aggravating factor (the defendant tore out the eyes of his victims prior to killing them) was cited to void the defendant's partial guilty plea of any effect in mitigation, resulting in a Category 1 conviction (death sentence).[43] At times, the Rwandan courts mention certain factors in aggravation even though they are not able to increase the level of punishment. Doing so serves multiple purposes. First, to promote an expressive or declaratory function that further stigmatizes the convict. Second, to emphasize why the convict was placed into a particular category in the first place.[44] Third, to explain why the court chose not to follow defense counsel's recommendation as to sentencing or chose to ascribe little weight to circumstances that might otherwise be mitigating.[45] The court also may use the amount of civil damages in a punitive sense (instead of merely compensatory or restitutionary) to operationalize aggravating factors.

My review of the case law reveals recourse to the following as mitigating factors:

(a) *Partial, incomplete, tardy, or irregular guilty pleas.* Proper guilty pleas, namely those that conform to the statutory requirements, carry significant weight in reducing sentence (this is quantified in the Organic Law). A guilty plea that falls outside of the statutory requirements, although void for the purposes of formally reducing the sentence, may still be given discretionary weight as a factor in mitigation.[46] A court is especially willing to reduce sentence when the irregular guilty plea is found to facilitate its work, contribute to the telling of the truth, evidence a request for forgiveness, or is sincere. The amount given as a discount in mitigation will not be as generous as the statutorily provided discounts. That said, this reduction may permit the defendant to receive a sentence below the minimum statutory sentence, for example, a sentence of twenty years or less for a Category 2 conviction for which the sanction is life imprisonment.[47]

(b) *Minor status.* Offenders under the age of fourteen cannot incur penal responsibility in Rwanda. Offenders between the ages of fourteen and eighteen at the time of committing the offense can incur penal responsibility, but are entitled to raise their status as minors as a mitigating factor in sentencing. The Rwandan courts give this factor considerable weight in mitigation. In fact, they avail themselves of this factor, enumerated in article 77 of the Rwandan Penal Code, even in situations where the statutory plea bargaining scheme applies. For example, in *Ministère Public v. Nzabonimpa*, the court cumulated the guilty plea made before the proceedings and the fact the accused was a minor under eighteen at the time of the offense to sharply reduce his sentence to five years' imprisonment plus legal costs.[48] The charges against this defendant involved his killing five Tutsi children between the ages of ten and fifteen years with a *masu* (a club studded with nails) and having informed others of their hideaway. The court did not justify why such a significantly discounted sentence for a perpetrator because of his youth, which might be apposite in the context of ordinary deviant crime, remains so in situations of the perpetration of extraordinary evil such as genocide. After all, a significant set of the reported cases involve minors, suggesting the complex agency of minors as both victimizers and victims in Rwanda. Minority also is given considerable cumulative weight in cases of irregular guilty pleas, moving defendants in such situations well below the statutory punishment scheme.[49]

The fact that minors between the ages of fourteen and eighteen can face criminal prosecution and punishment is another factor that distinguishes the domestic Rwandan process from the ICTR.

(c) *Coercion ("contrainte")*. In one case, the court viewed as a mitigating factor that accomplices obliged the defendant to participate by hitting him with a machete.[50] Elsewhere the courts have called this *contrainte*, which loosely translates as coercion.[51] Although ill defined, *contrainte* implies that the defendant was pressured into participating in the crimes. One complication here is that the Rwandan courts recognize duress as a substantive defense. It would be odd to define *contrainte* the same way as duress, insofar as the latter is a complete affirmative defense whereas the former only goes to mitigation of sentence. Therefore, logically *contrainte* should fall somewhere below the requirements for duress. This distinction, however, is not always clear in the jurisprudence. Following orders, a closely related mitigating factor, also surfaces in the case law.[52] The courts do not make an independent inquiry about coercion in the context of mass atrocity in considering it as a mitigating factor, once again transplanting it from its place within ordinary common criminal law despite the different regulatory purposes of criminalizing mass atrocity and criminalizing isolated deviance.

(d) *Individual characteristics*. Rwandan courts have considered the following in mitigation: that the defendant sheltered Tutsi during the genocide,[53] the ethnic status (Twa) of the defendants,[54] lack of education (cited both as a factor in mitigation[55] and as a factor reducing the defendant's criminal responsibility from that of a Category 1 offender to a Category 2 offender),[56] the defendant's weak physical health,[57] and that the defendant did not organize the attacks.[58]

Individuals convicted of genocide-related criminal offenses also face civil liability. This liability arises through collateral, private civil claims initiated by surviving victims and certain surviving relatives of deceased victims; claims also can be brought by the prosecutor on behalf of private parties. Private claims are brought by virtue of the *partie civile* process established under ordinary Rwandan law (applicable to all crimes) and are folded into the Organic Law.[59] Collateral plaintiff-initiated damages actions are common to civil law systems generally, but in Rwanda the process also draws from traditions of custom and reparation that animate *gacaca*. The criminal and civil avenues are not procedurally separate, as is the case in common law systems. *Partie civile* damage awards arise in the majority of the criminal cases published in the ASF database.

Partie civile lawsuits move in the direction of restitution and compensation for those victims most immediately aggrieved. However, these lawsuits can also serve retributive aims insofar as they permit a further marker of differentiation among perpetrators (even within the same category in a fixed scheme of mandatory sentencing) with regard to the gravity of their crimes. Civil liability can thereby constitute an additional layer of punishment. To be sure, it remains doubtful that successful claimants shall have their claims satisfied, as many problems arise with regard to the failure to pay compensation.[60] Most defendants are indigent. That said, those against whom unsatisfied claims have been entered ostensibly would be dogged by that civil liability for life. In some cases, the Rwandan state also is condemned as being jointly and severally liable (damages *in solidum*) because of its incapacity to prevent the massacres; however, the Rwandan government has eschewed payments and has in fact insulated itself from liability. Other than some modest funds raised through tax revenues, authorities in Rwanda balk when it comes to providing reparations to survivors or state compensation (even in the case of successful *partie civile* claims). That said, even when an award remains uncollectible, the *partie civile* process represents symbolic justice, promotes declaratory purposes, and constitutes another layer in the public narratives regarding victimization during the genocide. This process also permits victims some direct involvement in the legal proceedings.

Civil damage awards constitute a significant departure from the law-in-practice of the ICTR. One of the reasons why the ICTR has not issued a restitutionary award is that the defendants appearing before it have been declared indigent. However, failing to exercise the power to issue restitutionary awards for this reason alone is not terribly compelling, insofar as the domestic Rwandan experience reveals that ruling on civil claims can, at a minimum, serve important expressivist, declaratory, and truth-telling purposes.

In Rwanda, if an accused is acquitted of all charges, no civil damages are possible.[61] The criminal conviction is a prerequisite for civil liability. However, not all forms of individual criminal responsibility under the Organic Law trigger civil damage consequences. For example, in a 2002 decision by a trial court in Gikongoro, a defendant convicted of a Category 3 offense on the basis of associational liability (*association de malfaiteurs*) and sentenced to five years' imprisonment was found not to incur civil liability and the *partie civile* claim failed.[62] The court held that the defendant was not responsible for the losses of the claimants' family members (who were murdered) or possessions (which were pillaged). The defendant committed neither offense, and was criminally responsible only on the basis of a generalized associational presence. In any event, the criminal conviction ultimately was quashed on appeal at the Cour d'appel de Nyabisindu on December 11, 2002, and the defendant acquitted.

The size of the awards can be substantial. For example, in *Ministère Public v. Twahirwa*, the court awarded 144 million Rwandan francs against a Category 1 offender sentenced to death.[63] In *Ministère Public v. Higiro (Célestin) et al.*, a trial court in Butare sentenced one of the defendants, Basomingera (Category 2) to life imprisonment, *dégradation civique*, 1.5 million Rwandan francs to two victims each (for a total of 3 million) for the loss of their parents, plus miscellaneous expenses such as court costs; in the event of nonpayment the court ordered the forced sale of his possessions.[64] In 2004, the average exchange rate of U.S. $1 was 575 Rwandan francs; in 2000, the exchange rate was 1 to 400. At the 2004 rate, 1 million Rwandan francs equals U.S. $1,739, a sum larger than the per capita annual GDP in Rwanda.

At times the *partie civile* action is severed and to be determined later (for instance, to give the claimants time to collect justificatory evidence). But the action often is ruled upon immediately following the determination of the defendant's guilt or innocence. Rwandan courts examine the claimants' losses in great detail. In *Ministère Public v. Nteziryayo (Emmanuel) et al.*, the trial court grouped damages into two categories: moral damages (for pain of losses of certain relatives) and material damages (loss of goods that had been pillaged, stolen, or destroyed).[65] It prepared a detailed schema, in Rwandan francs, of the value to attribute to each of the heads of damage:[66]

Moral damages: 10 million for loss of a mother or a father
8 million for a child
5 million for a sibling
3 million for another close relative (i.e., uncle, aunt, nephew, niece)

Material damages: 300,000 for a cow
20,000 for a goat
2,000 for a chicken
1,000 for a rabbit
2 million for a house built out of wood and thatch
5 million for a house built out of bricks with metal doors
5 million for household articles
1 million for the harvest

In *Ministère Public v. Rwanteli et al.*, a trial court in Cyangugu reviewed damage claims for a broad array of losses, including pigs, goats, coffee, cement bags, bags of green beans, and also because one of the victims had to spend much time hiding in the weeds to escape from the killers.[67] In this case, a total of twenty-four million Rwandan francs was ordered, followed by the forced liquidation of the assets of all of the defendants. The quantification of the heads of damage in the *Rwanteli* case differed from the schema in the *Nteziryayo* case. Differences are found among other cases as well. For example, in *Auditorat Miltaire v. Ukurikiyimfura et al.*, the Conseil de Guerre awarded moral damages in the amounts of 10 million Rwandan francs for a spouse; 8 million for a child; 5 million for a parent or sibling; 3 million for a grandparent or grandchild; 2 million for an uncle, aunt, nephew, or niece; and 1 million for a brother- or sister-in-law.[68] The case law demonstrates significant discrepancies among courts sitting in different regions of the country (and even within the same court) with regard to the amount of loss awarded per type of damage.[69] This creates a certain level of inconsistency, insofar as plaintiffs are treated differently depending on the discretionary ("*selon sa sagesse*") or equitable exercise of authority by the court that adjudicates their case and whatever schematic it may generally or specifically apply. This contradicts the emergence of national standards, although it may be well tailored to do justice to the individual circumstances of the *parties civiles*.

These thorough discussions of the depth of the claimants' suffering allow their stories to be told in vivid, personal detail. It inks dignity and pain onto the pages of judicial documents often distinguished by antiseptic, sterile prose. Civil damages comprise a genre of compensation, storytelling, and sanction that has not occurred at the ICTR.[70]

b. *Foreign National or Military Courts*

A handful of foreign states have prosecuted Rwandans for genocide, crimes against humanity, or war crimes. There have been very few such trials.

   One example is the prosecution of Fulgence Niyonteze in the Swiss military court system. Niyonteze had been a mayor in Rwanda, but was living in Switzerland at the time the prosecution was initiated. He was accused of ordering the massacre of Tutsi and moderate Hutu in his village. On April 29, 1999, the Switzerland Military Court of First Instance convicted him of the murder of at least three people, attempted murder, and breach of international conventions (war crimes in internal armed conflict). The initial sentence was life imprisonment. On appeal, the sentence was reduced to fourteen years insofar as a number of convictions for common crimes were quashed.[71] In sentencing, the Military Court of Appeal alluded to retribution, noting the intrinsic gravity of the crimes. It observed that the murders were committed atrociously and that the corpses were denied a dignified burial in that they were left abandoned in latrines. The Military Court of Appeal mentioned Niyonteze's leadership role as mayor, noted his coldness and hatred (*grande froideur, haine*), and that he failed to express any remorse or empathy. The court did raise in mitigation, as the East Timor Special Panels have done on occasion, that Niyonteze faced a chaotic situation that left him with only limited room for decisionmaking. Niyonteze also was found to have saved the lives of some people who were close to him, for whom he had produced false documents.

   Proceedings by foreign courts can obstruct Rwanda's wish to prosecute alleged perpetrators at home. For example, Rwanda insists on bringing Wenceslas Munyeshyaka, a Catholic priest, to trial in Rwanda for his alleged involvement in atrocities in Kigali.[72] Yet Munyeshyaka is in France, where authorities are in the process of prosecuting him. The French prosecutions (which began in 1995) have been dismissed, appealed, and now restarted. Considerable controversy has arisen with regard to the question whether the French courts are competent to try crimes committed by a foreigner against foreigners in a foreign country. Questions of Munyeshyaka's responsibility have not yet been addressed. These complex jurisdictional questions would not arise were the proceedings to take place in Rwanda. In the interim, the accused continues to perform his pastoral duties in a parish near Paris. The desire by French courts to prosecute Munyeshyaka has deferred assessment of his actual responsibility and, by triggering this lengthy delay during which time the defendant exercises his vocation, has diminished the severity of whatever punishment might ensue.

   In 2001, a Belgian jury found four Rwandans resident in Belgium, including two nuns, guilty of multiple national and international crimes.[73] The court sentenced them to terms of twenty years, fifteen years, and two to terms of twelve years each. Although references were made to Belgian domestic law, no explicit elucidation was made of penological rationales as grounds for the variations in the sentences. The case contains one reference to a mitigating circumstance for each of the defendants: no evidence of prior criminal convictions.[74] This seems a fairly odd factor to consider in mitigation. Doing so effectively implies that extraordinary international criminals ought to see the severity of their sanction diminished because they had not been convicted of ordinary common crimes either before or after their acts of extreme evil. Given the multiple nature of the crimes, and the absence of any confession, plea, or remorse, the Belgian sentences are comparatively light in relation to what domestic Rwandan courts and the ICTR would issue. The defendants also faced civil sanction.

The occasional involvement of Belgian courts in punishing alleged perpetrators of genocide in Rwanda continues under Belgian legislation that permits its courts jurisdiction to prosecute certain extraordinary international crimes committed outside Belgium when the accused is a resident of Belgium. On June 29, 2005, two Rwandan businessmen were convicted by a Belgian jury of aiding and abetting war crimes and were sentenced to twelve and ten years.

A silent irony lurks in the Belgian judgments in that they do not demonstrate introspection regarding Belgium's colonial involvement in Rwanda, in which Belgium was a perpetrator of systematic rights abuses, and through which it also created conditions that eventually facilitated genocide in 1994. Belgian colonial administrators took a liking to the Tutsi, whom they treated preferentially. This angered the majority Hutu. In 1933, the Belgian colonial administration passed a law requiring every Rwandan to carry an ethnic identity card. The lines between Tutsi and Hutu, which traditionally had been porous and informal, suddenly became permanent and legalized. The ethnic identity card requirement persisted after Rwandan independence in 1960. Tragically, the continued presence of this requirement accelerated the genocide, insofar as persons unable to produce a Hutu card simply were slaughtered. Nor do the Belgian courts refer in their judgments to Belgium's role in failed international peacekeeping in Rwanda during the genocide.

The Belgian courts do not justify their interventions on the basis of Belgium's repaying a debt to Rwanda for historical events. The flattened historical narratives that emerge from individualized criminal trials, especially those conducted far away from Rwanda, do not elucidate the gnarled, and deeply complex, roots of responsibility for genocide. Instead, criminal trials permit the former colonial state to cleanse its wrongdoing and appear heroic in its quest for justice. These monodimensional and partial narratives pose a challenge to the expressive value of trials and punishment.

To be sure, there are times where proceedings conducted far away can be catalysts in the process of accountability at home, where they may help pry loose information that is deeply buried.[75] Arguably, this was the case with regard to extraterritorial prosecution of General Pinochet of Chile. Alternately, extraterritorial prosecutions can provide some justice when the territorial state's apparatus remains repressive, which is the case with regard to Spanish proceedings involving atrocity in Guatemala. In the case of Rwanda, however, the upshot of extraterritorial prosecutions is more difficult to discern and the interface of these proceedings with broader notions of justice remains quite complex.

c. *Gacaca*

Gacaca, which means "justice on the grass" in Kinyarwanda,[76] is a traditional method of dispute resolution. The Rwandan government has turned to this tradition, which it has significantly adapted, to promote accountability for offenses related to genocide and crimes against humanity committed between October 1, 1990, and December 31, 1994. With regard to these adapted proceedings, *gacaca* judges are elders and "people of integrity" (*Inyangamugayo*) elected from local communities throughout Rwanda. *In toto*, 170,000 judges sit on approximately 10,000 panels. The panels are composed at the lowest level (that of the *cellule*) of nine judges with five deputies.[77] There are two higher levels of panels at the *secteur* and appellate levels (each of these two levels has about 1,500 panels). All panels are to apply the same substantive criminal law that is applied by the national courts in proceedings related to genocide and crimes against humanity. Suspects are brought to the communities where they are alleged to have committed their crimes to face villagers and judges elected from the community. The notion of community in postgenocide Rwanda is dynamic, insofar as the community in the village that adjudges perpetrators generally does not correspond to the community that had been present at the time the crimes allegedly had been perpetrated. Many communities have become recomposed in the wake of the genocide owing to refugee movements, mass killings, internal displacements, immigration of Tutsi from Uganda, and government-driven resettlement programs.[78] This does not denude *gacaca* for genocide of its communitarian ethos, but suggests that the relationship of local *gacaca* initiatives with locally assembled populations certainly is nuanced.

Practically speaking, the decentralized nature of the *gacaca* process facilitates access to justice by reducing transportation costs for witnesses and victims, which has been cited as a shortcoming for the national trials and, especially, for the ICTR. Public involvement also is encouraged insofar as the proceedings are conducted in Kinyarwanda and businesses close (albeit by governmental order) on the days *gacaca* is in session. At the proceedings, the public (the General Assembly) can raise issues – discursively – that exceed the microscopic truths that would arise at trials. Members of the public can ask questions of suspects, to which suspects are permitted to reply. However, the judges are empowered to control the discussion, the flow of evidence, and maintain order at the proceedings. In the end, although the judges primarily adjudicate, they also act as mediators to help the gathered community attain both legal and extralegal goals. Lawyers are excluded, purportedly to ensure the open, participatory nature of the proceedings. Judges are laypersons who do receive limited legal training.

In practice, *gacaca* for genocide first began haltingly. The process was subject to numerous delays. A number of panels, however, began proceedings in March 2005.[79] In January 2006, it was reported that 4,162 individuals had been adjudged,

142 of whom were women.[80] Prior to appearing in *gacaca* courts, certain parolees had spent time in reeducation camps. All *gacaca* panels have undertaken investigations. Once proceedings begin in earnest throughout Rwanda, estimates vary widely as to how long it would take to process all detainees. Realistically speaking, it may take up to five or six years.

The government established *gacaca* courts for several reasons. One is managerial. After all, many detainees have been incarcerated since 1994 awaiting a putative trial date; given the pace of trials in the national courts, it could take as long as a century to clear all the cases. A second stated reason is to diversify the legal response to genocide by invoking mechanisms more steeped in reconciliation, reconstitution, and reintegration – each of which resonates in Rwandan sociolegal culture. This diversification, in theory at least, would move the focus away from retribution, in particular with regard to lower-level offenders. Consequently, the Rwandan government touts both retribution and reconciliation as goals of *gacaca* adjudication; and the *gacaca* framework notes the importance of penalties that permit convicts to "amend themselves" and reintegrate into Rwandan society.[81] A third reason is participatory – to involve the public in adjudication and discussion of genocide. A fourth reason is to "disclose the truth" (although the *gacaca* process, whether traditional or in modified form for the genocide, is not a truth and reconciliation commission).[82] And a fifth reason is one of sovereignty, namely the Rwandan government's perception that Rwanda needs to develop "by itself" solutions to the genocide and its consequences.[83]

These neotraditional *gacaca* courts initially were established in 2001 by virtue of an Organic Law.[84] In 2004, the 2001 Organic Law for *gacaca* courts was significantly amended.[85] The amended law, which collapsed and simplified elements of the preceding framework, categorizes offenders and punishments. In this regard, the approach is similar to that of the 1996 Organic Law for the Specialized Chambers of national courts, although there are important differences. For example, the form of punishment under *gacaca* includes incarceration as well as community service (*travaux d'intérêt general*), the length of sentence overall is slightly shorter than that set out in the 1996 Organic Law, and sentencers are given somewhat broader discretion. These changes – in particular with regard to punishment – are important insofar as it appears that, from now on, detainees will be processed through the 2004 *gacaca* legislation.

Article 51 of the 2004 *gacaca* legislation creates three categories of offenders. These are:

- Category 1: planners, leaders, notorious murderers, torturers (even when not resulting in death), rapists and sexual torturers, and those who committed dehumanizing acts against a dead body (in all cases, actual perpetrators and accomplices are implicated);
- Category 2: (1) murderers; (2) those who committed attacks with the intention to kill but did not succeed; and (3) those who committed other offenses against the person without the intention to kill;

- Category 3: those who committed property offenses (an offender in this category cannot be prosecuted if there is an agreement between the offender and the victim to settle the property harms caused).

Category 1 offenders are excluded from the local *gacaca* panels.[86] They are to be prosecuted more formally. Initially these prosecutions were to occur in the ordinary national court system. However, in November 2005, a new special court was created to hear these prosecutions. Local *gacaca* panels will only hear those cases involving Categories 2 and 3.[87] They will therefore have jurisdiction over those who killed (even intentionally), who assaulted persons, and who committed property offenses. That said, the *gacaca* law does create punishments for Category 1 offenders. This is because the determination of new Category 1 offenders (and the corroboration of evidence against others) can be made in the information-gathering pretrial stages of *gacaca*. Looking ahead, those individuals thusly determined to be in Category 1 shall, although processed by the new special court reconstituted following major legal reforms, apparently be entitled to the sentencing scheme established for them by the *gacaca* legislation, which differs from the sentencing scheme established by the 1996 Organic Law for the Specialized Chambers of national courts.

In all cases, investigations and compiling of evidence are carried out by the lowest-level *gacaca* panel, namely that of the *cellule*.[88] The community thereby becomes involved in developing lists of individuals accused of crimes and also in corroborating or removing charges the prosecution may have previously brought against parolees. It is through this process that an accused can be placed in a certain category (or removed therefrom). It is only when the investigatory and pretrial stages are completed that the *gacaca* panels adjudicate wrongdoing. Adjudication of Category 3 suspects occurs at the *cellule* level and Category 2 suspects at the *secteur* level.

The 2004 *gacaca* legislation provides a very detailed punishment schematic. It also meshes punishment with a confession and plea bargain regime that bears some similarities with, although also expands upon, that of the 1996 Organic Law for the Specialized Chambers. As set out in article 54 of the 2004 legislation, the focus is on confessions, pleading guilty, apologies (made publicly to surviving victims and to Rwandan society), and repentance; there also is a requirement to provide information regarding the whereabouts of victims' remains. The extent of the sentence discount is motored by when the accused confesses: namely, whether the confession is approved before the accused's name appears on a list drawn up by the *gacaca* courts in their investigative functions, or after. The General Assembly can reject an incomplete or insincere confession.

Article 72 states that Category 1 offenders who refuse to confess, or whose confessions have been rejected, incur either the death penalty or life imprisonment.[89] Given the current attitude of the Rwandan authorities toward the death penalty, it is likely that such offenders *de facto* will face life imprisonment. Category 1 offenders who confess as provided by the law incur a prison sentence ranging from twenty-five to thirty years.

Category 2 offenders who kill or who commit serious attacks with the intent to kill, and who either refuse to confess or whose confessions have been rejected, incur a sentence ranging from twenty-five to thirty years.[90] Those who confess after their names have appeared on the list compiled by the relevant *cellule*-level *gacaca* court incur a sentence from twelve to fifteen years, but out of this sentence they only serve half of their time in custody and the remainder is commuted into *travaux d'intérêt général* (community service). Those who confess before the list is drawn up incur a prison sentence ranging from seven to twelve years, half served in prison and half in community service. These sentence discounts are quite striking. The purpose of discounting sentence for persons who come forth and turn themselves in before investigations implicate them in atrocity and place them on the list is to save resources and encourage truthfulness.

Category 2 defendants who committed offenses against the person without the intention to kill face a term of imprisonment within the following ranges: five to seven years if they refuse to confess, or if the confession is rejected, half of which is in community service; three to five years if they confess after the list is drawn up, half of which is in community service; and one to three years if they confess before the list is drawn up, again half of which is in community service.

Members of Category 3 – those accused of property offenses – only can be sentenced to civil reparations for the damages they caused.[91] In the absence of an agreement concluded between the perpetrator and the aggrieved parties, the *gacaca* court quantifies the reparation due.

In addition to the recategorization and the simplification of the panel structure, the 2004 *gacaca* legislation effected two notable changes to the 2001 *gacaca* legislation that pertain directly to punishment. Whereas article 69 of the 2001 legislation sentenced a Category 2 offender who either did not plead guilty or whose plea was rejected to a sentence of twenty-five years or life, the 2004 legislation sets a maximum sentence of thirty years' imprisonment for a Category 2 offender. Second, under article 75 of the 2001 legislation, community service was cast as an option for the convict, namely, something that the convict could choose to do; in fact, the convict was free not to elect to serve half the sentence in community service but spend the whole sentence in prison. The 2004 legislation appears to eliminate the hitherto optional character of community service, thereby making it a mandatory component of many sentences. The motivations for these two changes to the punishment scheme are not readily ascertainable from the text or preamble to the legislation. They may reflect, on the first part, a move away from retribution and, on the second part, a desire to coax offender reintegration and victim restoration through labor.

In sum, *gacaca* offers a more diversified array of punishment than the Specialized Chambers of the Rwandan conventional courts, and certainly more so than international criminal tribunals. The community service aspect is the central vehicle for this diversity. In theory, this service might include tilling the fields of victims, donating produce or labor, obliging other members of the perpetrator's family to help the aggrieved family, constructing roads, and renovating houses partially destroyed during the genocide or building new houses for survivors.[92]

That said, it is too early in the practice of *gacaca* to make definitive assessments of the quality and form of community service projects, although the compensatory value appears to be underactualized.

Time spent in community service is conditioned on the convict's not committing another crime. Moreover, if a convict defaults on the community service commitments, then the time remaining on the sentence is to be served in custody.[93] It remains unclear exactly how the service shall be monitored and default determined. Monitoring costs could in fact be quite high. Default claims could tie up the *gacaca* system. On the other hand, if *gacaca* judges impose lengthy jail sentences (and too readily find default), then the problems of prison overcrowding and endless proceedings that plague the Rwandan legal and correctional system simply will reappear. In terms of the law-in-practice of *gacaca*, it is important to recognize that many suspects have been detained – some for over a decade – awaiting adjudication. In the event this pretrial detention counts toward any eventual sentence, a large number of individuals would simply be released for time served.

Dégradation civique also is contemplated as a sentence. According to article 76 of the 2004 Organic Law, for those convicted of Category 1 offenses this is *perpétuelle et totale*. Certain Category 2 offenders also are subject to *dégradation civique*. The 2004 Organic Law narrows the scope of convicts subject to *dégradation civique* from the 2001 Organic Law.[94]

The *gacaca* law also provides for restitution or repayment of looted or ransacked property, or carrying out the work required for the property to be repaired.[95] This is distinct from community service. At the initial *gacaca* proceedings, genocide survivors filled out forms requesting compensation, although perpetrators largely are illiquid and the Rwandan government has proven reluctant to commit funds. Given the great difficulty in enforcing the *partie civile* damage awards that emanate from the conventional court system, it may well be that the *gacaca* legislation's permitting offenders to carry out work to repair what they had destroyed becomes a more realistic method of restoration (although this, too, may be subject to tremendous monitoring costs, along with the potential for corruption and the possibility of involuntary servitude to private parties). For a society such as Rwanda, in which tens of thousands of families have been orphaned and for many years have been headed by children, financial reparation is not just a matter of commemoration or symbolic justice. It also could prove essential to rudimentary quality of life. That said, not all Rwandans wish to receive money or property as some sort of compensation for the loss of their loved ones.[96] This does not mean that they necessarily eschew the civil liability process. They may welcome its expressive and didactic value, as discussed earlier.

The 2004 Organic Law makes some reference, albeit quite parsimonious, to aggravating and mitigating factors. As for aggravating factors, article 52 states that position of leadership, which is a constitutive element of the categorization of the offender's degree of criminal liability, also is a factor that could expose the offender to the most severe punishment within the appropriate category. With regard to mitigating factors, the statutory framework makes great allowance for the process of confessing, pleading guilty, and apologizing. Minority, too, leads to discount and is explicitly referenced in a manner that is much more detailed than the statutory framework for the Specialized Chambers. Article 78 provides specially reduced punishment for minors between the ages of fourteen and eighteen at the time of the events.[97] Minors under the age of fourteen at the time of the events cannot face prosecution but can be placed in special solidarity camps.

The Organic Law is supplemented by a special manual that the Rwandan government has created for *gacaca* judges (*Manuel explicatif sur la loi organique portant création des juridictions gacaca*).[98] This document, initially created for the 2001 Organic Law, provides additional instruction for judges on how to conduct hearings. It also summarizes penalties for offenders and enumerates certain aggravating and mitigating factors in sentence (only 3 of over 100 pages are devoted to sentence). Having an authority position in the *cellule* is listed as an aggravating factor.[99] The *Manuel explicatif* also mentions as aggravating the fact that the offender may have been sentenced to concurrent convictions: in such a case, the sentencer is to exercise discretion (if available) to award the most severe sentence in the permissible range.[100] As for mitigating factors, the *Manuel explicatif* mentions vulnerability (*faible capacité d'esprit*), undue influence (*forte influence subie*), and whether the accused may have saved the lives of other victims.[101] In all cases other than what the Organic Law provides for minority and confessions, the incorporation of mitigating factors is a discretionary exercise. This discretion is fettered by article 81 of the 2004 Organic Law, which precludes judges from dipping below the minimum sentence statutorily provided.

Other than these factors, the positive law frameworks provide no explicit guidance to *gacaca* judges as to how they ought to exercise their considerable discretion in sentencing within the prescribed ranges (a discretion that exceeds that provided by the 1996 Organic Law). Furthermore, other than a few lines in the preamble, and extrinsic sources, the *gacaca* legislation makes no mention of the rationales for punishment generally. Although the *gacaca* court must present its reasons for judgment, it is under no obligation to present reasons for the sentence; the only requirement is for the penalties to be pronounced.[102] Despite the importance of community service, it is unclear whether judges can give voice to penological rationales, say retribution or restoration, through the choice of which kinds of service projects to assign to particular offenders. Nor is there any guidance regarding which sorts of projects intrinsically are more restorative, reparative, deterrent, or retributive; or how to differentiate modalities of community service from each other based on these different aspirations (in other words, what factors make a particular project more restorative than another, or more retributive than another). In the absence of such a schematic, it is unclear how the purposes of sentencing can be coherently individuated for the actual convict or victims implicated in a specific case.

Insofar as *gacaca* courts have only just begun their operations, there is limited law-in-practice. Statistics compiled by the Rwandan government in

June 2005 from initial *gacaca* adjudications throughout the country reveal that in all but one of twelve jurisdictions the maximum penalty of thirty years had been issued.[103] This is unsurprising insofar as the early *gacaca* proceedings involved more serious offenders, although many of them had confessed.[104] Minimum penalties issued range from one year to five years. Community service was ordered in about 45 percent of all judgments. In cases that have been adjudged, approximately 12 percent of defendants experienced a change in their category classification for reasons that remain unclear. The acquittal rate, reported in January 2006, was 12 percent (caveat: many initial cases involved confessions and guilty pleas) and about 25 percent of all judgments were appealed.[105]

ASF reports limited discussion of the rationales for punishment at the initial *gacaca* sessions its observers attended. It also reports that judges sentenced at the upper bands of the permissible range, which suggests that they exercised their discretion to impose the longest sentences possible and underplay mitigating factors.[106] *Gacaca* judges did not regularly award *dégradation civique* in the initial proceedings.[107] With regard to those sentenced by *gacaca* to community service, Human Rights Watch reports that the 750 individuals sentenced by September 2005 all were brought to work in one place (akin to a labor camp).[108] This seems to be at odds with traditional *gacaca*'s goal of diffuse local restitution or direct victim compensation.

It is now estimated that at least 760,000 individuals – perhaps even 1,000,000 (which would be over ten times the extant prison population) – eventually may end up facing a *gacaca* court.[109] Evidence emerging from the investigatory phases of *gacaca* proceedings suggests much broader levels of public participation in the Rwandan genocide than what many had previously believed (or wanted to believe), although a number of observers – myself included – consistently have maintained the populist nature of atrocity in Rwanda.[110] Through its investigations, *gacaca* may be unmasking these broad levels of complicity and the identification of perpetrators through public denunciations. Assuredly, some of the testimonial evidence proffered by detainees and accusers is likely unreliable, dated, uncorroborated, untruthful, and motored by ulterior motivation. But not all of it is so, and obviously the *gacaca* process will afford some occasion to verify the veracity of this evidence. In this regard, by permitting the adduction of evidence that expands the breadth of accountability for the Rwandan genocide, *gacaca* could distribute blame more evenly among those responsible.

The prospect that *gacaca* might implicate an additional one million people in genocide in Rwanda is deeply troubling to some observers. To be sure, this prospect presents significant administrative and bureaucratic challenges. It is unclear whether any system can accommodate such a volume of cases, especially in Rwanda where limited resources already are strained by the drive for accountability and where many suspects face substandard conditions of detention. Moreover, there is cause to fear that the state may turn to *gacaca* as an instrument to intimidate opposition. However, some of the concerns voiced by observers transcend the managerial or political. William Schabas, for example, finds that implicating one million people in genocide is a "terrible and totally unexpected result [...that...] ha[s] opened a Pandora's box [...] Charging 1,000,000 Rwandans with genocide amounts to an indictment of perhaps one-third of the country's adult population."[111]

But what if one-third of the country's adult population actually was involved – whether as perpetrator, accomplice, profiteer, or benefiting bystander – in the 1994 genocide? It may well be that expanding the array of suspects more accurately reflects the popular nature of genocide in Rwanda especially when, as *gacaca* does, property crimes and profiteering are included. I agree with Schabas that detaining suspects in "appalling conditions" is deeply problematic. I also acknowledge that managerial concerns arise with such a volume of cases and that there is evidence the government is deploying *gacaca* for social control purposes. Certain of the denunciations are politically motivated and, as is the case with all legal matters, some are unsubstantiated. However, these pragmatic concerns should not dissuade the contemplation of processes, such as *gacaca*, that have some potential to deracinate and examine the structural nature of genocide in Rwanda.

Frankly, one of the reasons why many observers are fearful of one million Rwandans facing *gacaca* is because *gacaca* for genocide looks and acts more like a liberal criminal court than what it traditionally is, namely a communal restorative mechanism. Community-based informal justice focusing on restorative and reintegrative shaming has a long history throughout Africa and takes various names and forms (e.g., *lekgotla* and *inkundla* in South Africa).[112] *Gacaca* shares in this history. However, *gacaca* as set out in the 2004 Organic Law differs from traditional *gacaca*:

> Charles Ntampaka, one of the leading experts on Rwandan customary law, observed that the traditional system of conflict resolution did not include any written rules; remained wary of legal prescriptions that adjudicate and convict; was closely related to the family unit; favored the role of the "head of the family"; involved forms of collective responsibility; did not promote equality; gave priority to community interests over individual rights; often deemed confessions to be a form of provocation; and drew on the sacred and the religious. [...] Such characteristics are in stark contrast to the present *gacaca* courts and their functioning.[113]

The structure of the genocide *gacaca* tribunals and the conduct of their trials therefore operates somewhere between traditionalism and liberal legalism. The movement, though, has been from the former to the latter. In effect, *gacaca* for the genocide is more like a court than its customary nature of communal gathering. It is more formal than informal. Article 39 of the Organic Law explicitly states that "[g]acaca courts have competences similar to those of ordinary courts," including the power to issue subpoenas and search warrants, summon witnesses, and confiscate goods. Although lawyers do not represent participants, the *gacaca* tribunals are counseled by appointed *conseillers juridiques* (legal advisers). A detailed appellate structure, including for sentencing appeals, is created.[114] Moreover, public participation in *gacaca* is not really voluntary. According to article 29 of the 2004 Organic Law, every Rwandan citizen has the duty to participate in the *gacaca* courts. A citizen can be sanctioned for refusing to testify.[115] In some cases, local people who fail to attend *gacaca* hearings have been punished. Whereas traditional *gacaca* excluded women from decision-making, and thereby was a deeply patriarchal institution, *gacaca* as envisioned by the 2004 Organic Law is encouragingly inclusive of women, including in the capacity of judges. That said, other aspects of traditional *gacaca* of which liberal legalism might be suspicious – such as its sacred, transcendental, revivalist, and religious aspects – might serve important transformative functions. Although differences persist between *gacaca* as contemplated by the 2004 Organic Law and the Specialized Chambers of the national courts (especially with regard to community service as a sentence and somewhat shorter terms of imprisonment), *gacaca* for genocide remains "tradition [. . .] cloaked in the mantle of a criminal trial, with a strict and written procedure."[116]

Traditional *gacaca* was not designed for mass atrocity (in fact it was geared for property, inheritance, and family law matters, but it did exceptionally encompass violent and serious crimes). However, just as it did not contemplate genocide, it did not contemplate long-term isolated imprisonment either. And, with a maximum sentence of thirty years' incarceration without community service for Category 2 offenders, there is something jarringly punitive about *gacaca* as contemplated by the 2004 Organic Law. A need therefore arises for vigilant monitoring insofar as the harsh sentences may prod the initiation of false denunciations lodged for ulterior motivations of acquiring land or dispossessing neighbors. The more *gacaca* trends toward punitiveness, the more due process ought to attach to its processes – else incarceration may be meted out to a person with insufficient guard against bias, error, or manipulation. On the other hand, were *gacaca* for genocide to focus on traditional restoration and reintegrative shaming, it would seem less terrifying even if it implicated the same vast number of people. If accountability were operationalized through remedies akin to those of traditional *gacaca*, then its implication of the many acts of lower-level offenders and benefiting bystanders that are necessary for atrocity to become truly massive might not be so disquieting. International lawyers' fears of *gacaca*'s capaciousness might diminish to the extent that the system contemplated traditional sanctions.

Notwithstanding my many concerns regarding *gacaca* for genocide, it remains an innovative approach to accountability and, in this vein, deserves some deference, particularly in the initial stages of its operation. That said, I believe *gacaca* had the potential to constitute a truly revolutionary approach to accountability for mass violence, but as time passes it is not fully actualizing this potential.[117] It could have been a locus for the revitalization of indigenous, local, and restorative mechanisms to stimulate a deeper accountability dynamic. However, attempts to diversify the accountability paradigm in Rwanda through popular measures such as *gacaca*, although partly successful, underachieve their restorative, cathartic, and reconciliatory potential. In effect, *gacaca* for the genocide is more akin to judicialized proceedings than the informal, flexible extralegal methods of traditional *gacaca* from whence it was inspired. This gives rise to two important questions. How did this come to be? And in this process of becoming, which international lawyers may equate with progress, has something been lost amid the gains?

I argue that a variety of pressures, some exogenous, have moved *gacaca* away from its restorative and reconciliatory goals and structures to something that is much more punitive and retributive. These include: (1) pressures brought by the international community, in particular rights monitors and donors, to push *gacaca* in the direction of criminal trials; (2) pressures by the Rwandan government to centralize and bureaucratize *gacaca*, thereby removing local autonomy and control, to suit its own ulterior motives; and (3) the reality that the *gacaca* system was not initially designed to prosecute perpetrators of extreme evil and the prospect of provisionally releasing, shaming, and rehabilitating murderers is daunting. The first two of these reasons are of particular concern. They also are interrelated insofar as one of the ways in which a process can look more lawlike is if local discretion and particularities are stifled through deep bureaucratization by the state. In the end, pressures exerted upon *gacaca* have inhibited the development of penological rationales that truly operationalize restoration and reintegration as goals of sanction; insofar as some of these pressures could be corrected over time, any assessment of the ultimate merit of *gacaca* for genocide is an ongoing relational one.

Turning to the first factor: the *gacaca* proposal has been subject to criticism by international lawyers, Western governments, and human rights activists, in particular regarding its lack of conformity with dominant understandings of due process.[118] Criticism was fiercest when *gacaca* first was introduced. Insofar as *gacaca* for genocide has responded to some of these criticisms, the outcry has moderated, but certain specific criticisms remain: the unavailability of defense counsel; limited appeal rights; that the process of gathering evidence is communal; and poor education and training (and often none in law), and potential partiality, of judges. The international community consistently has urged *gacaca* to resemble liberal legalist process and sanction, in which guilt instead of responsibility is the goal.

In 2003, the Rwandan government adopted a new Constitution that "draws on the main human rights treaties and institutions of Western democracies."[119] Certain constitutional provisions encompass due process protections.[120] Article 190 of the 2003 Constitution provides that international treaties and agreements that have been conclusively adopted are superior to organic and ordinary laws. The government has thereby recommitted Rwanda to universalized human rights as articulated in the major international human rights instruments (Rwanda had been a party to a number of these instruments prior to the genocide). These (re)commitments are motivated by a variety of goals, which include ideological buy-in, standing in the international community, credibility, and the desire to receive cases on referral from the ICTR (paradoxically, while committing to these rights-bearing instruments the Rwandan government also has been exasperated by their application to ICTR defendants, especially when occasioning an acquittal). The Rwandan government has been less successful at garnering buy-in for these constitutional and human rights instruments at the local level in Rwanda. This indicates a divide between state and society, central and local authority, and core and periphery that is common to legal reform in many developing nations. This divide can constitute an obstacle to the credibility of national modalities for justice when operationalized within local communities, particularly when communities remain ethnically divided. Justice as ordered by the state and state elites may be externalized from justice as understood by individuals whose lives primarily are lived locally.

Donor nations have been uninspired by, skeptical of, and in some cases hostile to *gacaca*,[121] especially without *gacaca* looking somewhat familiar to donor nations and corresponding to their expectations of what justice normatively should be. Rwanda, a very poor developing nation, cannot realistically remain impassive in the face of these expectations. There is a striking imbalance between, on the one hand, the response of the international community to the ICTR (quite generous, where international funding supports an average price tag of approximately U.S. $25 million to 30 million per verdict) and, on the other, to justice mechanisms in Rwanda itself (much more modest). One deficiency of these good faith criticisms by outsiders is that they construct *gacaca* primarily – if not exclusively – as a legal institution when, traditionally, and still to some extent neotraditionally, it wears many hats. These include the legal, but also extend to the political and the social. However, as *gacaca* becomes increasingly adversarial, it focuses more on the fate of the accused rather than the fate of the victim or the community.

Although, positivistically speaking, it is within the purview of the Rwandan government to decide how it wishes to respond to genocide, and how it wishes to react to international pressures, the Rwandan government is not without its own set of political motivations. This moves the discussion to the second of the three factors: pressures by Rwanda's RPF government to centralize and bureaucratize *gacaca* undermine local control while promoting the government's political agenda. Traditional *gacaca* fell outside the grasp of the formal state apparatus and did not occur in state-created institutions. This no longer is the case under the 2004 Organic Law. The centralization of *gacaca* has diminished popular ownership over the process and has permitted the government access to *gacaca* as a tool of social control. Some observers claim that *gacaca* courts are accusing individuals based not on what they did during the genocide, but based on their opposition to certain governmental policies.[122] Rwanda remains an authoritarian state under the auspices of the RPF. The government does not permit much criticism. Rwanda's President Paul Kagame received over 90 percent of the popular vote in the last election, which was marred by allegations of voting irregularities and intimidation. Understandably, Rwanda faces a precarious international and internal security situation, but RPF dominance is not a long-term solution. Whereas decentralizing authority could diversify the loci of power in Rwanda and, thereby, structurally mitigate the consolidation of influence that was one factor among many that accelerated genocide in 1994, the reality on the ground is that *gacaca* has not actualized meaningful decentralization. There are divides between the Tutsi elites governing the county and Tutsi survivors in the countryside.

In its traditional form, *gacaca* had considerable potential to serve goals of communal empowerment, "to reincorporate the person who was the source of the disorder"[123] and "thereby restore the balance of the community."[124] It still shares in this potential, which to my mind should be nurtured, but this has been whittled down quite deliberately. Assuredly, *gacaca* for genocide does open "a small, but real democratic space that creates the possibility for unforeseen, non-hegemonic discussions. . . ."[125] This is one of its most valuable aspects. These discussions could involve issues of accountability for genocide, but also could spill over into other areas unrelated to the genocide, thereby promoting political participation generally. There is thus a discursive aspect to *gacaca*. Phil Clark, noting that this discursive view (and the value of communal dialogue in and of itself) accords with the expectations of much of the general population, elaborates:

> According to the discursive view, participants in *gacaca* should feel free to discuss issues which are crucial to their personal and communal experiences during and after the genocide. Whatever "truth" may be discovered in *gacaca* will be reached through communal dialogue, not through the views of elites which they impart to the population. Such dialogue may be messy, may take a long time and may in the end produce rather inconclusive results. [. . .] In this view, *gacaca* encourages participants to discuss crucial issues in an open environment where the community as a whole may benefit from hearing, and contributing to, such dialogue.[126]

In practice, this discursive potential remains underexploited. For instance, the content of the conversations are regulated by the government: off the table is any discussion of human rights abuses by the government, or the reality that, in ousting the genocidal regime, the RPA massacred thousands of Hutu civilians. By eliminating jurisdiction over war crimes, the 2004 Organic Law cuts out much of the alleged RPA and RPF criminality.[127] Needless to say, discussion of RPF activity also is off the table in the national courts and at the ICTR. In fact, the Rwandan government lobbied against the reappointment of Carla Del Ponte as ICTR Chief Prosecutor in part due to her insistence that allegations of RPA crimes be investigated. The Security Council complied by deciding not to renew her mandate.[128] So it appears safe to say that the ICTR will not pursue this line of investigation.

Moreover, there are reports that indicate that some members of the public participate in the *gacaca* process out of a sense of coercion: they liken attendance at *gacaca* events to duties they owe the government and express fears of being branded as divisive should they not be seen as supporting the process.[129] These comments suggest the deep penetration of the formalized state apparatus into *gacaca*; they also hearken back to chilling talk of "work" for the state (*umuganda*) by which many Rwandans accounted for their participation in genocidal attacks in 1994. The formalism of the process has inhibited popular participation by both the Hutu and Tutsi populations. Furthermore, there is evidence that the RPF advances certain of its own ideologies at *gacaca* hearings.

Turning to the third factor: there is no denying that traditional *gacaca* was not designed with mass atrocity in mind. Understandably, the prospect of provisionally releasing extraordinary international criminals into the community, after many years of incapacitation, with a goal of reintegrating them is daunting. Unsurprisingly, there is concern among victims that *gacaca* too easily permits reintegration and punishes too lightly. Certain victims believe that the use of *gacaca* minimizes the seriousness of the underlying offense. From the victims' perspectives, *gacaca* will have to strike a difficult balance. It will have to maintain its distinctiveness without trivializing the wrongdoing that took place. That said, surveys of the Rwandan population, although revealing mixed attitudes among Hutu and Tutsi regarding *gacaca* (Hutu more favorably disposed than the Tutsi), also demonstrate that both groups are more supportive of *gacaca* than of ICTR trials, to which Rwandans as a whole remain relatively ambivalent and uninformed, and of trials in the national courts.[130]

The fact that restorative initiatives, such as those envisioned by traditional *gacaca*, have been downgraded in the justice matrix for mid- to lower-level offenders is of concern to me.[131] My concerns stem in large part from the limited success of retributive criminal trials in Rwanda in propounding acknowledgement of responsibility and atonement for genocide among detainees and defendants. The judicialization of atrocity in Rwanda has not sparked these important precursors to genuine reconciliation. In the Rwandan context, underdevelopment of these catalytic precursors is troubling insofar as, owing to two salient characteristics of the country's social geography, collective reconciliation is vital. These two characteristics are: (1) an ongoing need for victim and perpetrator to live together; and (2) massive popular involvement in terms of perpetration and victimization.[132]

Criminal trials in Rwanda have produced a limited sense of individual responsibility or blameworthiness among detainees. I first noted this disconnect in 1998, when I interviewed hundreds of genocide suspects in the central prison of Kigali.[133] Nearly every interviewee did not believe he or she had done anything "wrong," or that anything really "wrong" had happened, in the summer of 1994. Detainees who acknowledged that violence had occurred generally believed it was necessary out of self-defense. These detainees did not perceive the massacres as genocidal or in any way manifestly illegal. They saw themselves as honorable citizens tasked to do the dirty work of furthering the interests of the state. Even after years in jail, these detainees had not been disabused of the propaganda fed to them by extremist Hutu leaders, according to which the Tutsi were out to attack them, so, therefore, this attack had to be preempted by killing all the Tutsi. This violence therefore became legitimized as a preemptive war of survival, not condemned as genocide. Unsurprisingly, then, many detainees saw themselves as prisoners of war, simply ending up on the losing side. As a general rule, the trials, or the prospect of facing trial, failed to produce shame, contrition, regret, or remorse among the prisoners. They instead produced emphatic denial, buttressed by the group solidarity that then pervaded Rwandan prisons. Needless to say, this solidarity continues well past the 1998 period in which I conducted my interviews: some detainees continue to refer to their fellow detainees as "a community."[134]

Although the denials among detainees have thawed since the time I conducted my interviews, other researchers whose work postdates mine note that denials still persist.[135] I believe that the large number of confessions and guilty pleas – involving tens of thousands of detainees – that have occurred in recent years demonstrates that the disavowal of responsibility, although still a thread running through the Hutu detainee population, is dissipating.[136] The prospect of facing sentence by neotraditional *gacaca* panels prompted many of these confessions.[137] However, were *gacaca* for genocide to be more like traditional *gacaca*, and less like formal criminal trial proceedings, I posit that a larger number of individuals would come forth and confess – and would do so more sincerely – and acknowledge the harms caused and their unacceptability, offer apologies, and make amends. Accordingly, although neotraditional *gacaca* has encouraged detainees and defendants to become more contrite over time, and thereby has made a valuable contribution to reconciliation in Rwanda (much more so than the criminal trials in the Specialized Chambers, although these have advanced toward other goals), the extent to which *gacaca* has become judicialized and subject to governmental control has dampened its reconciliatory effectiveness.

Resistance to fully operationalizing restorative and reconciliatory measures in Rwanda appears misguided given the country's social geography. Rwanda is a dualist postgenocidal society, where in the aftermath of genocide both victim and aggressor must live unavoidably side by side within the same nation-state, occupy the same territory, and share common public spaces.[138] In today's Rwanda (as has been the case throughout its history), Hutu and Tutsi live geographically intermingled and in close economic interdependence. There is no separate Hutuland or Tutsiland, nor any possibility for such separation. Hutu and Tutsi speak the same language. Religious affiliations are not ethnically driven.

This commingling between Hutu and Tutsi operates in tandem with the high degree of public participation and complicity in the genocide, together with the pronounced level of victimization. Violence often was committed by neighbors upon other neighbors within local communities. Killings were committed publicly and were known to all. No attempt was made to conceal them. They were not sanitized through technology nor sterilized through anonymity. The killing was grueling, dirty, labor-intensive work – it takes many blows to kill someone with a machete, hoe, or stick. Many Rwandans provided lists of Tutsi in their region to the killers. Teachers identified students, physicians identified patients, and pastors identified the faithful. Significant numbers of Rwandans acquiesced in the face of genocide. Many of these individuals stood silent as murder plagued their streets, only to promptly move into a suddenly vacant home.

These characteristics, in turn, suggest that when considering objectives of punishment in the Rwandan context, reconciliation and reintegration ought to be given high priority. This does not mean that individuals should be spared accountability – quite the contrary, I believe the net should be cast broadly – but that the processes of accountability should encourage acknowledgement of responsibility and reconstruction of social norms. Until reconciliation and reintegration are deeply operationalized, Rwanda likely shall remain an ethnocracy with the fears of the minority Tutsi consolidating, instead of relaxing, their grip on the levers of power. When postgenocidal accountability measures consolidate instead of pluralize authority, and serve as conduits for state power at the expense of local empowerment, they remain inherently limited in the kind of transformation they can effect in removing preconditions to future violence. These concerns do not vitiate *gacaca* for genocide's innovative relevance in the accountability process, nor strip it of its entitlement to qualified deference on the part of the international community, but, rather, suggest that, as *gacaca* begins in earnest throughout Rwanda, its architects reflect upon how instantiating some of its informal and communal aspects could boost its restorative and reconciliatory potential.

(II) FORMER YUGOSLAVIA

The collapse of the Socialist Federative Republic of Yugoslavia (SFRY) triggered the dissolution of the union of its constituent entities. Croatia and Slovenia were the first to proclaim independence in 1991, followed by Bosnia and Herzegovina (in which there was a sizeable population of Bosnian Muslims, but also Bosnian Serbs and Bosnian Croats). This left the remaining provinces as the Serb-dominated Federal Republic of Yugoslavia (FRY). Fighting then began among Serbs, Croats, and Bosnian Muslims, in particular among militia forces, but civilians were deliberately targeted in pervasive violations of international humanitarian law. This violence raged until 1995, at which point a peace settlement was brokered. In 1998 and 1999, the FRY commenced a campaign of systemic human rights abuses against ethnic Albanians in Kosovo. In total, these conflicts among Serbs, Croats, Bosnian Muslims, and Kosovo Albanians claimed the lives of 200,000 to 250,000 individuals. These conflicts also saw the worst atrocities in Europe since World War II. Particularly egregious were brutalities committed in detention camps run by Serbs pursuant to policies of ethnic cleansing and, as has been found by the ICTY, genocide. Many of these brutalities were committed in Bosnia and Herzegovina.

Judicialization of atrocity in the former Yugoslavia proceeds through a number of institutions: the ICTY, a hybrid court (Kosovo), and national courts in several states within and outside of the states that emerged from the former Yugoslavia.

a. *Positive Law Frameworks*

The legislative framework for the punishment of extraordinary international criminals in the national courts of the states of the former Yugoslavia is extremely complex. This is so because several legal instruments might apply to the crimes. The SFRY Criminal Code is one such instrument. Each of the states that emerged out of the SFRY, however, has adopted its own domestic criminal code. And, what is more, many of these codes have over time been subject to amendment and, in some cases, significant reform. The legal framework in effect today, when a convict may be punished, differs from the framework in effect at the time the offense was committed, which itself was a period of rapid dissolution and reconstitution in terms of operative legal structures. Although principles of retroactivity suggest that the law in force at the time of committing the offense should govern (which is the approach the ICTY has taken), principles of lenity intimate that, if the current punishment is more lenient than the former punishment, then perhaps current punishment schemes ought to apply.[139] The ICTY is especially leery of being in any way bound by changes in domestic law that make punishment more lenient. Its fears are that "[i]n passing a national law setting low maximum penalties [...] States could then prevent their citizens from being properly sentenced by [the ICTY]. This is not compatible with the [ICTY's] primacy [...] and its overall mandate."[140]

The SFRY Criminal Code came into force in 1977.[141] At the time, regional criminal codes also were enacted in the SFRY's constitutive republics and autonomous regions. These legal frameworks coexisted in the federated system. When the republics and regions split from the SFRY, they originally retained both the SFRY Criminal Code and their regional codes, but in the following years enacted new codes that became the governing law. For example, in 2003, Bosnia and Herzegovina enacted a new criminal code on the state level; its main constitutive entities (the Serb-led Republika Srpska and the Federation of Bosnia and Herzegovina [Bosniak/Croat led]) also enacted their own criminal codes.

The 1977 SFRY Criminal Code permitted the imposition of capital punishment, imprisonment, confiscation of property, and fines.[142] The death penalty could be imposed only for the most serious criminal acts; the general range of imprisonment was from fifteen days to fifteen years. However, if a criminal offense was eligible for the death penalty, was perpetrated under particularly aggravating circumstances, or caused especially grave consequences, then a sentence of twenty years could be given.[143] In other words, the death penalty could be transformed by the court into a twenty-year prison sentence. In terms of specific extraordinary international crimes, article 141 of the SFRY Criminal Code punished genocide with imprisonment for not less than five years or by the death penalty; war crimes were subject to a similar scale.[144] Although in the former Yugoslavia the death penalty could attach to extraordinary international crimes, over time this penalty became abolished, thereby leaving the alternative punishment of imprisonment for a term of twenty years for criminal acts eligible for the death penalty.[145] The purposes of punishment under the SFRY Criminal Code were to prevent the offender from committing criminal acts, rehabilitation, to influence others not to commit criminal acts, and "to strengthen the moral fibre of the socialist society and to influence the development of the social responsibility and discipline of the citizenry."[146] The SFRY Criminal Code also specified aggravating and mitigating factors.

When the SFRY broke apart in 1992, the FRY maintained that it was the successor to the SFRY. This view was not shared by most in the international community, who instead maintained that the SFRY had dissolved and that the FRY was a newly emergent state. This question of status, however, was a matter relevant to the external relations of the FRY and not its internal legal structure. The 1992 FRY Constitution abolished the death penalty, although this did not affect the death penalty for offenses regulated by regional criminal codes in Serbia and Montenegro (although in the former case, the Constitutional Court of Serbia had declared the death penalty unconstitutional and, in 2002, the Serbian Parliament formally abolished it and replaced it with a term of forty years' imprisonment). For the most part, the FRY kept the SFRY Criminal Code in force, which it simply renamed the FRY Criminal Code, and which remained applicable to extraordinary international crimes. In 2002, an amendment to the FRY Criminal Code replaced the death penalty for offenses regulated in the FRY Criminal Code with a punishment of long-term imprisonment for forty years, although as of 1992 the imposition of the death penalty had already become impermissible for FRY Criminal Code crimes owing to the constitutional abolition thereof.[147]

In 2003, the FRY was transformed into the Confederation of Serbia and Montenegro. A further complicating development occurred in 2006, when Montenegro proclaimed independence following a plebiscite in which 55.4 percent of Montenegrans voted to end the confederation with Serbia.[148] This proclamation should not repercute strongly on the administration of criminal justice, insofar as the Confederation of Serbia and Montenegro did not have a federal criminal code: the competence to legislate in criminal matters operated at the level of Serbia and Montenegro. Serbia essentially reproduced the FRY Criminal Code as the Basic Criminal Code of Serbia, whereas Montenegro adopted a comprehensive new criminal code that entered into force in 2004. In Serbia, grave crimes are punishable by a fixed term of forty years' imprisonment, with possibility for parole after service of half the sentence (in exceptional cases, one-third).[149] War crimes and genocide are punishable in Serbia by imprisonment for not less than five years or by long-term imprisonment of forty years, thereby revealing vast judicial discretion.[150]

The Bosnia and Herzegovina Criminal Code contemplates long-term punishment in a range from twenty to forty-five years for the gravest forms of criminal offenses. The sentencing factors applicable to all crimes, even extraordinary international crimes, include: degree of criminal liability, motives for perpetrating the offense, degree of danger to the protected object, circumstances in which the offense was perpetrated, past conduct of the perpetrator, personal situation of the perpetrator, and conduct after the offense.[151] The goals of sentencing all types of offenses include the expression of the community's condemnation, reform of the perpetrator, deterrence, and raising the public's awareness of the danger of crime and the fairness of punishment.[152] Early release is contemplated, generally after service of one-half of the sentence, but a person punished by long-term imprisonment may be granted conditional release only after three-fifths of the sentence has been served.[153] Specifically enumerated ranges for certain extraordinary international crimes in the Bosnia and Herzegovina Criminal Code are a term of not less than ten years or long-term imprisonment, thereby investing considerable discretion in the judge,[154] and apparently setting a range of punishment that begins ten years lower than for long-term punishment of serious ordinary crimes. As for outer limits, as the ICTY has recognized in recent referral decisions, the maximum sentence for serious international crimes in Bosnia and Herzegovina is forty-five years.[155] A similar structure operates in the subnational entities within Bosnia and Herzegovina for long-term punishment, although extraordinary international crimes are not specifically addressed in these subnational codes. Bosnia and Herzegovina has the highest possible prison sentence currently operative in the states of the former Yugoslavia for extraordinary international crimes.

The Croatian Criminal Code entered into force in 1998, but has since been amended and revised on a number of occasions. In 2003 and 2004, Croatia adopted legislation to implement the Rome Statute of the International Criminal Court, resulting in the integration of new criminal offenses and procedures to national law. This law does not apply to the violence in the Balkans Wars of 1991–1995. The Croatian Criminal Code contemplates long-term imprisonment of between twenty and forty years for the most serious offenses, which is similar to the scheme in Bosnia and Herzegovina, but with an upper edge that is five years less. Although the 1998 Croatian Criminal Code does not specifically reference crimes against humanity, and hence differs from the Bosnia and Herzegovina Criminal Code, it turns to the similar structure of not less than ten years or long-term imprisonment for certain war crimes (although for most war crimes the minimum sentence is not less than five years) and genocide.[156] The lower range of the sentencing threshold for these extraordinary international crimes is ten years below (and in the case of many war crimes, fifteen years below) that for the most serious ordinary crimes.

Criminal code legislation enacted in Kosovo in 2004 in the hope of regularizing and standardizing the prosecution and punishment of ordinary crime established a sentence of long-term imprisonment of twenty-one to forty years for particularly serious offenses committed under aggravating circumstances.[157] Alternative measures such as suspended sentences, fines, and community service work also are contemplated. The Kosovo criminal justice system has processed, in ordinary courts, crimes of ethnically motivated violence. Initially, these prosecutions were deeply marred by ethnic bias.[158] This prompted the United Nations Mission in Kosovo to create (through Regulation 2000/64) internationalized hybrid panels to adjudge extraordinary international crimes, whose work I briefly mentioned in Chapter 3. The ICTY retains primary jurisdiction over serious international crimes committed in Kosovo but may begin to transfer cases to hybrid courts in Kosovo. Ethically motivated violence adjudged in the ordinary courts is not treated as extraordinary international crime. The ordinary courts in Kosovo continue to be faulted and the system is in disarray. Particular concerns have been noted regarding sentencing. These include lack of

appropriate reasoning or substantiation, inconsistency, excessive use of custo-
dial measures, and lack of institutional capacity.[159] Some local judges in Kosovo
reference the customary law of the Code of Lekë Dukagjini (otherwise known
as Kanun), first codified in the fifteenth century. The Kanun contains "detailed
rules for governing daily life and prescribes rights, obligations, duties, levies and
punishment."[160] It makes mention of retribution (*lex talonis*) and also reconciliation. The Kanun is of some influence in the determination of sentence in
Kosovo, especially by Kosovo Albanian judges.[161] It is not encouraged by the
new Kosovo criminal code.

The ICTY has exerted considerable influence on the legal systems of the
states of the former Yugoslavia. Much of the recent law reform, for example
reenactments of criminal codes (in particular procedural elements) in Bosnia
and Herzegovina and Kosovo, radically moved these systems to an adversarial model from what had hitherto been an investigatory/inquisitorial model.[162]
The 2003 reforms in Bosnia and Herzegovina constituted a "shift to a broadly
adversarial criminal justice system where – in contrast to the previous judge-led
mixed system – the trial is moved forward by the prosecutor and the defendant,
and the judge represents the neutral arbiter of the disputed issue."[163] A major
impetus in this process of law reform throughout the former Yugoslavia is the
reality that, by aligning domestic structures to those of the ICTY, these domestic structures become better positioned to receive cases from the ICTY, along
with international support, expertise, and resources. Furthermore, cooperation with the ICTY has become a central criterion on which Serbia's relationship
with the European Union has become contingent.

These developments attest to the influence of newly crystallized international processes to prosecute and punish perpetrators of mass atrocity, as well
as the migration of these operational norms back to the national level in places
that, heretofore, had not adhered to such methodologies. In the case of the former Yugoslavia, there is some evidence that these transplants are improving the
quality of justice by dissipating ethnic bias and promoting transparency in the
administration of justice. In terms of sentencing, many of the domestic reforms
mirror the ICTY's grant of considerable discretion to judges, although are not as
permissive. Insofar as national judges have few guidelines to fetter their discretion, a review of the case law, to which this discussion now turns, demonstrates
considerable variance in terms of sentence issued.

To be sure, some factors routinely increase or decrease the length of sentence in the national courts of states emergent from the SFRY. Guilty pleas
appear to be one factor consistently considered in mitigation. In the case
of Bosnia and Herzegovina, observers have noted that many plea-bargained
sentences dip below the proscribed minimum sentence, which is permissible
only in highly extenuating circumstances (article 49, Bosnia and Herzegovina
Criminal Code). This phenomenon particularly arises in cases where long-term
sentences are issued. There also is evidence of divergent and inconsistent judicial practice regarding sentencing individuals who plead guilty that, in turn,
threatens the principle that like cases are to be treated alike.[164] In terms of

aggravating factors, consistent reference is made to the heinous nature of the offense.

Ulrich Sieber and a team of experts interviewed judges in the former Yugoslavia.[165] In these interviews, commissioned in 2003, the judges stated that the fact that an offense was committed in times of war, as opposed to "normal circumstances," leads them to sentence more severely. As such, the extraordinary nature of the crime would constitute an aggravating factor (contrary to other situations, for example, in the East Timor Special Panels and in some of the domestic Rwandan cases, where the chaos of war has been seen as a mitigating factor).[166] At first blush, these interviews suggest that extraordinary international crimes are viewed as more serious than ordinary common crimes even when they embody a similar *actus reus* (e.g., rape, murder, or torture when committed as ordinary offenses or as war crimes). To this end, a penology for extraordinary international crimes might be emerging that grounds the differential sanction of these crimes in retributive or expressive goals tethered to the inherently greater gravity of offenses when committed in group conflict situations.

However, there are a number of wrinkles and limitations to the extrapolations that can be inferred from the interviews of judges in the former Yugoslavia published in Sieber's report. First, the interviews suggest that the differences between the punishment of wartime offenses and ordinary offenses are most distinct in cases of the commission of a single offense and drop sharply in cases of combined offenses of five to ten victims (where at the federal level in Bosnia and Herzegovina and in Croatia no differences were reported and, in fact, there was some evidence of more severe sanction for ordinary crimes).[167] Given the nature of extraordinary international crimes, a single offense is more an aberration than the norm. Second, the positive law frameworks in Croatia set a lower minimum punishment for war crimes than for serious ordinary crimes. So, too, do those in Bosnia and Herzegovina. Third, recourse by judges in the former Yugoslavia to the "special circumstances of war" as an aggravating factor is not in any way predictable. In fact, the researchers conducting the judges' interviews found that "judges had trouble explicitly considering concrete factors" in sentencing and that this, in turn, prodded a "retreat to the general sentencing criteria" and a replication of those mitigating factors explicitly stipulated in the general criminal legislation drafted with ordinary common crimes in mind.[168] Fourth, and most pertinent, these data emerged from model cases presented to a small sample of judges for them to determine sentences hypothetically based on their experience; this is quite a different exercise than sentencing actual perpetrators following actual convictions. In fact, there is a difference between what judges may in interviews say they are doing and what they actually do.

In the case law, the differentiation between crimes committed as extraordinary international crimes and ordinary common crimes is more inconclusive. Extant Croatian case law suggests a tendency to prosecute (and judge) ordinary crimes as extraordinary international crimes and then award them the lowest possible sentence. Ethnic bias and politicization corrode the retributive, expressive, and deterrent value of punishment in Serbia. There is frequent quashing of lower court decisions and remand by appellate courts in all jurisdictions. Although there are indications that, in very recent years, national courts are beginning to sentence perpetrators of international crimes to longer prison terms and are shedding the distorting effects of ethnic bias, there is no predictably conclusive movement in this direction.

b. *Courts in Bosnia and Herzegovina*

The Organization for Security and Cooperation in Europe (OSCE) has reported on the prosecution of extraordinary international crimes within the domestic (cantonal and district) courts of Bosnia and Herzegovina.[169] The OSCE Report focuses on proceedings before the ordinary courts, as the War Crimes Chamber of the State Court of Bosnia and Herzegovina had not yet come into existence at the time of its preparation.

The War Crimes Chamber, which focuses on serious extraordinary international crimes, was created in January 2005 primarily in response to the referral procedure initiated by the ICTY.[170] The Chamber formally opened in Sarajevo in March 2005.[171] Proceedings have commenced. The ICTY has referred cases. At the time of writing, the War Crimes Chamber had issued its first sentence, 13 1/3 years' imprisonment, to Neđo Samardžić, a Bosnian Serb convicted of crimes against humanity. In May 2006, it initiated its first genocide trial; these proceedings involve eleven Bosnian Serbs associated with the Srebrenica massacre. Looking ahead, the War Crimes Chamber shall be better equipped in terms of expertise to deal with the prosecution of extraordinary crimes than the ordinary domestic courts. That said, it remains unclear whether the Chamber's judges shall develop independent rationales of punishment insofar as pressures to conform to ICTY expectations in order to keep receiving referred cases will likely diminish the development of any *sui generis* approach, unless the ICTY itself moves in this direction.

Because the War Crimes Chamber is tasked only with the more serious cases, many charges of extraordinary international crimes will remain within the ordinary courts of Bosnia and Herzegovina.[172] The OSCE report determined that, in 2004, Bosnia and Herzegovina cantonal courts acquitted fifteen defendants, found nine guilty and, for these nine, issued sentences ranging from eighteen months to fifteen years of imprisonment.[173] The twenty-four defendants implicated in these proceedings divide into seven Bosniaks, ten Croats, and seven Serbs.[174] In 2005, the OSCE Report noted two additional convictions with sentences of 7 and 4.5 years.[175]

The OSCE Report also noted a number of important trends. First, it found that some courts and prosecutors had "made conscientious efforts to bring those responsible for war crimes to justice."[176] But numerous shortcomings were noted, principally ethnic bias, fear among judges and prosecutors for their safety, difficulties in terms of securing witnesses, and lack of structures for transborder cooperation.[177] Lack of coordination among courts and prosecutors also hampers efforts to obtain custody over and prosecute suspects. Observers also have

voiced concern with regard to due process, although these criticisms have qui-
eted over time. In terms of sentencing rationales, the OSCE Report is helpful
in delineating the operationalization of penality within these domestic courts,
and confirms an apparent lack of independent or cogent rationales for sentencing extraordinary international criminals (or, in many cases, an absence of any
stated reasons for aggravation or mitigation). The mean sentence of the cases
documented by the OSCE is slightly under nine years' imprisonment.[178]

On a different note, in July 2006 a reparations system for rape victims from the
Bosnian Wars was for the first time being considered by legislators in Sarajevo.
Also, a private Bosnian nongovernmental association is organizing a lawsuit
against the Republic of Serbia, in which it seeks reparations for women who
were raped or abused or who had family members killed during the conflict.
In both cases, these initiatives demonstrate attempts to pluralize modalities of
accountability.

c. *Courts in Serbia*

Ernesto Kiza reports that national courts in Serbia are not approaching the punishment of extraordinary international criminals in a predictable or structured
manner.[179] For the most part, the sentences issued remain quite lenient when
compared to ICTY sentences. This arises, in Kiza's estimation, for two reasons.
First, although there is evidence of the influence of the ICTY model of justice
in terms of affecting the perceived need to judicialize mass atrocity, and the formula of what that judicialization should resemble, what is lacking is reference to
ICTY sentencing jurisprudence (which is itself already unsystematized in terms
of the relationship between gravity of crime and severity of punishment).[180]
This lack of systematization is compounded by the inability of Serbian judges to
develop a comfort with or a methodology to punish extraordinary international
criminals. Kiza's empirical research leaves him with the sense that "domestic
judges [in Serbia] were simply overstrained by the prospect of punishing offenders of the gravest crimes committed during a state of widespread anomie. They
were just not sure how to handle the cases, although most of them were very
experienced concerning 'regular' murder, rape, and other violent crimes."[181]
What is more, there is considerable evidence of ethnic bias in the Serbian
judgments, pervasive clientelism, discomfort with analyzing the responsibility
of the political and military leadership, and a lack of support from the Serbian
government.[182]

International and foreign pressures upon the Serbian justice system, including demands explicitly raised as part of extradition negotiations, have dissipated
certain of the crudest manifestations of bias.[183] This result is desirable. These
pressures also have led to the establishment of a Special Court for War Crimes
in the Belgrade District Court. A War Crimes Prosecutor has been appointed.
Arrests have been undertaken, including for atrocity in Kosovo. No referrals
have yet been made from the ICTY to Serbia, unlike the case with Croatia, and
Bosnia and Herzegovina.

High-profile trials have begun at various levels in the Serb judicial system. In December 2005, a Serbian court convicted fourteen former Serb militia fighters for the killing of nearly 200 Croat prisoners in Vukovar; it issued sentences ranging from two to twenty years.[184] Trials have been undertaken in Serbia with regard to the Srebrenica massacre.[185] Proceedings have been initiated with regard to massacre in Kosovo.

That said, one thing these trials and convictions have not accomplished is to generate widespread acknowledgement within the Serbian population that Serb forces committed atrocities throughout the former Yugoslavia. A *contrario*: "[M]any Serbs say they are either unaware of war crimes or refuse to accept that their police or security forces could have committed them."[186] In the words of the Humanitarian Law Center, "Serbia is still stumbling under the burden of war crimes committed in the name of alleged patriotism."[187]

d. Courts in Croatia

Developments related to domestic prosecutions for extraordinary international crimes have been influenced by Croatia's relations with the ICTY, in particular the prospect of referral of cases to Croatia as part of the ICTY's completion strategy.[188] This prospect has encouraged Croatia to create a Special Court for War Crimes. At the time of writing, the ICTY has referred one case to Croatia. However, ordinary courts in Croatia have for some time prosecuted atrocity. Since 1991, Croatian courts have entered guilty verdicts against approximately 800 persons (many convicted *in absentia*) for war crimes (against civilians or prisoners of war) and genocide; at the time of writing, proceedings remain pending against another 1,400 to 1,500 individuals, with other investigations outstanding.[189] The OSCE has issued a number of detailed reports regarding domestic trials for extraordinary international crimes in Croatian courts.[190] These reports shed some light on sentencing practices and rationales.

The OSCE Report published in 2005 noted pervasive, albeit observably dissipating, ethnic bias resulting in Serb defendants' being disproportionately subject to investigation and prosecution for extraordinary international crimes. In 2004, Croatian prosecutors eliminated large numbers of unsubstantiated proceedings against Serbs.[191] This is an important step, in the OSCE's view, toward remedying a situation in which thousands of cases had been initiated against Serbs and only tens of cases against Croats, an extreme disproportion that "cannot be attributed only to different levels of criminality of certain members of the warring parties."[192] Whereas Serbs have been prosecuted for war crimes based on allegations of physical or psychological abuse, Croats have been almost exclusively prosecuted for conduct that involved killings; what is more, the Croatian judiciary "appears to apply a broader definition of genocide for which only Serbs have been convicted [...]."[193] Even when prosecutions have been initiated against Croats for killings and torture, ethnic bias has pervaded the initial judgments – requiring in some cases corrective action by the Croatian Supreme Court. On September 13, 2005, a domestic retrial of Croat military policemen accused of torturing and killing Serb prisoners of war in 1992 began following the overturning of acquittals by the Croatian Supreme Court in 2004. However, of the original eight defendants, only four reappeared in court, with the other four having fled into hiding following acquittal at the initial trial in 2002. The Croatian Supreme Court plays an important corrective function by reversing 55 percent of the trial court verdicts and ordering retrials and, in some of the affirmed verdicts, adjusting the sentence.[194] The figure of 55 percent, which is from 2004, is down from a reversal rate of 95 percent in 2002 and 60 percent in 2003.[195]

The OSCE Report also notes that, because so many lower-level Serbs are prosecuted, a large number of convictions become issued for "less serious offenses" that, when aggregated, result in the widespread imposition of less onerous punishment. For example, nearly 60 percent of the Serbs convicted of war crimes in 2004 received a sentence less than the statutory minimum of five years (the sentencing range for war crimes [against civilians or prisoners of war] and genocide is five to twenty years).[196] This creates an artificial downward pressure on the quantum of sentence in Croatian national courts for war crimes and genocide, which places this quantum out of proportion to that of the ICTY. The less serious charges pursued domestically (apparently done deliberately so as to convict large numbers of Serbs) account for the discrepancy.

Among the large number of cases (76 cases, covering 211 individuals) monitored by the OSCE Croatia Mission in 2004, 24 trials involving 47 individuals (42 Serbs, 4 Croats, and 1 Hungarian) were concluded that year.[197] Thirty individuals were found guilty, twelve were acquitted, and charges were abandoned against five.[198] More than half of those convicted received sentences less than the stipulated minimum of five years (it is permissible under Croatian law to dip below the minimum only if particularly obvious mitigating circumstances exist).[199] Overall, sentences ranged from a low of 1.5 years to a high of 15 years with an average sentence of approximately 5.5 years[200] (this is a decrease from an average sentence in 2003 of 9 years). Fifteen individuals received sentences in the one- to four-year range; eleven individuals in the five- to nine-year range; three in the ten- to fourteen-year range; and one in the fifteen- to twenty-year range.[201] In 2003, three monitored defendants received the maximum punishment of twenty years.[202] More specifically, in 2003, two individuals were sentenced to terms in the one- to four-year range; twenty-three to terms in the five- to nine-year range; five to terms in the ten- to fourteen-year range; and seven to terms in the fifteen- to twenty-year range.[203] Of these convictions, twenty-six were for war crimes against civilians, three for war crimes against prisoners of war, and eight for genocide.[204] As an aside, the ICTY has not held that genocide took place in Croatia. In 2002, fourteen individuals were sentenced in the one- to four-year range, eleven to the five- to nine-year range, fourteen to the ten- to fourteen-year range, and thirteen to the fifteen- to twenty-year range.[205]

Mitigating circumstances are frequently invoked to justify the lowering of sentences below the statutory minima.[206] These mitigating circumstances include the following, some of which are contradictory and none of which seem to be of the requisite importance to justify dipping below the statutory minima: the defendant is married; the defendant is divorced; the defendant has children; the defendant does not have a criminal record; the defendant is poor and does not own property; defendant's health and physical constitution, employment status, social status, susceptibility to coercion; and following orders or conveying orders.[207] Paradoxically, although conveying orders has been found by some Croatian courts to constitute a mitigating factor, others refuse to consider it as such.[208] Whereas service in the Croatian armed forces is a mitigating factor, service in the Yugoslav armed forces is an aggravating factor.[209] Whereas Croatian attacks are seen as defensive, Serb attacks are seen as offensive, the latter being graver for purposes of sentencing. Other aggravating factors include persistence in committing the act and groundless maltreatment,[210] and motivation to create a greater Serbia.[211]

The OSCE Report also concludes that the punishment imposed for comparable conduct differed drastically, thereby leading to inconsistent sentencing.[212] It cites among examples the following: "In the 'Virovitica' case, the Bjelovar County Court sentenced three Croats to one year each for having beaten two civilians, one of whom subsequently died. In contrast, the Osijek County Court sentenced Branko Stanković, a Serb, to 6 years' imprisonment for arresting and beating a civilian until he fainted."[213] The first of these decisions, however, was reversed by the Supreme Court and, as of 2005, a retrial is pending. There has been a trend toward improving the predictability and integrity of justice in Croatia, as in other jurisdictions in the former Yugoslavia. The increasing regularization of the activity of the Croatian courts through appellate review may lead to more principled systematicity in sentencing. However, the Croatian courts have not yet reached this point.[214] The main source of predictability in sentencing remains ethnic bias (i.e., violence being less grave when committed by Croats than by Serbs). Moreover, there is no indication of the development of broader-based remedies or theories of punishment specifically attuned to the atrocity perpetrator.

e. *Foreign Courts*

Trials have been conducted in national courts outside the former Yugoslavia. In some of these cases, principles of universal jurisdiction have been invoked. German courts have adjudged a number of defendants: Djajić (1997), Jorgić (1997), Sokolović (1999), and Kusljić (1999). Jorgić[215] and Kusljić[216] received life sentences for genocide. Djajić, convicted of war crimes for fourteen cases of aiding and abetting murder and one case of attempted murder, received five years.[217] Sokolović, convicted of aiding and abetting genocide and war crimes and of committing murder as a war crime, received nine years.[218] There is little discussion of sentencing considerations, although the *Jorgić* court found no elements of justification or exclusion of responsibility that would ordinarily serve to reduce a life sentence under German law.[219] Quite the contrary: the *Jorgić* court underscored the gravity of the crime,[220] thereby implying the importance of retribution.

In 1994, a Danish jury sentenced Refik Sarić, a Bosnian Muslim, to eight years' imprisonment for fourteen counts of serious bodily harm as war crimes.[221] Sarić had sought asylum in Denmark. The jury found aggravating circumstances under the applicable Danish law, but the judgment provides no elaboration.[222]

The jurisdiction of a Dutch court has been invoked in a compensation case against the Netherlands brought by relatives of victims of the 1995 Srebrenica massacre. Dutch soldiers had stood by while Bosnian Serb forces massacred at least seven thousand Bosnian Muslim men and boys in what had been declared to be a UN safe area. This kind of civil litigation can help spread responsibility for atrocity more broadly. Ironically, the Netherlands is the seat of the ICTY, where judgments regarding individual criminal responsibility for genocide in Srebrenica have been rendered and continue to be heard.

(III) WORLD WAR II

National military and criminal justice institutions actively prosecuted and punished perpetrators of Nazi aggression, the Holocaust, and systemic criminality in the Pacific Rim. Thousands of trials took place far away from Nuremberg and Tokyo in national courts, military commissions, and military courts all over Europe and the Far East. Although the accused were not as high-profile as those who appeared before the IMT, many came from senior ranks of Axis armed forces or were noted for particularly gruesome conduct during the conflict.

Allied military commissions zealously undertook prosecutions of Japanese war crimes: over 5,500 individuals were charged, 900 received death sentences, and 3,500 received prison sentences.[223] With regard to the war in Europe, many prosecutions took place in the British, French, American, and Soviet zones of occupied Germany and Austria. It is estimated that the Soviets alone tried over ten thousand cases. Trials of other Nazis occurred in the courts of those countries where they had committed their crimes, or elsewhere, and included Belgium, France, Yugoslavia, Italy, Poland, Norway, the Soviet Union, and Czechoslovakia. Although most of the defendants were nationals of enemy countries, in particular Germany, many courts tried their own nationals as well. For example, French national courts tried about 100,000 collaboration cases: 65,000 individuals were found guilty, although an amnesty law was passed in 1953.[224] The most famous collaborator trials involved Maréchal Henri Pétain and Pierre Laval (respectively, the Head of State and Prime Minister of France's wartime Vichy regime); and also Norway's Vidkun Quisling. In Italy, attempts to judicialize atrocity were weak. They were in fact largely superseded by "private revenge," which reasonable estimates suggest led to the disappearance or summary execution of 30,000 Italian fascists.[225] Even more so than was the case in Italy, in France accounts were settled extrajudicially. Carlos Santiago Nino reports that "[i]n 1944 alone, private citizens killed approximately 40,000 people accused of collaborating with the Nazis."[226]

The judicialization of the Holocaust and extraordinary international crimes committed by the Nazis has been considerably more pronounced than the judicialization of extraordinary international crimes committed by the Japanese. Proceedings involving Japanese defendants tapered off by the end of the 1940s, whereas those against Nazis and collaborators continued for many decades, albeit not steadily. Overall, trials for World War II atrocities have proceeded in waves: (1) military and civilian proceedings in the immediate aftermath of the war in both Europe and the Far East; (2) civilian proceedings that resurged in a variety of jurisdictions in the 1960s with regard to Nazi atrocity; and (3) a handful of high-profile cases, again with regard to Nazi atrocity, in civilian courts in the 1980s and 1990s. Courts continue to investigate, convict, and sentence perpetrators over sixty years after the Holocaust, although the number of defendants now has dwindled to a tiny handful of feeble and frail old men. Coincident with this third wave of criminal prosecution is acceptance by Germany and Austria, along with Swiss banks and other entities, of policies of restitution and reparations. German reunification also triggered the construction of commemorative memorials, for example in Berlin. One notable gap in the judicialization of wrongdoing from World War II is the absence of discussion of Allied conduct, for example, the firebombing of German cities and the dropping of two atom bombs.

These three waves of judicialization represent decreasing levels in the volume of defendants, although not necessarily in the symbolic value of convictions. That said, with the possible exception of the Adolf Eichmann trial in Israel and certain of the concentration camp trials, the expressive, pedagogical, and didactic value of national proceedings has not approached that of the Nuremberg prosecutions.

A qualitative review of the thick case law emerging from military instrumentalities and civilian courts prosecuting World War II atrocity reveals, in a manner consistent with my findings from other sites of judicialization, a paucity of discussion with regard to the purposes of punishment, the application of punishment, or how application may promote purpose. Judges were granted a tremendous amount of discretion in sentencing. Retribution and expressivism received stray mentions as purposes of punishment. Initially, sentences by military instrumentalities gravitated more toward the death penalty than in the Nuremberg or Tokyo proceedings. What is more, many of these death sentences quickly were carried out, especially in cases of former concentration camp officials appearing before military courts (for whom death sentences were the norm). For example, fifty-eight of the sixty-one defendants charged by an American Military Tribunal in relation to the Mauthausen Concentration Camp (*First Mauthausen Trial*) were sentenced to death (nine of these sentences later were commuted to life imprisonment).[227] Soviet military instrumentalities sentenced many individuals, including Russians and Ukrainian collaborators, to death.

In many cases brought in Germany in the 1960s, defendants – even those accused of involvement with concentration camps – were acquitted.[228] In terms of convicted defendants, sentences of national courts – especially German courts – were somewhat lenient. That said, leniency was not evident in all national courts. After all, the Israeli Supreme Court in 1962 upheld Eichmann's death sentence. However, even at the level of military instrumentalities run by the occupying powers, pressure soon emerged to parole most of those convicted. The onset of the Cold War dampened U.S. interest in prosecuting Nazi crimes. Amnesty laws were passed in a number of national jurisdictions. The situation of prosecutions in Austria is indicative: in immediate postwar years, 17,500 individuals were prosecuted in national courts (43 were sentenced to death, of whom 29 eventually were executed); in 1949 the Austrian government enacted an amnesty law for those only loosely implicated in the Nazi regime; and in 1957 a general amnesty was enacted for all members of the Nazi Party.[229] Looking back from a perspective sixty years after the end of World War II, it is clear that, although some perpetrators have faced legal process, many have evaded it.

a. *Immediate Aftermath of the War*

Many trials were held by military courts and commissions, along with national courts, in the late 1940s. Thousands of individuals were charged and convicted. These proceedings involved a medley of international law, municipal law, and military law. Although the Nuremberg judgments frequently were referenced, the proceedings largely remained dependent on provisions of ordinary municipal criminal law.

The case reports show very little, if any, thought given to penological purposes, although some discussion is found regarding the fixing of sentence and mitigating factors. This paucity of discussion occurs even in the handful of cases where national courts reviewed military commission sentences, such as the case of General Yamashita before the U.S. Supreme Court.[230] One exception is the judgment of the Netherlands Special Court of Cassation in the matter of Hans Albin Rauter. Here, the Netherlands Court discussed punishment for extraordinary crime and underscored the expressive value of punishment in this context. It noted that when a court punishes acts of extraordinary international criminality it has "the object of giving expression to the sense of justice of the community of Nations, which sense has been most deeply shocked by such crimes."[231] The Netherlands Court also underscored the relevance of the gravity of the acts and the need for punishment to be proportionate thereto.[232]

Overall, the sentences issued by national courts and military instrumentalities ranged from death (by hanging),[233] to long-term imprisonment (at times with hard labor), to shorter terms of imprisonment. Judges were given tremendous discretion in the sentencing process. For example, the Polish Law Concerning Trials of War Criminals provided for death, imprisonment (for life or a term sentence) and, similar to contemporary Rwanda, loss of public and civic rights and forfeiture of all property of the sentenced person.[234] The Netherlands East Indies Law allowed courts to punish war crimes through the death penalty, life imprisonment, or imprisonment from one day to twenty years.[235] The Chinese Law Concerning Trials of War Criminals restricted punishment to either death or life imprisonment in cases of crimes against humanity, crimes against the peace, and serious war crimes; with regard to other ostensibly less grave war crimes, punishment could encompass death, life imprisonment, or imprisonment for ten years and, with regard to other war crimes (ostensibly those of even lesser gravity), the choice was between life imprisonment and term imprisonment of not less than seven years.[236] Regulation 9 of the British Royal Warrant accorded a Military Court the ability to sentence a person found guilty to any one or more of the following punishments: death by shooting or hanging, imprisonment for life or any less term, confiscation, a fine, and – additionally – restitution.[237] The Canadian law basically was identical.

Interestingly, the Dutch Extraordinary Penal Law Decree increased the penalties for war crimes from those ordinarily available under municipal law for ordinary common crimes, suggesting the increased gravity that may be attached to these extraordinary international crimes; however, it still left significant discretion in the hands of the sentencing authority.[238] The Norwegian Law Concerning Trials of War Criminals also explicitly increased the sentences for extraordinary international crime over those available under ordinary domestic penal law. It permitted sentences to be doubled in the most serious cases from what would be ordinarily available; capital punishment was possible based on aggravating circumstances. The Norwegian government's reasons for enhancing the severity of punishment were explicitly retributive. It noted that ordinary Norwegian law "did not lay down sufficiently severe penalties" as it was "founded on the supposition of a normal social life."[239] This instance is one of the infrequent times where lawmakers expressly noted the difference between ordinary common crime and extraordinary international crime and turned to this difference to justify augmenting the retributive censure for extraordinary international crime. However, the French approach is more indicative of overall state practice. The French Law Concerning Trial of War Criminals in the French Zone of Germany simply stated that the penalties that can be applied to offenders are those provided in the ordinary penal code (for ordinary crimes).[240] There does not seem to be any predictable, or at times even explicable, basis upon which mercy reviews or confirmations of sentence were conducted.[241] These often reduced the severity of sentence initially issued, at times quite drastically. For example, two sentences of life imprisonment issued to two members of the Japanese Military Police by an Australian Military Court were each commuted to two-year sentences by the confirming officer.[242] Lieutenant General Kurt Maelzer's sentence was reduced from ten years' imprisonment to three years' imprisonment "by higher military authority."[243] In the Dachau concentration camp trial, thirty-six of the forty convicts initially were sentenced to death. However, the reviewing authority commuted three of the death sentences to terms of hard labor (life, twenty years, ten years) and then the confirming authority commuted five of the remaining thirty-three death sentences to various fixed terms of hard labor.[244] Despite a small number of additional trials that took place in Munich in the 1950s, 1960s, and 1970s, the crimes committed at Dachau largely remained unpunished.

As was the case at Nuremberg, a primitive typology of mitigating factors arose in cases prosecuted in the immediate aftermath of World War II. One factor was following superior orders, which, although largely incapable of exculpating an accused, routinely was considered in mitigation.[245] In this regard, many national courts and military commissions emulated the approach taken by the IMT judges. The more categorical the order, and the less the person to whom the order was made had any input regarding its content, the greater the tendency to mitigate the sentence. An individual's obeying laws and instructions while "exercis[ing] no initiative to any marked degree" was one factor that a U.S. Military Commission (Shanghai) found to "compel unusually strong mitigating consideration."[246] That said, pleas of superior orders did not mitigate sentence in every case.[247] Overall, however, superior orders was probably the factor most frequently accepted in mitigation.

Other mitigating factors, many of which were judicially created, include: age, experience, and family responsibilities of the offender;[248] that the offender's "mental faculties were defective and undeveloped";[249] minority (as per national law);[250] that the offender "stupidly allowed himself to be carried along with the criminal stream of German terrorism, rather than acted with intent on his own initiative";[251] and the "brief, passive, and mechanical participation of the accused."[252] A British Military Court was asked to take into account a defendant's "previous record as a brave, responsible soldier," but "nevertheless" sentenced him to death by hanging (the sentence was confirmed and implemented).[253] In the *Zyklon B Case*, which involved the complicity of German industrialists in the killing of Allied nationals in concentration camps, a British Military Court issued death sentences (subsequently confirmed and implemented) despite pleas of mitigation related to defendants' alleged lack of knowledge as to the use the gas was being put to, pressure from the military police, duress, and that one defendant had a wife and three children.[254] Also ineffective in the *Zyklon B Case* was a plea that, had the offender not cooperated, "the S.S. would certainly have achieved the aims by other means."[255] A Special Court in Amsterdam reduced a sentence to fifteen years' imprisonment for a crime against humanity in part because the offender "did not act on his own spontaneous initiative [but] was drawn into the whole abominable system of terrorism and brutality carried out under the higher German Nazi administration against civilians of the occupied nations."[256] Sometimes seemingly felicitous circumstances entirely beyond the offender's control were taken into account. For example, in a case involving the sentencing of a Japanese Navy Lieutenant convicted of subjecting prisoners of war to danger to seven years' imprisonment, a Netherlands Temporary Court-Martial took into account in sentencing that the ammunition depot to which the prisoners were dangerously exposed "was not actually hit as a result of allied bombing."[257]

Guilty pleas, which exercise considerable influence in sentencing in contemporary institutions, were viewed somewhat equivocally in World War II atrocity cases. For example, an accused facing charges of war crimes arising out of ill treatment of Allied prisoners changed his plea to guilty and was sentenced to death (the sentence was confirmed) despite his counsel's having delivered a closing speech calling for mitigation.[258]

Discussion of aggravating factors was more limited and often was mixed into consideration of the evidence of proof of individual criminal responsibility. Gravity of the offense was a routine factor; so, too, was the official power or status of the offender (although in cases of the crime of aggression or crimes against the peace this would seem to be a prerequisite for criminal responsibility). In affirming the death sentence awarded to Hans Albin Rauter, the Netherlands Special Court of Cassation signaled out the "reprehensible mentality" of the accused, the "reign of terror" he exercised, his zeal, his knowledge of the activities of the German administration in the Netherlands, and his "cowardly and furtively committed acts" against Jews and students.[259] The Court went out of its way to note that Rauter's commitment to furthering a German victory "provides no grounds for excuse or reasons for mitigation of punishment [...] as feelings of patriotism can never signify a license to conduct a war with criminal means [...] nor to apply inhumane measures of terrorism to the populations of occupied territories."[260] In cases of criminal groups, courts considered as an aggravating factor the extent of the involvement of the offender in the mutual criminal relationship.[261] Vulnerability of the victims also was cited. For example, the Netherlands Temporary Court-Martial at Batavia, which convicted Washio Awochi of the war crime of enforced prostitution, "took into consideration [in imposing punishment] the fact that the girls involved 'were mostly in poverty-stricken and difficult circumstances' and that the 'accused took advantage' of it for 'his own purposes' [...]."[262]

b. *From the 1960s Onward*

In contradistinction to trials conducted in the 1940s, trials that took place from the 1960s onward were completed overwhelmingly (though not exclusively) by national courts (as opposed to military instrumentalities). Also, the sentences issued tended to be more lenient, there were many acquittals, and many investigations were stalled (and eventually scuttled) by amnesties. The defense of following orders, which had been tightly circumscribed in the first wave of trials to serve only discretionarily as a mitigating factor, gained broader traction in this second wave of prosecutions with regard to determinations of individual criminal responsibility.

That said, these trials, particularly in West Germany, did bring to light several thousand Nazis living under assumed names and, in certain cases, prompted some sort of reckoning with the past. They also unpacked the brutalities of the concentration camps to the general public, although they did so in a manner that served to individualize responsibility, clouded the collective nature of criminality of the Nazi state, obscured complicity, and then punished without coherent penological purpose. Notwithstanding these shortcomings, however, trials in West Germany may have conveyed greater value to the German public than international or extraterritorial trials in that they were undertaken under the auspices of German officials.

In 1963 a trial began in Frankfurt, West Germany, involving a number of administrators and guards from the Auschwitz concentration camp. This was one of the most notorious camps, where millions of innocent detainees had been extirpated. Trials that had previously occurred in Poland and the German Democratic Republic with regard to Auschwitz personnel resulted in a number of executions. The West German proceedings concluded on August 19, 1965. Six defendants were given life sentences, eleven were given terms of imprisonment (ranging from slightly over three years to fourteen years), and three were acquitted. Rebecca Wittmann notes that, owing to West German laws, the prosecution could only prosecute those officials who had exceeded direct orders; this requirement ironically led, according to Wittmann, to a legitimization of the Nazi state and its legal framework.[263] As a result, attention fixated only on the most brutal and sadistic crimes while deeper questions about the normalization of violence in the Nazi era, and the automaticity of annihilation, were left unaddressed.[264] On the other hand, the Auschwitz trial appears to have had some expressive value in Germany. It also carries ongoing pedagogical currency. For example, there is an exhibit on the trial in the permanent collection of Berlin's Jewish Museum. This exhibit lauds the proceedings as having "laid the Nazi crimes before not only the people directly involved but also the German and international public."[265] It also notes that "[t]hese sentences, some of which were lenient, provoked intense public debate."[266]

Trials also were held in West Germany with regard to personnel, including officials, from camps at Belzec, Sobibor, and Treblinka. As with Auschwitz, these were places of absolute barbarity. Several hundred thousand individuals, mostly Jews, were exterminated at each of these camps. Many of the defendants were acquitted, often on the basis of following orders. For example, all but one of the defendants in the Belzec Trial (1963–1964) were acquitted and released. The one defendant actually convicted was punished with a 4.5-year sentence (although he had previously served time with regard to a different offense). A larger number of individuals were convicted in proceedings relating to the Sobibor camp. Sentences ranged from life to fixed terms of imprisonment, many as modest as three to four years. In the Sobibor trial, the court was sensitive to allegations of following orders and coercion (i.e., if the camp personnel did not obey they would have been punished, shot, or transferred). The Treblinka camp officials were treated somewhat more severely by the West German courts. It is estimated that 700,000 Jews were murdered at Treblinka. The Treblinka trial led to several convictions, for which sentences spanned from life imprisonment to fixed terms ranging from three to twelve years. Given the scale of torture and death in each of the camps, it seems quite a stretch to think of such sentences as proportionate to the enormity of the offenses.

Probably the most prominent trial in this second wave was held outside Germany. This was the prosecution of Adolf Eichmann in the Israeli courts. Eichmann, an SS Lieutenant-Colonel, was not a top Nazi, nor a policymaker, but was an official responsible for the implementation of the Final Solution. In 1960, Eichmann was kidnapped from Argentina by Israeli security agents. He was brought to Jerusalem to face charges of crimes against the Jewish people (which basically constitutes the crime of genocide), crimes against humanity, and war crimes. Unlike at Nuremberg, where the prosecutorial focus was on Nazi aggression and war crimes, in this trial the Holocaust occupied central stage.

The Jerusalem District Court convicted Eichmann on December 12, 1961.[267] His claim of superior orders was rejected insofar as the acts in question were found to be manifestly unlawful[268] and Eichmann's "inner attitude" was one of wholehearted and willing support of the Final Solution and, hence, belied any minimization of his moral responsibility.[269] The District Court held that "mere blind obedience could never have brought [Eichmann] to commit the crimes which he did with the efficiency and devotion with which he carried them out, had it not been for his fanatical belief that he was thereby fulfilling an important national mission."[270] Eichmann was "not lukewarm in his orders nor in his deeds, but energetic, full of initiative and active to the extreme in his efforts for the realization of the 'Final Solution.'"[271] The evidence established that, although Eichmann "received his principal orders from above,"[272] he held a key position in the architecture of the Final Solution and enjoyed considerable supervisory and discretionary authority. The District Court remarked:

> [Eichmann's] hatred was cold and calculated, aimed rather against the Jewish people as a whole than against the individual Jew, and it is for just this reason that it was so venomous and destructive in all its manifestations. To the task he devoted his alert mind, his great cunning and his organizing skill. He acted within the general framework of the orders which were given to him, but within this framework he went to the very limit to bring about the speedy and complete extermination of all Jews in the territories under German rule and influence. In saying all this we do not mean that the accused was exceptional in his evilness in the regime which had raised him. He was a loyal disciple of a regime which was wholly evil and malicious.[273]

Eichmann's death sentence was pronounced on December 15, 1961. This sentence was permitted by Israel's Nazis and Nazi Collaborators (Punishment) Law 5710/1950. In exercising its discretion to impose the death penalty, the District Court referenced the "unparalleled horror" of the crimes. The District Court noted that Eichmann's crimes differed "from criminal acts perpetrated against persons as individuals. It may be said that such comprehensive crimes, as well as crimes against humanity which are directed against a group of persons as such, are even more heinous than the sum total of the criminal acts against individuals of which they consist."[274] The District Court thereby intimated the need to enhance the severity of sentence in order to meet the additional retributive goals of punishment for such comprehensive crimes.

Eichmann's convictions and sentence were affirmed on appeal to the Israeli Supreme Court on May 29, 1962.[275] The Supreme Court dismissed superior orders insofar as it held that "within the framework of the order to carry out the 'Final Solution,' [Eichmann] acted independently and even exceeded the duties imposed on him through the service channels of the official chain of command [. . .]."[276] Eichmann was "the high and mighty one."[277] Following an unsuccessful plea for clemency to the President of Israel, Eichmann was hanged on May 31, 1962. His body was cremated. His ashes were scattered over the sea. In addition to giving Eichmann his just deserts – to the extent this ever could be possible – the trial achieved important expressive purposes. It officialized the stories of many Holocaust survivors. For some, testifying was cathartic. The trial proceedings and judgments provided a historiography of the rise of the Nazi party and its anti-Semitic ideology. It explained how this ideology was implemented country by country and camp by camp in frenzied pursuit of the Final Solution. Punishing Eichmann facilitated an important educational function. It also served a political function in terms of justifying the need for the state of Israel.

Trials held in the 1980s and 1990s involved perpetrators – once young – who, by the time they became defendants, had grown quite old. By and large, these individuals were not high profile. Their trials, however, quickly became spectacles owing to their symbolic value. Some of these trials postdated the formation of the ICTR and ICTY and, therefore, unfolded against the tapestry of the early case law of these institutions. In turn, the ad hoc tribunals refer back to these national decisions in the elaboration of their own jurisprudence.

Many national trials arose from a renewed, albeit anxious, interest on the part of states to investigate whether war criminals continued to lurk in their midst, including individuals who may have emigrated from the devastated Continent amid the confusion and labor shortages that followed the end of World War II, for example, to Canada (where the Deschênes Inquiry was established), the United States, and the United Kingdom. In some cases, deportation proceedings were instituted against suspected Nazi war criminals: the countries to which former Nazis immigrated following World War II have sought to strip those immigrants who became citizens of their citizenship because they had lied about their past on their entry papers. In some cases, denaturalization was obtained even though the individuals in question never were convicted criminally in the courts of the countries to which they were deported or extradited.

Many of these suspects, which investigations reveal engaged in acts of unfathomable barbarity, lived quite unremarkably for half a century. Some raised families and went about their own affairs quite tranquilly. They never got into trouble with the law. The case of Anthony Sawoniuk presents an example. Sawoniuk was convicted of war crimes in Crown Court in the United Kingdom in 1999; the conviction was upheld by the Court of Appeal (Criminal Division) in 2000.[278] He was sentenced to two life terms for murdering two Jews. Sawoniuk, originally from Domachevo in what is now western Belarus, had been living in the United Kingdom since 1946 (where he eventually retired as a British Rail ticket inspector). During World War II, he served in a police unit allied to the Nazis in Domachevo. At the time of conviction he was seventy-eight years old, deaf in one ear, nearly blind in one eye, diabetic, and suffering from heart disease, high blood pressure, and a mental condition.[279] He, the illiterate, illegitimate son of a washerwoman, had held a lowly rank in the hierarchy but, as Mr. Justice Potts noted at trial, "to the Jews of Domachevo it must have seemed otherwise."[280] Sawoniuk died in prison in November 2005.

A trilogy of cases – *Barbie, Touvier,* and *Papon* – decided in the French courts is noteworthy. Klaus Barbie, a German, was convicted on July 4, 1987, for crimes against humanity (as harmonized between international law, e.g., the Nuremberg Statute, and domestic French law) and sentenced to life imprisonment.[281] He died in prison in 1991. Barbie was the head of the intelligence section of the Gestapo in Lyon. He arrested and deported Jews to the concentration camp at Auschwitz. He also had been tasked to destroy the French Resistance. Following World War II, he had fled to Germany and then to Bolivia. Paul Touvier was convicted on April 20, 1994, for complicity in crimes against humanity. He had been sheltered by rightwing elements of the French Catholic Church and occasionally was seen dressed as a priest.[282] The convictions pertained to his killing of seven Jewish hostages while he served in the pro-Nazi *milice*. He was sentenced to imprisonment for life; and a symbolic one franc was awarded in damages upon request by the civil parties.[283] He, like Barbie and Sawoniuk, died in prison. As was the case in *Barbie*, the substantive law of the proceedings was a medley of French domestic law and international law as represented by the Nuremberg Charter and IMT judgments. Maurice Papon, at the time eighty-seven years old, was convicted by a French court on April 2, 1998, for complicity in crimes against humanity for his involvement in the deportation of Jews to concentration camps.[284] He had a higher position than either Barbie or Touvier.[285] In the 1960s, Papon had become the police chief of Paris. He was sentenced to ten years' imprisonment.[286] In 2002, Papon's sentence was suspended and he was released from prison owing to his age and poor health.

There are many other cases. These include Erich Priebke, a Nazi SS Captain initially sentenced in 1997 by an Italian military tribunal to fifteen years' imprisonment (reduced by ten years to account for an amnesty) for his role in the 1944 massacre of Italian civilians near Rome. Priebke's conviction subsequently became entangled in appellate litigation. In 1999, Alfons Goetzfried was sentenced in Stuttgart to ten years' imprisonment for his role in killing tens of thousands of Jews at the Maidanek concentration camp. The sentence, however, was waived on account of the time Goetzfried had spent in a Soviet camp. Anton Malloth was convicted in 2001 by a German court of *inter alia* beating and kicking a Jewish prisoner to death at the Theresienstadt prison camp in Czechoslovakia in 1944. Although at the time of conviction Malloth was eighty-nine years old, he was sentenced to life in prison.[287] Joseph Schwammberger (an Austrian Nazi who commanded a forced labor camp) was convicted in 1992 in Stuttgart and sentenced to life in prison. Schwammberger, who had hidden in Argentina for forty years, died in prison in 2004 at the age of ninety-two.[288] Julius Viel, a former SS officer, was sentenced by a German court in 2001 to twelve years' imprisonment for murders near the Theresienstadt camp. The judge noted that the exemplary life Viel had led after World War II, in which he became a respected journalist and won a government award of merit in 1983, did not reduce the enormity of the crime, although he chose not to hand down a life sentence owing to the length of time between the crime and the sentencing (although, given Viel's age of eighty-three at the time of sentencing, the punishment *de facto* is one of life).[289] In other cases from diverse jurisdictions, prosecutors have elected not to proceed, and judges have elected not to enforce (or to suspend) sentence, owing to the advanced age of the accused. These decisions, which do not seem to be made on any predictable basis, have, in turn, given rise to litigation and appeals.

What is the purpose of punishment in these cases? Leila Sadat, specifically referring to *Touvier*, concludes that "considering [the] age, neither specific deterrence nor rehabilitation appear particularly relevant [...]."[290] Sadat's conclusion is generalizable to all recent prosecutions of former Nazis. In any event, neither of these two factors receives much in the way of traction as a rationale of punishing extraordinary international criminals regardless of the time lag between commission of offense and conviction in any court at any level, whether national, local, or international. What about general deterrence? There is some evidence that punishment is directed to aspiring war criminals. For example, some of the media commentary with regard to the Sawoniuk conviction referred to its purported deterrent effects on the Kosovo atrocities then unfolding. The Malloth conviction was expressly categorized as a warning to deter today's neo-Nazis.[291] That said, today's neo-Nazis differ markedly from their predecessors insofar as the hate crimes of today's generation, albeit induced to some extent by group adhesion, amount to deviations from the accepted rules of a stable polity instead of complying with or furthering the dictates of a criminal state.

Retribution consistently remains a goal. As with deterrence, the value of retribution as a goal diminishes as the time between commission and conviction expands. The amount of pain that can be exacted from the convict, if pain is measured by length of sentence, diminishes sharply when the convict is ninety years old. Independent of physical realities of life span, some courts will consider that the time lag and the health of the accused serve as mitigating factors. The retributive value of punishment is further clouded by the fact that, in certain cases, the pain is dulled by the release of the offender or the suspension of sentence owing to advanced age. That said, age is not a predicable factor in mitigation. In some cases of comparable age, life imprisonment explicitly is awarded whereas in others it is not. In some cases, proceedings never are initiated (or become discontinued) because of the age of the accused, whereas in others defendants become more zealously pursued precisely because of their age and the perceived need to punish before they peacefully pass away. However, the overall pattern with regard to advanced age, if actually considered, is one where it mitigates sentence (as opposed, say, to increasing it insofar as elderly accused will often have avoided sanction for most of their lives). The ill health of the accused, if considered, will mitigate sentence although, once again, its admission as a mitigating factor remains unprincipled and discretionary.

Probably the most plausible justification for punishing aged former Nazis lies in the expressivist value of this punishment. Condemning these Nazis completes the tapestry of the past in the nick of time before they die. It promotes respect for the victims by casting the harms as transgressions of universal norms. In the cases of Touvier and Papon, judicial condemnation permitted French society to reflect upon its own internal divisions between those who collaborated with and those who resisted Nazi Germany. Admittedly, difficulties arise when courts, through their often convoluted rules of evidence, are called upon to officialize history. However, judging from national trials of World War II atrocities, they perform a reasonable job in this regard.

(IV) CONCLUSION

Penological goals and modalities of sanction are more diverse at the national and local levels than they are internationally. However, as is the case with international institutions, by and large sentencing is an afterthought and poorly conceptualized. Retribution remains a consistent goal, although national and local punishing institutions experience considerable difficulty in operationalizing enhanced retribution to accord atrocity perpetrators their comeuppance. Aggravating and mitigating factors derive from those applicable to ordinary common criminals. There are trends to consider certain factors in a typology of aggravation and mitigation, but recourse to these factors in actual cases is unpredictable and obscured by significant discretion. Other than with regard to expressivism, there is little evidence of any effort to theorize a penology reflective of or tailored to the criminality of mass atrocity. In terms of expressivist rationales, sanctioning at the national and local levels can serve important storytelling purposes, such as is the case with *partie civile* claims in Rwanda and popular trials like Eichmann's, although there are many other cases where the messaging value is obtuse or even contrary to prosecutorial intentions.

Pressures emanating from dominant international norms narrow the diversity of national and local accountability modalities. These pressures also whittle away operational differences between national modalities and these norms, in particular in the context of procedure and sanction. Insofar as international criminal prosecutions largely occur in states shattered by conflict, susceptibility to these pressures is particularly high. Developments on the ground in Rwanda and the states emerging from the former Yugoslavia suggest powerful patterns of legal migration.

Although national courts still punish with a broader *qualitative* variety of sanction and, in cases of punitive sanction, a broader *quantitative* range of length of imprisonment (sometimes even death), pressures from international institutions reduce both the variety and range of sentence available within national frameworks. In terms of imprisonment, for example, I contend that these pressures prompt the raising of minimum sentences – and embed duties to prosecute that might discourage alternate modalities of accountability – while lowering maximum sentences. These pressure points are proving to be of great relevance to the structure of punishment modalities for extraordinary international criminals although neither has much, if anything, to do with theoretical or applied determinations regarding the actual nature of extraordinary international crime.

Collaterally, this transplant from the international to the national may in fact be welcomed by many state actors, who enjoy the consolidation of power occasioned by centralized punitive criminal law frameworks and prefer it to the more free-ranging and authority-diffusing informal modalities of justice that may arise at local levels. The end result is the squeezing out of local approaches that are extralegal in nature, as well as those that depart from the methods and modalities dominant internationally. As I explore in greater detail in the next chapter, goals of retribution and general deterrence become injected into local legal cultures and institutions for which these goals may be neither indigenous nor innate. This places considerable stress on local approaches, especially those that traditionally are restorative in nature. Such has been the fate of *gacaca* in Rwanda.

CHAPTER 5

Legal Mimicry

The international legal system holds atrocity perpetrators accountable by prosecuting and incarcerating them. This approach also seeps into national and local legal systems. This seepage is animated by a number of factors, including internationalist pressures and the receptiveness of certain domestic actors to these pressures. Domestic actors often mimic international trendsetters, whose modern ideas they transplant to national and local contexts.[1] The result is a diffusion of liberal prosecutorial and correctional models. This diffusion is entangled with the diffusion of Western legalism generally.

Punishment for extraordinary international criminals is deeply associated with core liberal legalist assumptions manifested in the ordinary operation of the criminal law in Western states generally, regardless of their provenance (i.e., ideal-type civilian or common law systems). In this regard, Rama Mani notes that international justice evidences a predominance of Western-generated theories and an absence of non-Western discourse.[2] Most international lawyers are Westerners or members of Western-trained transnational elites. For Mani, this leads to "a troubling imbalance or 'injustice' in the study of justice," insofar as "international lawyers...have largely referred to and replicated their own legal systems, rather than catered to and built on local realities and needs."[3]

The question I pose in this chapter is whether this association with Western law spells, in Mani's terms, a "troubling imbalance or injustice" when it comes to holding perpetrators of extraordinary international crimes accountable for their wrongdoing. This chapter explores this question through an examination of the operation of international criminal tribunals, including the referral process of the ad hoc tribunals and the ICC's complementarity mechanism. Although both of these mechanisms are putatively geared to involving national entities in the accountability process, they serve as important, albeit not exclusive, conduits that funnel internationalized process to the national and local levels.[4] These conduits represent vertical applications of authority that radiate downward from the international to the national and, eventually, to the local. In assessing the legitimacy and effectiveness of these vertical applications of authority, I avail myself of two important indicia: (1) externalization of justice, which I identify as a situation where the outputs of the judicial process are methodologically distant[5] from populations directly afflicted by the violence; and (2) democratic deficits, which I identify as the exclusion of afflicted populations from the design, development, and operation of accountability mechanisms. I conclude that the implementation of international criminal law has occasioned – and, despite reform at the ICC tilting toward victim inclusion, remains prone to occasioning – a democratic deficit in part by placing considerable power in the hands of poorly accountable foreign experts. Assuredly, extraordinary international crimes are offenses against us all. However, I am troubled by a justice process that may favor the interests of those only morally affected by the violence over those actually physically afflicted by it.

The cultural foundations of the *modalities* of international criminal law means that their application to diverse spaces and places externalizes justice from the communities most traumatized by atrocity. One of the effects of these undemocratic externalizations is the sidelining of certain sanctioning mechanisms. The final sections of this chapter present restorative justice mechanisms as one such example. Since restorative mechanisms serve important goals in certain postconflict societies, sidelining them renders the justice paradigm less effective than it could be and stunts the development of a penological framework tailored to the peculiarities of mass atrocity. Rwanda serves as a case study insofar as restorative initiatives, as set out in Chapter 4, are underactualized despite their considerable potential. Although the ICC takes restorative initiatives more seriously, its treatment of the Ugandan situation demonstrates the limited restorative potential of ICC interventions as well as nettlesome conflicts between the goals of international prosecutors (indictment, trial, and imprisonment) and those of Acholi victim communities (peace, justice, and reintegration).

Much is to be welcomed in the fact that the international criminalization of genocide, crimes against humanity, and war crimes can prod national and local actors to hold perpetrators accountable. In some cases, no accountability would arise but for the creation of international institutions. These realities do not diminish the need for prudence, however, when it comes to the *migration* of procedural methods by which the accountability process is to unfurl and the *transplant* of monochrome schematics of sentencing by which punishment is to be visited upon perpetrators.

Assuredly, it is problematic to blindly glorify the local or that which otherwise differs from dominant discourse simply to promote pluralism as an end in itself. International intervention can be salutary to the extent that it purges corrupt practices, rebuilds shattered infrastructures, limits abusive sanctioning schemes, and promotes legitimacy. *In situ* legal institutions can be deeply susceptible to political interference and manipulation by state actors; many are profoundly undemocratic and themselves externalize justice from community members excluded from their formation and operation. In some cases, regime change in transitional societies results in bias within accountability institutions. In other contexts, pursuing accountability *in situ* destabilizes national security; or is flatly impossible, in that the atrocious regime still controls power. In all of these situations, there is a strong argument in favor of international intercessions.

However, the nature of these intercessions should incorporate local voices, foster capacity, and integrate indigenous approaches to justice (whether legal or extralegal). The value of punishment will increase to the extent that it resonates with local populations, is internalized in ravaged communities, and can form a coordinated part of postconflict transition instead of competing with other transitional justice mechanisms. I believe that international punishing institutions, as presently constituted, are insufficiently attuned to the national and local. These institutions, as is the case with many transnational bureaucracies, should take better care in the exercise of their institutional agendas to nurture the well-being of the societies whose tragedies they seek to redress.

(i) TRANSPLANTS AND LEGAL GEOLOGIES

Although my specific concern is the effectiveness of transplants with regard to the sanctioning of perpetrators of mass atrocity, it is helpful to begin with some discussion of legal transplants generally.

Transplants operate in all fields of law and regulation, including economic policy, investment, taxation, and property law.[6] The area of economic regulation is characterized by significant conformist pressures. The rapid marketization of formerly communist economies was accompanied by wholesale transplants of largely U.S. securities, banking, and capital markets law. These transplants, often boilerplate, took root in some jurisdictions while in others remained as potted plants.

Transplants also are occasioned by processes of regional integration. Chapter 11 of the North American Free Trade Agreement (NAFTA), for example, externalizes U.S. conceptions of expropriation for governmental action (takings) onto the Mexican and Canadian legal systems.[7] Chapter 11, which addresses foreign investment, purports to offer economic security and protection to investors from one NAFTA party who make financial investments in another NAFTA party.[8] Although this externalization initially was undertaken in the name of protecting U.S. investors in Mexico, the application of Chapter 11 has proven to be more nuanced. It has resulted in unanticipated attacks on venerated elements of the U.S. legal order, such as punitive damages in civil cases and the jury system, that, too, reveal conformist pressures exerted upon the U.S. system when it is the outlier.[9]

I contend that internationalists ought to pause before concluding that the replacement of the "other" by that which is familiar to them, namely the "international," is axiomatically beneficial. Although transplants are a fact of life where power meets rules in frameworks of supranational regulation, this does not dissipate the need to think critically about them. For example, writing within the context of NAFTA, Ari Afilalo urges caution when international arbitral panels are tasked with assessing the conformity of national legal practices with international norms.[10] My concern is different, insofar as my motivation is not for international institutions to preserve their legitimacy but, rather, for the regulatory goal at hand, namely the punishment of perpetrators of mass atrocity, to be as credible and effective as possible.

A fine line lies between chauvinism and constructive law reform, especially when the transplants emanate from the trendsetters of the international legal order and are insinuated into the domestic sphere of its objects. In this regard, as David Westbrook writes, "the diffusion of law cannot be separated from those social processes discussed under the rubric of globalization."[11] Accordingly, the legitimacy and effectiveness of Western legalist modalities of prosecuting and punishing perpetrators of atrocity cannot be assumed simply on the basis that these modalities now have become widely diffused. Rules agreed upon by elite international lawmakers are not necessarily in tune with bottom-up perspectives. Discord grows to the extent that diffusion is motored by behavior of powerful state actors to increase their influence, weaker state actors to protect their power within unsettled domestic polities, and influential transnational nonstate actors to further their own institutional goals.

Although transplants from international criminal institutions to national legal orders in Rwanda, Uganda, the Democratic Republic of the Congo (DRC), East Timor, or Kosovo are new, the process of transplanting is old. As such, I am concerned with a new wrinkle to a long-standing practice. The legal systems of many of the places currently receiving internationalized process and sanction for perpetrators of mass atrocity themselves are products of iterated processes of transplantation that have occurred throughout history, generally coincident with conquest, annexation, or colonial "discovery." In many of these places, broad swaths of commercial, public, and administrative law already are transplanted – and have been for generations. In other cases, the regulatory sediment is multilayered insofar as earlier transplants have been replaced by new ones. The legal geology is thick. Therefore, transplants in a relatively new area – namely, the punishment of extraordinary international criminals – can represent fresh law among fields of law that already have been tilled through frequent transplants. So, if the law already is transplanted, why is it of concern that more is becoming transplanted now, this time from the international level instead of directly from foreign conquering powers?

Three responses come to mind. First, just because law previously was transplanted does not mean that this law necessarily is viewed by local populations as legitimate; and, even if it is viewed as legitimate through processes of intergenerational socialization, this is no guarantee that the same will happen for freshly transplanted law. Second, as I set out in Chapter 6, the sentencing frameworks of international criminal law, although appearing modern and hence effective, operatively fall short of their aspirations and, thereby, cannot rely on their modernity as a proxy for their effectiveness. Third, national governments may welcome transplants for any number of self-serving reasons that have nothing to do with their merit or endogenous resonance within local communities. These reasons can involve preserving state authority, promoting centralized bureaucracy, quashing opposition, receiving foreign assistance, or shielding the state from international legal responsibility. Transplants may become implemented at the state level and retransplanted to local levels for ulterior purposes of state control over local affairs and to build up the apparatus of state authority in what are often fractious polities.

In the context of punishing extraordinary international criminals, transplants have encouraged uniformity of sanction. Should this uniformity be of concern? Indeed, it should if one listens to what victims in conflict societies want. Victims prefer more diversified responses instead of monosyllabic implementation of formal criminal trials. Moreover, when international lawyers state as a "first principle[]," as Judge Robertson of the Special Court for Sierra Leone recently did in a ruling exploring the interface between criminal trials and truth commissions in Sierra Leone, that "[c]riminal courts offer the most effective remedy," they advance an unproven academic argument and, in the name of that argument, institutionalize a series of expensive policy responses and establish a normative hierarchy at which they sit at the apex.[12] I believe the time has come to revisit the wisdom of this "first principle."

(II) EXTERNALIZATION OF JUSTICE

One of the limitations of Mani's work is its apparent crudeness in generalizing about "Western" legal systems. After all, Western legal process is not monolithic. Rudimentary comparative law analysis suggests that the Western legal family divides between common law (Anglo-American) and civil law (Continental European) branches.[13] Comparative legal scholars enunciate some generalized differences between these two branches.[14] For example, whereas ideal-type civil law systems are inquisitorial in nature, ideal-type common law systems are adversarial. Both systems, however, also share much in common. Moreover, there are differences within each of these two branches among various national jurisdictions.[15] That said, as Sir Basil Markesinis puts it, differences may be more a matter of style, in that, among Western legal systems, there is a growing convergence in terms of the questions asked, requirements established, and conclusions reached.[16]

The ICC reflects an amalgam of civil and common law approaches. Compromises are found throughout. The adversarial nature of ICC trials originates in common law systems, but the fact that the ICC Pre-Trial Chamber acts somewhat akin to an investigatory magistrate derives from civilian methodologies. Common law approaches have exerted considerable influence in the structure and functioning of the ICTY and ICTR, especially initially.[17] Specific examples include: stated recourse to precedent and inductive reasoning in formulating judicial opinions; extensive cross-examination within an essentially adversarial process;[18] the availability of plea bargaining; and the active role of defense counsel and of *amici*. However, ideal-type civil law methods have become influential in the operation of the ad hocs over time. One example is the structure of sentencing determinations, which are added on to the main proceeding in the form of closing arguments, as is the case in civil law jurisdictions, and not part of a separate sentencing hearing, which is the case in common law jurisdictions.[19] Other than in cases of proceedings on an admission of guilt, the Rome Statute permits the determination of sentence in the main proceedings, but also permits a separate sentencing hearing on motion of the Trial Chamber and requires a separate hearing at the request of the Prosecutor or the accused.[20] Evidentiary rules at the international tribunals also reflect a compromise between ideal-type civil and common law approaches.[21]

The procedural frameworks of international criminal law do express some novelty in that they represent hybrid cross-pollination between common law and civil law legal systems that, to some degree, pragmatically absorbs the particularities of mass violence. However, the limited novelty that exists is deeply *technical* in nature and, to paraphrase Markesinis, reconciles *stylistic* difference. It is not foundational. To suggest that this blended procedure is *sui generis* sets a low bar for a determination of jurisprudential originality.[22] The technical hybridization of common law and civil law approaches has been relatively easy to obtain because, within the rubric of criminal justice, both legal families evince a focus on punitive, retributive justice, as well as a preference for incarceration as a remedy.[23] Both common law and civil law methodologies are keyed to individualizing responsibility.[24] Both fear collective responsibility, at least rhetorically. George Fletcher observes that "[t]he generalization holds in our [common law] legal system as well as in the civil law tradition: Collective entities, their actions, their responsibility, and their guilt – these are ideas that run afoul of the methodological commitments of the legal mind."[25]

As Boaventura de Sousa Santos notes, Continental civil law and Anglo-American common law are "subcultures of Eurocentric political-legal culture."[26] These two Western traditions motor the liberal legalist approach to extraordinary international criminality. Ralph Henham contends that "the ideology and structures of punishment [in international sentencing] are closely aligned to maintaining the economic and political integrity of Western liberal democracies."[27] As a whole, international criminal process is not a genuine amalgam that accommodates the disempowered victims of mass violence – largely from non-Western audiences – already lacking a voice in international relations. Although the ICC takes some steps in this integrative direction, which I explore in this chapter, these are just the fledgling beginnings of meaningful inclusion.

Disconnects emerge when the pursuit of accountability and the imposition of punishment arise through processes that are distant from or alien to local populations. In such situations, justice is *externalized*. When justice is externalized from the afflicted societies for which it ought to be most proximately intended, it then becomes even more difficult for any of the proclaimed goals of prosecuting and punishing atrocity perpetrators – whether denouncing extreme evil, expressing rule of law, voicing retribution, or preventing recidivism – to take hold.[28] Although this justice becomes more intelligible for faraway audiences, this can come at the price of intelligibility for those at home whose neighbors were killers or victims.

Assuredly, there are pragmatic reasons in favor of externalizing justice. A particularly compelling case in favor of outsourcing trials arises in situations where proceeding locally or nationally would trigger political instability or insecurity.[29] Furthermore, externalized justice is better than no justice at all: ensuring that some justice is done is another pragmatic reason in favor of outsourcing trials to international or, in the case of universal jurisdiction crimes, foreign courts. After all, national actors may resist the pursuit of accountability or may be devastated in the wake of atrocity. Such was the case in the former Yugoslavia and Rwanda, respectively, at the time of the creation of the ICTY and ICTR. In these situations, physically externalizing the institution and its personnel may be one way to ignite an accountability process. However, in these situations it becomes all the more important for punishing institutions to coordinate their activities with political transition in the society whose atrocities are being judged, especially as time passes. What is more, just because an institution is physically externalized from the afflicted society does not mean that it must proceed in a manner that is methodologically externalized. It is this latter form of externalization that concerns me the most in the operation of the ICTY and, especially, the ICTR. Moreover, proceedings can be physically sited within the afflicted jurisdiction, but remain methodologically externalized. This, too, invites disconnects.

Although there is cause for greater optimism, there is no guarantee that hybrid institutions will internalize justice among local populations. East Timor is an example. Although traditional East Timorese understandings of justice emphasize compensation, restoration, and ritual, the East Timor Special Panels extensively imposed incarceration as a sanction. They did so despite the fact that:

> East Timorese view incarceration as an alien form of punishment and do not seek to avoid it with quite the same urgency as Western defendants. Because crime is conceived as creating an imbalance of values, traditional East Timorese justice mechanisms do not seek primarily to punish the offender, but aim rather to restore values and to re-establish the socio-cosmic order.[30]

In many postconflict societies, national dispute resolution institutions, especially courts, are viewed with tremendous skepticism as they had often served as instruments of social control in authoritarian regimes.[31] But the preference for international institutions cannot be based solely on the faults of national or local institutions. After all, in many cases the putative neutrality of international institutions, assuming *arguendo* that this is a *sine qua non* of justice and legitimacy, is lost on local populations. Chuter comments that "it is asking a great deal of people [in the former Yugoslavia] to credit that a court largely set up, funded, and staffed by Western powers that have intervened militarily in the Balkans can ever deliver verdicts that represent the truth or even would seek to do that."[32] In other cases, the competence of international institutions is viewed skeptically. The ICTR "has [...] been dogged by scandals including the discovery that genocide suspects themselves were on the tribunal's payroll as defence-team investigators."[33] One of the defense counsel appointed by the ICTR was in fact on a 2006 "most wanted list" of genocide suspects in Rwanda.[34] What is more, most Rwandans I have met simply do not see how the international community, which idly sat by during the genocide,[35] now has the moral legitimacy to punish individual Rwandans as perpetrators.

In the end, just because transnational lawmakers tend to see international judges as less susceptible to political manipulation or bias than their national counterparts does not mean that local populations see them that way, too. Similarly, just because an institution is international does not mean *ipso facto* that it is better or more legitimate. Transcending local parochialisms, which plays well for individuals operating transnationally, may actually feel quite empty to the vast majority of people, for whom politics, justice, and life are lived locally. Consequently, an international institution, such as the ICTR, can easily become "a rather distant reality."[36]

International judges may find this limitation difficult to digest. For example, the ICTY boldly stated in the *Furundžija* sentencing decision that "[i]t is the infallibility of punishment [. . .] which is the tool for retribution, stigmatization and deterrence. This is particularly the case for the International Tribunal: penalties are made more onerous by its international stature, moral authority and impact upon world opinion [. . .]."[37] Although having the ability to punish is central to the authoritativeness of an institution, it does not necessarily follow that the power to punish accords legitimacy to an institution. Osiel, citing political science research, notes that "[t]here has been vehement backlash against the [ICTY] within Serbia and Croatia."[38] Longitudinal research conducted in Sarajevo between 2000 and 2003 demonstrates a marked reduction in the percentage of respondents who believe the ICTY is the appropriate jurisdiction to adjudicate and punish offenders, with a corresponding increase in selection preference in favor of local institutions.[39] Postdating this research, Milošević's years of parrying with the ICTY left a great deal of public frustration among all constituencies in the former Yugoslavia that only was exacerbated by his death during the trial.

Certain victim communities may view sanction of atrocity perpetrators as *less* onerous *because* of the international provenance of the punishing tribunals. It often is the case that these perpetrators previously had been coddled or even supported by foreign powers, including the funders of international tribunals, who only became denunciatory after atrocity had been committed. On the other hand, there may be other local constituencies who may prefer international legal institutions over corrupted local ones.[40] All things considered, the reality on the ground is complex and it is not satisfactory generally to assume the enhanced legitimacy of international institutions.

Postgenocide Rwanda attests to the costs occasioned by externalized justice, as well as how easy it is for the process of operational and methodological externalization to be set in motion. The Rwandan public remains largely ignorant of, ambivalent to, or at times estranged from the ICTR.[41] ICTR trials are by and large inaccessible and have minimal impact on victims' lives. Perceptions of the ICTR vary among the Hutu and Tutsi communities, although lack of knowledge or interest in the ICTR prevails among both groups.[42] Some evidence indicates that the more Rwandans learn of the ICTR's work, the more inclined they become to view the institution more favorably.[43] However, other observers report that many informed Rwandans, regardless of ethnicity, see the ICTR as a foreign tribunal operating distantly under the aegis of the same entities that permitted the genocide to continue in the first place.[44] Interviews undertaken by Allison Des Forges and Timothy Longman led them to conclude that: "[M]any Rwandans felt that the work of the ICTR was far removed from their daily lives. Respondents complained that the trials were held far away from Rwanda and were organized using western-style judicial practices that place a heavy emphasis on procedure and have little concern for community interests."[45] One specific concern noted by Des Forges and Longman was that many of the Rwandans they interviewed "saw the adversarial legal approach applied in the ICTR as foreign to traditional Rwandan methods of conflict resolution."[46]

It is also understandable why Rwandans question the amount of resources consumed by the ICTR. For 2004–2005, the UN General Assembly appropriated for the ICTR a total biennial budget of U.S. $255,909,500 gross; for 2006–2007, a total budget of U.S. $269,758,400 gross was appropriated and 1,042 posts authorized. In previous years, budgets (at times biennial, at times annual) ranged from U.S. $29 million to U.S. $180 million. By the end of 2007, the cost of the ICTR's operations will have exceeded U.S. $1 billion. When appropriations by the UN General Assembly are totaled, and divided by the number of trial verdicts issued, the result becomes one of approximately U.S. $30 million for each person who has heard a verdict. This is a staggering sum of money in a country with a per capita economic output of about U.S. $1,500.[47] Surely, even just a part of these funds could have made a huge difference in terms of operationalizing restitutionary or reparative remedies for Rwandans.[48] Helena Cobban notes, by contrast, that amnesty applications in South Africa cost less than U.S. $4,300 per case and, in postconflict Mozambique, demobilization and reintegration programs for thousands of former combatants cost about U.S. $1,000 per combatant.[49] Similar disparities exist elsewhere: whereas in 2001 the total budget for governing East Timor was U.S. $65 million, the annual budget for the ICTY alone was U.S. $96.4 million.[50] The ICTY has over one thousand employees.

On the positive side, ICTR trials have raised international awareness of what happened in Rwanda in 1994 and have developed an historical record. ICTR jurisprudence has advanced and clarified numerous areas of substantive international criminal law. For example, the *Akayesu* decision provided a sophisticated definition of ethnicity (as an element of the crime of genocide) and also advanced a progressive understanding of sexual violence in which rape was found to be a tool of genocide.[51] The *Musema* decision extended command responsibility outside of the military context into a civilian corporate environment.[52] In *Barayagwiza*, an ICTR Trial Chamber issued a seminal verdict against media leaders for inciting genocide, in which it set a standard for differentiating statements of ethnic pride (protected by virtue of freedom of expression) from incitement to hate (not protected by freedom of expression).[53]

However, the main beneficiary of the ICTR's work arguably has been the international community – whether in terms of assuaging guilt or developing international criminal law – and not Rwandans. There is something disconcerting about externalizing justice so that it primarily resonates with certain extraterritorial audiences. Extraordinary international crimes create two sorts of victims: those actually attacked and, in more of an abstract sense, the rest of the world community. The victimology I envision would be one in which those directly afflicted by the violence have a greater moral claim to the internalization of justice – certainly methodologically – than global audiences.

Ironically, when Western societies become victimized by extraordinary international criminality, there is no question of externalizing justice for the benefit of transnational audiences. The 9/11 attacks – which I posit constitute crimes against humanity – present a stark example.[54] In the wake of these attacks, not only was a low premium placed on international criminal law as a mechanism to pursue justice, but the thought that an internationalized court adhering to internationalized legalist procedure would pronounce justice was also unacceptable to U.S. (and many, albeit not all, Western) policymakers. No such tribunal was created. In fact, no serious proposal ever was made; nor would such a proposal have gained traction.

Nationals of eighty-one countries perished on September 11[55] and nationals of thirty-nine countries were implicated to varying degrees in the attacks.[56] Subsequent Al-Qaeda bombings have occurred all over the world. Al-Qaeda is a transnational actor whose depraved crimes represent threats to international peace and security. Nonetheless, no serious attempt was made to empower neutral international criminal tribunals to punish terrorists and their financiers. The notion that Osama bin Laden, if caught, would have been spared the death penalty was unthinkable in U.S. discourse. The thought that erudite judges from outside the United States would determine his culpability, and that prosecutors from outside the United States would conduct the proceedings, would be simply unimaginable to most Americans.

Yet, this is precisely the kind of justice that the international community and Western, including U.S., donors have instituted elsewhere in the name of ethnic neutrality and the avoidance of ethnic bias. When victims in Rwanda and the states emergent from the former Yugoslavia – together with state officials and the general public – proclaimed their dissatisfaction with international criminal prosecutions, a typical response was that these prosecutions were necessary for the slow yet steady process of establishing rule of law, a culture of human rights, and combating impunity without propagating revenge.[57] The 2006 National Security Strategy of the United States notes that "the hard core of the terrorists cannot be deterred or reformed,"[58] yet the United States supports international criminal tribunals premised on the hope that their operation shall deter genocide. If suicidal terrorists are beyond deterrence, why should hardcore *génocidaires* be any different?

Instead of applying preexisting international criminal law precedents good enough for "others," U.S. officials invested tremendous energy in designing institutions and procedures for accused terrorists that minimize the scope of due process and public access. And even when, in its 2006 judgment in *Hamdan v. Rumsfeld*, the U.S. Supreme Court stepped in to invalidate one of these institutions – the military commissions – it certainly did not mandate that the commissions emulate the standards or modalities of international criminal law institutions.[59] In the wake of the *Hamdan* decision, the U.S. government affirmed that it would respect the most basic requirements of Common Article 3 of the Geneva Conventions in the treatment of Al-Qaeda detainees. It then enacted legislation, the Military Commissions Act, that may well fall below Common Article 3's minimum requirements. Even in the improbable event that, in the practice of the military commissions, the United States were to incorporate a generous understanding of the basic requirements contemplated by Common Article 3, any such understanding would be a far cry from the weighty due process and human rights standards for defendants that international criminal law obliges victims of atrocity in Rwanda and Bosnia to assimilate.

Whereas perpetrators of mass atrocity elsewhere are to be treated as persons, entitled to a raft of due process, perpetrators of violence in "our" neighborhoods are treated as something strikingly subaltern. Is it not disturbing when the nationality of the victims determines the perpetrators' level of due process entitlements? Although there is room to debate the precise value of due process for the legitmacy of a punishing institution, extolling the virtue of due process for other victims but shirking it for "ourselves" creates a glaring operational inconsistency that, at a minimum, corrodes the expressive value of the military commission process. More disturbingly, international criminal law should not be built upon the travails of the disempowered objects of international institutions while the masters of those same institutions pursue the sort of self-help, and systematic parsing of legalism,[60] forbidden to others.

(III) DEMOCRATIC DEFICITS

Instead of building accountability and restoration from the bottom-up through integration of indigenous laws, customs, personalities, politics, and practices, international criminal law interventions drop from the top-down. This unidirectionalism is most poignant in the Statutes of the ad hoc tribunals, which grant the tribunals primacy over all other courts in the exercise of their activities.[61] These tribunals were created for Rwanda and the former Yugoslavia by resolution of the Security Council; in the case of Rwanda, over the objection of a Rwandan government that was in place because its military forces were the only ones that actually ended the genocide. ICTY and ICTR judges are not directly accountable to populations in the former Yugoslavia or Rwanda. Although neither of these jurisdictions has a history of domestic judicial accountability,[62] this does not mean that international judges should follow in this same pattern. Both the ICTY and ICTR have, over time, demonstrated increased willingness to engage with national constituencies and, to this end, have established outreach programs.[63] These programs, however, have been modest and are geared to disseminating information about the tribunals to national constituencies. These programs certainly do not reassess the relationship between international legal institutions and aggrieved populations.

Primacy also is a feature of the Special Court for Sierra Leone.[64] This institution, however, is the product of negotiation between the government of Sierra Leone and the United Nations, which goes some way to address concerns over local disenfranchisement. Assuredly, as Chandra Lekha Sriram observes in the case of Sierra Leone, internationalized (as opposed to purely international) courts that remain formally separate from the national judicial system of the country in question do little to rebuild local capacity and expertise, or incorporate local manifestations of popular will, both of which often are touted as advantages for internationalized modalities as tools of political transition.[65] However, the infusion of international officials into a process that is vested with and anchored in local capacity may augment credibility and, thereby, represent some potential for healthy coconstitutive local engagement.[66]

The ICC makes a number of improvements over the ad hoc tribunals with regard to concerns over democratic deficits. The ICC only will admit a case once it deems that the complementarity principle has been satisfied.[67] According to this principle, which I unpack later in this chapter, the ICC only will assume jurisdiction when a state is unable or unwilling genuinely to investigate or prosecute. This improvement, however, does not materially redress the democratic deficit insofar as the local is not necessarily included in the machinery of international criminal law. Another improvement lies in the fact that the ICC is an institution created by international treaty. Accordingly, participation in the ICC depends on the consent of states. It therefore seems reasonable to contend that those states that consent to the ICC indicate, through their consent, their support for the modalities of justice and punishment pursued by the ICC. The reasonableness of this proposition, however, is not self-evident. States, after all, do not always reflect society. The process by which many states (particularly illiberal states) consent is far from democratic insofar as there may be minimal to no bottom-up participation or debate during the ratification process. Moreover, states consent to international treaties for a variety of reasons, not all of which are indicative of endorsement of the actual content of those treaties. Motivating reasons include, although certainly are not limited to, considerations such as maintaining standing in the international community, pursuing the appearance of legitimacy and modernity, and pressure from donor states.[68] Decisions to sign onto (and, to a lesser degree, subsequently to ratify and implement) the Rome Statute are contoured by a broad array of factors, including international economic and political considerations.[69]

Nor do state decisions to refer matters to the ICC necessarily represent a normative preference for criminal trials as policy responses to episodes of cataclysmic atrocity. In terms of penology, the ICC is not mandated to take into account local or national sentencing practices; nor is reference to these practices even suggested in the Rome Statute.[70] In this regard, the Rome Statute formally differs from the Statutes of the ICTY and ICTR. Moreover, the ICC can exercise jurisdiction over nationals of states that do not consent to be bound by it; or it can, as is the case with the Sudan, exercise jurisdiction over an atrocity by virtue of Security Council referral – a process that does not materially differ from the anatomy of the institutional creation of the ICTR or ICTY.

International criminal law interventions as currently structured therefore represent grist for the mill of those who posit the antidemocratic nature of international law generally. Allen Buchanan, for example, fears the influence of an unaccountable global technocratic elite.[71] With regard to the ICC, I would note that it has independent lawmaking capacity through which it becomes more than the agent or delegee of consenting states. This is part of a broader trend among international organizations whereby treaty secretariats acquire quasilegislative or judicial powers. This emergence of a treaty-centered international administrative bureaucracy can remove important matters – including those that relate to the actual obligations assumed – from the control of consenting states. This phenomenon is similar to the twentieth-century growth of the administrative apparatus of modern welfare states, and resultant technocracy, which also induces a whittling down of democratic input in important aspects of national lawmaking.

Jed Rubenfeld remarks that international efforts toward transitional justice, which often include scripting constitutional and foundational documents, proceed in top-down fashion.[72] Rubenfeld identifies "international constitutionalism" as a viewpoint from which it is "not particularly important for a constitution to be the product of a national participatory political process."[73] Rather, from this viewpoint, the goal is to implement an agenda agreed to by the international human rights community. Although "[n]ational ratification of a new constitution might be instrumentally valuable, ... having a committee of expert foreign jurists draw up a constitution would be perfectly satisfactory in principle."[74] In fact, according to Rubenfeld's description of the prevailing viewpoint, "interpretation by a body of international jurists is ... not only satisfactory but *superior* to local interpretation, which invariably involves constitutional law in partisan and ideological political disputes."[75]

Rubenfeld's observations are somewhat apposite to international criminal law interventions in that these interventions tend to look beyond local interpretation in favor of administration by a transnational expert community. This leads to a paradox: the society reeling from violence becomes disenfranchised from the redressing of that violence, which, instead, becomes a task suited to the technocratic savvy of international lawyers. Assuredly, many of these societies may never have experienced democracy nor may they foresee realistic short-term prospects for democratization (some may even trend in the opposite direction). This, however, surely is not a valid reason to further add to popular disenfranchisement in these same places.

The ICC's framework has been informed by lessons regarding victim disengagement from the ICTR and ICTY. These lessons have led to another improvement in the ICC approach, namely that the ICC is more welcoming of victims than the ICTR and ICTY have been in practice.[76] Victim opportunities to participate in ICC investigations and proceedings are subject to judicial permission and subordinate to the defendant's due process rights. Just as is the case with the ICTR and ICTY, there are no juries at the ICC. That said, early indications are that ICC judges are open to victim participation. An ICC Pre-Trial Chamber ruled that victims can become involved in ICC investigations in the DRC and present their views and concerns, file documents, and request the ordering of specific measures.[77] The ICC Prosecutor, who opposed the victims' applications, immediately appealed this decision, fearing an encroachment on his freedom of action. There are, therefore, conflicts between his office, on the one hand, and victim communities, on the other. As of the time of writing, the appeal has not been adjudged. Furthermore, conflicts are emerging between victim communities and the Prosecutor with regard to investigations and indictments in Uganda, which I explore later in this chapter. Although both seek justice, the Prosecutor and victim communities do not necessarily share a synergistic relationship, despite the accommodation made to victims in the Rome Statute, thereby suggesting the complex victimology at play. Whereas in Uganda the ICC Prosecutor seeks justice through criminal prosecutions, victim communities seek justice through peace and traditional reintegration ceremonies.[78]

As it grows and matures, international criminal law should continue to reconceive its relationship with local politics. In light of their growing professionalizaton and bureaucratization, often coordinated from faraway centers of power, it becomes all the more important for international criminal lawyers to integrate with local entities. Chapter 7 provides some ideas regarding how this might take place by proposing a horizontal expansion in the operation of international criminal law such that it interfaces more actively with political institutions and, thereby, pursues a more holistic vision of justice.

Although there are some indications that the ICC will chart a more inclusive orientation, the accumulated practice of international criminal tribunals thus far demonstrates discomfort with local politics and, as a result, tends to exclude locals, in particular members of the afflicted society, from the administration of justice undertaken for their benefit. One of the reasons why there is skittishness regarding the involvement of locals in capacities that exceed that of witness or defendant is because of fears that such involvement would taint institutional operation owing to ethnic or national bias. Certain influential international punishing institutions in fact tether their legitimacy to their ethnic and national neutrality.[79] I believe that, although there certainly is something to be gained in minimizing bias, something also is lost when the pursuit of minimizing bias excludes those with the greatest interest in accountability for the conflict and transition to peace. Furthermore, international lawmakers should not be oblivious to the fact that the pursuit of neutrality itself can politicize.[80]

As I briefly inquired in the context of externalization of justice: do distant, impartial, and disinterested parties necessarily have greater moral authority to adjudicate atrocity? In some cases, the same disinterested parties that now judge had, through their disengagement, permitted atrocity to continue. The violence that escalated in Rwanda in April 1994 did not come as a surprise. There were many indicators that a carefully constructed plan had been plotted since at least 1992 to eliminate the Tutsi. Many of these indicators were known to the international community. However, they were ignored, undervalued, or downplayed by international organizations and foreign states. The passivity of the international community enabled hate-mongers to normalize their hatred; this same passivity encouraged ordinary Hutu to see this hate not as deviant or reprehensible behavior, but as something that properly formed part of Hutu civic duty. Powerful states refused to call the violence in Rwanda genocide even as news reports emerged that the killings met the legal definition of genocide.

In the immediate prelude to and actualization of the genocide, international peacekeeping efforts in Rwanda were weak. There is evidence that more effective deployment of peacekeepers may have reduced the severity of the genocide, although it is far from apparent that it would have fully prevented genocide.[81] There also is evidence that, were radio communications to have been jammed and other media dissemination of hate propaganda to have been impeded, the extent of the violence and its ferocity may have been attenuated.[82]

The bulk of the peacekeeping effort fell upon the shoulders of the United Nations Assistance Mission in Rwanda (UNAMIR). This was headed by a Canadian, Lt. Gen. Roméo Dallaire, and was constituted by soldiers from several countries. UNAMIR had been present in Rwanda prior to and during the genocide. Its size was reduced in early April 1994 with the murder, by Hutu extremists, of a number of Belgian peacekeepers, which prompted the withdrawal of the remaining Belgians. UNAMIR, despite brave and dedicated efforts, was understaffed and crimped by extremely tight rules of engagement that prevented it from fighting back against genocidal killers or intervening more directly.[83]

Dallaire bluntly has stated that the international community lacked the will to intervene decisively in Rwanda.[84] Although Dallaire communicated to senior UN officials the intelligence he had received from informants well ahead of time that genocide was being planned in Rwanda, institutionally speaking the United Nations remained unmoved. The execution of the actual genocide corresponded closely to what Dallaire had been told months in advance would take place. Dallaire's requests for more forces, better equipment, and a more aggressive mandate went unheeded. Tragically, over a decade later, dithering now is occurring with regard to peacekeeping and peaceenforcement intervention to mitigate atrocity in the Darfur region of the Sudan.

Ironically, once the international community did become active in Rwanda near the end of the genocide, its interventions served beneficial as well as troubling purposes. *Opération Turquoise*, led by the French, helped protect Hutu refugees as they escaped areas occupied by the RPA. That said, *Opération Turquoise* also allowed many perpetrators of genocide to flee and set up shop in refugee camps in the DRC, Rwanda's neighbor to the west. These perpetrators terrorized Rwandans inside the camps and, with these as a base, made incursions into Rwanda itself, prompting further military action by the Rwandan

government that, ultimately, led to protracted multistate armed conflict throughout the Great Lakes region of Africa.

Given this tragedy, it simply cannot be assumed that an international tribunal
created by the UN Security Council and supported by the same states that
failed so miserably in preventing genocide in Rwanda carries much legitimacy
in the eyes of Rwandans. To Rwandans, the international community is far from
neutral. Consequently, shuttering Rwandans out of its decisionmaking in the
name of neutrality becomes especially alienating.

(IV) REFERRALS

The ICTY and ICTR have adopted "completion strategies."[85] One of the central
mechanisms in service of these strategies is for the ICTY and ICTR to refer
cases to national courts.[86] These could be courts in the states of the former
Yugoslavia or in Rwanda, but also could be courts in other countries. The
referral mechanism preserves the primacy of the ad hoc tribunals over national
institutions, but allows some cases to be processed at the national level. Referrals
are to involve mid- to low-level perpetrators. In some cases, referrals concern
individuals actually indicted by the ad hoc tribunals; referrals of nonindicted
cases to national authorities also are contemplated.[87]

There are important limitations to the referral process as a mechanism to
internalize justice and democratize its administration. In particular, referrals
create a situation in which defendants may have spent many years in international custody only to be returned to national jurisdictions, in part because those
defendants are no longer sufficiently important to the international tribunals or
because those same tribunals now are facing financial pressures, thereby revealing the contingency of criminal liability at the international level.

As of December 2005, the ICTY Prosecutor has filed twelve referral motions
involving twenty accused; one case has been referred to Croatia and two to the
War Crimes Chamber of the State Court of Bosnia and Herzegovina.[88] Not all
motions for referral have been granted. ICTY referrals are undertaken pursuant
to Rule 11bis and its new amendments. According to Rule 11bis,[89] a case can be
referred to the national jurisdiction where the crime was committed, in which
the accused was arrested, or that otherwise has jurisdiction and is willing and
adequately prepared to accept the case.[90] It is the ICTY, through its Referral
Bench, that determines whether or not to refer. In making this determination,
the Referral Bench is to consider the gravity of the crimes charged and the level
of responsibility of the accused; it also must be satisfied that the accused will
receive a fair trial and that the death penalty will not be imposed or carried out.[91]
The request for referral is to be made by the ICTY Prosecutor or by the Referral
Bench of its own accord. In all cases, "upon referral of a case, the [ICTY] still
may be called upon to take back those cases where an accused is not afforded
a fair trial in the State to which they were referred."[92] The Referral Bench in
fact requires regular reports following a decision to refer and, depending on the
information contained therein, may recall the case.

The effect of this process is to induce national courts that seek jurisdiction to conform to a variety of modalities that mimic those found in international criminal law regarding sanction (i.e., no death penalty) and procedure (i.e., a fair trial).[93] Thus, those national courts that emulate these modalities become able to prosecute perpetrators of extraordinary international crimes, albeit not the most serious offenders, nor those highest in the chain of command, nor those whose offenses were not geographically contained.[94] In practice, a number of national jurisdictions compete over the chance to receive a referral. This adds a further incentive to conform as closely as possible with ICTY practice, process, and penalty in order to improve the chances of prevailing in this *de facto* tournament. The decision where to refer a case remains, within the auspices of the statutory framework, a discretionary one on the part of the Referral Bench.[95] The ICTY has in a number of cases decided not to refer cases to the national courts of Serbia and Montenegro despite requests to do so.

A review of the case law of the Referral Bench suggests that the ICTY takes its substantive review of the relevant domestic law quite seriously. This incentivizes national courts that seek custody to emulate the ICTY's process in order to maximize chances of success in receiving referrals. National judges participate in ICTY training initiatives, geared to "ensur[ing] that due process is accorded in cases referred" and "to build local capacity."[96] Although there are many advantages to this process, referrals do have a flattening effect on the diversity of national legal frameworks. The result is a standardization of law and practice, transplanted from the international level back down to diffuse national contexts, masking its initial origin in the domestic legal fabric of those states that dominate the international sociolegal order. Referrals also encourage national jurisdictions to create separate atrocity crime courts or chambers, which has happened throughout the states emergent from the former Yugoslavia. There is significant upshot to creating these institutions. That said, given finite resources, edifying specialized courts or chambers means that alternate accountability mechanisms become disadvantaged. Also potentially disadvantaged are investments into the general court system, which seems a perverse result in that the general system may actually end up processing a vastly larger number of suspects than the specialized system. All in all, high-profile specialized chambers may divert resources and attention from the general judicial system, thereby occasioning tension.[97]

Somewhat perplexing with regard to the allegedly retributive, deterrent, and expressive superiority of international prosecutions over those of national courts is the fact that certain defendants in referral cases have strenuously resisted transfer to the national courts to which they were eventually referred, preferring to have their case adjudicated by the ICTY. One defendant argued that the referral would violate his decision voluntarily to surrender to the ICTY, suggesting that he never would have surrendered to the Bosnian national courts.[98] Other defendants went so far as to contend that the gravity of the crimes charged against them was so serious, and their position in the command structure so high, that it would be inappropriate to refer their case out of the ICTY.[99] These defendants so preferred adjudication at the ICTY that, in resisting referral elsewhere, they were willing to risk precluding their ability ultimately to raise lack of gravity or command authority as mitigating factors in sentencing.[100]

The retention of the death penalty on the books in Rwanda creates a significant obstacle to its ability to receive high-profile referrals from the ICTR. Rwanda already has responded to these international abolitionist pressures. For example, it has not carried out death sentences since 1998. The number of individuals who receive death sentences in national courts has declined progressively with each passing year. Insofar as Rwanda continues to resist these international pressures and retains the death penalty, even if only symbolically, the ICTR may simply refer cases elsewhere.[101]

In fact, the first ICTR Rule 11bis motion filed by the ICTR Prosecutor (on February 15, 2006) requested transfer not to Rwanda, but to Norway.[102] The case involved Michel Bagaragaza, former director general of the office controlling the Rwandan tea industry. The ICTR Prosecutor contends that the transfer of cases under Rule 11bis to jurisdictions other than Rwanda would "provide for wider understanding of how genocide can happen" and, in Bagaragaza's case, would assist the administration of justice insofar as Bagaragaza may be able to provide information on other genocide suspects who have falsely claimed refugee status in Norway.[103] Except for these incidental contacts, Norwegians have no connection to the Rwandan genocide other than being victims in the sense that all individuals everywhere are the victims of the crimes committed by the enemies of humankind. Bagaragaza supported the transfer of his case to Norway. The Rwandan government objected to the transfer.

On May 19, 2006, an ICTR Trial Chamber denied the ICTR Prosecutor's referral motion on the basis that Norway lacked jurisdiction over the crimes alleged in the Bagaragaza indictment.[104] This denial was subsequently upheld by the Appeals Chamber.[105] Norway had not codified genocide or complicity in genocide in its domestic criminal law. For the judges who heard the matter, it was not acceptable that Bagaragaza would be prosecuted only for ordinary crime (i.e., murder).

The dispute over where Bagaragaza should be tried reflects Rwanda's vulnerability. An international official (the ICTR Prosecutor) and very distant foreign government (Norway) – in both cases, over which the Rwandan population has no control – agree to prosecute a high-profile suspected génocidaire. They reach this agreement because they deem the judicial process in Rwanda too out of synchronicity with liberal legalist values to deserve to prosecute him. The concern over Rwanda's compatibility with these values, including appropriate modalities of sentencing, is so great that it threatens to oust strongly presumptive grounds of jurisdiction such as territoriality and nationality. In the end, ICTR judges disagreed with the Prosecutor's recommendation. However, the Rwandan population remains marginalized insofar as it has no control over ICTR judges. Although there is reason to question why the Rwandan government retains the death penalty on the books (i.e., for social control?), as well as its general motivations, the result of this jurisdictional maneuvering and intrainstitutional feuding over an accused genocidal leader's apparent entitlement to avoid Rwandan legal process is disempowering to those who survived the litany of abuses he is alleged to have committed.

At the time of writing, the ICTR Prosecutor also has made other requests for transfer of ICTR detainees to member states of the United Nations. In the event that Rwanda agreed *ex ante* not to pursue the death penalty against anyone referred by the ICTR, which might allow it to hear these cases, a retributive imbalance would be triggered. Those higher-level defendants that have been in custody at the ICTR would thereby become exempt from Rwandan law as applicable to all other Rwandans. Alternately, the prospect of referrals may simply change Rwandan law.

(v) COMPLEMENTARITY

Article 17 of the Rome Statute of the ICC, which governs the admissibility of cases, operationalizes the complementarity principle.[106] According to this principle, states are given the first opportunity to investigate or prosecute individuals alleged to have committed the crimes proscribed by the Rome Statute. States, through their courts, could obtain jurisdiction over alleged perpetrators in a variety of ways, including the traditional exercise of jurisdiction based on nationality (i.e., citizenship of the accused) or territoriality (i.e., where the crimes were committed). It is only if states are unwilling or unable genuinely to investigate or prosecute these crimes that the ICC can admit the case (assuming, of course, that ICC jurisdiction otherwise exists and that the case properly has been referred). Accordingly, the complementarity mechanism provides a vivid *situs* for broader comparative law concerns regarding the integration of diverse legal traditions into international institutions.[107]

The complementarity mechanism operates in conjunction with article 20 of the Rome Statute, which addresses *ne bis in idem*. Article 20(3) prevents the ICC from asserting jurisdiction over a person who has been tried by "another court" for the same conduct unless the proceedings in the other court: (a) were for the purpose of shielding the person concerned from criminal responsibility; or (b) "were not conducted independently or impartially in accordance with the norms of due process recognized by international law and were conducted in a manner which, in the circumstances, was inconsistent with an intent to bring the person concerned to justice." The ICC thereby incentivizes states to undertake their own domestic proceedings and accords states some leeway in exactly how to implement them. But the scope of the leeway is fettered and remains subject to review.

A number of thorny questions arise. What exactly does "unwilling or unable genuinely to carry out the investigation or prosecution" mean for the purposes of article 17? What is a proceeding that is "not conducted independently or impartially in accordance with the norms of due process recognized by international law" for the purpose of article 20 and, also, for the determination of "unwillingness" under article 17?

In some cases, such as sham proceedings designed to shield an accused or proceedings designed gratuitously to humiliate good faith witnesses, the answer will be clear-cut. These proceedings are, after all, not exactly "genuine," if the term is understood to connote good faith efforts. Also clear-cut are situations where there has been a total collapse in the administration, judiciary, or constabulary of the state in question, which is not an infrequent occurrence in a postconflict society. But what about proceedings that, although well intentioned, are not prosecutorial in form? Or are investigatory, but lead in good faith to truth commissions instead of adversarial and individualized criminal prosecutions? Complexities also arise even if the investigations lead to criminal prosecutions. What if the prosecutions fail to comport with internationalized due process standards? What if they follow methodologies that differ from ICC methodology? Differences in punishment also might run afoul of the complementarity regime. This could be because punishment is viewed as too harsh (i.e., the death penalty) or too lenient (i.e., community service, reparations, or apology instead of the internationalized norm of incarceration in distant prisons).

It is likely that the ICC shall approach complementarity determinations with some restraint. The ICC probably will focus its efforts on national systems that avoid bringing offenders to justice, rather than on places that do so but in a manner that provides less due process than the ICC. In particular, the ICC presumably would tolerate the diversity of national initiatives regarding lower-level offenders because its purpose trends toward the prosecution and punishment of those who bear the most serious responsibility, for example, leaders and other "big fish."[108] Moreover, article 17 mostly concerns objective criteria (especially as regards the inability genuinely to investigate or prosecute). However, notwithstanding my predictions of restraint by the ICC, it appears that subjective review of national practices simply may be inevitable in terms of the determination whether the activities of a state amount to a genuine unwillingness to investigate or prosecute.[109] Subjective review also may be inevitable in assessing the conformity of national practices to the "principles of due process recognized by international law." To be sure, this review is not as explicitly directed at the quality of justice as that mandated by Chapter 11 of the NAFTA, but does implicitly involve the reviewability of national decisions and the nature of national initiatives to respond to mass atrocity (or decisions whether to respond at all).

Serious comparative law assessments therefore are likely to occur within the context of Rome Statute articles 17 and 20. These comparative law assessments could also arise within the context of article 53(1)(c), which sets some guidelines for the ICC Prosecutor in his decision whether or not to initiate an investigation: the Prosecutor shall consider whether "[t]aking into account the gravity of the crime and the interests of victims, there are nonetheless substantial reasons to believe that an investigation would not serve the interests of justice."[110] This provision can cover situations where a state may have chosen to respond to endemic violence through truth commissions or national amnesties, and affords the Prosecutor some discretion to elect not to pursue a matter otherwise admissible.[111] It is foreseeable that the Prosecutor might determine it unwise to investigate a matter where national authorities have implemented truth-seeking mechanisms coupled with qualified amnesties. But there is no express mention of criteria that differentiate acceptable amnesties or mechanisms from unacceptable ones. In any event, any decision by the Prosecutor not to proceed based entirely on article 53(1)(c) must be subsequently confirmed by an ICC Pre-Trial Chamber.[112]

To summarize: there remains some subjective discretion in determining genuine unwillingness to investigate or prosecute, and a greater level of subjective discretion regarding the determination whether ICC investigation would not serve the interests of justice. In these instances, the ICC Prosecutor would consider a range of factors, including the quality of justice proffered at the national level, along with broader political ramifications. In assessing the quality of justice, there may be recourse to contrast the proffered national proceedings to those envisioned by international criminal law. After all, the dominant view among international criminal lawyers is that the processual content of international criminal law is central to its legitimacy.[113] In particular, the need may arise to consider the due process of the proceedings as a measure of their legitimacy, and in this regard it seems inescapable that the due process guarantees[114] of international criminal law once again shall enter the analysis as some sort of template.

Robert Cryer observes that "the system of complementarity creates a strong interest in States not to cheat by failing to prosecute. [. . .] States, particularly in relation to offenses by their nationals, are more likely to prefer to investigate at the national level, rather than have an investigation proceeded with in public by an independent international investigator."[115] Both the language of the complementarity provisions as well as the psychology of judging (after all, the ICC will judge its own jurisdiction to judge) suggest that the more a national legal process approximates that of the ICC, including its specific trial and sanctioning modalities, the greater the likelihood that this process will be palatable and pass muster. This, in turn, suggests that one permutation is that national institutions will model themselves along the lines of the ICC in order to maximize their jurisdiction.[116] Complementarity, therefore, may encourage heterogeneity in terms of the number of institutions adjudicating international crimes, but homogeneity in terms of the process they follow and the punishment they mete out. In the end, the content of local practices may be excluded regardless of the legitimacy with which these practices are perceived. Because the preferred practice is that which dominates in Western societies, excluded local practices overwhelmingly will be those present in non-Western societies. Moreover, because the political realities of international criminal law institutions suggest that the focus of their efforts will be – at least initially – directed to redressing systemic criminality in non-Western spaces, the end result is the exclusion of the local in those places where atrocity is most likely to be criminalized.

There is a second behavioral permutation. Not all states may pursue mimicry. Some states simply may acquiesce in an ICC exercise of jurisdiction or may self-refer a matter to the ICC. The decision by the Ugandan government to self-refer atrocity committed by a rebel group, the Lord's Resistance Army, in northern

Uganda illustrates this phenomenon. The Ugandan situation is one of a number of cases, largely unexpected, where national and territorial jurisdiction join in the same state and that state refers what is largely an internecine conflict, albeit one with transnational implications and of serious concern to the international community as a whole, to the ICC.[117] The Lord's Resistance Army has engaged in a nearly twenty-year-long conflict in which practices of crimes against humanity, child abduction and soldiering, and sexual violence abound. Much of this conflict is centered among the Acholi people of northern Uganda, who are implicated on both sides of the violence. In the Ugandan context, it is unclear whether the domestic court system is unable to prosecute or whether domestic sociolegal institutions are unable to hold perpetrators accountable. Yet, the ICC is investigating and has issued indictments.

Why did the Ugandan government self-refer this situation to the ICC? One reason may well have been control. Fearing that the ICC Prosecutor may have exercised his *proprio motu* power to investigate in any event, the Ugandan government may have self-referred out of an anticipatory hope that, were the ICC to assume jurisdiction based on a self-referral instead of acting independently, this would give the Ugandan government greater control over the situation. The Ugandan government may have craved control for eminently rational reasons: namely protecting itself and promoting its interests. Specifically, the Ugandan government may wish to obfuscate atrocities allegedly committed by its own armed forces. Although the ICC has not precluded investigation of these specific allegations,[118] it is unclear how seriously they will be pursued. The arrest warrants issued in October 2005 by the ICC – its first – were for the leader and four members of the Lord's Resistance Army (it has been reported that one indictee was subsequently killed by the Ugandan army). At this juncture, it bears mentioning that the Ugandan government is an illiberal regime with an uneven human rights record. This is the same government that, while requesting ICC intervention, was condemned by the International Court of Justice for violations of international humanitarian law – and ordered to pay reparations – with regard to its responsibility for unlawful armed activity, plundering, and massive human rights violations in the DRC between 1998 and 2003.[119]

Ugandan political elites also may have turned to the ICC in the hopes it would promote their own interests by targeting rivals[120] and allowing elites to manage, and dissuade, calls by local community leaders to settle matters through traditional forms of dispute resolution. One example of a traditional practice is *mato oput* (drinking bitter root herb). Another is *nyouo tong gweno* (a welcoming ceremony incorporating eggs and twigs). To the extent that these forms of dispute resolution gain currency, they portend a decentralization of power from the centralized apparatus of the state or the state's delegation of power to an international organization.

Ugandans, particularly residents of the northern parts of the country most affected by the violence, have expressed reservations to the idea of ICC intervention.[121] A number of parliamentarians and religious leaders from northern Uganda in fact have traveled to The Hague to oppose the ICC investigation.[122]

Joanna Quinn notes that "to the people of northern Uganda, the international legal process is almost completely foreign."[123] Instead, members of victimized communities value traditional approaches such as *mato oput* and *nyouo tong gweno*.[124] Many community members feel that these social institutions respect the fact that the line between victimizers and the victimized, particularly in the case of child soldiers, is opaque.[125] In local eyes, the fact that the ICC was invited by the Ugandan government spoils its putative impartiality.

Predictably, both *mato oput* and *nyouo tong gweno* have been subject to the pressures of the internationalized legal paradigm. Desperate for some semblance of these mechanisms to be invoked in Uganda's settlement of these terrible atrocities, "Acholi parliamentarians have drafted an addendum to the ICC bill, the implementing law, to attach penalties to their traditional justice mechanism in an effort to fall within the complementarity principle and prevent criminal prosecution of such cases."[126] This suggests how complementarity initiates a drive toward homogenization by massaging the traditional into the neotraditional. Similarly, William Burke-White reports that, although the Congolese president may have referred atrocity in the DRC to the ICC to discredit his political opponents, these opponents, who prefer that any prosecutions remain within the domestic judiciary, in turn push judicial reform of the domestic courts so as to reduce the likelihood that the ICC will admit these cases.[127] The ICC, by virtue of the complementarity regime, therefore plays a role in changing domestic sociolegal structures, instead of serving as a temporary substitution or stopgap for these structures.[128] This brings the discussion back to the hypothesis that the complementarity regime encourages mimicry.

Returning to the Ugandan situation, in addition to their sense that ICC justice will be externalized justice (and hence that the justice payoff will be low), local constituencies, comprised of people who actually live in the area ravaged by violence, have expressed concern with the political effects of ICC indictments. A Ugandan delegation actually implored the ICC not to indict the leaders of the Lord's Resistance Army because delegees felt that doing so removes the bargaining chip of amnesty for such individuals in settling the country's civil war.[129] Although amnesty tends to be a dirty word in the lexicon of international criminal lawyers, it may not be so in the lexicon of local populations; moreover, it appears that amnesties have more appeal[130] and favorable long-term results than international criminal lawyers may care to admit. Local communities in northern Uganda also express concern that the ICC will not be able to guarantee the security of those witnesses called to testify. Now that indictments have been issued, as a matter of formal law amnesties seemingly have been pushed off the table – while, paradoxically, local pressures for peace discussions that actively contemplate the prospect of amnesty increase in stridence. In 2006, the Ugandan government guaranteed Lord's Resistance Army leader Joseph Kony's safety, and even amnesty, in exchange for serious efforts to negotiate peace, which it then participated in. The ICC and its Western backers promptly expressed deep reservations about such a proposal, insisting that Uganda apprehend Kony and refusing to drop its arrest warrants. Tension therefore is emerging between the pursuit of peace, which is relevant to communities torn by strife, and satisfaction of international arrest warrants, which is relevant to the functionality of international criminal law. At the time of writing, the situation in Uganda delicately remains in flux, although the prospect of amnesty apparently is what has stopped the violence.[131]

In summary: even in cases where they self-refer, states may be animated by a complex array of motivations, including the prospect of avoiding *proprio motu* intervention by the Prosecutor. Consequently, instead of pursuing mimicry by reforming domestic institutions, the state may invite the ICC to investigate. This, however, leads to a similar (and perhaps even more troubling) result, namely the simplistic superimposition of selective exogenous criminal law on terribly complex conflicts. The existence of the ICC may offer illiberal governments a tool to consolidate power and avoid enfranchising the policy preferences of afflicted local populations by providing these governments an option to refer matters to a distant institution focused on the reductionism of punitive criminal law. The ICC thereby creates an option of exit for national governments to externalize complex processes of justice onto a foreign entity. This availability of exit creates a risk that little is done genuinely to place domestic sociolegal structures in the service of postconflict transition. In the case of Uganda, this risk has been attenuated only by dint of the vigor of the Acholi community, which has been unexpectedly forceful in the bottom-up articulation of its preferences. Partly as a result of Acholi mobilization and partly as a result of learning that it cannot control the ICC intervention, Ugandan authorities, despite having self-referred the matter in the first place, have begun to openly hedge regarding the exact role that they wish the ICC to play.[132]

One reaction to my concerns over the remodeling effects of complementarity is that I overstate these effects. After all, the ICC targets "the most serious crimes of concern to the international community as a whole."[133] At first blush, the ICC appears to be designed only to pursue a handful of leaders. *Arguendo*, the ICC would have limited interest in the vast majority of perpetrators, namely those lower-level offenders who undertake the dirty work of atrocity. Consequently, it follows that the ICC would have little to no interest in how national and local institutions deal with such offenders.

In response, it is not altogether clear that the ICC never would prosecute lower-level offenders. In some places, such prosecutions may be necessary in order to begin to compile the judicial record with regard to higher-level offenders and develop familiarity with the facts of the atrocity. After all, the ICTY's initial prosecutions involved low-level thugs, such as Dusko Tadić, and one individual of diminished mental capacity; even a more recent conviction of great jurisprudential value – namely, criminalizing and punishing sexual violence – involved a relatively low-level paramilitary commander named Dragoljub Kunarac. Furthermore, the East Timor Special Panels essentially only prosecuted lower-level offenders. But, assuming *arguendo* that the ICC's focus will be on high-level defendants, I would agree that the ICC should prove to be predisposed to act generously toward national and local institutions with regard to how they process low-level offenders. And I would certainly agree that an international system keyed to a handful of perpetrators is less invasive in its migrations than one that explicitly captures all perpetrators.

However, national and local actors will take their cues, and model their behavior, from how international institutions process those deemed most responsible for atrocity. Gauging by international responses to *gacaca* in Rwanda, and traditional mechanisms in Uganda, there is in fact palpable concern over processing lower-level perpetrators in a manner that deviates from the norms of international institutions. The fact that international institutions exert influence over the modalities of accountability for individuals in whom they have little, if any, interest merely attests to the influence these institutions wield.

In sum, although by virtue of complementarity "the majority of prosecutions for international crimes are expected to take place in domestic courts,"[134] the form of these proceedings may become monochrome. Admittedly, it is probably inevitable that international institutions exert some downward pressures on the process of domestic law. It also is probably unavoidable that domestic law has some trickle-down effect on local law. In both cases, these pressures also may create considerable good. However, should these pressures lead to the externalization of justice and the creation of democratic deficits, then they no longer serve salutary ends. Therefore, international lawmakers ought to consider how to control these pressures so as to minimize their undesirable effects. In this regard, Chapter 7 proposes to substitute *qualified deference* for complementarity as a pluralistic interpretive lens for the vertical application of authority. Qualified deference gives more leeway to local variation from the trial and punishment modalities of contemporary international criminal tribunals.

(VI) CONCLUSION

The international community increasingly is holding atrocity perpetrators accountable. That said, the accountability process remains narrowly oriented to incarceration following liberal criminal trials. It is not a broader process that is yet comfortable with meaningful restorative initiatives,[135] indigenous values,[136] qualified amnesties, reintegrative shaming, the needs of victims, reparations, collective or foreign responsibilities, distributive justice, or pointed questions regarding the structural nature of violence in the international system. International criminal law pursues some individuals – cast as enemies of humankind – in some places. In so doing, it punishes these individuals and, thereby, cleanses, purifies, and salves. This process, however, conveniently or unwittingly swaddles the myriad structural factors that permitted the guilty to perpetrate evil on such a large scale. With pronouncement of sentence comes a rush to closure, absolution for the acquiescent, and the evaporation of collective responsibility. This results in the punishment of certain individuals but does not lead to the reform of criminogenic conditions. Scholars of international crime have not yet satisfactorily examined the relationship between these conditions and the long-term peaceful resolution of disputes within and between afflicted societies.

When the ascendancy of criminal trials discourages the development of alternate approaches to accountability, the result is a troubling reductionism. Moreover, given the difficulties criminal trials experience in attaining their stated retributive and deterrent objectives in contexts of collective cataclysm, to which I turn in the next chapter, there is some urgency to the investigation of alternate rationales for and modalities of sanction.

Research suggests that lasting social order in societies roiled by internecine conflict is restored by a "forgiveness process characterized by truth telling, redefinition of the identity of the former belligerents, partial justice, and a call for a new relationship."[137] Assuredly, criminal trials could form an element of some of these goals, notably partial justice and truth telling.[138] But restorative mechanisms also could form an element of these, and other, goals as well. Victimological surveys indicate that aggrieved individuals seek polycentric mechanisms, including those consonant with restoration.[139]

This is not to say that restorative initiatives by definition always are salutary. Some restorative justice initiatives, such as the Sierra Leone Truth and Reconciliation Commission, served ritualistic importance, but did not actualize local reconstructive practices nor stimulate much in the way of truth-telling. Restorative modalities are no panacea; local justice must not be sentimentalized. Restorative modalities that draw parallels from mechanisms used to reintegrate ordinary deviant transgressors in settled times will likely run afoul of the complexities of reintegration in situations of mass atrocity. Restorative shaming theory predicated on a majority of the community's disapproval of the impugned conduct may not be directly transposable to contexts where a majority of that community may not have actually disapproved of atrocity. Moreover, restorative mechanisms that inject alien methodologies will likely prove of limited effect. We cannot blithely assume the suitability of a truth commission whose *logos* is one of Western psychoanalytic theory generalized from the single patient to an entire society. It is critical not to implement restorative mechanisms that may be faulted for the same kind of externalization and transplantation that shadow internationalized criminal process.

Postconflict justice is terribly and terrifically complex. There are no simple solutions. Chauvinism that views truth commissions as a one-size-fits-all hegemonic remedy succumbs to the same frailties as judicial romanticism. Consequently, one important lesson is the need to avoid methodological parsimoniousness. Instead, consideration should be given to consolidating diverse mechanisms more closely attuned to the social geographies of the afflicted societies.

CHAPTER 6

Quest for Purpose

The stated values of the punishment of extraordinary international criminals principally are retribution, deterrence, and expressivism. In this chapter, I consider whether extant sentencing modalities at the local, national, and international levels attain these aspirations. I conclude that, although these modalities go some way to meet retributive and deterrent goals, they fall well short of operationalizing these goals in any meaningful sense. Extant modalities experience greater, albeit still limited, success in attaining expressive goals.

At the outset, it is important to underscore that the three theories of punishment discussed here are not mutually exclusive. Despite the potential for tensions among these theories, courts often refer to them overlappingly when it comes to punishing a single defendant. This creates some tautness insofar as the goals of deterrence (to punish to prevent future crime) at times may conflict with those of retribution (to punish because the criminal deserves it). On the other hand, this overlap also may generate synergies. For example, retribution may have some positive utilitarian effect in deterring violence by discouraging vigilantism among the general public during periods of political transition.[1] That said, the French prosecution of 100,000 collaborators following liberation from the Nazis did not quash vigilantism, insofar as thousands of individuals believed to be collaborators were privately killed. Furthermore, despite the existence of the ICTY, Kosovo Albanians carried out "revenge killings" against Serbs in 1999 following NATO's Operation Allied Force; despite the existence of the ICTR, the RPF committed violent reprisals against Hutus.[2] Retribution and expressivism also share connections: a public that sees a wrongdoer punished in a manner that accords with perceptions of that individual's just deserts can augment the value of the legal system in the eyes of that same public. This prospect, in turn, has given rise to the notion of expressive retribution, which has emerged in recent ICTY jurisprudence.

Punishing atrocity perpetrators on occasion purports to promote other goals, such as rehabilitation, incapacitation, and reintegration. Insofar as these goals remain on the penumbra of sentencing practice, I do not consider them here.[3] This is not to deny their normative worth. They are, in fact, immensely important to any project of transitional justice. International criminal law, however, has not yet accorded these goals much in the way of jurisprudential emphasis and, in cases where such emphasis fleetingly has been given, the goals remain – as set out in Chapters 3 and 4 – rather poorly operationalized.

Reconciliation, another goal, has been given some attention in the judgments of the ad hoc tribunals and a little more so in those of the East Timor Special Panels. Much of this attention, however, is rhetorical, in that international legal institutions expend little effort in practically (and consistently) thinking about how their punishment schematics actually can be made to help victims and offenders (not to mention victim and offender communities) reconcile. National and local institutions, perhaps because they are more deeply embedded in domestic transitional frameworks, often are forced to engage more practically with the operationalization of reconciliation. To this end, reconciliation has somewhat greater currency in certain *in situ* institutions, such as *gacaca*; on the other hand, *gacaca*'s reconciliatory potential is crimped by its operational structure. Overall, there is insufficient evidence to support the inclusion of reconciliation among the principal objectives that existing institutions ascribe to the imposition of sentence upon extraordinary international criminals. There is much to be said in favor of reconciliation as an objective, both in theory and in practice, especially given its on-the-ground importance in many afflicted communities.[4] The challenge, however, is to assess how much reconciliation actually can be generated by criminal trials. In Rwanda, although national criminal trials have developed a jurisprudential record and have involved ten thousand defendants, the promotion of national reconciliation is not among their successes.[5] Laurel Fletcher notes from her research in the Balkans that, although under certain circumstances trials can contribute to what really is a very private personal decision to reconcile, these circumstances are not common and, hence, it is difficult to generalize correlations between trials and collective reconciliation.[6]

(i) RETRIBUTION

Immanuel Kant understood retribution to mean that criminals should be punished because they deserve it.[7] For the retributivist, criminals are not mere cogs in a process of social engineering. Rather, they are ends in themselves – actors deserving of condemnation. G.W.F. Hegel, although generally holding to a restorative view of justice, also recognized the merit of retribution. Hegel noted in *Philosophy of Right* that "as the criminal has done, so should it be done to him."[8]

Retribution is the dominant stated objective for punishment of atrocity perpetrators at the national and international levels.[9] In practice, though, extant punishing frameworks experience a number of challenges in attaining their retributive ambitions. These challenges, which operate at both the national and international levels, include three distinct phenomena: (a) selectivity; (b) severity of sanction and discretion of sentencing judges; and (c) plea bargaining. Although each of these phenomena may promote a variety of salutary goals, each also hampers the fulfillment of retributive aspirations.

a. *Selectivity*

The retributive function is hobbled by the fact that only some extreme evil gets punished, whereas much escapes its grasp, often for political reasons anathema to Kantian deontology. Assuredly, I recognize that criminal law always is contingent on politics. Selectivity is inevitable in the operation of law even in a robustly ordered and purportedly egalitarian domestic polity. However, as Robert Cryer notes, selectivity poses a greater challenge to international criminal law than it does to national criminal law.[10] The contingency of international criminal law is pronounced, including when enforced by international institutions.

Only a few atrocities ever become judicialized. Diane Marie Amann notes that "[a] random confluence of political concerns produced *ad hoc* tribunals for just two out of a number of conflicts that warranted such treatment."[11] These inconsistencies do not eviscerate the retributive value of punishing the guilty in Bosnia or Rwanda. Rather, they underscore the difficulty in ascribing retributive purposes to international criminal law as a whole when a "confluence of political concerns," and not the inherent gravity of the crimes, prods the punishment of offenders. Owing to these concerns, and the contingencies they sow, plenty of perpetrators of extremely grave crimes simply avoid any entanglement with a punishing institution.

Even when a punishing institution is established, however, the reach of the criminal law only attaches to a small subset of alleged perpetrators. The ICTY Prosecutor, for example, has been forced to select a modest number of cases from many thousands of targets.[12] Selection decisions often are discretionary in nature.[13] Prosecutorial discretion tends to be exercised in favor of those cases where there is a better chance of securing a conviction. In some cases, the better chance arises because of the inherent gravity of the crime, in that the crime was planned, organized, brutal, and vast in scope and, therefore, left a deep evidentiary footprint. In these cases, an overlap with retributive goals may arise, in that discretion is exercised in favor of the worst cases where the perpetrators most deserve to be punished. However, in other cases, the exercise of prosecutorial discretion is contingent on variables (such as the cooperation of states, utility of convicting a low-level thug for strategic purposes, and availability of material resources) that have little to do with the inherent gravity of the alleged crime.

At the ICTR and the East Timor Special Panels, selectivity arises insofar as the jurisdiction of these punishing institutions is formally or practically limited to an artificial and politically convenient time frame. Large numbers of killers and killings are therefore left unexamined. Katzenstein offers the following explanation for the truncated temporal jurisdiction of the Special Panels:

> Limiting the investigations exclusively to referendum-related violence of 1999, despite a mandate that provides for jurisdiction over acts committed during a much broader time frame, was not simply a decision based upon resource constraints. Rather, it was also motivated by a concern that a more expansive inquiry could lead to the indictment of U.S. officials who countenanced the

Indonesian invasion and helped to equip and train the Indonesian military both prior to and throughout the occupation.[14]

At first blush, there is less selectivity in a permanent institution, such as the ICC, than in ad hoc institutions created by the UN Security Council. And, indeed, to a large degree the ICC operates independently of the Security Council.[15] However, selectivity intractably affects, and will continue to affect, the ICC's work. The Rome Statute places considerable power within the office of a single individual: its Prosecutor, currently Luis Moreno-Ocampo.[16] The ICC Statute "is almost totally silent with respect to the larger policy questions about which potential accused should be pursued by the Prosecutor."[17] There is limited judicial oversight of Prosecutorial decisions not to investigate. Although there may be very important and eminently justifiable reasons for the Prosecutor to decline to investigate or prosecute – reasons that I would avidly support – it remains that these reasons, however laudable, if applied to extremely grave cases undermine retribution as a principled objective.

Moreover, regardless of institutional oversight of the ICC Prosecutor's discretion, it is impossible to squeeze out the political contingency of criminal liability in the ICC's practice.[18] Looking ahead, there will likely be a large disparity between the cases the ICC could potentially prosecute and those that it will effectively prosecute.[19] The ICC Prosecutor, for whom resources remain limited, will face "competing situations of crisis."[20] Ineluctably, this means that only some crises will be selected for investigation and prosecution. The Rome Statute provides limited guidance regarding how to comparatively evaluate crisis situations.[21] Pragmatically speaking, in order for the ICC institutionally to maintain resource support, it is incentivized to investigate wrongdoers in politically powerless places.[22] Decisions whether or not to investigate or prosecute therefore become contoured by concerns over how they affect the ICC's political standing, funding, and support among states. Cases may be turned away because of politics and initiated because of politics, instead of cases initiated or turned away solely because of the gravity of the alleged violations of international law that they actually present. In the end, the permanent ICC could *de facto* resemble an ad hoc institution contingent on international political consensus. However, even when such consensus exists – as is the case with the Security Council's referral of the Darfur situation to the ICC – resource availability will affect the ICC's ability to do its work. In the Darfur situation, for example, it does not appear that the Security Council is paying for investigatory or prosecutorial costs occasioned by the referral. Contingency and selectivity triggered by funding vagaries may lead to a situation where culpable individuals evade accountability.

To his great credit, Moreno-Ocampo has expressed interest in examining the broader context in which mass violence occurs, in particular links to international economic dynamics and corporate behavior. This development would be salutary (although it is limited by the fact the ICC only has jurisdiction over natural persons). After all, prosecuting only a small number of individuals in cases of massive levels of violence leads to a very partial print of justice. Atrocity is often the result of structural factors. Slobodan Milošević, Saddam Hussein, and Pol Pot emerged from deeply globalized forces, including acts and omissions of international agents and foreign governments; the sources of genocide at Srebrenica and Rwanda are complex and multicausal. Frankly, for many Rwandans and Bosnian Muslims, retribution might well include accountability for the UN and foreign governments, whose peacekeepers were ineffective while genocidal massacre occurred in their midst. Just because these entities are not, or cannot be found to be, criminally guilty does not mean that they are in no way responsible for genocide. In the end, however, the operation of international criminal law occasions a retributive shortfall in that too few people or entities receive just deserts while many powerful states and organizations are absolved of responsibility. So, too, are bystanders – many of whom are not so innocent. Although it may seem counterintuitive, restorative justice modalities and institutions that push reintegrative shaming could in fact augment overall retribution by capturing a far greater number of individuals and organizations in the accountability process, albeit not to the severity or depth characteristic of the criminal conviction.

At the national level, courts that adjudicate extraordinary international criminals face many of the same selectivity challenges that hinder their international counterparts. National courts that assert jurisdiction based on nationality or territoriality additionally face their own proximity to the violence and their own susceptibility to domestic political pressures. They may be preoccupied with maintaining their own legitimacy during periods of political transition. These concerns contour decisions regarding who to prosecute and can disaggregate prosecutorial decisions from the gravity of the underlying offenses. This certainly appears to be the case in national courts throughout the former Yugoslavia, where many proceedings are corroded by ethnic bias, thereby undermining the principled attainment of retributive objectives.

Furthermore, the retributive value of punishment at the national level can be compromised by two diametrically opposite phenomena that do not arise at the international level: (1) overcapture and (2) intentional undercapture through amnesties.

Overcapture most acutely involves pursuing individuals for atrocity when that pursuit is motored by concerns other than the gravity of the alleged atrocity offense. For example, denunciations have been lodged with *gacaca* that appear to be motivated by ulterior purposes of land acquisition, romantic disputes, political vendettas, and relationship breakdowns. In such cases, one way to get even with an uncooperative colleague or unfaithful lover is to denounce him or her as having been involved in genocide. In some cases, accusations may be entirely false, in other cases they may be partially true, and in some they may be fully true but brought not to seek justice for acts committed in 1994 but, rather, acts – often not criminal – initiated much later that have nothing to do with genocide. In each of these scenarios, there is a dilution in terms of the retributive value of the punishment that is meted out: this dilution is greatest when punishment is undeserved, but also arises when punishment is pursued because of concerns unrelated to the gravity of the initial atrocious conduct. Due process can filter out those denunciations that lack foundation and, hence, serve a gatekeeping or corrective function with regard to overcapture.

Undercapture is trickier. National courts often must face the prospect of amnesties. These erode the retributive value of prosecution and punishment for mass atrocity or politically related violence. Generally, amnesties are unavailable for ordinary domestic crime, yet they arise frequently in situations of mass atrocity.[23] In some cases, amnesties are unqualified. In other cases, they are qualified, in that they require the person seeking amnesty to tell the truth, apologize, or make amends. Whereas the amnesties (self-)accorded to Argentine and Chilean military leaders were unqualified, amnesty in South Africa was qualified. Regardless, even in the case of South Africa, "[f]rom a retributive point of view, it is not immediately clear why a murderer who kills for political reasons should be entitled to amnesty in return for the truth, while one who kills out of passion or greed should not."[24] This disparity in treatment is particularly vexing for the retributivist because the gravity of the conduct of the extraordinary international criminal is supposed to be *greater* than that of the ordinary common criminal. Assuredly, as noted in Chapter 5, much can be said in favor of amnesties. Amnesties have many justifications that can be coherently grounded in moral theory, popular will, and pressing political realities. That said, these justifications – however attractive – do not attenuate the reality that amnesties selectivize punishment of extraordinary international criminals at the national level in a manner that hampers retribution as a principled penological goal.

b. *Severity of Sanction and Discretion of Sentencing Judges*

Retribution requires proportionality between the gravity of the offense and the severity of sanction. In this section, I consider challenges to the retributive metric posed by three realities revealed by the data presented in Chapters 3 and 4 regarding the sentencing of extraordinary international criminals. These realities are:

(1) Regardless of the level at which punishment is imposed, sentences for extraordinary international crimes are not generally longer than for serious ordinary common crimes;

(2) Sentences for extraordinary international crimes are not as a rule longer when pronounced by international tribunals than when pronounced by national courts (nor are conditions of imprisonment harsher or stigma weightier), even though international tribunals exercise jurisdiction over the most serious offenders; and

(3) There is significant disparity within and among institutions when it comes to the severity of sentence, and this disparity is not consistently explainable on the basis of the gravity of the offense.

Let us consider each of these realities in turn, and investigate how they obstruct the retributive goals of international criminal law.

(1) **Overwhelming Gravity of the Crimes.** The data reveal that, at both the national and international levels, sentences for multiple international crimes are generally not lengthier than what national jurisdictions award for a single serious ordinary crime. The length of a term of imprisonment is, obviously, not the *only* possible indicator of retributive value. Nor is it evident that the mere addition of several years to a sentence necessarily augments its retributive force; or that shortening a sentence by several years guts that force. However, length of sentence constitutes the central – and, basically, only –measurement device that liberal legalist institutions practically avail themselves of when it comes to operationalizing punishment in extant sentencing frameworks. According to the proportionality metric: the graver the offense, the longer the term of imprisonment. Therefore, the length of a prison term is used as a meter for retributive value. As such, these frameworks must be judged by their own terms.

Some positive law instruments at the national level, such as in many Western countries, provide longer sentences for extraordinary international crimes than for ordinary serious common crimes; this also was the case in certain jurisdictions that punished atrocity committed in Europe or the Pacific Rim in the immediate aftermath of World War II. On the other hand, this is not a universal practice – far from it – among positive law instruments in all national legal orders. What is more, the practice of contemporary courts that punish offenders for extraordinary international crimes, for example in the former Yugoslavia, reveals that, for the most part, sentences for multiple international crimes range from as severe to less severe than for a single serious common crime.[25] As the states of the former Yugoslavia develop specialized war crimes chambers to process atrocity cases, average sentences might increase through the ordering of harsher minimum sentences. Such an upward – and, for the moment, largely conjectural – trajectory in the severity of sentence, however, would do no more than place such sentences in the same ballpark as sentences for serious ordinary crime.

The East Timor Special Panels appeared in their practice to be supportive of greater retribution for international crimes than for ordinary crimes. As a hybrid tribunal with dual jurisdiction over ordinary and extraordinary crimes, the Special Panels constitute an interesting case study. The data reported in Chapter 3 demonstrate that, with regard to mean sentences, the ratio between ordinary crimes and international crimes was 1:1.58. Therefore, the mean sentence for extraordinary international crimes was about 50 percent longer than for ordinary common crimes. However, the data interpretation remains subject to a number of important caveats. First, the mean sentence for serious ordinary crimes was 6.3 years. The median sentence was five years. These sentences are very modest when compared to the treatment that serious ordinary crimes receive in the domestic law of many states, thereby suggesting that the disparity between sentences for ordinary and international crimes in the practice of the Special Panels emanated in part from lightly punishing ordinary crimes. Second, three

sentences of 33 ⅓ years issued by the Special Panels for crimes against humanity deviated considerably from the median sentence and, thereby, artificially
boosted the mean. These sentences eventually were reduced by *ex post* Presidential Decree to twenty-five years. Third, over time the trend in East Timor
arced toward more lenient sentences, including extremely modest sentences in
the two- to seven-year range for crimes against humanity. These three caveats
cloud the apparent practice of the Special Panels to pursue greater retribution
for extraordinary international crimes.

One major impediment to the retributive aspirations of international criminal law is that widespread crime cannot be reflected in punishment owing to
human rights standards, which cabin the parameters of sanction. In particular, these standards limit the amount of pain that institutions can inflict upon
detainees. The gravity of atrocity crimes can quickly become overwhelming – so
much so that, from a retributive perspective, gravity becomes unintelligible and
immeasurable. How, then, to make punishment proportionate to the amplitude
of harm caused?[26]

Faced with the prospect of "trying" the former Romanian dictator Nicolae
Ceausescu and his wife, Elena, the prosecutor bitterly noted that his entire
professional code of ethics became upended. He famously remarked:

> [A]s a lawyer, [I] would have liked to oppose the death sentence, because it is
> inhuman. But we are not talking about people. I would not call for the death
> sentence, but it would be incomprehensible for the Romanian people to have
> to go on suffering this great misery and not to have it ended by sentencing the
> two Ceausescus to death.[27]

The evil was simply so overwhelming that the prosecutor had no way to punish
the perpetrators other than resorting to a sanction that fell outside the values
he associated with the law. For the Romanian prosecutor, the wrongdoing – to
borrow from Arendt – simply exploded the limits of the law.

But the wrongdoing can explode the limits even of a legal process that
favors the death penalty as an ultimate retributive sanction. If retribution
truly were to reflect the gravity of extraordinary international criminality, death
might even fall short. As the Supreme Court of Israel frustratedly observed in
Eichmann:

> We know only too well how utterly inadequate the sentence of death is as
> compared with the millions of unnatural deaths he decreed for his victims.
> Even as there is no word in human speech to describe deeds such as the deeds
> of [Eichmann], so there is no punishment under human law sufficiently grave
> to match [his] guilt.[28]

In correspondence with her mentor Karl Jaspers, Arendt observed that, for
extraordinary international crimes, "no punishment is severe enough [. . .] this
guilt, in contrast to all criminal guilt, oversteps and shatters any and all legal
systems. [. . .] We are simply not equipped to deal . . . with a guilt that is beyond

crime [...]."²⁹ If the retributive value of punishing extraordinary international criminals truly were to be engaged, perhaps punishment would have to exceed anything ordinary.³⁰ Truly proportionate sentences then might involve torture or reciprocal group eliminationism. That is a terrifying path. In such a scenario, survivors would become as depraved as their tormentors.

In sum: for those who commit the most egregious crimes of concern to the international community as a whole, sanctions tend to range from less severe to as severe as the punishments for ordinary murder in many countries.³¹ But extraordinary international crimes are supposedly graver than serious ordinary common crimes. The fact that punishment does not match this enhanced gravity weakens retribution's credibility as a penological goal for international criminal law.

(2) Treatment of High-Level Offenders. When it comes to punishing extraordinary international criminals, although the retributive value of international convictions is supposed to be greater than that of national convictions,³² the sentences of the international criminal tribunals are not predictably lengthier than those meted out in those territorial jurisdictions where atrocity is over-lappingly prosecuted as extraordinary international crimes through national or local institutions.³³ Nor are the conditions of imprisonment at international institutions more onerous; nor is the stigma of conviction weightier.

Let us begin with length of sentence. The overall evidence is inconclusive regarding the existence of differences in terms of absolute length of sentence between international and national institutions. Although IMT sentences were harsher than those of many national civilian courts that prosecuted World War II atrocity, they were not more severe than the sentences issued by certain national military instrumentalities. The enhanced severity of international sanction is even less apparent in the case of contemporary institutions, particularly when factoring in that international tribunals assert jurisdiction over the most serious offenders. Elemental retributive theory suggests that these offenders proportionately deserve harsher punishment. Therefore, the fact that the evidence is inconclusive with regard to whether contemporary international tribunals issue harsher sentences than national or local institutions, which generally process lower-level offenders, is of concern to the viability of retributive theory.

Evidence introduced in Chapter 4 suggests that national courts in the states that emerged from the former Yugoslavia have punished extraordinary international criminals less harshly than the ICTY. This, however, is not due to the particularly lengthy nature of sentences issued by the ICTY. Rather, it is largely due to the prevalence of ethnic bias and unprofessionalism in national courts (e.g., in Croatia), which often results in modest sentences for low-level offenders. Looking ahead, though, the situation in these national courts is set to change. I predict an increasing alignment of the practice of these courts (in particular, specialized war crimes chambers) with that of the ICTY as these courts receive referrals from the ICTY and begin independently to prosecute higher-profile cases as a matter of course. This alignment would diminish sentencing differences between the two levels of judicialization.

The ICTY does not as a matter of course sentence its convicts to terms of imprisonment that exceed what it determines to be available under domestic law. As a benchmark, the ICTY often adopts twenty years as the maximum term available in the sentencing practice of the former Yugoslavia (this seems to come from the fact that, under the SFRY Criminal Code, the most serious offenses that were eligible for the death penalty could be transformed by the court into a twenty-year sentence).[34] Many ICTY sentences dip below twenty years (and the mean and median sentences are well below that figure); on the other hand, some sentences have exceeded that maximum and, in fact, the ICTY has as a matter of law affirmed that it has the discretion to exceed this maximum.[35] However, as set out in Chapter 4, current sentencing frameworks in the states that emerged from the former Yugoslavia, although abolishing the death penalty, permit maximum sentences in the forty- to forty-five-year range depending on the state. Although in some cases the ICTY acknowledges this maximum range, it rarely issues such sentences (as of May 2006, it has only done so twice – under 5 percent of its total sentences). In the end, it is not surprising that survey research demonstrates that residents of afflicted communities in the former Yugoslavia view ICTY sentences as lenient.[36] Moreover, ICTY defendants tend to resist referral of their cases to national courts in the former Yugoslavia. The prospect of referral apparently played a part in one ICTY defendant's decision to plead guilty.[37] The fact that perpetrators demonstrate greater fear of punishment at the hands of national authorities seems at odds with the supposedly enhanced retributive value of punishment at the ICTY.

Because Rwandan domestic law still provides for the death penalty, the defendants found guilty by the ICTR (mostly senior officials) in theory receive sentences lower than what they likely would receive under Rwandan law. Overall, the Rwandan national courts issue death sentences to about 10 percent of all defendants, although that percentage has progressively declined since 2002 and no individuals have been executed since 1998. To be sure, Rwanda's practice of no longer enforcing death sentences suggests that, *de facto*, the death penalty may no longer be a practical sentencing option in Rwanda. That said, as an ICTR Trial Chamber recently noted in *Prosecutor v. Muhimana*, the death sentence does remain on the books.[38] This reveals a paradox: namely, leaders of the genocide are formally punished less severely than lower-level offenders. This paradox also is evident in Sierra Leone, which "retains the death penalty under its domestic law [leading to a situation] where the worst offenders are eligible for lower punishments because they are tried at the international tribunal."[39]

The ICTR sentences slightly under half of its convicts to life terms. Because it has acquitted three individuals so far, this means that just over 40 percent of all ICTR defendants who have gone to trial receive life sentences. This is a higher proportion of life sentences than that issued by the Rwandan national courts, including the Specialized Chambers. But when the number of death sentences in the national courts is added to the mix, the result is that approximately

40 percent of defendants receive life or death. The proportion of life or death sentences has been dropping annually in the Rwandan national system (there is no evidence of such a trend regarding life sentences at the ICTR). With regard to fixed terms of imprisonment, my research, set out in Chapter 4, identified a median term of 11 years and a mean term of 15.25 years in the Rwandan courts; to be contrasted with the ICTR's practice among finalized sentences of a mean fixed term of 20.9 years and a median fixed term of 15 years (among unfinalized sentences, the mean increases to 23.5 years and the median jumps to 25 years).

Given the figures regarding fixed-term sentences, and the trends in the domestic courts, the overall length of sentence is therefore higher at the ICTR than in the domestic courts. However, the defendants prosecuted before each institution are not similarly situated. Account must be had that, when it comes to high-status offenders, sentences in Rwandan courts are stiffer. For example, in *Prosecutor v. Semanza*, the ICTR Appeals Chamber found that, although the defendant's sentence may have been more severe in Rwandan courts, "the Trial Chamber acted within its discretion when it imposed a lesser sentence."[40] Under Rwandan law, Semanza would have received at least life imprisonment (maybe even a death sentence). In *Prosecutor v. Bisengimana*, a case from 2006, an ICTR Trial Chamber recognized that the *gacaca* law subjects a person of the stature of the defendant who pleads guilty to crimes against humanity to a sentence between twenty-five years to life.[41] It then sentenced the defendant to fifteen years' imprisonment. In the case of *gacaca*, preliminary evidence from Rwanda suggests a tremendously wide range of sentence. The maximum sentence under *gacaca* for Category 2 offenders is thirty years' imprisonment. This dips below what the ICTR can issue. However, the ICTR would have virtually no interest in prosecuting an individual whose culpability is alleged to be tantamount to that of a Category 2 offender.

On a different note, as set out in Chapter 3, the ICTY permits convicts access to conditional and early release. Eligibility for pardon or commutation of sentence hinges upon the domestic criminal law of the state where the prisoner serves sentence.[42] ICTY convicts are imprisoned in Western European states whose domestic law permits application for commutation or early release to be made after two-thirds of the sentence has been served. This process disempowers the afflicted society by superimposing the ordinary common criminal law of a faraway state (and judgments of state officials in these faraway places) as a template to attenuate punishment after the fact. Interestingly, however, the ordinary domestic laws of some states emergent from the former Yugoslavia have been revised to provide for early and conditional release, even in the case of extraordinary international criminals. This reveals the emergence of some consensus in these states in favor of permitting atrocity perpetrators access to the same early release possibilities that are available for common criminals. I posit that this domestic law reform is in part influenced by the perceived need to mimic modern international methodologies. Regardless, it is unclear how the putatively enhanced retributive value of punishing extraordinary international criminals is satisfied by permitting these criminals access to (and in many cases granting) early release in the same manner as for ordinary common criminals.

Early or conditional release has not yet begun at the ICTR. But it soon might, given that the ICTR has concluded agreements to house prisoners in Western European countries. If ICTR convicts begin to serve sentence in these countries and then become entitled to early release provisions that neither Rwanda nor Mali (where ICTR convicts currently serve sentence) contemplate, the retributive gap between the treatment accorded those most responsible for genocide and those less responsible will grow. In the case of the East Timor Special Panels, the retributive value of punishment, already threatened by conditional release, is additionally undercut by the exercise of Presidential Decrees that reduce the duration of imprisonment. The application of these Decrees promotes an added layer of selectivity and unequal treatment among convicts.

When it comes to assessing whether the retributive value of international proceedings exceeds or falls short of that of national proceedings, a truly purposive comparative analysis must transcend strict quantitative measurement of length of imprisonment. In this regard, I consider two other aspects of the retributive value of punishment: (1) conditions of imprisonment and (2) stigma.

Qualitatively speaking, conditions of incarceration arranged at the international level tend to be much less harsh than those available to defendants sentenced nationally. When compared to the domestic Rwandan prisons, the ICTR detention unit is luxurious. Although prisons in Mali, where most ICTR defendants serve sentence, are not as comfortable as the ICTR detention unit, they are superior to options available in Rwanda.

Moreover, defendants awaiting trial at the ICTR detention unit receive a quality of health care that exceeds that accorded to defendants in national trials or *gacaca* and, more starkly, victims living in Rwanda. ICTR defendants have access to treatment, medication, and services that few victims can claim.[43] These disparities are galling given the prevalence of HIV/AIDS in Rwanda generally and in particular among genocide survivors.[44] Victims' groups in Rwanda have made antiretrovirals available to some members of the public; nonetheless, affordable and accessible medical treatment is scarce. Prosecuting and punishing perpetrators is supposed to voice retribution. However, in the case of ICTR defendants, the fact they are accused of extraordinary international crimes ironically may keep them alive and healthy to enjoy a quality of life that exceeds that of victims and probably exceeds that which they would experience were they not to be "punished" at all.

A similar concern arises regarding the retributive value of the pain and punishment inflicted by the ICTY. In the recent plea-bargained sentence of Biljana Plavšić (a Bosnian Serb leader known as the Serbian Iron Lady), "victims reacted with predictable outrage" at the fact that "Plavšić was sent to serve her term in a posh Swedish prison that reportedly provides prisoners with use of a sauna, solarium, massage room, and horse-riding paddock, among other amenities."[45] While in jail, she was even "presented a birthday cake on her birthday."[46]

Similarly, research on popular attitudes toward punishment in East Timor reveals profound externalization of justice concerns as well as a deep retributive shortfall. Legal scholar Nancy Amoury Combs concludes: "[I]n the eyes of many East Timorese, detention constitutes precious little punishment since prisoners are fed and housed in jail, and in some cases can avoid their compensation obligation."[47]

If severity of sanction is construed to include level of stigmatization, then there is cause to believe that international sanctions are more denunciatory.[48] International proceedings reach a worldwide audience. They are broadcast on television screens everywhere. The stigma is spread widely. Paradoxically, though, the broadcasting often is more accessible outside of the afflicted locality than within it. But it is important not to underestimate the stigmatizing value of national proceedings.[49] Sometimes, the shaming value of sentencing is more acute when carried out by a community of one's immediate peers.

And, finally, other differences persist between international and national modalities of punishment that, in certain cases, render the retributive value of punishment at the international level less onerous than at the national level. Rwanda once again presents an example. In Rwanda, the national courts through the *partie civile* process routinely award very substantial (although largely uncollected) financial damages to victims and survivors; also, the accused, if found guilty, will be ordered to pay the costs of the proceedings. Both of these additional remedies represent an interesting diversification of the accountability paradigm that adds to the retributive weight of punishment. Although the ICTR Statute contemplates some restitutionary and reparative possibilities, these have not been pursued in practice. My review of the Rwandan national jurisprudence notes cases where, in order to execute these orders, the convicted person's assets are auctioned off. The prospect of a lifetime of work or community service to pay off these civil damages can be of a high punitive force and, hence, can go far in pursuing retributive goals.

(3) Variability in Sentencing. At the international level, trial judges have unfettered discretion to affix the period of imprisonment for convicted extraordinary international criminals. Moreover, appellate judges, who also benefit from broad discretion in sentencing, actively intervene as well. Assuredly, sentencers at the international level are assisted by a typology of aggravating and mitigating factors. But the predictability or clarity this typology provides is limited. Parties do not have much of a sense of what evidence to present in sentencing hearings (if there even is a separate hearing) and which aspects to emphasize. There is considerable inconsistency – both cardinally and ordinally – in terms of the sentences issued. Although there is some indication that the sentencing jurisprudence of international criminal tribunals is deepening in depth and rigor, it still remains confusing, unpredictable, and without the ordering benefits of a viable heuristic. There is also, dating back to Nuremberg, confusion with regard to the mixing of factors implicating liability with factors to consider in aggravation of sentence.

At the national level, there is much greater diversity in terms of the discretion accorded sentencers in determining the period of imprisonment. Some national frameworks tie the hands of sentencers. Some, such as Rwanda's, set parameters within which some discretion is retained. Others are very permissive.

Discretion in sentencing carries with it certain advantages, such as flexibility and the opportunity to individualize punishment. Discretion, however, poses challenges to the attainment of the claimed retributive purpose of punishment. It can lead to a lack of consistency in sentencing that, in turn, could cloud the public's ability to assess the gravity or seriousness of crime. This obfuscation might diminish public respect for the legal system.

As outlined in Chapter 3, at the international level considerable variability persists within institutions in terms of the length of sentences meted out to similarly situated defendants. Moreover, sentences vary considerably not only within but also among the various international tribunals. For example, the sentences of the East Timor Special Panels for extraordinary international crimes are the most lenient. Does this mean that atrocity in East Timor is of the least gravity? The most proximate comparison is between the two ad hoc tribunals. ICTR sentences are longer than ICTY sentences; in addition, the ICTY welcomes early release, which has not (yet) been operationalized at the ICTR. In order for the retributive justification to explain this disparity, it might assume that the gravity of the Rwandan violence exceeds that of the former Yugoslavia.

Intuitively, making comparative assessments of the gravity of systemic violence does not seem patently unreasonable. That said, these are difficult comparisons to make and can degenerate into hairsplitting. Punishing institutions have not yet articulated any framework of comparative assessment that determines the yardsticks by which to measure the greater gravity of, for example, Rwanda's tragedy over Bosnia's, or Sierra Leone's over East Timor's. No punishing institution has justified the enhanced or diminished length of its sentences on the basis of the more repugnant nature of one nation's atrocity over another's.

Two other rationalizations could coherently explain why ICTR sentences are longer than ICTY and East Timor Special Panel sentences. The first involves the incorporation of the norms of the afflicted community. Domestic sentences, in particular those maximum sentences that would be imposed on high-level or notorious convicts, are more punitive in Rwanda (death, life imprisonment) than in the former Yugoslavia (long-term fixed imprisonment).[50] The second rationalization posits that sentences by the ICTR appropriately are harsher because the ICTR has convicted much more frequently for genocide, which has been described as the "crime of all crimes,"[51] and, therefore, for those who accept this description, it follows that perpetrators of genocide simply deserve harsher sentences.

In principle, I would welcome a policy whereby international institutions sentenced differently based on incorporation of national norms. Such a policy militates against a democratic deficit. This policy is particularly desirable when national positive law instruments, or court activity, represent what populations on the ground envision as legitimate sentencing practice. In my opinion, accommodating representative national sentencing practices is intimately connected to the meaningfulness of sanction. This accommodation, however, would not necessarily be grounded in the retributive value of punishment, but, instead, in other penological justifications and, even, broader justifications such as democratic legitimacy.

That said, the international criminal tribunals have not explicitly recognized differences in national sentencing practices to justify the longer sentences at the ICTR. In fact, the incorporation of national sentencing practices in the decisionmaking of international punishing institutions remains unpredictable. The ad hoc tribunals refuse to view national practices as in any way binding. In fact, an ICTY Trial Chamber recently held that national sentencing practices are "purely indicative."[52] The ICTR has held it has no obligation to conform to general practice regarding prison sentences at the national level, although it is to refer to this practice.[53] The East Timor Special Panels took a similar approach to the incorporation of domestic law.[54] The Special Panels sporadically integrated *adat*, a traditional notion regarding taking responsibility and paying respects, into the sentencing framework. However, they never predictably stated when *adat* ought to be referenced. The ICC does not appear to be under any obligation to recognize national or customary practices. In sum: although the incorporation of national and local law into international sentencing practices is a salutary goal, the extant process of incorporation seems to undermine consistency without providing the real legitimizing benefits of local and contextual involvement.

With regard to the second rationalization, it is true that many of the convictions at the ICTR have been for genocide, whereas nearly all ICTY convictions have been for crimes against humanity and war crimes. Looking more carefully, however, the ICTY's actual genocide convictions do not incur as stiff a penalty as the ICTR's. An ICTY Trial Chamber sentenced Blagojević to eighteen years (on a count of complicity to commit genocide)[55] and the Appeals Chamber sentenced Krstić to thirty-five years (for aiding and abetting genocide).[56] The ICTY's harshest sentences have been for crimes against humanity. Factually, many perpetrators in Rwanda were convicted as primary perpetrators of genocide, not as aiders and abettors, and this more serious level of responsibility does problematize the comparison somewhat. Fundamentally, though, the international tribunals have not consistently stated that, *ceteris paribus*, genocide merits a more severe sanction because its inherent gravity exceeds that of crimes against humanity or war crimes.[57]

c. *Plea Bargaining*

Plea bargains present another challenge to the retributive value of punishing extraordinary international criminals. This challenge operates at both the national and international levels.

Plea bargains can take several forms. The confession and pure guilty plea constitutes one form. Here, an offender unilaterally confesses, admits guilt, and foregoes the trial. The matter proceeds directly to sentencing.[58] Other forms involve bilateral negotiation. The plea agreement, for example, arises from negotiations between prosecution and defendant. This quasicontractual process, which has gained traction at the international criminal tribunals, incorporates pragmatic elements that are commonplace to U.S. domestic criminal law. For example, prosecutor and defendant can conclude a sentence bargain, where they agree upon underlying facts and negotiate regarding a sentencing range. This range is then presented to the international tribunal for approval together with the guilty plea. Another form is the charge bargain. In charge bargaining, the prosecutor may drop certain charges (including serious charges) as part of the plea negotiations. In some cases, the defendant may only plead guilty to one omnibus charge that generalizes the specifics of the factual record (and may exclude facts regarding certain dropped charges and details regarding others). Charge bargaining has occurred at the international tribunals, although less frequently than sentence bargaining.

Plea bargains have many benefits. The confession and guilty plea often reflects atonement, apology, and recognition of responsibility on the part of the offender who self-convicts. In a case involving a controversial charge bargain, ICTR judges noted the offender's genuine desire to tell the whole truth, ask for pardon, and publicly express remorse.[59] Plea bargains are cited for their ability to promote reconciliation.[60] Moreover, plea bargains promote managerial efficiency. Accordingly, they appeal to prosecutors facing tight completion strategies, funding shortfalls, or political pressures, each of which has dogged international institutions. Plea bargains ensure that some justice is seen to be done. They also can facilitate the acquisition of evidence that implicates other defendants.[61]

That said, negotiated plea bargains compete with the notion that perpetrators deserve to be punished. In this quasicontractual exchange, punishment becomes disconnected from desert or gravity and contingent on what the convict knows, who else the convict is willing to implicate, and the vulnerability of the punishing institution. Perpetrators having information on others will likely be given a better bargain than those with nothing to offer. A perpetrator involved in a joint criminal enterprise with high-level accused could benefit the most from the liability or sentencing discount regardless of the egregiousness of the crimes, the perpetrator's ability to encourage recidivism among others, or the expressive value of stigmatizing that perpetrator through public denunciation.

Assuredly, these disparities also are found in domestic criminal law, in particular regarding the sentencing of drug offenders and criminal syndicates (where they have prompted a broad array of critical commentary). Concerns, however, are even more pronounced when a plea-bargaining model designed to process ordinary crimes in select adversarial domestic criminal law systems is extended to the context of extraordinary international crimes. An institutional policy that differentially punishes extraordinary international criminals based not on the gravity of their offenses but, rather, on judicial economy, strategic system interests, and bureaucratic contingencies splinters the deontological basis of retribution.

The ICTY has noted that another benefit to plea bargains is that they protect victims from having to testify.[62] Although experience indicates that testifying is traumatic for many victims, this is not the case for every victim. In fact, for some victims, testifying might have significant cathartic value. Accordingly, if one of the purposes of retribution is for individual victims to see punishment inflicted on the criminal, victims should play a role in determining whether or not a plea should be accepted and, if so, on what terms.

Plea bargains of diverse forms have occurred at each of the ICTY, ICTR, and East Timor Special Panels. Prosecutors from each institution have pushed plea bargains. Defendants at each institution have responded differently. ICTY defendants have been receptive to plea agreements owing to an appetite for sentencing concessions.[63] Admittedly, the actual mitigating discount that plea bargaining will obtain is difficult to measure and remains unpredictable. As of November 2004, the mean and median sentences of those ICTY defendants convicted following a plea bargain were 2.6 and 6 years shorter than the mean and median sentences of those convicted following trial.[64]

The willingness of ICTY defendants to plead guilty recently has abated owing to decisions by the Trial Chambers to impose sentences that exceed the range that the ICTY Prosecutor and defendant had agreed upon.[65] In these cases, the Trial Chambers were motivated by the perceived excessive lenity of punishment in these agreements.[66] The ICTY positive law instruments stipulate that the Trial Chambers are not formally bound by a sentence recommendation contained in a plea agreement.

The *Momir Nikolić* case presents an example. Nikolić was a security and intelligence officer at Srebrenica, where he played a command role. He was the first Serb officer to admit to participating in the Srebrenica massacre. The Trial Chamber sentenced him to twenty-seven years.[67] This exceeded the recommendation of the plea agreement (where the ICTY Prosecutor had agreed to recommend a fifteen- to twenty-year sentence and the defense a ten-year sentence). Nikolić had pled guilty to one count of persecutions as a crime against humanity. The Trial Chamber had expressed a number of reservations with regard to plea bargains for cases of extraordinary international criminality, and did not follow the plea recommendation, although it still found the guilty plea to be significant and to constitute an important factor in mitigation. Nikolić appealed. The Appeals Chamber did not quarrel with the Trial Chamber's approach to the guilty plea. However, for other reasons it reduced the sentence to twenty years.[68] This meant that the sentence fell within the range the Prosecutor had recommended.

Although there have been other cases in which ICTY judges have voiced some reserve regarding the general suitability of plea bargaining for serious crimes of concern to the international community, the Trial and Appeals Chambers have accepted many of the plea agreements that have come before them, at times in spite of articulated concerns.

Sentences issued by the ICTY following plea bargains have little retributive rhyme or reason. On the one hand, Biljana Plavšić, who was responsible for planning some of the gravest atrocities in Bosnia (forced expulsion of hundreds of thousands of nonSerbs, destruction of 850 nonSerb villages, killings of many thousands of individuals, widespread sexual assault, and inhumane destruction),[69] was sentenced to eleven years. (This fell below the Prosecutor's recommended range of fifteen to twenty-five years). On the other hand, rebel Croatian Serb leader Milan Babić, further down on the leadership hierarchy – and who, unlike Plavšić, testified against Slobodan Milošević – received a sentence of thirteen years for his role in a campaign to expel non-Serbs.[70] Whereas Plavšić was given significant discount for her post hoc efforts at peace negotiation, Babić was not given such discount despite the ICTY's recognition of the salience of his efforts.

To be sure, Plavšić was in her seventies at the time of sentencing and the ICTY took account of her age as a mitigating factor. That said, Plavšić's sentence is only four years longer than that imposed on Miodrag Jokić, who pled guilty to a number of war crime charges related to the shelling of Dubrovnik (the charges against Jokić related to the destruction of cultural property and the deaths of two civilians and the wounding of three others).[71] In 2005, an ICTY Trial Chamber sentenced Lieutenant-General Strugar, who was initially charged together with Jokić with regard to the 1991 Dubrovnik attacks, to eight years' imprisonment for attacks on civilians and destruction/willful damage to heritage/charitable institutions.[72] Strugar is roughly the same age as Plavšić and was sentenced to only three years less imprisonment than her despite the yawning gap between the two in terms of the gravity of their impugned conduct.[73]

Whereas Darko Mrdja was sentenced to 17 years for pleading guilty to direct involvement in the shooting of 200 persons (only 12 of whom survived),[74] Ranko Češić, a Bosnian Serb police reservist, was sentenced to 18 years for pleading guilty to beating to death 10 prisoners and sexually assaulting 2 others.[75] Češić was a de facto subordinate to Goran Jelisić, who had previously pled guilty to thirteen murders at the same camp where Češić had committed his crimes. Jelisić, however, had received a sentence of forty years: by any measure, an incredible disparity in sentencing.[76] The Češić sentence also should be juxtaposed against the ten-year sentence meted out to Miroslav Deronjić, an influential civilian leader who substantially participated in a joint criminal enterprise that ordered the razing of the village of Glogova, in which sixty-four Bosnian Muslim civilians were killed and many more forcibly displaced.[77] In Deronjić's case, the Trial Chamber ruminated about the suitability of plea bargains for situations of mass atrocity, but ultimately affirmed the plea bargain as well as the light sentence recommended by the Prosecutor.[78] On appeal, the sentence was upheld.[79]

While there are inherent difficulties in comparing the specific situation of individual defendants, such comparisons are possible, valuable, and – above all – necessary if the sentencing regime is to have predictability or consistency. These comparisons suggest that, by injecting considerable indeterminacy into the allocation of punishment, plea bargains undermine its retributive value.[80] To be sure, nothing is *per se* improper about basing punishment on managerial economy, pragmatics, incentivizing rewards, and prosecutorial strategizing.

When taken together, these factors can constitute a compelling basis on which to justify the allocation of punishment. However, this basis never has been articulated as an explicit goal or objective of punishment by the international tribunals. To this end, basing punishment thereupon only can be assessed in relation to how it plays with the avowed goals of sentencing, in this case retribution. And it does not seem to play well. Plea bargaining may mix more easily with reconciliatory, restorative, or reintegrative aspirations of punishment but, insofar as these are only distantly conceptualized or operationalized by the ad hoc tribunals, this relationship is more one of conjecture than actual practice.

Perhaps responding to the ICTY's lead, national courts in the states emerging from the former Yugoslavia also have implemented plea bargaining (for example, Bosnia and Herzegovina's criminal procedure saw the introduction of plea bargaining in 2003). Many judges in domestic courts award huge discounts for guilty pleas in the name of administrative economy. These discounts make it difficult for punishment to retain retributive value.

Many (at least half) of the extraordinary international criminals prosecuted by the East Timor Special Panels pled guilty.[81] Resultant plea agreements often were encouragingly affirmed by the Special Panels, who extolled how plea agreements aided in the administration of justice.[82] In terms of quantification of sentence, those who pled guilty in East Timor received a significant discount. Overall, the Special Panels had shown a "markedly lenient approach" to those who pled guilty, cutting around half of the sentence that would otherwise have been imposed.[83]

Many East Timorese defendants pled guilty, however, not because of sentencing concessions (many may not even have understood the plea-bargaining process) but, rather, because of a "cultural[] commit[ment] to a world view that places tremendous value on confession, apology, and reconciliation."[84] This suggests that the motivation for guilty pleas as gleaned from domestic common law legal systems, namely the desire for a reduced sentence among ordinary common criminals, does not *ipso facto* apply to all contexts of extraordinary international criminality. The incorporation of plea bargaining from its entrenched status in these systems to the very different context of the punishment of international crimes represents yet another example of borrowing from the familiar to ground the extraordinary. However, "the wholesale transplant of plea bargaining practices that successfully procure guilty pleas in the context of domestic crimes is likely to prove inefficient and ineffective in the context of many international crimes."[85] The East Timorese situation thereby demonstrates the value of an accountability paradigm that is implemented through differentiated kinds of procedures keyed to the sociolegal particularities of the afflicted society, instead of a simple transplant.

The ICTR also has incorporated plea agreements, including charge bargaining.[86] For example, Paul Bisengimana, a former mayor, was sentenced by an ICTR Trial Chamber in April 2006 to fifteen years' imprisonment for his role in the murder of one thousand Tutsi who had sought refuge in a church.[87] He had pled guilty to two charges of murder and extermination. In return, the

Prosecutor dropped eight other counts, including genocide, complicity in genocide, and rape. Overall, though, plea bargaining has not been particularly prevalent at the ICTR. This is so for a number of reasons. One reason is that the ICTR's
first guilty plea, which involved Jean Kambanda (the Rwandan Prime Minister
during the genocide), led to a life sentence. This sentence was imposed over
Kambanda's objections and, arguably, his understanding during the plea discussions. Kambanda certainly did not intend a life sentence to issue from the guilty
plea and, unsurprisingly, this outcome placed the plea-bargaining process into
a certain level of disrepute. As an aside, it is noteworthy that Kambanda was
given absolutely no sentencing discount for the reconciliatory and truth-telling
value of his timely guilty plea, unlike the ICTY's treatment of Plavšić's plea.[88]
This constitutes yet another example of the evident – and poorly justified –
sentencing disparities between the ICTY and ICTR.

Another reason why there has been infrequent plea bargaining at the ICTR
is because, according to Combs, many ICTR defendants are dissuaded from
pleading guilty by ideological factors.[89] This behavior also would appear to erode
international criminal law's deterrent capacity as well, insofar as this capacity
is predicated on the assumption that individuals shall modify their behavior in
light of the threat of punishment. The fact that defendants are insufficiently
moved by the prospect of reduced punishment to alter their behavior *ex post*
belies the possibility such defendants would be willing to alter their behavior *ex
ante*.

Guilty pleas are more frequent in the domestic Rwandan legal system than
at the ICTR. This is the case *despite* the fact that the requirements of pleading
guilty are more onerous within Rwanda than they are at the ICTR. What might
account for the greater frequency? One possible explanatory factor is that, within
the Rwandan system, the sentencing discounts for those who confess and plead
guilty are somewhat predictable (at least in terms of ranges). Another possible
explanation is that nearly all defendants at the ICTR are high-level accused
who, by virtue of their status, are less inclined to plead guilty owing to a deeper
ideological commitment. A third is that Rwandan defendants – particularly
lower-level accused – are more willing to plead guilty within the neotraditional
gacaca process than within an adversarial criminal trial.

In Rwanda – at the levels of the conventional courts as well as *gacaca* – the
confession and guilty plea process is not as much of a contractual exchange
as it is at the ad hoc tribunals. The *in situ* process (albeit inescapably affected
by downward pressures from the international) involves greater adherence to
standards of truthfulness and apology, although it is very far from a guarantor
thereof. Plea negotiations do not appear to be the norm. Rather, there is a
tendency toward pleading guilty to the charges as stated. Partial or dubious
guilty pleas are rejected, although judges can (and do) count such pleas outside
of the statutory scheme in mitigation of sentence. In the case of *gacaca*, the
General Assembly (namely, the population of the afflicted community) is able
to reject confessions considered to be incomplete or insincere. This provides an
important democratizing element that contrasts with the exclusion of afflicted

populations from plea-bargain negotiations undertaken at the ad hoc tribunals. If the plea is accepted, the offender becomes subject to a somewhat standardized regime of discount in which there is discretion within established ranges (this discretion is contoured by some determined mitigating and aggravating factors). Overall, I believe that the domestic Rwandan legal system (both the national courts and *gacaca*) demonstrates greater predictability, rhyme, and reason in handling plea discounts than is the case with the ad hoc tribunals.

(II) DETERRENCE

Deterrence theory justifies punishment not because it is deserved, but rather because punishment consequentially builds a safer world.[90] Insofar as deterrence assumes that individuals will be dissuaded from offending (or reoffending) because they fear getting punished, it posits that law is capable of fulfilling a social engineering function. Deterrence can be specific to individual offenders or general to the community of potential offenders. There is some scattered reference to the merits of specific deterrence in the jurisprudence of institutions that punish extraordinary international criminals.[91] However, the focus overwhelmingly is on general deterrence, namely the notion that if one person is punished, this will reduce the likelihood that another person in that same place or somewhere else will offend in the future.[92] As an ICTR Trial Chamber intoned, punishment "dissuade[s] for ever[] others who may be tempted in the future to perpetrate such atrocities [...]."[93] The UN Secretary-General has explicitly endorsed the value of the international criminal tribunals in "deter[ring] further horrors."[94]

Can criminal law deter atrocity? Although there are scattered anecdotal reports that suggest that potential extraordinary international criminals are deterred by the punishment of others following criminal trials,[95] no systematized or conclusive evidence has been proffered.[96] In any event, any anecdotal research must absorb the reality that at times atrocity has continued to occur in places following the creation of criminal tribunals to punish perpetrators. The ICTY stands out as an example. It was created in 1993. However, some of the gravest atrocities in the former Yugoslavia, including the Srebrenica massacre (1995) and Kosovo ethnic cleansing (1998), occurred while the ICTY was in full operation. Assuredly, it is somewhat facile to conclude that deterrence may not be actualized just because atrocity continues after the establishment of a punishing institution. After all, we can never know how much worse atrocity might have been if no institution ever had been created. That said, all things considered, just because we may have some cause to think that some deterrence has been achieved does not mean that the extant paradigm effectively deters. Other approaches to sanctioning universally repugnant crimes might be more adept in attaining deterrent aspirations.

One reality that deterrence theory must contend with is the very low chance that offenders ever are accused or, if accused, that they ever are taken into the custody of criminal justice institutions. Selectivity is especially corrosive to the deterrent value of prosecution and punishment. Criminologists long have posited that it is the chance of getting caught and the promptness of punishment, and not the severity of punishment, that affects behavior.[97] International tribunals are particularly vexed by the difficulties they experience in capturing indictees. Insofar as international tribunals lack their own police force or agents of enforcement, they can become dependent on the cooperation of the same national authorities whose jurisdiction they may have ousted. In its early years, the ICTY was stymied by the difficulty it experienced in capturing indictees. ICTY officials tenaciously persevered, however, and, as of December 2005, only 6 out of a total of 161 indictees remain at large (although, for the moment, this group includes high-profile suspects such as Mladić and Karadzić).[98] Eighteen of the ICTR indictees remain at large (the ICTR has arrested seventy-two individuals). Before closing up shop, the East Timor Special Panels were able to prosecute only 87 of 370 indicted individuals. Many indictees roam around free in Indonesia.

Moreover, being brought into custody to face trial is one thing; actually being convicted is another. International criminal law's focus on individual culpability provable beyond a reasonable doubt – a hallmark of liberal legalism – sharply reduces the number of people who can plausibly be brought into the dock because there always is a risk that insufficiently compelling evidence will lead to an acquittal. This risk is cited as one of the reasons in favor of introducing vicarious liability theories into international criminal law, such as JCE, to which the field exhibits considerable skittishness. Although JCE may promote deterrence by increasing the number of potential convicts, any such increase is a minor one at the margins. There are only a small number of defendants for whom JCE has played a material difference in terms of the prospect of conviction.

In some cases, national institutions are more successful in obtaining custody over accused offenders. In Rwanda, well over one hundred thousand accused have been taken into custody. However, in other contexts few (and sometimes no) suspects are indicted or taken into custody by national authorities. National institutions often are crimped in the exercise of criminal punishment by amnesties that, in certain cases, may be implemented for eminently laudable goals of political transition or peace. In other cases, national authorities simply elect to forget the past.

In sum, the chances of getting caught for committing egregious violations of human rights – certainly for heads of state and superior officers – are higher today than they were prior to the establishment of institutions at the international level. That said, notwithstanding the fact that the prospect of getting caught is greater than it once was, it still remains tiny.

At this juncture, an interlocutor committed to deterrence theory might respond: if the problem is limited to a lack of institutions, constabulary, and finances, that problem is easy to rectify. Just create more institutions! Provide more money! And, thereby, increase the likelihood of getting caught. Accordingly, so goes the argument, shortcomings with deterrence are not intrinsic to the theory. Instead, they derive from the functionally inadequate way in which the theory currently is implemented: the deterrence objective is attainable, but remains underachieved by virtue of administrative limitations.

At first blush, it seems plausible that creating new institutions might go some way to augment deterrence. However, I remain unconvinced that, fundamentally, the existence of more liberal legalist punishing institutions would *effectively* deter committed extraordinary international criminals. This is because deterrence's assumption of a certain degree of perpetrator rationality, which is grounded in liberalism's treatment of the ordinary common criminal, seems particularly ill fitting for those who perpetrate atrocity. This assumption already is hotly debated within the context of isolated common crime. However, its viability is even more problematic in the context of the chaos of massive violence, incendiary propaganda, and upended social order that contours atrocity. Do genocidal fanatics, industrialized into well-oiled machineries of death, make cost-benefit analyses prior to beginning work? In the specific case of terrorism, will a suicide bomber be deterred by fear of punishment in the event of capture? Although certain people may be deterred from killing or raping in pursuit of eliminationist goals by a fear of imminent retaliation (i.e., an enemy army coming around the corner), there is little to suggest that the threat of punishment by a distant international court would deter. I am not alone in my skepticism.[99] Mégret opines that "[i]t beggars belief to suggest that the average crazed nationalist purifier or abused child soldier . . . will be deterred by the prospect of facing trial."[100] He adds that this assumption is "a typical case of liberalism's hegemonious tendency of constructing the other in its own self-image, preferably along the lines of some reductionist form of economic rational choice theory."[101]

Let us examine two painful realities that jeopardize the assumption of perpetrator rationality amid cataclysmic events. These are: first, gratification; and, second, survival.

First, many perpetrators *want* to belong to violent groups.[102] They find comfort and solidarity in these groups. For many participants, violence has meaning and is compelling. Although certain group organizers may be coldly motivated by bureaucratic ambitions (such as Adolf Eichmann's goal of advancing his career) that might be deterred by the threat of eventual punishment or demotion, many individuals organized as foot soldiers of evil share an affective motivation for discriminatory killing. They are captured by angry social norms or, at least, are captivated by them. As Jaime Malamud-Goti observes, many participants believe that they are acting for the benefit of the collective, not their own personal gain.[103] It is simply not evident that the risk of punishment will deter people from engaging in violent behavior that they, at the time, believe is morally justifiable and perhaps even necessary – if not downright gratifying.[104]

Even assuming *arguendo* that rational choice were possible in the cataclysm of mass violence, for some people the value of killing or dying for a cause exceeds the value of living peacefully without the prospect of punishment. Participants often are motivated by immediate approval from their peers. Cravings for such approval easily can outweigh the dissuasive effect of distant, and often hypothetical, punishment by an alien international criminal tribunal. Why incur immediate ostracism in situations where, as perpetrators themselves note, one person's insubordination would have made no difference anyway? Alette Smeulers reports:

> Many perpetrators [. . .] convince themselves that they do not really have any control and that it would not have made a difference if they had stood up and refused to carry out the order. Stangl, commander of Treblinka, said: If I had sacrificed myself, if I had made public what I felt and had died . . . it would have made no difference. Not an iota. It would all have gone on just the same, as if it and I had never happened.[105]

Second, amid the social disintegration and group-based reconstitution that usually precedes mass violence, individuals often end up joining a marauding group because to do so is the only viable survival strategy. Anthropologists have documented such motivations in a variety of contexts, including among child soldiers in Sierra Leone.[106] After all, if one is not part of the group, one is alone. Being alone makes it all the easier to become victimized or perceived as belonging with or sympathetic to the "other." Fears of aloneness are particularly pronounced among many militia recruits – orphaned children, adolescents, and young men without families: in many cases poor and without occupational skills. Even those individuals for whom violence is not gratifying may willingly join, insofar as participating in massacre can guarantee survival to the next morning. There is something luxurious, if not utopian, in the notion that individuals in such desperate circumstances are amenable to being deterred by the prospect of some distant international or domestic institution that might punish them several years after their side might lose the conflict they currently are embroiled in. This requires a heavy burden of proof on the part of deterrence theorists. This burden has not been satisfactorily discharged. Although individuals who join a marauding group for petty material gain might be deterred by the criminal law, the same cannot be said for those who join to survive. And those who join for survival purposes become much more committed and rigorous in their killing than those who join merely to acquire incidental material trinkets.

Accordingly, criminal trials face significant obstacles in achieving their goal of deterring killers. Criminal trials face even greater difficulty in reaching benefiting bystanders, another key group identified in Chapter 2. Essentially, liberal criminal law leaves the masses unaccountable: its narrow focus persists *despite* the fact that support and acquiescence of the masses is the singular prerequisite for atrocity truly to become epidemic. Violence becomes normalized when neighbors avert their gaze, draw the blinds, and excitedly move into a suddenly available apartment. This broad public participation, despite its catalytic role, is overlooked by criminal law, thereby perpetuating a myth and a deception. The myth is that a handful of people are responsible for endemic levels of violence. The deception, which inures to the benefit of powerful states and organizations, involves hiding the myriad political, economic, historical, and colonial factors that create conditions precedent for violence.[107]

Because the silence of the majority, the acquiescence of the bystander, the enrichment of neighbors, and the nonfeasance of international organizations never is implicated by a system based on criminalization, any such system does little to deter these essential prerequisites to mass violence. Although the trial represents closure, this closure may be chimeric; and, more ominously, prematurely might divert attention from more expansive reconstruction efforts or dull our sensibilities regarding the inadequacies of criminal trials in unearthing many of the root causes of systemic violence. On the other hand, a broader-based approach that contemplates diverse, including collectively based, sanctions might reduce the appeal of passively acquiescing and, thereby, turn some erstwhile bystanders into gatekeepers who shutter out and shut down conflict entrepreneurs before it becomes too late. I contend that the passive support of the public that benefits from eliminationism but is not intoxicated by it might, to some degree at least, be dissipated by regulatory structures that sanction passive support. I develop this idea in Chapter 7. Although it is not evident that collective sanctions actually will dissuade public acquiescence (perhaps the passive public also lies beyond deterrence?), what is evident is that a regulatory system based on select criminalization, which never even reaches the key constituency of the passive public, forecloses this possibility and with it a valuable line of research and inquiry.

International criminal law is deeply paradoxical: it courageously operates in opposition to state interests while stubbornly protecting state interests.[108] To the extent that international criminal law pins blame for atrocity on a small number of horrible individuals, who generally control a state apparatus, it achieves some justice and curbs atrocity as a tool of a state's foreign or domestic policy. However, if in the process of attributing guilt it pulls our gaze away from the many other actors involved in the tapestry of atrocity – including malfeasant, complicit, or distracted states and their officials, along with decisionmakers in international organizations – then it will do little to root out atrocity's multicausal origins. A fuller picture of responsibility for wrongdoing will emerge only to the extent that we resist simple, and comforting, criminal explanations and reach deeper to a more embarassing place. The institutionalization of some accountability through criminal trials – and the conversations these trials produce – must not lull us into thinking we have attained justice, but should prod us to go much further.

(III) EXPRESSIVISM

Expressivists contend that trial, conviction, and punishment appreciate public respect for law. The expressivist punishes to strengthen faith in rule of law among the general public, as opposed to punishing simply because the perpetrator deserves it or because potential perpetrators will be deterred by it. Expressivism also transcends retribution and deterrence in claiming as a central goal the crafting of historical narratives, their authentication as truths, and their pedagogical dissemination to the public. Overall, expressive objectives receive less attention than retribution or deterrence in the jurisprudence of institutions that pursue extraordinary international criminals, although they are reliably invoked as justifications for imposing sanction.[109]

Much of expressive theory relates to trial and conviction. For example, Judge Patricia Wald observes that taking indictees into custody and prosecuting them "put[s] the flesh of situational application on the bareboned definitions of war crimes, crimes against humanity, and genocide [...]."[110] It is tempting for the expressivist who extols the norm-generating and dramaturgical function of law to focus on trial and conviction. However, punishment, too, has significant messaging value – both as an end in and of itself and, also, as contributing to the force of prosecution and conviction. David Garland posits that punishment "communicates meaning ... about power, authority, legitimacy, normality, morality, personhood, social relations, and a host of other tangential matters."[111] The fact that consequences follow a guilty verdict makes law all the more real to the community.[112] This sends a message that the law is to be taken seriously. Emile Durkheim observed that by expressing condemnation, punishment in fact could strengthen social solidarity.[113] Punishment internalizes – and even reinforces – social norms among the public and, thereby, from the expressivist perspective proactively promotes law-abiding behavior. Moreover, punishment can serve a prophylactic purpose – carrying with it significant therapeutic value for victims.

If punishment signals the absolute immutability of core values – for example, the universal repugnance of discriminatory group-based killings – then initial plans by conflict entrepreneurs to inveigle and habituate killers may stall. Punishment can thereby impede the early indoctrination phases in which average citizens become assimilated into the machinery of mass violence. This objective of punishment differs from deterring individuals from killing after they have become habituated into killing by desire or desperation. Whereas it seems problematic to deter – through fear of distant and deferred punishment – violence once it is imminent or has already begun, it seems somewhat more plausible to inhibit the mainstreaming of hatemongering as politics owing to the consolidation, through law and punishment, of a social consensus regarding the *moral unacceptability* of such politics. Law and punishment may be able to decelerate indoctrination because potential indoctrinees to the inchoate stages where hate is normalized have come to see discrimination-based massacre as manifestly illegal. Assuredly, it is difficult to combat the dizzying effects of propaganda. But if punishment can create principled citizens who value a normative structure that repudiates group-based eliminationism, then the size and attentiveness of the propagandists' audience would drop. In this vein, punishment operates as moral educator.[114]

Legal process can narrate history and thereby express shared understandings of the provenance, particulars, and effects of mass violence; punishing the offender contributes yet another layer of authenticity to this narration. Truthtelling (or, more colloquially, "discovering the truth") has been acknowledged by international criminal tribunals and is itself tied to a number of other goals, including the consequentialist goal of national reconciliation.[115] Discovering the truth also is frequently evoked by atrocity victims as an important objective of retrospective legal interventions. Trials create archives of information: either through documents, as at Nuremberg, or through testimony, as at Eichmann's trial in Jerusalem. The ICTY's dogged prosecution of the Srebrenica massacre led to "an archive of eyewitness accounts and often gruesome photographs and videos."[116] These materials can turn tragedy into a teaching moment. Trials can educate the public through the spectacle of theater – there is, after all, pedagogical value to performance and communicative value to dramaturgy.[117] This performance is made all the more weighty by the reality that, coincident with the closing act, comes the infliction of shame, sanction, and stigma upon the antagonists. Prosecution and punishment in response to extraordinary crimes can thereby serve a broader didactic purpose that meets the interests of history and memory.[118]

The ICTR's judicial characterization of the massacre that took place in Rwanda in 1994 as genocide serves the purpose of indelibly memorializing the violence; the ICTY Appeals Chamber also very consciously used its judgment in *Krstić* as a vehicle to pursue declaratory objectives so as to officialize the Srebrenica tragedy as genocide.[119] Prosecution and punishment can manufacture an authoritative version of the truth and, thereby, narrate a story that later becomes history. The IMT at Nuremberg put a repertoire of Nazi barbarities on display and condemned – before the international community – those of its architects who had survived so as, in the words of Robert Jackson, to "establish incredible events by credible evidence."[120] Now, sixty years later, the Nuremberg judgment remains a fixed anchor of our children's education.

There is good reason to believe that the punishment inflicted by an international tribunal operating prominently on the global agenda at the cusp of history has enhanced expressive value in asserting the importance of law, the stigmatization of the offender who transgresses that law, and the authenticity of the historical narrative that ensues. International trials have a better chance of becoming the kinds of "popular trials" that define a debate, remind us of the content and value of law, or serve as intergenerational "signposts" in history.[121] This is in part because international trials reach a global audience.[122] Their liberal legalist modalities are intelligible to communities in the epicenters of global power. Their reliance on due process may help justice to be seen to be done. On the other hand, too much due process may give rise to technical proceedings seen to be overly tilted in favor of iniquitous defendants, who become able to grandstand and humiliate witnesses.

The didactic value of international proceedings is not preordained. The Tokyo Tribunal has not become a pedagogical anchor in a manner comparable to the Nuremberg Tribunal. Contemporary international institutions must be careful not to overlook the audience that matters more than any other – namely, directly afflicted populations. Perceptions among such populations that contemporary institutions lack clean hands will not be dissipated by fastidious adherence to due process alone. In determining a process to be just, audiences will assess much more that simply whether it accords with liberal legalism.

Other than *Eichmann*, national trials of Nazi atrocity – whether conducted by civilian or military instrumentalities – have not reached Nuremberg's expressivist level.[123] That said, national proceedings regarding Nazi atrocity did produce salient expressive content, even when it came to the implication of non-Germans. The *Barbie, Touvier*, and *Papon* trials were, at least for the French nation, didactically valuable popular events. Other proceedings, despite resulting in lenient sentences completely disproportionate to the gravity of the underlying offenses, narrated the horrors of the Nazi concentration camps to a bewildered public. These proceedings – many of which were undertaken by West German courts – filled a critical gap in the historical tapestry insofar as the Nuremberg prosecutions were directed toward Nazi aggressive war, not crimes against humanity or the Holocaust.[124] Furthermore, one of the strengths of certain national institutions is the diversity of mechanisms they rely upon to didactically weave narratives. In Rwanda, for example, the *partie civile* lawsuits adduce and personalize stories of suffering and loss in a victim-centered manner. *Mato oput* in Uganda relies on ritual to reintegrate offenders while respecting their own suffering, which seems particularly apt in the case of child soldiers.

Assuredly, whether liberal criminal trials narrate historical truths that, in turn, have expressive legitimacy remains a contested question.[125] I believe they are capable of such a function, although I certainly recognize that alternate forms of accountability may have equivalent or even enhanced truth-telling capacity. I also recognize that criminal prosecution, followed by incarceration, is limited in its truth-telling function. In particular, four specific aspects of criminal process and sanction challenge the quality of the narrative output. These aspects are: (1) selective truths; (2) interrupted performances; (3) management strategies; and (4) plea bargains. I consider each of these in turn.

a. *Selective Truths*

Criminal trials are deliberately selective in terms of the truths they produce. The application of modern rules of evidence and procedure frames this selectivity. These rules favor the production of logical and microscopic truths over the dialogic and experiential truths that emerge phenomenologically from restorative justice initiatives.[126] For Miriam Aukerman, the formalism and rigidity of trials make them at times "excruciatingly boring."[127]

The rules may create more than just tedium. Although bolstering the authenticity of the narrative, these rules paradoxically also may crimp it. For example, Martti Koskenniemi writes that evidentiary rules and due process may undermine memory by allowing the accused to belittle accusers in cross-examination and reduce their accusations to "panicky 'I don't know' statements."[128] Rules may truncate victim storytelling, thereby sowing disappointment;[129] but, on the other hand, may control the extent to which victim storytelling serves ulterior political purposes unrelated to the guilt or innocence of the accused. Rules also exclude as nonprobative certain facts that local audiences might find deeply relevant and, in this regard, distort the historical narrative. The situation of Belgian courts adjudging Rwandan *génocidaires* constitutes an example. Although the Belgian prosecutions should be lauded for bringing systematic human rights abusers to justice, they also rewrite the historical record by presenting Belgium as a font of justice, instead of weaving into the judicial narrative the much more complicated role Belgian colonial interventions played in exacerbating ethnic divisions in Rwanda that laid the groundwork for eventual genocide.

Expressive value is further threatened by the reality that this value often is externalized from afflicted local communities owing to the distance and mistrust evident between such communities and international criminal tribunals. Procedural differences between liberal criminal trials and expectations among local populations, in particular non-Western populations, also diminish the prophylactic value of verdict and punishment.

b. *Interrupted Performances*

The death of Slobodan Milošević in the midst of his trial (which, at the time of his death, had gone on for four years) illustrates the frailties of criminal process. To be sure, a trial that stops short of verdict and punishment is not denuded of all expressive value. Prosecuting Milošević allowed a worldwide public to learn in dribs and drabs of the charges against him and the details of the atrocities he allegedly coordinated. Instrumentally speaking, some of the testimonial and documentary evidence introduced during the Milošević proceedings will be used against other defendants. But Milošević's death denied the possibility of a final sentence: infallible and authoritative. The curtain fell before the closing act. When the antagonist dies before the protagonist's pursuit is complete, the script becomes frustrated. The performance reaches an end, but it is an anticlimax. A formal adversarial trial cannot continue posthumously, at least not under current understandings of internationalized due process.

Milošević's premature death is an obstacle to the ICTY's narration of an overarching story of death and destruction in the Balkans. The ICTY has mitigated the impact of this obstacle by indicting 161 individuals in total; and, quickly following Milošević's death, by moving ahead with other high-profile trials, including regarding atrocity at Srebrenica and in Kosovo. That said, the ICTY had plea-bargained with other defendants, giving up reduced sentences in exchange for the promise of prized testimony against Milošević. These bargains crimped the expressive value of punishing those defendants in the hopes of a blockbuster impact in ringingly convicting Milošević.

The expressive vulnerabilities of criminal trials, and the impact of an interrupted performance, can be minimized to the extent that the net of accountability is broadened. In particular, if accountability ranges beyond high-profile criminal trials, the resultant greater methodological diversification diminishes the risk that an interrupted performance scuttles the overall truth-telling process.

The prosecution of leaders rendered frail through the passage of time necessarily involves a race against time. The sooner justice is delivered the better. Wily defendants can dither, piddle, and delay. Popular trials create a platform that places the defendant onto the world's center stage. If the defendant can make the trial all about himself, and selfishly control the stage though grandstanding, histrionics, and manipulation, then the proceedings drift away from the victims and their terrible losses.

c. *Management Strategies*

The Milošević trial's performativity was susceptible to interruption in part because the trial had dragged on for so long. The Iraqi High Tribunal (IHT) applied some lessons learned from the languidness of the Milošević proceedings to its prosecution of Ba'ath Party leaders, including Saddam Hussein.

First, IHT judges exhibited greater vigilance than their ICTY counterparts in controlling the courtroom and the content of the discussions. On the one hand, tight control secures managerial and bureaucratic goals, streamlines process, dissipates inflammatory controversy, and preserves judicial authority. On the other hand, though, as levels of control become too tight, they may strangle the judicial record and thereby inflict credibility costs. Flattening the narratives to protect power drains some of their transformative content.

Second, IHT prosecutors elected to proceed through a series of minitrials instead of, as had been the case with Milošević, one overwhelming omnibus sixty-six count proceeding. The first minitrial, which led to convictions for crimes against humanity and war crimes against seven defendants (and a variety of sentences, including a death sentence for Saddam Hussein), involved the killings – at the hands of the Iraqi state – of 148 residents of the Shiite village of Dujail.[130] In 1982, Dujail had been the site of a failed assassination attempt against Hussein. In response, Iraqi security forces detained suspects. The Iraqi Revolutionary Court subsequently sentenced these villagers to death. Executions were carried out. Hussein's signature was on the orders.

Subsequent IHT minitrials do involve a higher-stakes context: for example, proceedings related to the Anfal (Arabic for "spoils of war") campaign, which had resulted in the allegedly genocidal massacre of at least (a conservative estimate) 50,000 Kurdish civilians in 1988, and the crushing of the 1991 Shiite uprising in the south. By proceeding sequentially, IHT prosecutors ensure cyclical episodes of gratification and closure, thereby reducing the risks that long-term proceedings lead to a deferred all or nothing outcome. They allow different victim groups, for example Kurds and Shias, to express outrage at the travesties inflicted upon them through context-specific proceedings. This is a prudential move. However, it is not without its own drawbacks. It results in a dramaturgical methodology in which the narrative is told through iterated vignettes. IHT officials need to be diligent that the digestible parts add up to a compelling, overarching whole. If discontinuous lower-stakes convictions remain narratively fragmented, then the IHT may, in the name of prudence, have forsaken the opportunity to leave a hardier historical footprint. Moreover, hanging Hussein for the Dujail conviction before the remaining minitrials took place induced an interrupted performance detrimental to the expressive value of these other proceedings.

d. *Pleading Out*

Can plea bargains attain truth-telling objectives? Indeed, offenders who plead guilty may admit wrongdoing, apologize, express remorse, dignify victims, and provide details regarding the crimes. Self-convicting offenders may even implicate others, although this is not always the case (nor is there any guarantee of the veracity of the evidence subsequently proffered).[131] With regard to high-level accused, where the exacting nature of the criminal law requires the leader to be traced to the bodies interred in the mass grave, plea bargains can offer a partial print of the truth whose value exceeds that of the acquittal that might result should the prosecution be unable to meet the high threshold of proof demanded in the pursuit of microscopic and logical truths.

Although the ad hoc tribunals affirm that plea bargains contribute to truth-telling objectives,[132] certain institutionalized aspects of plea bargaining at the ad hoc tribunals whittle down the narrative value of plea-bargained convictions and sentences. Although some agreements contain a detailed factual basis, in other cases the offender pleads guilty to fairly bare allegations. In the latter case, the offender avoids contending with the gruesome, detailed evidence that would be admitted at trial. Deronjić's plea agreement, which was judicially affirmed, cursorily established the truth only regarding the tragedy that encompassed one village on one particular day, thereby burying several other potential truths – namely, accusations involving other spaces and places in Bosnia.[133]

Charge bargaining, in particular, jeopardizes expressive storytelling. Plavšić, in an agreement affirmed by the ICTY, pled guilty to one umbrella count of persecution as a crime against humanity and the Prosecutor dropped the remaining seven charges, including two counts of genocide and complicity in genocide.[134] In Milan Simić's case, the ICTY Prosecutor "agreed to withdraw several counts, including the most serious – persecution as a crime against humanity relating to Simić's mayor-like role [. . .]."[135] Simić, a paraplegic, was sentenced to five years' imprisonment. Combs notes that "such a sentence would have been unthinkable had the factual basis for Simić's conviction encompassed all the conduct for which he was initially charged."[136] As discussed earlier in the context of retribution, charge bargains push certain allegations off the agenda, thereby precluding the truth of those allegations from being officially unearthed. It is true that pleading guilty to an umbrella charge of persecution, a result that obtains in certain plea bargains, permits a broad array of facts, which may well support the substance of all of the original charges, to be included in the judicial record. However, the practice of the ad hoc tribunals has been spotty in this regard.

(IV) CONCLUSION

The preference for incarceration following what liberal international lawyers deem to be an acceptable criminal trial on the whole falls short of its penological objectives, in particular retribution and deterrence. This may be because those objectives are too ambitious. It may also be because the criminal law, standing alone, simply is not enough nor can ever be enough.

CHAPTER 7

From Law to Justice

In this chapter, I outline two proposals. These proposals begin a conversation. They do not seal a conclusion. The proposals respond to two major, and interconnected, shortcomings of dominant modalities of prosecution and incarceration: (1) the democratic deficits and externalization of justice that they trigger; and (2) the difficulties they experience in attaining stated penological objectives.

The two proposals, which I present as reforms, are: (1) *vertical*: to rescript the division of labor toward greater inclusiveness of *in situ* sociolegal institutions and bottom-up input; and (2) *horizontal*: to look beyond criminal process and welcome the general regulatory power of law, as well as extralegal interventions, to holistically capture the broad-based complicity that inheres in mass atrocity.

These two reforms are synergistic. When twinned, they promote a pluralistic understanding of accountability; their goal is to activate a broader sense of justice in the aftermath of atrocity. These reforms aim to move the agenda from law to justice: initially, by advancing international criminal law to a capacious law of atrocity and, ultimately, to an enterprise that constructively incorporates extrajudicial initiatives.

Of course, international criminal law as currently implemented through prosecution and incarceration goes some way to promote justice. But it is intrinsically limited. A richly multivalent approach could go further. It could push penological objectives, for instance reintegration and restoration, which heretofore have been given short shrift. Moreover, a richly multivalent approach could consolidate, and better attain, expressivism; and, perhaps, offer new ways of thinking about how deterrence and retribution – much more difficult objectives – might be operationalized. Such an approach also reminds international lawyers of an important lesson, wonderfully articulated by Paul Roberts, that international criminal law is only – and can only be – part of the justice picture.[1]

One implication of these reforms is that sanction might look different and assume different calibrations in each case of atrocity. Sanction might involve court proceedings *and* interventions by institutions other than courts. This recognizes the distinctiveness of each individual atrocity. Recognizing this distinctiveness is a valuable exercise. After all, although all three are genocides, the atrocities of the Holocaust, Rwanda, and Srebrenica (Bosnia) are not identical. Variation in sanction, however, creates some unevenness, perhaps even some messiness. Clarity, and our expectations for clarity, could cloud. I envision a penology that gains its independence through its embrace of procedural diversity. How does this accord with the position, to which I subscribe, that discrimination-based atrocity constitutes universal great evil? Might pluralist implementation fragment the coherence of the repudiation of the universal nature of the evils at hand? Before elaborating on the proposed reforms, I sketch a response to these questions. I draw from cosmopolitan theory to justify a position that holds that, although genocide and discrimination-based crimes against humanity are universal evils, they coherently can be sanctioned in diverse manners that may take different forms in light of the distinctive social geographies of various atrocities.

(i) PLURALIST PROCESS FOR UNIVERSAL EVIL?

Martti Koskenniemi engages with the notion that international law fundamentally is a European tradition derived from a desire to rationalize society through law.[2] From this general perch, it is not too far to jump to the specific conclusion that condemning the repugnance of extreme evil through law reflects a rationalization that may not be universally shared. Koskenniemi, however, goes on to conclude – in no uncertain terms – that "[t]he fact that international law is a European language does not even slightly stand in the way of its being capable of expressing something universal."[3]

And substantive international criminal law does express something universal, recognized by deep traditions in moral philosophy: namely, the condemnation of acts of great (or, in Arendt's phrasing, extreme) evil and wickedness. Stuart Hampshire sagely advises that "[t]here is nothing . . . culture-bound in the great evils of human experience, reaffirmed in every age and in every written history and in every tragedy or fiction [. . .]. That these great evils are to be averted is the constant presupposition of moral arguments at all times and in all places [. . .]."[4] David Luban, whose work bridges law, ethics, and morals, pointedly adds: "There is no society [. . .] in which gratuitous infliction of the great evils is tolerable."[5] No human being wishes to be victimized by the wicked or the evil. The concomitant to this right is a remedy. This remedy reflects another universally shared moral value, namely that the victims of great wickedness can demand that those who inflicted such acts upon them be held accountable.

It is one thing to agree to the universal repudiation of the great evils and to agree that victims are entitled to accountability. It is another matter to accept the universality of categorizing the great evils as crimes. This categorization is widely accepted among international lawmakers. It is one that the architecture of international criminal justice has internalized. Larry May finds deep justification for the universal categorization of the great evils as crimes.[6] May's work bears parallels to the *Eichmann* judgment, in which the Supreme Court of Israel affirmed the universal criminality of Eichmann's wrongdoings because they "constitute[d] acts which damage vital international interests," "impair[ed] the foundations and security of the international community," and violated "universal moral values and humanitarian principles."[7] One of the benefits of criminalizing the great evils is that the proscriptive certainty required by the criminal law has triggered fairly precise definitions of genocide and crimes against humanity.[8]

My argument regarding the universal condemnation of the great evils does not hinge upon proof of the universality of categorizing the great evils as crimes. I accept this categorization, at least functionally, insofar as I routinely invoke the settled category of extraordinary international criminality and contrast it to ordinary domestic criminality. Nonetheless, law can condemn behavior and repair victims in many ways. Behavior also can be condemned through sources exogenous to the law entirely. Accordingly, it could be argued that casting the great evils as crimes represents another imposition of Western juridical categories to a diverse world order. In the West, the most odious social transgressions are viewed as crimes sanctionable by the state through imprisonment or, exceptionally (and decreasingly), execution. This may not be the case everywhere, however. In other places, the most odious social transgressions may be cast as delicts sanctionable by society through restitution, reparation, or countermeasures. However, for the purposes of my argument, what matters is the universality of the condemnability of the underlying substantive harm, this being the infliction of great evil, and the universality of the notion that victimizers are to be held to account. In fact, as I unpack later in my discussion of horizontal pluralism, there is considerable value in classifying the great evils as something *more than just* crimes. Doing so expands the lexicon of international justice and, thereby, permits prudent application of the broader panoply of accountability modalities and methods that are available under law generally. Outreach to private law – such as obligation, tort, contract, and restitution – and to quasilegal initiatives – such as public inquiries and truth commissions – enhances the quality of accountability.

It is crucial to separate the substantive goals at hand, namely the condemnation of great evil and the promotion of accountability in its aftermath, from the process regarding *how* these goals are to be operationalized and the institutions *where* this process is to occur. All national legal systems know a distinction, albeit often blurred,[9] between process and substance. Supranational legal orders also know such a distinction.

It is at the level of the procedural, broadly defined, and the institutional, broadly understood, that international criminal law as *technique* is most susceptible to the claim of pyrrhic universalism, deeply rooted in Western visions of what process *should* look like. As May intuits: "Those of us raised in the Western legal tradition often have a visceral reaction to attempts to sidestep legal trials."[10] International criminal law does not exclude individuals outside this tradition through its condemnation of great evil but, rather, through the ascension and now expatriation of a particular mode of reporting evil and punishing perpetrators. It is at the procedural level that the contingency of international criminal law's universalism seems starkest. Assuredly, certain aspects of international criminal process tap into something genuinely universal in the human experience. For example, all legal systems envision the need for some relationship between wrongdoing and sanction. However, international criminal process has other modalities whose cultural contingency does not resonate universally, in particular with regard to sanction. One-size-fits-all application of these modalities creates dissonance, which is evident in places whose atrocities currently are being judicialized.

The modalities of international criminal law, in particular those related to punishment and sentence, tend to universalize through ideological preference instead of through an independent assessment of the social psychology of the violence, comparative reflection about how diverse justice traditions might punish, and development of multilateral interinstitutional conversations. The choices are not binary: namely, either to accept the received wisdom of extant internationalized institutions, on the one hand, or the void of impunity, on the other. It is disappointing that so much of the brilliant work of international criminal law, namely the definition of the substantive crimes and the march past impunity, has been accompanied by a seemingly casual path dependence in delineating institutions and methodologies capable of putting that work into action.[11]

That said, we must ask: are some legal processes simply better suited than others to denounce extreme evil, condemn it, and prevent its reemergence? If so, are Western methodologies of adjudication and punishment the best we have? Indeed, were this to be the case, then there would be some experiential or empirical justification for their influence over international discourse and their transplant back to national legal orders, even to those orders where they may not be indigenous. Clearly, there is much good in replacing the many things that do not work, or that work poorly, with the one that does work, or at least works better. Despite the monochrome that may result, the question at hand is not one of aesthetics.

However, in the case of internationalized modalities of punishment, this argument is not persuasive. The prevailing way of doing things fails to meet the principal goals that it places upon itself: namely, retribution and deterrence. I am not convinced that individualized criminal trials and incarceration self-evidently are the best that we can do. In fact, diversifying processual and penological methodologies could be a step toward augmenting our collective experiences, and empirical knowledge, with regard to the role and effectiveness of law in the aftermath of atrocity.

May notes "a strong Western bias" in the ICC and he provides starkly procedural examples of this, namely the adversarial method and cross-examination.[12] He then implies that some sort of procedural uniformity might be inevitable, "since courts must follow some model, whether Western or non-Western."[13] Assuredly, institutions must abide by *some* procedure, and May is wise to insist on this. But that procedure need not be the same everywhere. *Some* model does not ineluctably lead to the *same* model. Multiculturalist theorists such as Charles Taylor and Radhika Coomaraswamy teach us that the enforcement of positive human rights need not be static and flat. Coomaraswamy notes that "internationally accepted standards and norms do exist, in defiance of postmodernist tendencies. [...] What must be seen as negotiable are the strategies of enforcement and implementation [. . .]."[14] In a similar vein, the enforcement of humanity's right to hold its enemies accountable can proceed through diverse methodologies and integrated sanctions. In the end, humanity can coherently strive to implement universal values through pluralistic procedures and institutions.

(II) COSMOPOLITAN THEORY

The supple model of accountability that I propose is compatible with cosmopolitan visions of law and authority in the international context. Essentially, cosmopolitanism is a tradition in sociopolitical and legal philosophy according to which all human beings belong to a single community. This community derives from, and in turn fosters, certain shared values. Cosmopolitans differ as to the number, nature, and depth of the values that are shared.

Cosmopolitans hold in common a belief that we all owe some duties to each other. We have obligations and entitlements based on our status, in Diogenes the Cynic's phrasing, as "citizens of the world" rather than as citizens of a particular state.[15] Accordingly, we cannot think of distributive justice obligations as stopping at our national borders. Our responsibilities do not end at the customs and immigration desk. Instead, they seep beyond, to strangers in faraway lands. Cosmopolitanism, therefore, offers a philosophical basis for global governance over a global public.

As with all theoretical perspectives, cosmopolitanism is diverse. A wide variety of views can be called cosmopolitan. Although cosmopolitans often are depicted as avid universalists who shutter out local or national identities, this is a caricature. A more textured reading of cosmopolitan theory reveals much greater nuance. Even ancient cosmopolitans such as the Stoics recognized that the citizen of the world need not give up his or her local identifications. These identifications, in fact, enrich the citizen's life. Accordingly, the Stoics understood an individual's identity as ranging through concentric circles that extend outward from the personal, to the local, and, ultimately, to humanity as a whole: each circle constitutes an important element of overarching identity.[16]

Many contemporary cosmopolitans also engage with the diversity of the familial, local, and national. They accept that human beings have conservative sensibilities that find comfort and meaning in inherited localism. They acknowledge local identities as part of the complex nature of human agency and thereby recognize the pull of partiality and pluralism. The work of leading cosmopolitans such as Martha Nussbaum,[17] David Hollinger,[18] David Held,[19] Kok-Chor Tan,[20] Kwame Anthony Appiah,[21] and Paul Schiff Berman[22] recognizes, and in most cases welcomes, multiple affiliations and overlapping associations.

Among contemporary cosmopolitans, Nussbaum is blunt about her belief that an emphasis on patriotic pride is "morally dangerous."[23] She warns that "patriotism is very close to jingoism."[24] However, even Nussbaum refuses to negate the fact that "all profound human matters are differently realized in different societies."[25] She holds to the position that "[n]one of the major thinkers in the cosmopolitan tradition denied that we can and should give special attention to [...] our own ties of religious and national belonging."[26] Appiah is bolder in arguing that it is possible for a person to be a cosmopolitan and also a patriot.[27] Humanity can commit to universal standards while celebrating difference. For Appiah, cosmopolitanism in fact delights in the diversity of human cultures. Institutions can have cosmopolitan obligations (as envisioned by Nussbaum) that, I would add, they can articulate through local conduits, even those that may strike the sophisticated global citizen as parochial. Institutions, for instance the ICC, could host the kind of conversations that Appiah believes bridge encounters among "people from different ways of life."[28]

Tan, while recognizing certain universal moral concerns, takes national and patriotic attachments seriously. For Tan, these attachments have a defined place within a cosmopolitan theory of justice. In *Democracy and the Global Order*, Held explores how power could be exercised beyond the jurisdiction of states at the global level for a global public, but he also recognizes that such an exercise of power could promote a democratic deficit. Berman offers a particularly interpenetrative and flexible approach to cosmopolitanism. He notes: "A cosmopolitan conception of law [...] aims to capture a middle ground between strict territorialism on the one hand and expansive universalism on the other."[29] Attachments can be fluid, multilayered, and malleable. Consequently, cosmopolitanism is not inhospitable to pluralism. Berman concludes:

> A cosmopolitan conception [...] makes no attempt to deny the multirooted nature of individuals within a variety of communities, both territorial and non-territorial. [...] [C]osmopolitanism offers a promising rubric for analyzing law in a world of diverse normative voices. [...] [I]t celebrates diverse normative orders in multiple communities and need not insist on homogenizing that diversity into one global culture of one international legal framework.[30]

The model I propose recognizes the universality of our shared membership in a moral community that condemns great evil and entitles victims thereof, in particular those most directly affected, to accountability. This aligns the model with the basic precept of cosmopolitanism. Moreover, the model adopts cosmopolitanism's acceptance of the richness of local identifications, particularly when this richness helps promote justice and the ability for people to lead (and live) a good life. The notion of diverse procedure for universal wrongdoing thereby fits within a cosmopolitan theory of law, tending toward the pluralist end of the continuum. I avail myself of the term "cosmopolitan pluralism"[31] to describe this position. Cosmopolitan pluralism would support substantive censure at the global level, but endeavor to allay democratic deficit concerns through optimistic incorporation of local control, process, and sanction. Another advantage to reforms that promote cosmopolitan pluralism horizontally and vertically is that these reforms recognize that, although instances of genocide and crimes against humanity are universally condemnable, each particular instance is original in its own regard and thereby retains a level of distinctiveness. Cosmopolitan pluralist reform would preserve the expressive value of punishing the universal while respecting the importance of not flattening the particular by permitting accountability modalities to vary in each individual case.[32] It is through this relational interplay between universal accountability and pluralistic enforcement that an independent criminology and penology for mass atrocity can emerge.

A premise of this book is that one of the reasons international criminal law falls short is because it treats the extraordinary international criminal like the ordinary common criminal. One extrapolation that could be made from this premise is the need to develop a cosmopolitan vision of punishment the content of which, different than that applied to ordinary criminals, becomes universally applicable to all extraordinary international criminals everywhere. This is not the direction I take. Such a direction, in fact, runs counter to a pluralized vision of punishment in which local attachments are to be welcomed and in which applications of authority ought to begin with the bottom-up and not push down from the transnational top. Within this pluralized vision, some societies might decide that it is in their best interests to subject the extraordinary international criminal to common processes of adversarial prosecution and isolated incarceration. Obviously some polities – for instance, in the West – already have done so. It is possible that many polities freely come to the same conclusion.[33] It is probable that some will not, while others will come to a more nuanced position. Regardless of the direction that actual pluralism takes us, the current internationalization of the preference for prosecution and incarceration is not the result of bottom-up consensus but, rather, the product of powerful state and political interests. This leads to disquieting results insofar as the application of international criminal law overwhelmingly occurs in non-Western localities where formal state institutions that propound criminal trial modalities may do so for ulterior motivations. Western prosecution and punishment for deviant criminals has become transplanted to (and for) places where it may not reflect what afflicted populations would in good faith come up with on their own for group-based tragedies.

Until the voices of afflicted populations are more clearly heard, and loosened from the primacy or complementarity of internationalist visions, we simply do not know exactly what values pertaining to the punishment of the enemies of humankind truly are shared among us all. Herein lie the beginnings of a *sui generis* penology for mass violence. Creating a safer space than what presently exists for the articulation of such voices is an important step. Insofar as the evidence on the ground is that afflicted communities seek a diverse array of legal and extralegal initiatives to respond to atrocity, the emergence of liberal legalism as the preferential and dominant response seems more pragmatic than genuine. It seems more political than reflective. In the next section, I consider how a somewhat safer discursive space can be created.

(III) VERTICAL AUTHORITY ALLOCATIONS: A CASE FOR QUALIFIED DEFERENCE

I propose a test of *qualified deference* – in contrast to primacy or complementarity – in the vertical allocation of institutional authority, which currently radiates downward from the international, over extraordinary international criminals.

I draw some guidance from European Union experiments with subsidiarity as an ordering principle. Subsidiarity, a lynchpin of European constitutionalism, requires "any infringements of the autonomy of the local level by means of pre-emptive norms enacted on the higher level to be justified by good reasons."[34] But there are limits to the range of lessons that can be learned from experiments with subsidiarity. It is difficult to transpose the value of subsidiarity to the context of punishing extraordinary international criminals. After all, subsidiarity aims to harmonize local law with the supranational in stable periods. What is more, subsidiarity does not involve the kinds of widescale collective action problems that are intrinsic to mass atrocity. National and local entities ought to be entitled to deference in times of postconflict justice, but subsidiarity could prove to be too generous.

Qualified deference does not involve a blind retreat to national or local institutions. Such a retreat would be problematic. In some postconflict societies, juridical institutions are devastated, illegitimate, corrupt, manipulable, complicit in violence, or in the service of repressive social control; not all post-conflict societies move toward democracy or peace, some trend in the direction of authoritarianism; some postconflict societies look more like societies between conflicts. Complementarity, however, is too controlling – whether intentionally or unintentionally – given the incentives it creates for local institutions. Qualified deference strikes a middle ground between subsidiarity and complementarity. It creates a rebuttable presumption in favor of local or national institutions that, unlike complementarity, does not search for procedural compatibility between their process and liberal criminal law and, unlike primacy, does not explicitly impose liberal criminal procedure.

I also draw some guidance from the margin of appreciation doctrine, a rule of judicial interpretation most famously applied in the case law of the European Court of Human Rights. Margin of appreciation doctrine "encourages international courts to exercise restraint and flexibility when reviewing the decisions of national authorities."[35] Shany identifies two major characteristics of margin of appreciation: (1) a certain degree of judicial deference with regard to the execution of international law obligations that (2) becomes applicable to situations of normative flexibility (i.e., to international norms that are open-ended, unsettled, "intrinsically uncertain," and that preserve a significant zone of legality).[36] Although margin of appreciation is a more expressly legal doctrine than subsidiarity, and animates much human rights jurisprudence, it – too – has limitations as precedent. The substantive nature of the normative prohibition of genocide, crimes against humanity, and war crimes is not open-ended, "intrinsically uncertain," or unsettled. It is very important for procedural diversity not to cloud the shared nature of the condemnation of great evil. Fears of such a muddied outcome are one reason why margin of appreciation has not been actively contemplated by international criminal courts. Qualified deference would better resist troubling conflations of the substantive and the procedural.

As an ordering principle, qualified deference meets important utilitarian objectives in promoting legitimacy, in warding off what I have elsewhere called globalitarianism,[37] in dissipating the top-down incentives created by complementarity, and in minimizing unrealistic expectations of local legitimacy upon which subsidiarity is predicated. Qualified deference does not purport to resolve all concerns of mediating the particular with universal essentials, but does take us down a new and, I believe, fruitful path.

There is considerable value to the most traditional bases of jurisdiction – namely, territoriality and nationality – that should not be overlooked. Although institutions of international criminal punishment profess that the legitimacy of punishment is enhanced by an institution's international provenance, the experiences of postconflict societies reveal a more complex picture. This should not be surprising, insofar as interpretations of justice are often multilayered and, for many people, take root in national and local institutional and procedural contexts. Practically speaking, too, some advantages arise in proceeding locally in terms of culling and interpreting information, with regard to cultural coding, and requiring less in the way of immediate translation. For example, much has been lost in translation from Kinyarwanda into English and French in hearings at the ICTR; likewise, the East Timor Special Panels have experienced considerable difficulty with translation. But the translation issue cuts both ways. Obligations to translate into French, English, or Portuguese have rendered the judicial record accessible to a much broader transnational audience, with the corresponding benefit of a wider dissemination of information and denunciation (thereby augmenting the expressive value of the judicial output). However, nothing precludes a local process under local control from becoming disseminated to, and subsequently translated for, a global audience.[38]

If accepted, what would the operation of qualified deference look like? It falls to those individuals, including members of afflicted communities, who enforce the universal goal of condemning the great evils at the national and local levels to fine-tune the interplay and overlap that emerges from the dialogue between the local and the universal. I propose that the following interpretive guidelines contour the implementation of qualified deference:

(1) *good faith*;

(2) the *democratic legitimacy* of the procedural rules in question;

(3) the *specific characteristics of the violence* and of the *current political context*;

(4) the *avoidance of gratuitous or iterated punishment*;

(5) the *effect of the procedure on the universal substance*; and

(6) the *preclusion of the infliction of great evils on others*.

These interpretive guidelines would operate disjunctively. In other words, not all of them must be met in order for the presumption of qualified deference to a local or national accountability measure to remain satisfied. However, a gross failure on the part of the measure to meet one of the guidelines could suffice to reverse the presumption in favor of qualified deference. In cases of failure to meet the guidelines, internationalized interventions should not replace *in situ* modalities, but, to the extent possible, work in tandem with local actors to develop harmonized structures that respond to the shortcomings.

Let us consider these interpretive guidelines in somewhat greater detail, beginning with *good faith*. The construction of good faith envisioned by qualified deference matches that of virtue ethics.[39] For the virtue ethicist, character is tied to actions; and character, in turn, affects whether ethical actions are appropriate. This gives rise to the proposition that "whether laws are just is a matter of whether they express or display sufficiently good motives on the part of the legislators."[40]

Democratic legitimacy is not assured by legislative vote. Measures adopted through legislative vote tend to have greater legitimacy than those adopted by executive fiat. But, as explored in Chapter 4, centralized state institutions (even putatively representative ones) may not reflect on-the-ground values in afflicted communities. To this end, by democratic legitimacy I intend not a formal positivist process but, rather, a substantive form of social legitimacy.[41] In many places, the state cannot be taken as a proxy for society or for social legitimacy. Consequently, there is a need to effect a more fine-grained assessment.

The *specific characteristics of the violence* and of the *current political context* consider the degree to which the violence was popular, whether it has ended, and whether the society has transitioned into peace and relative security. This interpretive guideline also asks: What are the effects of retrospective accountability on prospective stability? Are national or local sociolegal institutions without capacity? Were they, and their officials, complicit in the violence? Are they corrupt, susceptible to political pressure, or authoritarian? Postconflict, is the society transitioning toward democracy or drifting toward a new totalitarianism? Before rescinding qualified deference for capacity reasons, decision-makers ought to consider whether the international community could help build capacity to effective levels. The level of destitution in the country ought to trigger our cosmopolitan distributive justice obligations to build up general infrastructure within and for members of the afflicted community instead of strikingly expensive criminal courts that stand apart from that community.

The *avoidance of gratuitous iterated punishment* means something slightly different than typical understandings of *ne bis in idem*. For example, the International Association of Penal Law understands *ne bis in idem* as precluding "double prosecutions and sanctions."[42] It considers that "non-criminal prosecutions and decisions with an equivalent punitive effect likewise bar a new prosecution."[43] Qualified deference would trend toward a more nuanced analysis. A local initiative that sequentially pursued civil liability after a criminal conviction had been obtained would not be suspect on that basis alone, even if the civil liability had a "punitive effect." Mere differences in the nature or scope of punishment with regard to what Western legalist institutions would award would not constitute a basis to rescind deference.

Another guideline for qualified deference is that the *procedural methods not void the substantive content* of the shared universal value, this being the condemnation of great evil. This guideline prohibits procedural mechanisms that directly or indirectly redefine the meaning of that evil so as to trivialize it or render it so elastic that it loses its specificity. This does not mean that different societies are incapable of adopting slightly different substantive understandings of the meaning of great evil. In the event a society decides to use as a proxy for the meaning of these great evils the definitions of these evils found in substantive international criminal law, it should be free to do so; in the event the society tinkers with these definitions this would not necessarily run afoul of qualified deference. After all, the development of norms often arises through patterns of healthy accretion. That said, there is a need for vigilance given the *erga omnes* nature of our shared values regarding the moral unacceptability of the great evils.

The final element of qualified deference is that the local or national modalities *not inflict great evils on other individuals*, whether perpetrators or third parties. This element sets parameters to the kind of punishment that can be imposed. Punishment cannot take the form of what cosmopolitan values condemn as a great evil.

Some real-life examples should help illustrate these guidelines. I take up three case studies where, at the time of writing, the presumption of qualified deference would be reversed: Sudan, Afghanistan (with regard to customary law, the *Pashtunwali*), and Iraq.

Civil war has raged in the Sudan since the country achieved independence in 1956. Historically, much of the internecine conflict has been between the northern government (Arab Muslim) and rebels (Christian or animist) in the south, although a peace agreement has been concluded between these parties. Starting in 2003, however, a new conflict flared up in the western part of the country, specifically in the province of Darfur, when different rebel groups (African Muslim) attacked the Arab Muslim government.[44] The government of Sudan retaliated through a campaign directed against civilian targets. It recruited and equipped members of Darfur's Arab tribes in this campaign. Most notorious among the conscripts are the mounted *janjaweed* militia.[45] *Janjaweed* engaged (and, as of mid-2006, continue to engage with the not-so-discreet support of the Sudanese government) in gruesome incidents of pillage, rape, murder, and the razing of entire villages. It is estimated that at least two hundred thousand black Africans have been killed and two million more displaced (many into neighboring Chad). Many of the displaced refugees are ravaged by famine and disease.

An international commission found evidence of crimes against humanity and war crimes but concluded that the government of Sudan had not pursued a policy of genocide.[46] This commission found that, together with other actors, the government of the Sudan was responsible for crimes under international law. The commission report formed the basis of the United Nations Security Council referral of the Darfur situation to the ICC.[47] By virtue of this referral, the ICC is mandated to investigate and prosecute crimes against humanity and war crimes in the Sudan. A list of suspects has been compiled. Sudanese President Omar

Hassan Bashir opposes ICC intervention and has stated that he will not hand over any suspects to the ICC.[48] Sudanese officials have obstructed the gathering of evidence by ICC investigators.[49] Notwithstanding, it looks like international prosecutions are to begin.

The Sudanese government has done nothing to materially combat ethnic oppression or disarm the *janjaweed*; in fact, it has exacerbated the violence. Yet this same military government, in response to the prospect of judicialization through the ICC, has implemented its own set of legal proceedings through a court system that it controls. Sudanese courts have convicted and sentenced some members of the Sudanese army for "waging war" in Darfur, and others for torturing and killing civilians.[50] These Sudanese proceedings would not be entitled to qualified deference. Atrocities continue in Darfur under the auspices of the very government that conducts the trials. This certainly does not demonstrate any basis to impute any good faith to the Sudanese trial process. The government's good faith is compromised by the reality that it continues to be involved in the atrocity that it is purportedly punishing.

The *Pashtunwali* is customary law in the Pashtun region of Afghanistan.[51] It presents a second case study of a local legal system that would not meet the qualified deference guidelines. The *Pashtunwali* is not formal state law. As such, it does not by definition apply to all cases of extraordinary international criminality in Afghanistan. In fact, the preference of the Afghan government is to process such cases through the formalized state court system.[52] However, the *Pashtunwali* remains influential in the rural areas of Afghanistan. Many of these areas lie outside of central control and, at the time of writing, are the dominion of warlords who share an affinity with the *Pashtunwali*. Attempts by central authorities to supersede the *Pashtunwali* have been unsuccessful.

The *Pashtunwali* is a complex code of conduct that regulates diverse areas of private and public life, including process and remedies for the infliction of violence and serious human rights abuses. For these situations, it propounds a restorative justice approach in which the family of the human rights abuser is called upon to make restitution to the family of the abused. Restitution takes the form of, but is not limited to, transfer of money and livestock. So long as one of the sanctions contemplated by the *Pashtunwali* (even if only *in extremis*) – namely, the transfer of young girls or women from the family of the human rights abuser to the family of the abused in order to restore the harm – remained operative, the *Pashtunwali* would not be entitled to qualified deference.[53] This is because that sanction would impose a new great evil, namely sexual violence and terror, on uninvolved third-party children. There is a second reason why the *Pashtunwali* would lose its presumptive entitlement to qualified deference. It lacks democratic legitimacy. The *Pashtunwali* emerges from the *diktat* of patriarchal elites who serve as nonrepresentative religious or military leaders. It is not a consensual project.[54] Who exactly gets to participate in the determination of local sanctions and processes is of great importance to any assessment of the democratic or social legitimacy thereof.

The Iraqi High Tribunal (IHT) would not be entitled to qualified deference because of the specific characteristics of the security situation prevalent in Iraq at the time of writing.[55] The choice to prosecute Saddam Hussein (and other defendants) and to showcase these trials as instruments for transitional justice initially was made under the false belief that foreign troops and an Iraqi police force would be able to maintain order. Tragically, Iraq is wrought with pervasive insecurity. There are daily reports of bombings and murder. The IHT itself has been plagued by violence. Since the proceedings opened on October 19, 2005, several individuals associated with the IHT (including, thus far, a judge and three defense lawyers) have been assassinated; another defense lawyer was seriously injured in an ambush.[56] Personnel have received death threats: some have fled the country.[57]

Any accountability process must reasonably guarantee the safety of its participants and its audience. One that cannot do so cannot pass muster. Although it may well be deflating for those, such as I, who prefer *in situ* accountability methods, perhaps the time has come for a serious discussion of moving trials out of Iraq. Although exceptional, there are times where it benefits roiled societies for accountability to be pursued elsewhere.[58] This is the case if *in situ* trials cannot proceed securely or if they induce significant insecurity. That said, sometimes it makes sense to defer the pursuit of justice, instead of ousting it from local hands, until a certain level of stability can be established.

In contrast to these three *in situ* modalities, neotraditional *gacaca* as implemented for genocide through the 2004 Organic Law in Rwanda would not upend the qualified deference presumption. It underachieves its restorative, reintegrative, and reconciliatory potential, but this alone is not a basis to vitiate the deference entitlement. Although I am deeply concerned about the Rwandan government's use of *gacaca* to consolidate power – and evidence that *gacaca* is manipulated to serve political ends – I do not believe that this evidence yet rises to the level of lack of good faith, akin to that demonstrated by the Sudanese government, that would oust the presumption in favor of qualified deference. That said, once *gacaca* panels engage their operations in earnest, the extent to which the process practically serves political ends and shields the RPF from allegations of its own wrongdoing (for example, war crimes, which currently are excluded from the panels' jurisdiction) would chip away at the deference presumption. Unlike the case with the *Pashtunwali*, *gacaca*'s sanctions do not include the infliction of great evils on uninvolved third parties. *Gacaca* sanctions are not gratuitously iterated. Another key distinction from the *Pashtunwali* is that *gacaca* for genocide, although not as democratic as it could be, retains central markers of public participation. Judges are elected by the public. Judges and other decision-makers are not barred from their work on the basis of gender or religion, although they can be barred if they are suspected to be *génocidaires*. All community members can speak at sessions. Admittedly, the *gacaca* process cannot guarantee the security of all of its participants. There have been murders of witnesses. Some of these cases have been prosecuted. In Iraq, on the other hand, there is poor accountability for the egregious sectarian violence committed today, including that which targets the IHT. With thousands of *gacaca* panels set up throughout Rwanda and tens of thousands of defendants implicated in the process, it may simply be inevitable that some conflict develops.[59] That said, Rwanda is not in a situation of pervasive instability akin to that in Iraq.

(IV) HORIZONTAL DIMENSIONS: OBLIGATION IN MULTIPLE ORDERS

Cosmopolitan pluralism grounds a horizontal outreach beyond the criminal law to other dimensions of law and to extrajudicial regulation. The goal of this proposed outreach is to acknowledge the group-based nature of atrocity, a task for which criminal trials are not well suited. Were the project of international justice to horizontally integrate a broader swath of regulatory mechanisms, it would become more responsive to group dynamics. To the extent that cosmopolitan pluralism favors this capaciousness, it has much to offer as an ordering framework.

I begin by proposing an integration of the law of obligation, which includes areas of law such as tort, contract, and restitution. This integration spawns an overarching *law of atrocity*. In some jurisdictions, these dimensions of law remain *judicialized law* in that they involve civil awards that are meted out by judicial actors to private parties. In these cases, obligation tends to incorporate basic tenets of liberalism in that it is predicated on individual agency, proximate causation, and adherence to adversarial modalities of proof, including cross-examination, that formally occur in a courtroom. Judicialized approaches to responsibility are subject to a similar cultural and ideological contingency for which I fault international criminal law. These approaches cannot be assumed to be universal exemplars of legal responsibility and blindly superimposed upon cultural contexts that may conceptualize responsibility differently. In other jurisdictions, for example, obligation is not judicialized or privatized but is articulated through communal social institutions. In my opinion, an indigenous liability scheme would retain its entitlement to qualified deference even if it did not emulate liberal approaches to fault and liability; qualified deference, however, would operate to diminish the hazards of abusive communitarian punishment.

When implemented horizontally, cosmopolitan pluralism encourages responses to mass atrocity to attach to law as a whole and not just parochially to one small subset of law, namely international criminal law. However, development of a law of atrocity that captures both judicialized and nonjudicialized process is only the first step in horizontal expansion. The second step takes the form of outreach to quasilegal or fully extralegal mechanisms such as truth commissions, legislative reparations, public inquiries, and the politics of commemoration. This outreach pushes the enterprise of atrocity law toward the holistic promotion of *justice for atrocity*. Just as accountability for extraordinary international crimes can be enhanced by the richness and connectivity of local process, so, too, can it be enhanced by the richness and connectivity of alternate disciplines.

Private law and extrajudicial mechanisms already form part of the practice of states in response to atrocity. At national levels, for example, extrajudicial mechanisms are quite commonly invoked in the aftermath of atrocity. However, the internationalized paradigm generally views these mechanisms as separate from, subaltern to, and in competition with criminal trials. Complementarity has poorly thought out how the potential of extrajudicial initiatives could be harnessed. Instead, complementarity creates incentives that may squeeze such initiatives out of the justice matrix. Those international instruments that recognize reparations to victims view their importance as adjunct to international criminal law.[60] Tellingly, while universal criminal jurisdiction for genocide is well established, the notion of universal civil jurisdiction is not.[61]

Although international law historically viewed responsibility in terms of the state, the emergence of the paradigm of individual criminal responsibility has put pressure on the doctrine of state responsibility. The interface of international criminal courts with international courts having civil liability powers, such as the International Court of Justice (ICJ), remains uneasy in matters related to accountability for the great evils.[62] The ICJ was established in 1946 as the principal judicial organ of the United Nations. It only has jurisdiction over states. The ICJ's rapidly expanding docket includes cases regarding boundary disputes, treaty interpretation, and the responsibility of states for international wrongs. Victim states have filed claims with the ICJ that allege that other states bear legal responsibility for serious violations of international humanitarian law and, even, genocide. These claims have led to some unease among international lawmakers. Although the law of state responsibility traditionally provides that breaches of international law trigger a duty to provide reparations, applying this general duty to the specific instance of the crime of genocide is proving particularly contentious.

The sidelining of obligation[63] within the official project of international justice reduces the project's diversity. The project's ability to coordinate and tap the full power of law and regulation to respond to atrocity is thereby impeded. A cosmopolitan pluralist vision would encourage the dominant model, in which deviance-based criminal law is transplanted to situations of collective cataclysm, to release this preference and welcome the myriad ways in which law and politics can capture atrocity's group-based nature.

Tort, contract, and restitution implicate involved masses more effectively by permitting more carefully calibrated measurements of degrees of responsibility beyond the scarlet letter of guilt. These alternate sources of regulation offer a more textured understanding of the key roles played by many otherwise neglected actors. Tort, contract, and restitution can promote different goals – such as restoration, reconciliation, and reparation – which may be more capable of actualization. Restorative justice conceptions of accountability, downplayed by international criminal law, could serve important purposes of reintegrative shaming that resonate with the transitional needs of many postconflict societies.[64]

Tort permits declaratory or monetary relief for violations of state responsibility and potentially for group liability outside the confines of the state. This relief might provide an additional layer of justice insofar as the criminal law does not reach the state as an actor. Tort also permits strict liability, which, in theory, could monitor groups that know they are about to do something dangerous and incentivize them to establish proactive duties to intervene. Consideration could be given to how contract law might impose *ex ante* conditions on influential offices in politics, media, and the clergy in which the occupancy of such offices hinged on an officeholder's refusal to disseminate hate and, in a situation where others preach hate, a commitment to engage in countervailing action. Contract law also could mandate action on the part of international organizations, peacekeepers, and private transnational actors. The law of restitution could integrate private reparations well suited for situations where much of the violence is committed locally by perpetrators known to victims and by neighbors upon neighbors. Looking beyond, a pluralized law of restitution that avoids liberalist standing requirements could facilitate group recovery and oblige the disgorging of the benefits of group violence. In the past, international law has experienced tensions between liberal approaches to standing and recovery, on the one hand, and the expectations of victims seeking relief, on the other.[65]

Going further, I propose a broader integration of extrajudicial and extralegal modalities such as truth commissions, legislated reparations, public inquiries, lustration, the politics of commemoration, redistributing wealth, and fostering constitutional guarantees that structurally curb the concentration of power. The impulse to broaden the response to mass atrocity must extend beyond legal proceedings. This impulse should welcome communal sociolegal institutions, in particular indigenous institutions, and thereby expand the template of policy options. At present, the interface between these institutions and criminal tribunals is poorly thought out. It is marked by squabbling and controversy. Institutions feel pressure to judicialize in order to be deemed complementary or to receive funding. Instead, a more nurturing interface could be developed. The *de jure* or *de facto* primacy of criminal courts over reconstructive efforts may not reflect what the societies under reconstruction actually want. Victims seek diverse remedies.[66] For victims, justice does not singularly involve the incarceration of a handful of offenders in distant, and often comfortable, prisons. A cosmopolitan pluralist paradigm might better coordinate victim preferences interinstitutionally. Contemporary international criminal tribunals exercise jurisdiction without being comprehensively linked to other entities central to postconflict reconstruction, in particular institutions and interventions that promote economic development and constitutional stability. After all, what would the Nuremberg prosecutions have amounted to without the Marshall Plan and the Basic Law?

Extant international criminal law institutions resist horizontal expansion for a number of reasons. One is territorial. The field, and the sophisticated experts well versed in it, has acquired official leadership as the preferred and pragmatic response to atrocity. It is asking much of international criminal tribunals to cede (or even share) that influence. Another reason is ideological. International criminal lawyers often equate civil and political remedies with collective forms of accountability. For many international criminal lawyers, collective forms of accountability raise the specter of the collective guilt of an entire nation or ethnicity. I believe that it is unfair to raise this specter. Although pursuing obligation through civil and political remedies does capture a broader number of individuals involved in atrocity, and hence moves toward collectivization, it does not invariably lead to collective guilt. Guilt, among many other things, is a liberal criminal law concept. It is what is imputed to those who are convicted pursuant to a criminal trial and subsequently incarcerated (or, in outlier cases, executed). Equating civil liability or restorative community service with collective guilt is overreach. In theory, it could be possible to determine an entire nation criminally guilty and incarcerate each member of the nation.[67] This is decidedly *not* what my proposal for horizontal diversification contemplates. Instead, it aims to move us *away* from the current dependence on criminal law.

Rather, my proposal turns to the fundamentally different notion of *collective responsibility*. There is a yawning gap between guilt and responsibility.[68] Whereas many individuals are responsible for atrocity, a much smaller number are criminally guilty. A much larger number of individuals are responsible than can (and deserve to) be captured by criminal trials. Civil liability implicates those individuals and institutions found to bear some responsibility for discrimination-based mass atrocity. This can be a large group, hence the recourse to the phrase collective responsibility. We would do the project of international criminal justice a disservice if, in implementing international criminal law, out of unfounded fear of imposing collective guilt we marginalized or sneered down modalities of accountability that promoted the collective responsibility of groups.

Collective responsibility understandably makes many observers nervous. After all, civil liability, community service, and, especially, public reintegrative shaming are powerful measures. Their use as collective sanctions for collective responsibility merits extremely careful analysis. Probably the most evident starting point for this analysis is to explore how, exactly, to define the responsible group. I propose that the responsible group can be defined either *crudely* or *carefully*.

The *crude* way structures the responsible group along its most evident characteristics or combinations thereof: for example, nationality, ethnicity, inhabited territory, or religion. So, for example, it renders all Germans as blameworthy for the Holocaust; all Arab Sudanese for Darfur. The crude way assigns responsibility to the group in whose name atrocity was undertaken independently from the actions of its individual members. The crude way therefore can include individuals who are not personally responsible. It can even include individuals who were incompetent, or unable to do anything, so long as the atrocity was committed in their collective name. In cases where atrocity is committed at the behest of a state, the crude way includes within the group all those individuals living within the jurisdiction of that state. This can have particularly harsh consequences. Levying sanctions against a collectivity when that collectivity contains both per-petrators and victims would hinder the victims' recovery efforts. In sum, the crude way does not limit the group to the aggregate of those individuals whose action or inaction culminated in atrocity. Damages ultimately pass through to and are borne by all group members, regardless of how bravely they resisted, how servilely they complied, how eagerly they killed, or how much hurt they suffered. At first blush, the crude way of group designation is anathema to liberalists.[69]

The *careful* way, on the other hand, pays attention to individual agency. It limits the group to those individuals who, by virtue of their action or inaction, are demonstrably responsible for atrocity. The careful way requires a more fine-grained analysis. The careful way thereby abides by Western legalist assumptions of causation and individual agency. The careful way can be so careful that it can appear in criminal prosecutions, albeit controversially: for example, doctrines such as joint criminal enterprise that implicate very small groups acting in concert.[70] In cases of civil responsibility, however, the careful way still conditions group membership on some sort of demonstrable linkage between action (or nonfeasance) and the great evil. Individuals or entities for whom no connection can affirmatively be delineated would avoid membership in the sanctioned group. This renders the careful way dependent on similar modalities that limit the effectiveness and universality of criminal trials.

The claim filed in 1993 by Bosnia and Herzegovina against Serbia and Montenegro at the ICJ presents a case study of collective responsibility, and a template for the directions in which collective responsibility could hypo-thetically head.[71] In its claim, Bosnia and Herzegovina asserts that Serbia and Montenegro, the state into which the FRY was transformed in 2003,[72] violated its obligations to prevent and punish genocide under the Genocide Convention. Bosnia and Herzegovina asserts that these violations constitute wrongful acts attributable to Serbia and Montenegro that entail its international responsibil-ity. Remedies sought include the payment of compensation for damages and losses. Oral arguments closed in May 2006. The ICJ has reserved judgment. Regardless of how the ICJ eventually disposes of this matter (a decision may well be handed down while this book is in production), Bosnia and Herzegovina's genocide claim can stimulate a discussion, which transcends the actual jurisdic-tion of the ICJ, regarding what crude or careful group designation might look like in a cosmopolitan pluralist accountability framework.

Bosnia and Herzegovina's claim – along with a similar one brought against Serbia and Montenegro by Croatia[73] – has caused jitters in the international law community. These jitters are understandable. After all, a damages award against the state of Serbia and Montenegro could run in the billions of dollars. Such an award might be paid for by the tax contributions of all individual citizens of Serbia and Montenegro. Alternately, it might be paid for by withholding foreign aid, which means that projects intended for the benefit of all individual citizens become halted or decelerated. A stinging declaratory award against the state would trickle down and, by association, mark all state citizens. These citizens could become international pariahs. Take Serbia and Montenegro's World Cup soccer team. No longer could the players say, "You've got those responsible: they're the guilty ones in the ICTY dock," and then keep on playing with the expectation of full reciprocal respect from the rest of humanity. Instead, the players, too, would be responsible, in their own small way, and have to pay for it in cash, reputation, or both.

The practical effects of collective responsibility frameworks are unsettling. Signs of discomfort with collective responsibility had already surfaced in 1996, when the ICJ initially found jurisdiction over Bosnia and Herzegovina's claim and dismissed preliminary objections thereto.[74] One of the preliminary objections was that the allegations of state responsibility brought by Bosnia and Herzegovina simply fell outside the scope of the Genocide Convention. The majority of ICJ judges dismissed this preliminary objection. This group tersely found that the plain language of the Convention, in particular the compromissory clause, did not exclude any form of state responsibility.[75] Four judges disagreed. Two of these four judges – Judges Shi and Vereshchetin – ultimately ruled that the ICJ had jurisdiction over the Bosnian claim. However, they appended a separate declaration to the ICJ's judgment. In this declaration, they expressed their "disquiet" with the holding that the Genocide Convention does not exclude state responsibility. They reasoned that the Genocide Convention:

> is essentially and primarily directed towards the punishment of persons committing genocide or genocidal acts and the prevention of the commission of such crimes by individuals. [. . .] In substance, the Convention remains an instrument relating to the criminal responsibility of individuals. The determination of the international community to bring *individual perpetrators* of genocidal acts to justice [. . .] points to the most appropriate course of action.[76]

Judges Shi and Vereshchetin referenced the perniciousness of collective guilt as a basis for the preference for individualized criminal prosecutions. They explicitly cited the ICTY as having been created for the prosecution of persons responsible for serious violations of humanitarian law committed in the territory of the former Yugoslavia. The preference for the ICTY as the appropriate forum for judicialization works to the detriment of other fora. In a statement whose pronounced hedging belies its normativity, Judges Shi and Vereshchetin concluded that "it might be argued that [the ICJ] is perhaps not the proper venue for the adjudication of the complaints [. . .] raised."[77] So, although both judges ultimately concluded that the compromissory clause of the Genocide Convention afforded a jurisdictional basis for Bosnia and Herzegovina's claim, they felt "obliged to express [their] concern" over this aspect of the case and, thereby, sent a strong signal regarding how the merits of this aspect of the case ultimately ought to be decided. These concerns, although not derailing Bosnia and Herzegovina's case at the preliminary stage, inevitably shall weave into the resolution of the substantive claim and the kind of state responsibility the ICJ believes the Genocide Convention actually creates. These concerns therefore form a leitmotiv. Obliquely, they may even have informed the reasons why a majority of the ICJ dismissed (upon preliminary objection and for jurisdictional grounds) Serbia and Montenegro's claim that, when NATO countries bombed the FRY in 1999, they violated their international obligations.

It is obvious that a larger number of citizens of Serbia and Montenegro than those actually indicted by the ICTY, or by national prosecutors, were responsible for genocide at Srebrenica. An even greater number acquiesced in the carrying out of atrocity generally in the name of Serb nationalism. All such complicit and benefiting bystanders bear some responsibility. So long as those responsible foresee that they shall never face any sanction, the law does nothing to dissuade them from acquiescing in atrocity in its inchoate stages, when the enterprise of atrocity is most vulnerable. Accordingly, I do not believe it is effective for international criminal responsibility to entirely displace state responsibility in matters of the great evils.

On the other hand, not all citizens of Serbia and Montenegro were responsible for genocide at Srebrenica or atrocity in general. Moreover, equating the group with the state does a particularly great disservice to those citizens of Serbia and Montenegro who resisted genocide, spoke out against it, or were themselves harmed by it. To this end, a judgment in favor of Bosnia and Herzegovina would punish those who individually bear no responsibility. Looking at it from the Bosnian perspective, a successful claim would inure to the benefit of all its citizens. Included among the beneficiaries are individuals who were victimized, those who were not, and those who were complicit in the violence or actually committed it. Similar tracking problems abound. Although Srebrenica's Bosnian Muslims were the target of genocide, not each of Srebrenica's Bosnian Muslims equally was a victim. European Jewry was the target of the Holocaust, but some European Jews served as *kapos* (guards) and inflicted great brutality upon Jewish detainees. In the end, if Bosnia and Herzegovina's claim were successful, it would restitute some individuals while unjustly enriching others. One poignant paradox is that "[w]ithin Bosnia, the Republika Srpska is actively opposed to the Bosnian lawsuit and does everything in its power to obstruct it."[78]

The ICJ, hampered by its own jurisdictional limits, therefore faces a difficult choice. If it finds in favor of Bosnia and Herzegovina, it avoids impunity for the many Serbs responsible and ensures some reparation for the many Bosnian victims; but it also sanctions nonresponsible Serbs and enriches Bosnian Muslims with dirty hands.

One response is to alter the incentives to reduce the starkness of the trade-off. This reflects implementation of the *careful way*. Currently, implementation of the careful way is manifestly problematic for the ICJ insofar as its jurisdiction is limited to states, not individuals, associations, or governmental departments or subunits. That said, assuming hypothetically (1) that the ICJ were able to engage broader forms of civil liability and jurisdiction and (2) that Bosnia and Herzegovina were successful in establishing the substantive elements of its claim (namely, infringement of the Genocide Convention),[79] then the ICJ's conjectural pursuit of the careful way would, were it so empowered, allow it to make fine-grained assessments of the group that is actually responsible (and, separately, of the group entitled to damages). In such a scenario, civil damages or declaratory denunciation would perhaps only be awarded against individual members of the state government. Or against members of associations with control over the apparatus of the state. Or against corporate entities who funded and equipped genocide. But the careful way would obstruct liability from trickling down to *all* citizens of the state.

A second response is to defend the collective responsibility of the entire population of Serbia and Montenegro. This is the *crude way*. Assuming once again that Bosnia and Herzegovina were successful on its substantive claim, an ICJ adhering to the crude way would enter damages and denunciatory declarations against the state, as it is empowered to do, and no eyebrows would be raised regarding a trickle-down effect to every individual citizen of Serbia and Montenegro. The details of who did what, and which Bosnian receives what, would become irrelevant in the name of a greater good. Sanctioners minded toward the crude way also might invoke proxies to associate the actions of the Serbian state with the Serbian people. One possible proxy is the electoral/political behavior of the majority, or a plurality, of the population. Thomas Franck proposes that: "Where the people whose leaders are committing international crimes have the option to vote them out, or to stage mass protests against those acts, and fail to do so it is not only morally appropriate but good social policy that they be made to assume a degree of responsibility for the things done in their name."[80]

Whereas the careful response may soothe some liberal sensibilities, the crude position as applied to atrocity is bound to be controversial – at least to a Western audience. Of course, some of this controversy amounts to posturing. After all, collective sanctions that capture the nonresponsible are found with some frequency within the domestic law of Western states.[81] Collective sanctions that capture the innocent exist, often to a greater degree, in other sociolegal orders as well.[82]

Bosnia and Herzegovina's ICJ claim reflects the inevitability that international criminal lawyers will have to juristically deal with collective responsibility. Even if Bosnia's claim were to be dismissed on all fronts, it will not be the last kind of collective responsibility claim ever brought. In fact, the ICJ issued a collective responsibility award in another case, *DRC v. Uganda*, which primarily involved use of force matters, although also implicated violations of international criminal and humanitarian law (albeit not genocide).[83] The ICJ ordered Uganda to pay reparations in light of its responsibility for armed activity, plundering, and massive human rights violations in the DRC. Specifically, the ICJ located Uganda's responsibility for *inter alia* killing, torture, training of child soldiers, incitement of ethnic conflict, and other forms of inhumane treatment.[84] The pursuit of collective responsibility is a strong preference among victims, who exhibit great cleverness in attempting to articulate this pursuit through juristic channels. The inevitability of assessing the place of collective responsibility within the project of international justice, however, should be a cause for contemplation and optimism, not embarrassment or annoyance.

By turning collective responsibility into a *bête noire*, skeptics properly remind us of dark days: for example, the results of the Treaty of Versailles, which imposed "victor's justice" reparations on an entire nation and arguably promoted cycles of further violence. On the other hand, as I have argued elsewhere, I believe that international criminal lawyers' fears of collective responsibility have inhibited dispassionate conversations about its potential in thwarting atrocity and retrospectively promoting justice.[85] Any realistic analysis of discrimination-based mass atrocity teaches us that the violence is deeply collective in nature and, what is more, that its collective nature surpasses the aggregate of all individual action. Just as it is counterproductive to downplay the role of the collective as a factor that induces the impulse toward atrocity, it also is counterproductive to eschew considering how collective remedies can confront collective action. I believe there is value in debating collective responsibility for reasons rooted in communitarian moral theory, as developed by George Fletcher,[86] and also, as noted by Larry May,[87] for reconciliation. Let me advance a third reason, which I find more compelling: utilitarianism.

Many atrocities begin with the devious kindling of conflict entrepreneurs, who seek to inflame and exacerbate communal tensions. Community responses to this kindling are not predestined. How the community responds is the central determinant regarding whether violence subsequently erupts and, if so, of its amplitude. If community members ignore these flames, and look past attempts to habituate them into violence and hatred, then the conflict entrepreneur remains marginal. If community members are attracted to the flames, and identify with violence and hatred, then the wheels of atrocity are set in motion. And once set in motion, these wheels quickly become unstoppable by anything other than the use of countervailing force.

I argued in Chapter 6 that criminal punishment goes some way to developing expressive values that edify a moral consensus regarding the manifest illegality of discrimination-based violence. This consensus might serve as a bulwark against exhortations by conflict entrepreneurs in favor of such violence. I also argued in Chapter 6 that the threat of criminal punishment will not deter committed individuals acculturated into hatred from implementing their own final solutions. Criminal law does little to deter eliminationist killers. However, let me suggest here that collective responsibility might go some way *ex ante*, in a utilitarian sense, to diminish the mainstreaming of conflict entrepreneurship and the festering of cultures of hatred. If normalized, collective responsibility could augment the likelihood of sanction for a much broader number of individuals. Collective responsibility could reach the catalytic group of benefiting bystanders I identified in Chapter 2.

Group members are in an advantageous position to identify, monitor, and quash the behavior of conflict entrepreneurs before it metastasizes. Because the criminal law paradigm does not reach group members, it provides them no incentive to cabin or control the behavior of conflict entrepreneurs. Collective responsibility might do more to encourage group members to control conflict entrepreneurs early on, and hence serve as gatekeepers, because they would be called to task afterwards. A collective responsibility paradigm could thereby serve a monitoring function. Group members would, as Mark Osiel suggests, begin to police each other's activities and responses.[88] The threat of collective sanctions may activate group members to marginalize the conduct of conflict entrepreneurs or, in the best-case scenario, snuff it out. Cosmopolitan pluralism would encourage an interface with collective responsibility mechanisms that, in turn, could go some way to plugging an important gap left by criminal trials. Given that passive acquiescence rarely – if ever – is implicated by a system based on individualized criminal law, it is unclear how this system can deter this fundamental prerequisite to mass atrocity.

States have duties to their citizens; to which I would add that citizens also have certain duties to the state. One of these is a duty to prevent the state from actualizing extraordinary international crimes. This duty becomes all the more onerous to the extent that citizens have input into political decisionmaking. Citizens should be put on notice that they cannot stand by while hatemongering becomes normalized.

Collective responsibility frameworks can implicate benefiting bystanders. These frameworks can thereby affix a cost to an individual's drawing the blinds, receiving a promotion at work because the "other" got fired, moving into a suddenly vacated apartment, and acquiescing in the hijacking of the state by extremists. It is well-nigh impossible to deter a suicide bomber or crazed ideologue. Once an individual has passed a threshold of habituation in or affection for violence, has deeply imbibed hatred, or needs to kill to survive, the law can offer little in deterrence. However, the law may more plausibly reach the much larger group of people that passively allow the conflict entrepreneur to assume office, procure weapons, and build a power base of habituated killers. Any structure that incentivizes the masses to root out the conflict entrepreneur before that individual can indoctrinate and brainwash will diminish the depth of perpetrator moral disengagement that is a condition precedent to mass atrocity. Such a structure thereby inhibits early on, when inhibition still remains possible, the "escalating commitments" that psychologist James Waller believes demarcate the "road to extraordinary evil."[89] The social death of the victims – a precondition to their actual deaths – may thereby be impeded. Capturing all individuals in a responsible collective might make it much more difficult for individuals to hide within the collective, seek exoneration in its anonymity, benefit from the diffusion of responsibility, and proffer excuses in Milgram's agentic state of transposed responsibility. Collective responsibility could inject a risk allocation and management analysis into the minds of the general population in the very inchoate stages of atrocity. I believe this would help move extant frameworks from being essentially *reactive* to tragedy to a somewhat more *proactive* position.

Moreover, collective responsibility frameworks would monitor more than just the activities of individuals. Monitoring also could extend to corporate entities, thereby implicating very relevant actors that fall outside the reach of international criminal law (for example, the ICC or ad hoc tribunals only have jurisdiction over natural persons). Corporate entities are major facilitators of genocide, insofar as they produce the tools by which genocide is executed. They provide the means to industrialize atrocity. Moreover, collective sanction does not have to limit itself to agents of the perpetrator group. Would international institutions and foreign states have responded with the same nonfeasance to genocide in Rwanda or Srebrenica were they to be subject to the reach of collective sanctions? This is a particularly poignant question given empirical research that indicates that mass violence, particularly state-centered violence, can be slowed or stopped by military interventions, led for example by the international community or foreign states, which directly challenge the perpetrator or aid the target of the policy.[90]

That said, this is a discussion of what might be, not what obviously is. Experiments have not been concluded. Data have not been generated. It may well be that a collective responsibility framework would fall short of these utilitarian goals, or would attain some of them in certain places but not in others. For example, it is not implausible that the existence of a collective sanctions framework would induce group members to permit atrocity and then simply devote their energies to covering it up. It is possible that the existence of collective responsibility would prompt groups to insure against the civil liability that results from genocide, thereby creating moral hazard. Perhaps benefiting bystanders are not rational thinkers; perhaps they are no different than *Interahamwe* militia or suicide bombers.

But we will never be able to evaluate the potential or limitations of a horizontally expanded law of atrocity that contemplates group-based sanction unless we shed our fears and dispassionately engage with collective responsibility as a regulatory mechanism and as a possible tool in the justice toolbox. My point here is to spark renewed discussion and research.

Ultimately, my proposal for horizontal cosmopolitan pluralism is a humanistic one that supports collective claims but endeavors to straddle the gap between crude and careful group demarcation. I believe the group can be defined crudely, with the subsequent opportunity for group members to affirmatively demonstrate why they should be excluded from the liable group. Reasons for exclusion would include members' activities prior to or during the atrocity. This creates a strong incentive to resist or, at least, not to acquiesce. Victims, too, would be excluded from liability. With regard to Bosnia and Herzegovina's claim, in the event genocide were attributable to the Serbian state, I would proffer a hypothetical liability framework in which the Serbian state could be sanctioned, but in which individual or institutional members of Serbian society could be permitted to avoid footing the bill, or foot less of the bill than others, by affirmatively demonstrating what they did to prevent genocide or to oppose the state. Such a process could open up a wide discursive space about who did what during times of atrocity, thereby serving powerful didactic and expressive purposes. Looking at the other side of the coin: I believe the claimant group also can be defined crudely if this is how it elects to define itself. Victims should be entitled to constitute themselves as they see fit for the purpose of filing claims and should be given qualified deference if not every individual member of the group meets exacting standing rules. I am less concerned over unjust enrichment for some members of victim communities than I am over sanction for some members of perpetrator communities who actively resisted.

(v) CONCLUSION

The cosmopolitan pluralism I envision would permit criminal trials and punishment to stake a claim in the justice matrix and, hence, be a participant in the justice process, but would cast this claim as procedurally deferential (with qualifications) to the local *and* as conceptually porous to alternate private law and extrajudicial modalities. In both cases, the result is that the universal norm of accountability for great evil enters into dialogic relational intercourse with local procedure *and* the richness of the legal landscape beyond the narrowness of ordinary criminal law.

In the end, an independent theoretical understanding of the organic and myriad sources of mass atrocity shall not come from a process of reduction animated by a strong preference for deviance-based criminal law. Rather, it more readily emerges from a process of accretion that recognizes that mass atrocity arises when, collectively, groups fail to respect fundamental obligations owed to humanity and individuals within those groups either actively or passively facilitate that failure. Encouraging multiple forms of accountability through diverse, and different, legal orders might go some way to recognize the truly extraordinary nature of the evil at hand and, thereby, promote the attainment of penological goals.

Justice for atrocity is not synonymous with international criminal trials. It entails much, much more. Any value that selective adversarial prosecutions of individuals deemed most responsible for atrocity, which is the mandate of the ICC, actually convey will only appreciate if these prosecutions concurrently operate within, as opposed to shutter out, a multilayered and diverse array of initiatives – legal as well as political – that promote accountability.

CHAPTER 8

Conclusion: Some Immediate Implications

The trajectory I have traced began with the compilation and review of sentences issued by domestic courts and international tribunals in cases of great evil. Courts and tribunals affirm that they punish extraordinary international criminals mainly to promote retribution, deterrence, and expressivism. It turns out, however, that there is a shortfall between retributive and deterrent goals and the realities of sentence. This shortfall can be explained in part by international criminal law's reliance on the modalities of ordinary liberal criminal law, which is designed for deviant individuals in select jurisdictions and not for the obedient masses that, to varying degrees, are associated with discrimination-based atrocity. Expressive aspirations, although more obtainable, remain quite frail.

In response to this shortfall and frailty, I propose a process of critique and renewal that portends changes in the way in which perpetrators of atrocity are to be punished. These reforms would encourage looking beyond stated punitive rationales to consider other justifications, including currently undervalued goals such as restoration. Societies with a collective as opposed to individualist ethos would have more space to pursue accountability mechanisms other than adversarial criminal trials. Vertical and horizontal reforms would splinter the present focus on a handful of retrospective trials motored top-down by internationalist modalities; these reforms also would fragment the powerful remedial preference for incarceration. For a variety of reasons exogenous to the quality of justice, liberal internationalist modalities, with their preference for trial and incarceration, have migrated to the national and local levels even in those places where such process and sanction are neither innate nor indigenous.

Ultimately, the cosmopolitan pluralist vision I propose fosters an obligation-based preventative model, operationalized from the bottom-up through diverse modalities that contemplate a coordinated admixture of sanctions calibrated to each specific atrocity. The toolbox of sanctions could include imprisonment, reparations, community service, lustration, declaratory relief, restitution, affirmative duties to promote human rights, and institutional and constitutional reforms to diminish the likelihood that discrimination-fueled hatemongers (re)assume power.

Instead of the tight social control and scripted narrative envisioned by individualist criminal law, more free-ranging approaches that uproot the many sources of violence – a much more accurate, albeit inconvenient, topography – could be encouraged *in situ* when local authorities pursue these in good faith. Punishment frameworks could thereby transcend those of preexisting criminal law formulations, harness broader sociological forces, attend to the local needs of the places directly afflicted by mass atrocity, and strive to integrate alternate methodologies.

These proposed reforms are ambitious and wide-ranging. They demand much in the way of intellectual and financial support. Although keyed to the long term, these proposals also are capable of gradual and incremental articulation. Accordingly, the reform process need not be overwhelming. Existing hard-won frameworks, whether institutional or conceptual, can be modified to accommodate the beginnings of a cosmopolitan pluralist vision. By way of conclusion, I identify several short-term adjustments.

(1) LEGAL INSTITUTIONS AND JURISPRUDENCE

Proposed adjustments include:

(1) Retool the division of labor by recognizing, either expressly through textual amendment or implicitly through interpretative canon, a presumption of qualified deference toward national or local institutions in the following processes:

- Referrals from ad hoc tribunals to national courts;
- Rome Statute article 17 admissibility determinations;
- Referrals from the Security Council or states party to the ICC;
- Decisions by the ICC Prosecutor to investigate or prosecute *proprio motu*;
- Security Council decisions to create new punishing institutions (e.g., on an ad hoc basis); and
- Determinations of the "interests of justice" under Rome Statute article 53(1)(c).

(2) Integrate non-Western legal traditions into globalized understandings of the adequacy of due process; insert comparative law methodologies more deeply into the international jurisprudence.

(3) Recognize the difficulties that extant modalities of sentence experience in attaining their avowed aspirations (retribution, deterrence, and expressivism); develop the separate sentencing hearings contemplated by the Rome Statute such that they involve a rich, principled, and textured discussion of punishment; integrate the sociopsychological aspects of individual agency in collective cataclysm into the sentencing metric.

(4) Encourage the ICC in the inchoate steps it has taken to involve victims in its processes; assess the potential and limits of victim impact testimony, including

in sentencing; adequately support the ICC's Trust Fund; and provide similar funds for those places whose atrocity currently is judicialized by international or internationalized institutions.

(5) Eliminate charge bargaining, and permit plea bargaining only in cases of confessions with apologies and where the defendant admits the full scale of his or her involvement (even if pleading guilty only to one umbrella charge). This admission should take the form of a detailed signed document, read into the judicial record, in which the defendant allocutes to all of the facts that serve as a basis for the charges. Such a requirement would move plea bargaining in the direction of restorative initiatives (e.g., those practiced by the South Africa Truth and Reconciliation Commission).

(6) While the need for diversity of punishment structures must be appreciated, work on "bringing law to sentencing"[1] once a structure has been developed for a specific atrocity so that outcomes within that jurisdiction become predictable and referenced to a stable heuristic. Such reform would allow involved parties to know what type of information to adduce and what weight to place thereupon. To the extent that "bringing law to sentencing" opens a discussion regarding the establishment of sentencing guidelines or tariffs, that discussion should be welcomed (recognizing that, when implemented crudely, mandatory tariffs can depersonalize punishment and lead to excessively rigid outcomes).

(7) Expand the language of judgments, as Laurel Fletcher advises, to explicate the role of bystanders.[2]

(8) Clarify and synthesize jurisprudential linkages between the International Court of Justice, on the one hand, and criminal justice institutions at the domestic and international levels, on the other hand, in cases of extraordinary international crimes.

(9) Consider collective sanction, in particular monetary sanction, on a group (state or otherwise) when it reasonably could have prevented extraordinary international crimes but declined to do so; once the group is delineated, permit group members an opportunity to affirmatively demonstrate why they should be excluded from responsibility (e.g., based on their opposition to the violence or their own victimization).

(10) Welcome the participation of citizens from afflicted conflict zones in the accountability process so that a technocratic transnational expert community does not dominate; also, dovetailing with the general principle of qualified deference, exert a preference to site justice institutions locally with concomitant investment in outreach.

(11) Preclude early release/conditional release based on the ordinary criminal law of the state that agrees to detain the convict if that state has no territorial or national connection to the violence.

(II) POLITICAL INSTITUTIONS AND BEHAVIOR

Proposed adjustments include:

(1) Explore how international organizations can become contractually bound to intercede when conditions of conflict entrepreneurship arise; in this process, link with UN reform as contemplated by the New Threats Panel Report and broader notions of humanitarian armed intervention and humanitarian communications intervention so that *ex post* punishment does not substitute for *ex ante* prevention.

(2) Explore how national frameworks can place duties on influential public and private offices to diminish the chances that persons occupying such offices convert them into platforms for conflict entrepreneurship.

(3) For donor communities and human rights activists: resist exerting pressure on national institutions to conform to the procedural modalities of international legal institutions; decouple funding from mimicry, but not from fine-grained qualified deference assessments.

(4) Resist the tendency to look for simplicity in response to fundamentally complex crimes.

(5) Setting of scholarly agendas: track convicts over time and analyze the ability of local mechanisms, such as *gacaca* and *mato oput*, to attain regulatory objectives.

(III) CLOSING NOTE: CRITIQUE AND RENEWAL

The ICC has come of age. Universal criminal jurisdiction is settled. National courts prosecute extraordinary international crimes. These developments, while striking, are only the beginning of the justice metric. They certainly are not the end. To view them as such would evince a perilously narrow understanding of justice. Much work remains to be done in order for the punishment of the great evils to develop a meaningful doctrinal method tied to a penology that truly is its own. Should international criminal law fail to push in this direction, it risks consigning itself to a perpetual stage of adolescence or, in the much more eloquent words of Cherif Bassiouni, to no more than "Potemkin justice."[3] Extant institutions can become more relevant for communities reconstructing themselves in the wake of mass atrocity. Courts and tribunals are not ends in themselves. Rather, they are elements of a much broader project.

The choice is not one between safeguarding extant institutions, on the one hand, or living lawlessly in a world of impunity, on the other. This is a false dichotomy. There is another option: one of critique and growth. This option recognizes the potential (and limits) of law to enhance human welfare. It also recognizes that deficiencies must be addressed, not glossed over. International law is to be studied, not venerated. Only through hard work, and modesty regarding past accomplishments, can humanity move from law to justice.

Notes

1. EXTRAORDINARY CRIME AND ORDINARY PUNISHMENT: AN OVERVIEW

1. *Prosecutor v. Nkinamubanzi et al.* (April 17, 1998, 1 ière instance, Kibuye), RMP 50919/S4/ GM/KBY/97, RP CH.SP.014/01/97, p. 2.
2. *Id.* p. 1 (identifying him as a "*chauffeur*").
3. *Id.* p. 14.
4. Rory Carrol, *Rwandan Priest Goes on Trial for Genocide*, THE GUARDIAN (Sept. 21, 2004).
5. *ICTR/Seromba – Man Who Bulldozed Church Accused of Being Paid to Change Testimony*, Information, Documentation and Training Agency (Tanzania) News (April 6, 2006). Nkinamubanzi was supposed to appear as a prosecution witness at the International Criminal Tribunal for Rwanda (ICTR) in proceedings against the head priest of Nyange parish, Father Athanase Seromba. Nkinamubanzi was to testify that Seromba instructed and paid him to level the church. However, he then changed his story to exculpate Seromba, allegedly in exchange for bribes. *Id.* Seromba was convicted by an ICTR Trial Chamber in December 2006 of genocide and extermination as a crime against humanity and sentenced to fifteen years' imprisonment.
6. Such as Mika Muhimana, convicted in 2005 by the ICTR and sentenced to life imprisonment, who among other brutalities grotesquely "cut a pregnant woman from her breasts down to her genitals and remove[d] her baby, who cried for some time before dying." *Prosecutor v. Muhimana*, Case No. ICTR-95-1B-T, ¶¶ 612, 614 (ICTR Trial Chamber, April 28, 2005). Moreover, "[a]fter disemboweling the woman, the assailants [. . .] then cut off her arms and stuck sharpened sticks into them."
7. Hannah Arendt, EICHMANN IN JERUSALEM: A REPORT ON THE BANALITY OF EVIL (rev. ed., 1965). For other accounts of the banality theme, *see* Christopher Browning, ORDINARY MEN: RESERVE POLICE BATTALION 101 AND THE FINAL SOLUTION IN POLAND (1992); Mark Osiel, MASS ATROCITY, ORDINARY EVIL, AND HANNAH ARENDT (2001).
8. Amartya Sen, IDENTITY AND VIOLENCE: THE ILLUSION OF DESTINY 2 (2006).
9. *See, e.g.*, M. Cherif Bassiouni, INTRODUCTION TO INTERNATIONAL CRIMINAL LAW (2003); Antonio Cassese, INTERNATIONAL CRIMINAL LAW (2003); Bruce Broomhall, INTERNATIONAL JUSTICE AND THE INTERNATIONAL CRIMINAL COURT: BETWEEN SOVEREIGNTY AND RULE OF LAW (2004); Leila Nadya Sadat, THE INTERNATIONAL CRIMINAL COURT AND THE TRANSFORMATION OF INTERNATIONAL LAW: JUSTICE FOR THE NEW MILLENNIUM (2002); William Schabas, GENOCIDE IN INTERNATIONAL LAW (2000).
10. Eric A. Posner & John C. Yoo, *Judicial Independence in International Tribunals*, 93 CALIF. L. REV. 1, 7–8 (2005); Laurence R. Helfer & Anne-Marie Slaughter, *Why States Create International Tribunals – A Response to Professors Posner and Yoo*, 93 CALIF. L. REV. 899, 905 (2005).
11. Ruti Teitel, TRANSITIONAL JUSTICE (2000); Osiel, MASS ATROCITY, *op. cit.*

12. *See, e.g.,* Bassiouni, *op. cit.* (devoting 18 pages out of a total of 740); Cassese, *op. cit.* (devoting 3 pages out of a total of 458).

13. Viktor Frankl, MAN'S SEARCH FOR MEANING: EXPERIENCES IN THE CONCENTRATION CAMP (trans. 1959); Primo Levi, SURVIVAL IN AUSCHWITZ (reprint 1995).

14. Robert Cryer, PROSECUTING INTERNATIONAL CRIMES: SELECTIVITY AND THE INTERNATIONAL CRIMINAL LAW REGIME 36, 38 (2005); Peter Maguire, LAW AND WAR: AN AMERICAN STORY 90 (2000); Carlos Santiago Nino, RADICAL EVIL ON TRIAL 5–6 (1996).

15. This view persists today. *See, e.g.,* Kenneth J. Campbell, GENOCIDE AND THE GLOBAL VILLAGE 28 (2001) (citing UN Secretary-General Annan as stating that "the crime of genocide against one people truly is an assault on us all"). This view derives from the actual events at the Nuremberg trials and, perhaps more importantly, subsequent interpretation thereof. Telford Taylor, NUREMBERG AND VIETNAM: AN AMERICAN TRAGEDY 13–14 (1970) (noting also that "'Nuremberg' is both what actually happened there and what people think happened, and the second is more important than the first").

16. Hannah Arendt, THE HUMAN CONDITION 241 (1958). *See also* Nino, *op. cit.,* at vii, ix.

17. C. Fred Alford, *Augustine, Arendt, and Melanie Klein: The (De)Privation of Evil,* 10 J. FOR THE PSYCHOANALYSIS OF CULTURE & SOC'Y 44, 50–51 (2005) (describing developments in Arendt's thinking from the ORIGIN OF TOTALITARIANISM (1951) to EICHMANN IN JERUSALEM (1963)). For Arendt, only good "has depth and can be radical;" evil was like a "fungus" on the "surface" that could spread and "lay waste [to] the whole world." *Id.* I also use the term *great evil* to describe this violence.

18. Hannah Arendt, *Letter from Hannah Arendt to Karl Jaspers (August 18, 1946),* in Hannah Arendt & Karl Jaspers, HANNAH ARENDT, KARL JASPERS: CORRESPONDENCE, 1926–1969, 54 (Kohler & Saner eds., 1992).

19. *Prosecutor v. Deronjić,* Case No. IT-02-61-A, ¶ 136 (ICTY Appeals Chamber, July 20, 2005) (quoting ICTY Appeals Chamber judgment in *Čelebići,* ¶ 806: "The cases which come before the [International] Tribunal differ in many respects from those which ordinarily come before national jurisdictions, primarily because of the serious nature of the crimes being prosecuted, that is 'serious violations of international humanitarian law.'"); *Prosecutor v. Tadić,* Case No. IT-94-1 (ICTY Appeals Chamber, Oct. 2, 1995) (warning of the "perennial danger" that international crimes might be characterized as ordinary crimes and citing this danger as justifying ICTY primacy).

20. For use of this term, *see* David Luban, *A Theory of Crimes Against Humanity,* 29 YALE J. INT'L L. 85, 90 (2004); Steven C. McCaffrey, UNDERSTANDING INTERNATIONAL LAW 184 (2006) (surveying practice and policy that extends the appellation "enemy of all humankind" to the torturer and other perpetrators, including of genocide, crimes against humanity, war crimes, and the slave trade).

21. I contend that the proscription of widespread attacks by terrorists deliberately undertaken against civilian populations and the financing thereof, which are criminalized within transnational criminal law, have moved from this level to that of international criminal law, becoming in the least an obligation *erga omnes.* I consider such attacks as atrocity crimes, both on their own and, if the legal tests are met, as crimes against humanity (for example, the September 11, 2001, attacks). *See* Mark A. Drumbl, *Judging the 11 September Terrorist Attack,* 24 HUM. RTS. Q. 323 (2002). The Rome Statute of the International Criminal Court, which precedes the jurisgeneration triggered by the international community's response to the September 11 attack, does not create jurisdiction to prosecute terrorism. Rome Statute of the International Criminal Court, U.N. Doc. A/CONF.183/9 [hereinafter Rome Statute].

22. Rome Statute, *op. cit.,* art. 7. Acts include murder, enslavement, extermination, deportation, persecution, rape, torture, sexual slavery, enforced prostitution, and forced pregnancy.

23. *Id.* art. 6.

24. War crimes cover two sorts of activities: crimes committed in international armed conflict and violations of the laws and customs of war, a residual category applicable to noninternational armed conflicts. *Id.* art. 8.

25. The *dolus specialis* of genocide entails proof of intent to wipe out a target group in whole or in part. I construct this intent as (in the least) discriminatory in nature. Formal proof of discriminatory intent is not a required element in all jurisdictions for all crimes against humanity. *Mugesera v. Canada (Minister of Citizenship and Immigration)*, 2005 S.C.R. 40, ¶ 144 (Supreme Court of Canada (2005)); *but see* Larry May, CRIMES AGAINST HUMANITY 124–128 (2005) (arguing in favor of requiring discriminatory intent in cases of crimes against humanity). Persecution is an example of a crime against humanity for which there is a settled requirement of discriminatory intent. *Mugesera v. Canada*, ¶ 145; *Prosecutor v. Bralo*, Case No. IT-95-17-S (ICTY Trial Chamber, December 7, 2005); *Prosecutor v. Barros and Mendonca*, Case No. 01/2004, ¶ 22(e) (Dili Dist. Ct. Serious Crimes Spec. Panel, May 12, 2005, *aff'd* East Timor Ct. App.). The requisite intent is the denial of a fundamental right on discriminatory grounds. Hate speech may rise to this level (*see, e.g., Prosecutor v. Nahimana*, Case No. ICTR-99-52-T, ¶ 117 (Summary of Judgment) (ICTR Trial Chamber, Dec. 3, 2003)) or it may not (*see, e.g., Prosecutor v. Kordić and Čerkez*, IT-95-14/2-A (ICTY Appeals Chamber, Dec. 17, 2004)). When taken as a whole, what distinguish crimes against humanity from ordinary crimes is that the acts in question become crimes against humanity if they are committed as part of a widespread or systematic attack directed against any civilian population or any identifiable group. *Mugesera v. Canada*, ¶ 151. Systematic attacks will include some sort of common policy or plan that operates on a patterned basis; they are not random. *Mugesera v. Canada*, ¶ 155. The interpretation of "widespread" involves the large-scale nature of the act: in the language of the ICTR, that it is "carried out collectively with considerable seriousness and directed against a multiplicity of victims." *Prosecutor v. Akayesu*, Case No. ICTR-96-4-T, ¶ 580 (ICTR Trial Chamber, Oct. 2, 1998); *see also Prosecutor v. Kayishema*, Case No. ICTR-95-1-T, ¶ 123 (ICTR Trial Chamber, May 21, 1999).

26. Nuremberg was a watershed. That said, the notion that alleged war criminals should be tried and punished if found guilty certainly existed prior to Nuremberg. *See generally* Anthony Ellis, *What Should We Do With War Criminals?*, in WAR CRIMES AND COLLECTIVE WRONGDOING 97, 97 (Jokić ed., 2001). In fact, the pre–World War II period was important for international criminal law in that it saw the development of proposals for the field and enforcement; a few trials occurred for alleged World War I crimes, for example domestically at Leipzig. Nuremberg, however, practically operationalized the perceived need to punish within an international criminal tribunal. And, looking beyond Nuremberg, this practical operationalization has blossomed in earnest over the past decade.

27. *See* Martti Koskenniemi, *Hersch Lauterpacht and the Development of International Criminal Law*, 2 J. INT'L CRIM. JUST. 810, 824 (2004) (noting that "'individualism' is a recent aspect of Western thinking that may undermine forms of experience or ways of life that cannot be articulated in the individualist terms familiar to the (developed) West").

28. Judith Shklar, LEGALISM: LAW, MORALS, AND POLITICAL TRIALS 152 (1964).

29. Miriam J. Aukerman, *Extraordinary Evil, Ordinary Crime: A Framework for Understanding Transitional Justice*, 15 HARV. HUM. RTS. J. 39, 40 (2002) (concluding that participants in the debate over the use of prosecutions in transitional justice "share a basic assumption: prosecuting perpetrators of injustice is the optimal method for dealing with past atrocities"); Stephen Landsman, *Alternative Responses to Serious Human Rights Abuses: Of Prosecution and Truth Commissions*, 59 LAW & CONTEMP. PROBS. 81, 83 (1996) (concluding that the best response is vigorous prosecution). Moreover, preferences in a context of finite resources can lead to exclusivity.

30. Laurel E. Fletcher, *From Indifference to Engagement: Bystanders and International Criminal Justice*, 26 MICH. J. INT'L L. 1013, 1031 (2005). Fletcher also refers to this concept as "international legalism." *Id.* at 1015. She also refers to "liberal law adjudication." *Id.* at 1062.

31. *Id.* at 1031. Other scholars also turn to "liberal legalism" as a descriptive tool. *See, e.g.*, Sanja Kutnjak Ivković & John Hagan, *The Politics of Punishment and the Siege of Sarajevo: Toward a Conflict Theory of Perceived International (In)justice*, 40 LAW & SOC'Y. REV. 369

(2006); Eric A. Posner & Adrian Vermeule, *Transitional Justice as Ordinary Justice*, 117 HARV. L. REV. 761, 792 n.92 (2004) (referring to "liberal procedural legalists").

32. *See also generally* David Chuter, WAR CRIMES: CONFRONTING ATROCITY IN THE MODERN WORLD 94 (2003) ("[I]nternational criminal law's vocabulary and concepts are not neutral. They are culturally specific, constructed and manipulated by a very small number of countries...."). As Gary Bass notes, the "pursuit of war criminals can only be explained with reference to domestic political norms in liberal states." Gary J. Bass, STAY THE HAND OF VENGEANCE: THE POLITICS OF WAR CRIMES TRIBUNALS 35 (2002).

33. History has bestowed this legitimacy upon international institutions despite Arendt's relative equivocation as to whether these extraordinary crimes were more suitably dealt with at the national or international levels.

34. *See* Alain Pellet, *Internationalized Courts: Better Than Nothing...*, in INTERNATIONALIZED CRIMINAL COURTS 437, 438 (Romano, Nollkaemper, & Kleffner eds., 2004) ("[I]t must be kept in mind that only crimes which 'deeply shock the conscience of humanity' can justify an internationalization of their prosecution, which involves a far-reaching blow to the competence of domestic courts on an issue which otherwise would come under 'matters which are essentially within the domestic jurisdiction of States'.... [W]hen such serious crimes are at stake ... it is then important that they not be 'confiscated' by any particular state, including the one in which the crime has been committed or of which the victims or the authors are nationals."). *See also generally* Arendt, EICHMANN IN JERUSALEM, *op. cit.*, at 269.

35. May, CRIMES AGAINST HUMANITY, *op. cit.*, at 99, 106; Larry May, WAR CRIMES AND JUST WARS 15 (2005) (monograph on file with the author); Michael J. Matheson, *United Nations Governance of Post-Conflict Societies*, 95 AM. J. INT'L L. 76, 83 (2001). For May, crimes against humanity always implicate international interests given their group-based or systematic nature, whereas war crimes do not. War crimes, for May, are crimes against humaneness rather than crimes against humanity.

36. Universal jurisdiction, in particular, is predicated largely on the fact that the extraordinary international criminal offends the interests of all of humanity. *See* Kenneth C. Randall, *Universal Jurisdiction Under International Law*, 66 TEX. L. REV. 785, 803 (1988); *see also The State of Israel v. Adolf Eichmann* (S. Ct. Israel, May 29, 1962), 36 INT'L L. REP. 277, 291 (1968) (universal international crimes arise from the fact that they "constitute acts which damage vital international interests," "impair the foundations and security of the international community," and violate "universal moral values and humanitarian principles").

37. Foreign influences also inform the operationalization of justice at the national and local levels.

38. For example, although I consider the Iraqi High Tribunal (also referred to as the Iraqi Higher Criminal Court) to be a national legal institution, it embodies foreign and international elements. *See generally* Statute, Law No. 10 2005 (October 9, 2005), Official Gazette of the Republic of Iraq, No. 4006 (October 18, 2005). The Iraqi High Tribunal [hereinafter IHT] receives expertise from the United States, was created pursuant to the invasion of Iraq by foreign powers, and directly incorporates certain of the crimes and liability theories from the constitutive documents of international criminal tribunals. The IHT was established on December 10, 2003, and approved by the Iraqi Transitional National Assembly on August 11, 2005. Its purpose is to prosecute high-level members of the former Iraqi regime. The IHT's Statute, initially drafted in 2003, was amended in 2005 and approved in October 2005. The IHT is empowered to prosecute genocide, crimes against humanity, war crimes, and certain violations of Iraqi law committed between July 17, 1968, and May 1, 2003. It adheres to a civil law model with investigative judges. The IHT is to have primacy over all other Iraqi courts with respect to the extraordinary international crimes within its jurisdiction. Its personnel are Iraqi. In its interpretation of the crimes within its jurisdiction, the IHT may resort to relevant decisions of international criminal courts. *Id.* art. 17. The IHT shall also turn for guidance to the sentences of international

criminal courts when it comes to affixing punishment for the extraordinary international crimes within its jurisdiction. *Id.* art. 24. In addition to sentences previously issued by other international courts, the IHT is to take into account factors such as the gravity of the crime and the individual circumstances of the convicted person. However, punishment is that prescribed by domestic Iraqi law, which includes the death penalty. The IHT's Rules of Procedure and Evidence permit guilty pleas. The Rules mandate the IHT when sentencing offenders to take into consideration aggravating and mitigating circumstances. Only one specific example is given, this being a mitigating factor: substantial cooperation. On guilty pleas and mitigating/aggravating factors, *see generally* Rules of Procedure and Evidence, The Official Gazette of the Republic of Iraq, No. 4006, Rules 37, 65 (October 18, 2005). The October 2005 version of the IHT Statute identifies in a postscript its "justifying reasons" for imposing punishment as follows: to expose the crimes committed in Iraq; to lay down rules and punishments to condemn the perpetrators after a fair trial; to form a high criminal court; to reveal the truth, agonies, and injustice; to protect the rights of Iraqis; and "alleviating injustice and for demonstrating heaven's justice as envisaged by the Almighty God." The IHT's first judgment was issued in writing and translated in December 2006. This judgment involved culpability for state executions in the village of Dujail. The sentencing part of the IHT judgment was so terse that it did not involve discussion of penological goals, even those noted in the Statute, nor any explanation of why each convict received the sentence he was awarded (Saddam Hussein received the death sentence).

39. The ICC, which entered into force on July 1, 2002, was created by the Rome Statute of the International Criminal Court. *See* Rome Statute, *op. cit.* It is a permanent institution mandated to investigate and prosecute the most serious crimes of international concern, namely genocide, crimes against humanity, and war crimes. At the time of writing, 100 nations have become parties to the Rome Statute. *See* U.N. Treaty Collection, Ratification Status, *available at* http://untreaty.un.org/ENGLISH/bible/englishinternetbible/partI/chapterXVIII/treaty11.asp (last visited May 25, 2006). The Rome Statute has been signed by 139 nations. The ICC is investigating allegations of crimes in a number of places, including Sudan, the Democratic Republic of the Congo (DRC), and Uganda. It has arrested its first individual: alleged Congolese militia leader Thomas Lubanga.

40. The ICTR was established as an ad hoc institution by the Security Council. *See* Statute of the ICTR, U.N. SCOR, 49th Sess., 3453d mtg. at 15, U.N. Doc. S/Res/955 (1994). It investigates and prosecutes persons responsible for genocide and other serious violations of international humanitarian law committed in the territory of Rwanda and Rwandan citizens responsible for genocide and other such violations committed in the territory of neighboring states, between January 1, 1994, and December 31, 1994. In 1994, an extremist government headed by members of the Hutu ethnic group fostered a populist genocide that resulted in the murder of 500,000 to 800,000 members of the Tutsi ethnic group.

41. The ICTY was established as an ad hoc institution by the Security Council to investigate and prosecute persons responsible for serious violations of international humanitarian law committed in the territory of the former Yugoslavia since 1991. *See* Statute of the ICTY, U.N. SCOR, 48th Sess., 3217th mtg. at 29, U.N. Doc. S/Res/827 (1993). These conflicts involved fighting among Serbs, Croats, Bosnian Muslims, and Kosovo Albanians. In total, approximately 250,000 individuals were killed in this fighting.

42. The Sierra Leone Special Court, which has begun operations, was established jointly by the government of Sierra Leone and the United Nations to prosecute those who bear the greatest responsibility for serious violations of international humanitarian law and Sierra Leonean law committed in the territory of Sierra Leone since November 30, 1996. *See* Statute of the Special Court for Sierra Leone, art. 1, S.C. Res. 1315, U.N. SCOR, 55th Sess., 4186th mtg. at 1, *available at* http://www.sc-sl.org/scsl-statute.html. The violence in Sierra Leone arose from conflict between government and rebel forces during the 1990s.

43. The various hybrid institutions contemplated here are internationalized to different degrees insofar as the division of labor between the international and the national varies from institution to institution.

44. *See* United Nations Interim Administration Mission in Kosovo, Reg. 2000/64 (Dec. 15, 2000). These special panels (also called "Regulation 64 panels") adjudicate violations of domestic criminal law that include those occurring in 1998 and 1999 in the course of the armed conflict then ongoing in Kosovo between Kosovo separatists and the forces of the Federal Republic of Yugoslavia. Organization for Security and Cooperation in Europe Mission in Kosovo, KOSOVO'S WAR CRIMES TRIALS: A REVIEW 9 (Sept. 2002). Regulation 64 panels do not have exclusive jurisdiction over such crimes. Many of the crimes within the jurisdiction of the panels are international crimes that have been enacted in domestic law. Bert Swart, *Internationalized Courts and Substantive Criminal Law*, in INTERNATIONALIZED CRIMINAL COURTS 295 (Romano, Nollkaemper, & Kleffner eds., 2004). These include genocide, crimes against humanity, and war crimes. International judges or prosecutors can be assigned to these panels upon request by prosecutors, the accused, or defense counsel in order to ensure judicial impartiality or the proper administration of justice. One of the motivations for the creation of these hybrid courts in Kosovo is the "problem of ethnic bias, both actual and perceived [. . .]." International Judicial Support, UNMIK – Police & Justice, *available at* http://www.unmikonline.org/justice/ijsd.htm.

45. East Timor was admitted (as Timor-Leste) on September 27, 2002, as the 191st member of the United Nations (I use the former name in this book). In 1999, following a plebiscite in which a majority of East Timorese favored the region's independence from Indonesia, militia forces supported by the Indonesian army massacred over one thousand East Timorese civilians and engaged in a widespread campaign of deportation, property destruction, and sexual violence. The Indonesian administration of East Timor collapsed following the violence. The United Nations Transitional Administration in East Timor ("UNTAET") facilitated East Timor's transition to independence. Suzanne Katzenstein, *Hybrid Tribunals: Searching for Justice in East Timor*, 16 HARV. HUM. RTS. J. 245, 249 (2003). Courts were organized in East Timor with the assistance of UNTAET. *On the Organization of Courts in East Timor*, U.N. Transnational Administration in East Timor, U.N. Doc. UNTAET/REG/2000/11 (Mar. 6, 2000), *available at* http://www.un.org/peace/etimor/ untaetR/Reg11.pdf, *amended by* U.N. Doc. UNTAET Regulation 2001/25 (Sept. 14, 2001), *available at* http://www.un.org/peace/etimor/untaetR/2001-25.pdf. These include District Courts and a Court of Appeals. *Id.* § 4. One District Court, located in Dili, had two Special Panels for Serious Crimes with exclusive jurisdiction over "serious criminal offenses," namely genocide, war crimes, crimes against humanity, murder, sexual offenses, and torture committed between January 1 and October 25, 1999. *Id.* § 9; *On the Establishment of Panels with Exclusive Jurisdiction over Serious Criminal Offences*, U.N. Transnational Administration in East Timor, § 1.3, U.N. Doc. UNTAET/REG/2000/15 (June 6, 2000), *at* http://www.un.org/peace/etimor/untaetR/Reg0015E.pdf [hereinafter UNTAET Regulation 15]. The applicable law was both international criminal law, including customary international law, and national criminal law (predominantly Indonesian law). UNTAET Regulation 15, §§ 4–9. The substantive international crimes were nearly fully taken from the Rome Statute. Sylvia de Bertodano, *East Timor: Trials and Tribulations*, in INTERNATIONALIZED CRIMINAL COURTS 90 (Romano, Nollkaemper, & Kleffner eds., 2004). Judges were of mixed national and international provenance. UNTAET Regulation 15, § 22. The mandate of the Special Panels ended on May 20, 2005. At that point, fifty-five trials had been completed; eighty-four individuals had been convicted and three acquitted. Before ceasing operations, the Special Panels only were able to try about one-quarter of all individuals indicted for serious crimes pertaining to the East Timorese violence. Those who bear primary responsibility for the violence have yet to be held to account. *See generally* Press Release, *available at* http://www.jsmp. minihub.org/Press%20Release/2005/May/050524%20End%20SPSC.pdf. The closing of the

Special Panels also terminated a number of investigations into human rights violations. *Id.* In January 2006, the East Timor Commission for Reception, Truth, and Reconciliation issued its report. It concluded that Indonesian security forces and the militias they supported had killed at least 100,000 East Timorese since 1975. Colum Lynch & Ellen Nakashima, *E. Timor Atrocities Detailed*, WASHINGTON POST (Jan. 21, 2006) at A12.

46. *Khmer Rouge Trials, Annex Draft Agreement Between the United Nations and the Royal Government of Cambodia*, G.A. Res. 57/228, U.N. Doc. A/RES/57/228 (May 22, 2003); Law on the Establishment of Extraordinary Chambers in the Courts of Cambodia for the Prosecution of Crimes Committed During the Period of Democratic Kampuchea, *available at* http://www.derechos.org/human-rights/seasia/doc/krlaw.html. From 1975 to 1979, the Khmer Rouge executed, tortured, and starved to death approximately 1.7 million Cambodians. These agreements created Extraordinary Chambers in the Courts of Cambodia for the prosecution of Khmer Rouge leaders and others most responsible during the period April 17, 1975, to January 6, 1979, for serious violations of Cambodian penal law, international humanitarian law and custom (including genocide), and international conventions recognized by Cambodia. A number of countries have pledged sufficient funds to sustain the Extraordinary Chambers. Physical plant has been arranged. Judges and prosecutors have been sworn in. It appears as if prosecutions will begin in 2007.

47. *See generally* Bassiouni, *op. cit.*, at 11, 588 (arguing that the goals of international criminal law are an extension of the goals of national criminal law and that international criminal law lacks its own juridical method); Cassese, *op. cit.*, at 18 (stating that "international criminal law . . . results from the gradual *transposition* on to the international level of rules and legal constructs proper to national criminal law or national trial proceedings"); Tom J. Farer, *Restraining the Barbarians: Can International Criminal Law Help?*, 22 HUM. RTS. Q. 90, 91 (2000) (casting the purpose of penal sanctions in cases of international crimes as "largely coextensive" with the purpose of penal sanctions in national legal orders); Bass, *op. cit.*, at 16–28 (observing that international criminal law emerges from legal liberalism that analogizes to the domestic); Leila Sadat Wexler, *The Interpretation of the Nuremberg Principles by the French Court of Cassation: From Touvier to Barbie and Back Again*, 32 COLUM. J. TRANS. L. 289, 364 (1994) (noting that the normative aspect of international criminal law is "international in character," but that "punishment and procedure is necessarily municipal in character").

48. Typically, common law criminal procedure is adversarial in nature, whereas the civil law tradition is inquisitorial. There has, however, been some convergence among national legal systems in the West in matters of criminal procedure, including the importation of adversarialism into archetypically nonadversarial systems. As I examine further in Chapter 5, this convergence has been obtainable owing to underlying philosophical similarities among Western legal systems, which share a basic liberal legalist predisposition.

49. *See* Ralph Henham, *Some Issues for Sentencing in the International Criminal Court*, 52 INT'L & COMP. L.Q. 81 (2003) (describing this harmonization as a pragmatic political settlement among powerful international actors).

50. Molly Moore, *Trial of Milosevic Holds Lessons for Iraqi Prosecutors*, WASHINGTON POST (October 18, 2005).

51. Robert Jackson, *Opening Speech for the Prosecution at Nuremberg* (Nov. 21, 1945), reprinted in Robert Jackson, THE CASE AGAINST THE NAZI WAR CRIMINALS 7 (1946).

52. Moore, *op. cit.*

53. *See* Mark A. Drumbl, *The Expressive Value of Prosecuting and Punishing Terrorists: Hamdan, the Geneva Conventions, and International Criminal Law*, 75 GEO. WASH. L. REV. (forthcoming 2007).

54. International law defines a *jus cogens* norm as a customary rule applicable to all states from which no derogation is possible.

55. Mark A. Drumbl, *Punishment, Postgenocide: From Guilt to Shame to Civis in Rwanda*, 75 N.Y.U. L. REV. 1221, 1290–1292 (2000).

56. Mark A. Drumbl, *Pluralizing International Criminal Justice*, 103 MICH. L. REV. 1295 (2005) (review essay); *see also* Meir Dan-Cohen, *Responsibility and the Boundaries of the Self*, 105 HARV. L. REV. 959 (1990) (noting that the criminal law's ethic of individualism seems to trump the implementation of collective responsibility).

57. "[. . .] American criminal law does not always condition criminal liability on a clear show-ing of personal culpability, as demonstrated by the rules on felony murder, *Pinkerton* conspiracies, and liability under the Racketeer Influenced and Corrupt Organizations Act (RICO)." Mark Osiel, *The Banality of Good: Aligning Incentives Against Mass Atrocity*, 105 COLUM. L. REV. 1751, 1754 n.9 (2005). But Osiel then notes the "near exclusive reliance of domestic criminal law on individualistic premises." *Id.* at 1841. Osiel goes on to conclude that "[t]hese doctrines remain controversial, however, precisely because of their arguable departure from that principle." *Id.*; *see also id.* at 1786 n.155 (noting that *Pinkerton* liability is rejected by the U.S. Model Penal Code).

58. Furthermore, regulators at the national level do not rely exclusively on penal sanction to promote compliance with the law. In many jurisdictions, civil suits play an important role. This even is the case in places that evidence a preference for the criminalization of transgressive behavior. International legal institutions overwhelmingly regulate atrocity through the criminal law instead of other forms that law commonly takes. The ICC envi-sions a slightly more diversified approach, insofar as it is joined by a Trust Fund for Victims that might serve restitutionary and restorative goals, although it is unclear exactly how the practice of the Fund shall unfold.

59. Payam Akhavan, *The International Criminal Court in Context: Mediating the Global and Local in the Age of Accountability*, 97 AM. J. INT'L L. 712, 712 (2003) (noting that the "eupho-ria" surrounding the ICC's establishment creates a "sympathetic posture" that "obscures a more critical discourse on the efficacy of managing massive atrocities in distant lands within the rarified confines of international legal process"); Jan Klabbers, *Just Revenge? The Deterrence Argument in International Criminal Law*, XII FINNISH Y.B. INT'L L. 249, 250 (2001) (noting that "we have all fallen under the spell of international criminal law and the beauty of bringing an end to the culture of impunity"); Frédéric Mégret, *Three Dangers for the International Criminal Court: A Critical Look at a Consensual Project*, XII FINNISH Y.B. INT'L L. 193, 201 (2001) (writing that there is "a flow of rhetoric endowing the ICC with almost mythical powers," including the management of international affairs through criminal law). *See also generally* Antonio Cassese, *Reflections on International Criminal Justice*, 61 MOD. L. REV. 1, 6 (1998); Jackson Nyamuya Maogoto, WAR CRIMES AND REALPOLITIK 8 (2004) ("[I]nternational tribunals . . . have become the international community's primary response to humanitarian crises . . . ").

60. Lawrence Douglas, THE MEMORY OF JUDGMENT: MAKING LAW AND HISTORY IN THE TRIALS OF THE HOLOCAUST 257–261 (2001) (insisting that the legal response to crimes as extraor-dinary as the Holocaust must take the form of a show trial that can serve both the interest of justice as conventionally conceived and also a broader didactic purpose serving the interests of history and memory); John M. Czarnetzky & Ronald J. Rychlak, *An Empire of Law? Legalism and the International Criminal Court*, 79 NOTRE DAME L. REV. 55, 62 (2003) (noting that "faith in the ICC" is "held quite strongly in Western intellectual circles").

61. *See generally* Benedict Kingsbury, *Is the Proliferation of International Courts and Tribunals a Systemic Problem?*, 31 N.Y.U. J. INT'L L. & POL. 679, 688 (1999) (citing John Bolton, *Reject and Oppose the International Criminal Court, in* TOWARD AN INTERNATIONAL CRIMINAL COURT? 37–38 (Frye ed., 1999)).

62. *See* William Schabas, *Sentencing by International Tribunals: A Human Rights Approach*, 7 DUKE J. COMP. & INT'L L. 461, 515 (1997); *see also* Stuart Beresford, *Unshackling the Paper Tiger – the Sentencing Practices of the Ad Hoc International Criminal Tribunals for the Former Yugoslavia and Rwanda*, 1 INT'L CRIM. L. REV. 33, 89 (2001) ("It is paradoxical, therefore, that while they were once the champion of prisoners' rights, the human rights

community is now at the forefront and in many cases the instigator of the international community's desire to punish.").

63. *Hearing Before the House Comm. on Int'l Relations*, 107th Cong., 2nd Sess., at 25 (Feb. 28, 2002) ("The United States remains proud of its leadership in supporting the two ad hoc tribunals and will continue to do so in the future.") (statement of Pierre Prosper, U.S. Ambassador at Large for War Crime Issues); Bass, *op. cit.*, at 24–25 (discussing U.S. involvement in promoting due process for Nazi war criminals); Juan E. Mendez, *Human Rights Policy in the Age of Terrorism*, 46 ST. LOUIS U. L.J. 377, 388 (2002) (reporting that the ICTY and ICTR "enjoyed decisive support – of a bipartisan nature – from the United States"); Beth K. Dougherty, *Combating Impunity: The Charles Taylor Case at the Special Court for Sierra Leone* 1 (unpublished manuscript on file with the author) ("The U.S. is the largest single donor to the Sierra Leone [Special Tribunal]."). That said, the United States currently is pressuring the ad hoc tribunals to complete their work by 2008, a prospect that appears improbable. S.C. Res. 1503, U.N. SCOR, 58th Sess., 4817th mtg., at 1 (2003); Nancy Amoury Combs, *International Decisions*, 97 AM. J. INT'L L. 923, 935 (2003).

64. Rupert Cornwell, *US Will Deny Aid to Countries that Refuse Court Immunity Deals*, INDE-PENDENT (U.K.) (Nov. 4, 2003) (reporting official statements made by then U.S. Under-secretary of State John Bolton). The United States did not oppose the Security Council's referral of the Darfur situation to the ICC. *See generally* Nora Boustany, *A Shift in the Debate on International Court*, WASHINGTON POST (Nov. 7, 2006) at A16.

65. Drumbl, *Punishment Postgenocide, op. cit.*; Mark A. Drumbl, *Victimhood in Our Neigh-borhood: Terrorist Crime, Taliban Guilt, and the Asymmetries of the International Legal Order*, 81 N.C. L. REV. 1, 75–92, n.30 (2002); Mark A. Drumbl, *Rights, Culture, and Crime: The Role of Rule of Law for the Women of Afghanistan*, 42 COLUM. J. TRANSNAT'L L. 349 (2004).

66. Carl Schmitt, THE CONCEPT OF THE POLITICAL (Schwab trans., 1996).

67. George F. Kennan, AMERICAN DIPLOMACY 99 (1951); *see also id.* at 95 (arguing the "most serious fault" of U.S. foreign policy is "a legalistic-moralistic approach to international problems"). Henry Kissinger frets that an "unprecedented movement has emerged to sub-mit international politics to judicial procedures... [which] risk[s] substituting the tyranny of judges for that of governments." Henry A. Kissinger, *The Pitfalls of Universal Jurisdiction*, 80 FOREIGN AFF. 86, 86 (July/Aug. 2001).

68. Posner & Yoo, *Judicial Independence, op. cit.*; Jack Goldsmith & Eric Posner, THE LIMITS OF INTERNATIONAL LAW (2005).

69. Helfer & Slaughter, *op. cit.* (commenting on Posner & Yoo article); Paul Schiff Berman, *Seeing Beyond the Limits of International Law*, 84 TEX. L. REV. 1265 (2006) (review essay commenting on Posner & Goldsmith).

70. I define legitimacy as the condition that arises when authority is exercised in a manner seen as justified. Criminology is the study of crime, criminals, and criminal behavior. Vic-timology is the study of crime victims. Penology is the study of punishment and prisoners.

71. In November 2006, as this book was going to press, the ICTY Appeals Chamber sentenced Stanislav Galić to life – thereby resulting in the first actual life sentence. On an earlier occasion, the Appeals Chamber overturned a life sentence that had been issued by an ICTY Trial Chamber.

72. Data current to May 2006. Although the ICTR convicts a significantly larger proportion of its defendants for genocide than the ICTY or Special Panels (both of which convict mainly for crimes against humanity), it is not apparent that this fact coherently explains the ICTR's more severe sentences. After all, ICTR genocide sentences are longer than genocide sentences at these other tribunals. In Chapter 6, I also consider two other explanations for this differential judicial behavior: incorporation of national law and the sheer gravity of atrocity in Rwanda. The ICTY thus far has issued two genocide convictions. The Special Panels did not issue a genocide conviction, although the East Timor Court of Appeal did convict one defendant for genocide contrary to the Portuguese Penal Code following

acquittal by the Special Panels for crimes against humanity and sentenced that individual to twenty-five years' imprisonment. *Prosecutor v. dos Santos*, Case No. 16/2001, ¶ 75 (East Timor Ct. App., July 15, 2003). Insofar as it remains unclear whether genocide actually was committed in East Timor, the more useful comparison is between the ICTY and ICTR sentences for genocide.

73. Just like in many influential ordinary justice systems, rehabilitation is given little effectivity. *See, e.g., Prosecutor v. Deronjić*, Case No. IT-02-61-A (ICTY Appeals Chamber, July 20, 2005); *Prosecutor v. Kordić and Čerkez*, Case No. IT-95-14/2-A, ¶ 1079 (ICTY Appeals Chamber, Dec. 17, 2004). On reconciliation, *see Prosecutor v. Babić*, Case No. IT-03-72-A (ICTY Appeals Chamber, July 18, 2005) (refusing to reduce a sentence even though finding that the Trial Chamber erred in failing to consider the activities of the accused toward encouraging peace and reconciliation in the region). Although the jurisprudence displays some movement toward discussing reconciliation as a penological goal, this goal is poorly operationalized.

74. On transplants generally, *see* Alan Watson, Legal Transplants: An Approach to Comparative Law (2d ed., 1993).

75. Rome Statute, *op. cit.*, art. 17.

76. Complementarity and referrals are only two of many pressure points exerted on national jurisdictions to mimic the process of international criminal tribunals. Other pressure points include: instrumental needs to obtain financing and legitimacy; defensive maneuvers to shield from criticism; selfish concerns regarding the eliding of actual systemic responsibility that protects state power and interests and curtails deeper examinations of state responsibility for violence; and jurisdictional goals to receive cases from foreign national courts (for example, through extradition).

77. Decision of January 17, 2006, on Participation of Victims, ICC Pre-Trial Chamber, *available at* http://www.icc-cpi.int/library/cases/ICC-01-04-101_tEnglish-Corr.pdf. Chapter 5 explores conflicts between victim communities in Uganda and the ICC with regard to ICC investigations and indictments. Prosecutor and victim communities do not necessarily share complementary interests.

78. Immanuel Kant, The Metaphysical Elements of Justice (Ladd trans., 2d ed., 1999). For discussion of retribution, *see also* Michael Moore, *The Moral Worth of Retribution*, in Principled Sentencing: Readings on Theory & Policy 150 (von Hirsch & Ashworth eds., 1998); Joshua Dressler, *Hating Criminals: How Can Something that Feels So Good Be Wrong?*, 88 Mich. L. Rev. 1448 (1990) (review essay); Jean Hampton, *Correcting Harms versus Righting Wrongs: The Goal of Retribution*, 39 UCLA L. Rev. 1659, 1686 (1992); Jeffrie G. Murphy, *Kant's Theory of Criminal Punishment*, in Retribution, Justice, and Therapy: Essays in the Philosophy of Law (1979).

79. On the influence of international human rights standards on international criminal tribunals, *see* Allison Marston Danner & Jenny Martinez, *Guilty Associations: Joint Criminal Enterprise, Command Responsibility, and the Development of International Criminal Law*, 93 Cal. L. Rev. 75 (2005).

80. This broad discretion recently was reaffirmed in *Prosecutor v. Semanza*, Case No. ICTR-97-20-A, ¶ 312 (ICTR Appeals Chamber, May 20, 2005) ("Trial Chambers are vested with broad discretion to tailor the penalties to fit the individual circumstances of the accused and the gravity of the crime."); *Prosecutor v. Kvočka et al.*, Case No. IT-98-30/1-A, ¶ 668 (ICTY Appeals Chamber, February 28, 2005) (recognizing that there is "no definitive list of sentencing guidelines"), ¶ 669 ("Sentencing is essentially a discretionary process on the part of a Trial Chamber."), ¶ 715 ("[T]he Trial Chamber has discretion as regards the factors it considers in mitigation, the weight it attaches to a particular mitigating factor, and the discounting of a particular mitigating factor.")

81. Osiel, *The Banality of Good, op. cit.*, at 1804, 1829 (positing differing incentives faced by international and national prosecutors in bringing to book perpetrators of extraordinary international crime).

82. Peter Uvin & Charles Mironko, *Western and Local Approaches to Justice in Rwanda*, 9 GLOBAL GOVERNANCE 219, 223 (2003); Timothy Longman, *The Domestic Impact of the International Criminal Tribunal for Rwanda, in* INTERNATIONAL WAR CRIMES TRIALS: MAKING A DIFFERENCE? 33, 37 (Ratner & Bischoff eds., 2004).

83. *Prosecutor v. Kordić and Čerkez*, IT-95-14/2-A, ¶ 1076 (ICTY Appeals Chamber, Dec. 17, 2004) ("both individual [n.b. specific] and general deterrence serve as important goals of sentencing" and also discussing reintegrative deterrence).

84. *See, e.g.,* William W. Burke-White, *Complementarity in Practice: The International Criminal Court as Part of a System of Multi-level Global Governance in the Democratic Republic of Congo*, 18 LEIDEN J. INT'L L. 557 (2005) (noting also the methodological limitations to his careful research and the impossibility of turning to these data to provide statistically meaningful evidence that the ICC has direct deterrent effect).

85. Diane Marie Amann, *Message as Medium in Sierra Leone*, 7 ILSA J. INT'L & COMP. L. 237, 238 (2001).

86. *Prosecutor v. Kordić and Čerkez*, IT-95-14/2-A, ¶¶ 1080–1082 (ICTY Appeals Chamber, Dec. 17, 2004) (referring to the "educational function of a sentence" that "aims at conveying the message that rules of humanitarian international law have to be obeyed under all circumstances . . . [and] seeks to internalize these rules and the moral demands they are based on in the minds of the public"; also noting that: "The unfortunate legacy of wars shows that until today many perpetrators believe that violations of binding international norms can be lawfully committed, because they are fighting for a 'just cause'. Those people have to understand that international law is applicable to everybody, in particular during times of war").

87. Douglas, *op. cit.*, at 2–5.

88. The Confederation of Serbia and Montenegro was dissolved in May 2006 when, following a plebiscite, Montenegro narrowly voted for independence. Serbia now is the successor state to Serbia and Montenegro.

89. This term is from Anthony Giddens, THE THIRD WAY: THE RENEWAL OF SOCIAL DEMOCRACY 66 (1998). Giddens writes within the starkly different context of reforming social democracy, specifically in Great Britain. He does include a chapter on the cosmopolitan nation and cultural pluralism, in which the term cosmopolitan pluralism is not developed.

2. CONFORMITY AND DEVIANCE

1. M. Cherif Bassiouni, INTRODUCTION TO INTERNATIONAL CRIMINAL LAW 585 (2003).

2. *Id.* at 583.

3. *See, e.g.,* 15 LAW REPORTS OF TRIALS OF WAR CRIMINALS 1, 197 (1949) (commenting with regard to World War II atrocity proceedings that "[i]n general the rules of evidence applied in War Crime trials are less technical than those governing the proceedings of courts conducting trials in accordance with the ordinary criminal laws of states"). In addition, international evidence law also represents a harmonization of ideal-type common law and civil law approaches to admissibility.

4. Miriam J. Aukerman, *Extraordinary Evil, Ordinary Crime: A Framework for Understanding Transitional Justice*, 15 HARV. HUM. RTS. J. 39, 41 n.15 (2002). *See also* Martti Koskenniemi, *International Law and Hegemony: A Reconfiguration*, 17 CAMBRIDGE REVIEW OF INTERNATIONAL AFFAIRS 197, 210 (2004) (noting that the ICTY is ideologically dependent on its Western supporters).

5. Hersch Lauterpacht, PRIVATE LAW SOURCES AND ANALOGIES OF INTERNATIONAL LAW (1927).

6. Sanford Levinson, *Responsibility for War Crimes*, 2 PHIL. & PUB. AFF. 244, 245 (1973) ("There seems to be an inverse relationship between the number of individuals involved . . . and the efficacy of traditional legal analysis as a mode of comprehending it . . .").

7. Andreas L. Paulus, *Legalist Groundwork for the International Criminal Court: Commentaries on the Statute of the International Criminal Court*, 14 EUR. J. INT'L L. 843, 859 (2003) (citing Otto Triffterer, *Preliminary Remarks: The Permanent International Criminal Court – Ideal and Reality*, in COMMENTARY ON THE ROME STATUTE OF THE INTERNATIONAL CRIMINAL COURT 17 (Triffterer ed., 1999)).

8. Or, in the matter of sentencing, the convict.

9. This ill fit is of particular concern insofar as the methods of international criminal process, through mechanisms such as primacy, referrals, and complementarity, now are being assimilated into the fabric of the legal orders of communities that do not share a predisposition toward liberal legalism.

10. Moreover, it is possible to be both a perpetrator and victim (for example, in the case of child soldiers) or a perpetrator and a rescuer (for example, Hutu killers in Rwanda occasionally saved a favored Tutsi).

11. Richard J. Goldstone, *The International Tribunal for the Former Yugoslavia: A Case Study in Security Council Action*, 6 DUKE J. COMP. & INT'L L. 5, 7 (1995).

12. Lower-level offenders have been prosecuted by international tribunals for a number of reasons, including strategic concerns such as ability to obtain custody, lower-level offenders' willingness to implicate others, and availability of (or access to) inculpating evidence.

13. *Prosecutor v. Krstić*, Case No. IT-98-33-T, ¶ 709 (ICTY Trial Chamber, Aug. 2, 2001) (conclusion left undisturbed on appeal); *Prosecutor v. Plavšić*, Case No. IT-00-39 & 40/1-S, ¶ 134 (ICTY Trial Chamber, Feb. 27, 2003) (sentence of eleven years for Bosnian Serb leader); *Prosecutor v. Kvočka et al.*, Case No. IT-98-30/1T, ¶¶ 752-67 (ICTY Trial Chamber, November 2, 2001) (more severe sentence issued to lower-ranked offender in the Omarska camp crimes and lesser sentences to those occupying supervisory roles).

14. Several ex-officials of Gen. Pinochet's secret police, including DINA and its successor, have been prosecuted and convicted in Chile. They received sentences ranging from life imprisonment to three years. Pinochet died on December 10, 2006, as this book went to press.

15. A Spanish court sentenced Adolfo Scilingo, a former Argentine naval officer, to 640 years in prison for crimes against humanity, torture, and terrorism for his involvement with death flights. *640 years for Argentine in Spain*, CNN (April 19, 2005) (document on file with the author). Under Spanish law, thirty years is the maximum time that Scilingo can serve. *Id.*

16. *Special Report: Establishing the Rule of Law in Iraq*, U.S. INST. OF PEACE 8 (Apr. 2003).

17. David Luban, *Intervention and Civilization: Some Unhappy Lessons of the Kosovo War*, in GLOBAL JUSTICE AND TRANSNATIONAL POLITICS 107 (De Greiff & Cronin eds., 2002).

18. Luis Salas, *Reconstruction of Public Security and Justice in Post Conflict Societies: The Rwandan Experience*, 26 INT'L J. COMP. & APPLIED CRIM. JUST. 165, 175 (2002). "Many of the victims died because their bodies were so badly torn after repeated rapes in which sharpened sticks, gun barrels or boiling water often replaced penises.... Others died because their attackers tried to gouge out their genitalia or otherwise sexually mutilate them with machetes after raping them." *Id.*

19. Mahmood Mamdani, WHEN VICTIMS BECOME KILLERS 18 (2001). *See also* Amy Chua, WORLD ON FIRE 170 (2004) (noting that "a majority of the Rwandan people supported, indeed personally conducted, the unspeakable atrocities").

20. Organic Law establishing the organization, competence and functioning of Gacaca Courts charged with prosecuting and trying the perpetrators of the crime of genocide and other crimes against humanity, committed between October 1st, 1990 and December 31, 1994, pmbl, Nos. 40/2000 (January 26, 2001) and 33/2001 (June 22, 2001).

21. Rosa Ehrenreich Brooks, *The New Imperialism: Violence, Norms, and the "Rule of Law,"* 101 MICH. L. REV. 2275, 2327 (Hutu leaders "succeeded in dramatically shifting the normative commitment of several million Rwandan Hutus"). *See also* José E. Alvarez, *Crimes of States/Crimes of Hate: Lessons from Rwanda*, 24 YALE J. INT'L L. 365, 368 (1999) (positing that implementation of genocide in Rwanda was a communal crime of hate).

22. Judith Shklar, LEGALISM: LAW, MORALS, AND POLITICAL TRIALS 172 (rev. ed., 1986).

23. H.L.A. Hart, PUNISHMENT AND RESPONSIBILITY: ESSAYS IN THE PHILOSOPHY OF LAW 114 (1968).

24. Patrick Burgess, *Justice and Reconciliation in East Timor: The Relationship between the Commission for Reception, Truth and Reconciliation and the Courts*, 15 CRIM. L. F. 135, 147 (2004). There was an embedded group element to the East Timorese violence. *See, e.g., Prosecutor v. Fernandez*, Case No. 02.C.G.2000, 4 (Dili Dist. Ct. Serious Crimes Spec. Panel, Mar. 1, 2000, sentence reduced by East Timor Ct. App., October 29, 2001) ("the victim was tied, beaten and suffering and [. . .] the crowd was shouting 'kill him, kill him' ") (case prosecuted as ordinary murder but revealing communal nature of violence).

25. Iris Chang, THE RAPE OF NANKING: THE FORGOTTEN HOLOCAUST OF WORLD WAR II (1997).

26. BBC, *Srebrenica massacre list compiled, available at* http://news.bbc.co.uk/2/hi/europe/4310310.stm (last visited June 6, 2006).

27. *Id.*

28. Peter A. French, *Unchosen Evil and Moral Responsibility*, in WAR CRIMES AND COLLECTIVE WRONGDOING 29, 32–34 (Jokić ed., 2001).

29. *Id.* at 32.

30. *Id.* at 33.

31. *Id.*

32. *Id.* (noting also that perpetrators "are described as brimming with righteousness while carrying out the atrocities of ethnic cleansing"). *See also* Donal Coffey, Seminar Paper (Washington & Lee University, Fall 2004) (on file with the author) (theoretically modeling influences and incentives faced by individual perpetrators).

33. Daniel Jonah Goldhagen, HITLER'S WILLING EXECUTIONERS: ORDINARY GERMANS AND THE HOLOCAUST (1996).

34. *Id.* at 9, 14, 450–454.

35. James Waller, BECOMING EVIL: HOW ORDINARY PEOPLE COMMIT GENOCIDE AND MASS KILLING 39 (2002) (describing the Goldhagen thesis).

36. Goldhagen, *op. cit.*, at 480 (Appendix 3: foreword to the German edition).

37. For criticism, *see* Waller, *op. cit.*, at 39–49. French makes a similar argument to Goldhagen in the Serbian case. He contends that perpetrators of mass atrocity in the Balkans have been "immersed in their culture of ethnic hatred, baptized in it from birth. It is an unquestioned, unexamined part of their lives." French, *op. cit.*, at 42. *See also generally* Michael A. Sells, THE BRIDGE BETRAYED: RELIGION AND GENOCIDE IN BOSNIA (1996).

38. Goldhagen, *op. cit.*, at 478 (Appendix 3: foreword to the German edition).

39. *Id.*

40. *Id.* at 482. For supplemental discussion, *see also* David Cooper, *Collective Responsibility, "Moral Luck," and Reconciliation*, in WAR CRIMES AND COLLECTIVE WRONGDOING 205, 208 (Jokić ed., 2001).

41. Goldhagen, *op. cit.*, at 481 (Appendix 3: foreword to the German edition).

42. Alix Christie, *Guarding the Truth*, WASHINGTON POST MAGAZINE (Feb. 26, 2006) at W08. There were nearly one million men in the Waffen-SS alone.

43. *Id.* The White Rose, a resistance group that operated in Munich during World War II, distributed pamphlets throughout German universities until its leaders were caught and executed. White Rose Leaflet II made explicit reference, *inter alia*, to the murder of Jews in Poland. It then inquired: "Why are we telling you these things, since you are fully aware of them – or if not of these, then of other equally grave crimes committed by this frightful sub-humanity? . . . Why do the German people behave so apathetically in the face of all these abominable crimes . . . ?" THE WHITE ROSE: THE RESISTANCE BY STUDENTS AGAINST HITLER 45–46 (1991).

44. Laurel E. Fletcher & Harvey M. Weinstein, *Violence and Social Repair: Rethinking the Contribution of Justice to Reconciliation*, 24 HUM. RTS. Q. 573, 605 (2002) (citing social science and psychological research).

45. *Id.* at 607–610.

46. Hannah Arendt, EICHMANN IN JERUSALEM: A REPORT ON THE BANALITY OF EVIL 252 (1965).

47. An East Timor panel recognized this nuance but then sentenced the individual perpetrator (a head of a militia contingent) to seven years' imprisonment for abduction and murder as a crime against humanity. *Prosecutor v. Agustinho Atolan*, Case No. 3/2003, ¶ 23 (Dili Dist. Ct. Serious Crimes Spec. Panel, June 9, 2003).

48. Immi Tallgren, *The Sensibility and Sense of International Criminal Law*, 13 EUR. J. INT'L L. 561, 573 (2002).

49. Discussed in Waller, *op. cit.*, at 30–32.

50. *Id.* at 87. *See also id.* at xiii (noting how "[a]s collectives, we engage in acts of extraordinary evil, with apparent moral calm and intensity of supposed purpose, which could only be described as insane were they committed by an individual").

51. *See, e.g.,* Tim Judah, THE SERBS 233 (1997) (reporting on sadists and psychopaths).

52. Waller, *op. cit.*, at 70.

53. Douglas M. Kelley, 22 CELLS IN NUREMBERG: A PSYCHIATRIST EXAMINES THE NAZI WAR CRIMINALS (1947). *See also* discussion in Waller, *op. cit.*, at 61–71 (subsequent interpretation of the initial data compiled at Nuremberg).

54. Waller, *op. cit.*, at 63. *See also id.* at 66 (summarizing extensive research by a group of psychologists as demonstrating that the leaders of Nazi Germany were "for the most part, extremely able, intelligent, high-functioning people. [. . .] There was no evidence of thought disorder or psychiatric condition in most of these men.").

55. *Id.* at 67. *See also* Christopher R. Browning, ORDINARY MEN: RESERVE POLICE BATTALION 101 AND THE FINAL SOLUTION IN POLAND (1992).

56. Stanley Milgram, *Behavioral Study of Obedience*, 67 J. OF ABNORMAL AND SOC. PSYCH. 371 (1963); Stanley Milgram, OBEDIENCE TO AUTHORITY: AN EXPERIMENTAL VIEW (1974).

57. Stanley Milgram, OBEDIENCE TO AUTHORITY, *op. cit.*, at 133, 143–147.

58. Waller, *op. cit.*, at 151, 167.

59. Peg Birmingham, *Holes of Oblivion: The Banality of Radical Evil*, 18 HYPATIA 80, 84 (2003) (reproducing text from a 1951 letter from Arendt to Jaspers).

60. *See also* Tallgren, *op. cit.*, at 575.

61. It is often "second-hand and speculative, based upon imagination, others' reports and hostile encounters." David Downes & Paul Rock, UNDERSTANDING DEVIANCE: A GUIDE TO THE SOCIOLOGY OF CRIME AND RULE BREAKING 1, 23–24 (1998).

62. *Id.* at 26.

63. *Id.*

64. *Id.* at 27.

65. *Id.* at 149 (citing Albert K. Cohen, DELINQUENT BOYS: THE CULTURE OF THE GANG (1955)).

66. Travis Hirschi, CAUSES OF DELINQUENCY 16 (1969).

67. Downes & Rock, *op. cit.*, at 240.

68. Larry May, CRIMES AGAINST HUMANITY 99, 106 (2005).

69. *See* Robert Cryer, PROSECUTING INTERNATIONAL CRIMES: SELECTIVITY AND THE INTERNATIONAL CRIMINAL LAW REGIME 268 (2005) ("While a state may be fairly confident that its officials will not commit genocide or crimes against humanity, the same cannot be said for war crimes, which are an omnipresent danger in times of armed conflict.").

70. Rome Statute of the International Criminal Court, U.N. Doc. A/CONF. 183/9, art. 124 [hereinafter Rome Statute]. Only France and Colombia have availed themselves of this opportunity. Article 124 shall be reviewed at the first Review Conference in 2009.

71. Stathis N. Kalyvas, *The Ontology of "Political Violence": Action and Identity in Civil Wars*, 1:3 PERSPECTIVES ON POLITICS 475 (2003).

72. Marko Milanović, *State Responsibility for Genocide*, 17 EUR. J. INT'L L. 553, 603 (2006) ("Genocide is indeed a state crime: there is not a single instance of genocide in recorded history which was not committed either directly by a state, or by a state through one of its proxies.").

73. ERIC D. WEITZ, A CENTURY OF GENOCIDE: UTOPIAS OF RACE AND NATION (2003) (arguing that genocide is organized by states but is operationalized only with widespread popular participation). Nor can international criminal courts punish corporations.

74. George P. Fletcher, *Collective Guilt and Collective Punishment*, 5 THEORETICAL INQUIRIES IN LAW 163 (2004).

75. Cherie Booth, *Prospects and Issues for the International Criminal Court*, in FROM NUREMBERG TO THE HAGUE 184 (Sands ed., 2003). I discuss the collective responsibility notion in my review essay, *Pluralizing International Criminal Justice*, 103 MICH. L. REV. 1295, 1317 (2005), and the short section that follows draws from this work.

76. *Prosecutor v. Momir Nikolić*, Case. No. IT-02-60/1-S, ¶ 60 (ICTY Trial Chamber, December 2, 2003) (emphasis in original).

77. Philip Allot, THE HEALTH OF NATIONS 67 (2002).

78. Fletcher & Weinstein, *op. cit.*, at 580.

79. Karl Jaspers, THE QUESTION OF GERMAN GUILT (Ashton trans., 1978) (1947).

80. *Id.* at 31–32, 73–74.

81. Lyn S. Graybill, TRUTH & RECONCILIATION IN SOUTH AFRICA 113 (2002) (discussing the work of Jaspers).

82. *Id.* (citing Jaspers).

83. Fletcher & Weinstein, *op. cit.*, at 604.

84. Laurel E. Fletcher, *From Indifference to Engagement: Bystanders and International Criminal Justice*, 26 MICH. J. INT'L L. 1013, 1034–1035 (2005). *See also id.* at 1070 (referring to the ICTY's *Simić* judgment as locating "the cause of the mass and systemic persecution in the choices made by individual criminals. Simić and his identified cronies are liable and not the collective Serb population: bystanders witness the evil 'innocently' from the sidelines.").

85. Robert Meister, *Human Rights and the Politics of Victimhood*, 16 ETHICS & INTERNATIONAL AFFAIRS 91, 107 (Oct. 2002).

86. *See, e.g.*, Peter E. Quint, *The Border Guard Trials and the East German Past – Seven Arguments*, 48 AM. J. COMP. L. 541, 542 (2000) (analyzing whether the principle that a person may not be convicted of a criminal offense unless that offense was established by law at the time the act was committed ought to apply to the East German border guards who used deadly force to prevent citizens of East Germany from escaping into West Germany); UNIVERSAL DECLARATION OF HUMAN RIGHTS art. 11(2) (adopted and proclaimed by General Assembly Resolution 217 A (III) Dec. 10, 1948), *available at* http://www.un.org/Overview/rights.html.

87. May, *op. cit.*, at 161. May describes this defense as follows: "For guilt is normally assigned only when there is a difference among people – one person intentionally acting wrongly where everyone, or nearly everyone, else is acting rightly – where the perpetrator is a monster and everyone else is a 'normal' member of society." *Id.*

88. One example is the conviction in December 2005 of Dutch businessman Frans van Anraat by the Hague District Court (a national court in the Netherlands) for complicity in war crimes committed in Iraq. Van Anraat was sentenced to fifteen years' imprisonment. Van Anraat had supplied raw materials to the Iraqi government that, in turn, were used for the development of mustard gas and chemical weapons. These chemical weapons were used to attack the Kurdish population of Halabja in 1998. The Hague District Court deemed these attacks to rise to the level of genocide (van Anraat was acquitted of genocide insofar as the Hague District Court did not find sufficient evidence of his knowledge of the Iraqi government's genocidal intent). An estimated five thousand people perished in the Halabja violence. The van Anraat case bears some parallels to a prosecution, also initiated in the Netherlands, against Guus van Kouwenhoven, a Dutch arms dealer associated with Charles Taylor, for war crimes and gun smuggling. *Taylor's Dutch Ally Accused of War Crimes*, Business Day (South Africa) (April 25, 2006), *available at* http://www.businessday.co.za/PrintFriendly.aspx?ID=BD4A190341 (visited on April 27, 2006). The van Anraat punishment condemns and the Kouwenhoven prosecution relates a

broader story of collaborators, business interests, and transnational networks that facilitate and finance atrocity.

89. *See* Fletcher & Weinstein, *op. cit.*, at 580, 601.

90. Mark Osiel, *The Banality of Good: Aligning Incentives Against Mass Atrocity*, 105 COLUM. L. REV. 1751, 1754 n.9, 1786 n.155 (2005).

91. Drumbl, *Pluralizing International Criminal Justice, op. cit.*, at 1304–1305. It is by no means an exclusive principle.

92. "Crimes against international law are committed by men, not by abstract entities, and only by punishing individuals who commit such crimes can the provisions of international law be enforced." Andrew Clapham, *Issues of complexity, complicity and complementarity: from the Nuremberg Trials to the dawn of the new International Criminal Court, in* FROM NUREMBERG TO THE HAGUE 32–33 (Sands ed., 2003) (citing Trial of German Major War Criminals (Goering et al.), International Military Tribunal (Nuremberg), Judgment and Sentence, 30 Sept. & 1 Oct., 1946, p. 40).

93. *See Prosecutor v. Dragan Nikolić*, Case No. IT-94-2-S, ¶ 60 (ICTY Trial Chamber, Dec. 18, 2003) (elucidating the predicate of avoiding collective guilt within the context of sentencing). Another example is the controversy over the notion of state crimes within the law of state responsibility that roiled members of the International Law Commission.

94. Norman Cigar & Paul Williams, INDICTMENT AT THE HAGUE: THE MILOŠEVIĆ REGIME AND THE CRIMES OF THE BALKAN WAR 30 n.7 (2002).

95. Molly Moore, *Trial of Milosevic Holds Lessons for Iraqi Prosecutors*, WASHINGTON POST (October 18, 2005).

96. *Id. See also* Patricia M. Wald, *The International Criminal Tribunal for the former Yugoslavia Comes of Age: Some Observations of Day to Day Dilemmas of an International Court*, 5 WASH. U.J.L. & POL'Y 87, 95 (2001) ("[A] fair trial by capable judges is indispensable to the Tribunal's reputation as a legitimate vehicle of international accountability.").

97. *See, e.g., Prosecutor v. Kajelijeli*, Case No. ICTR-98-44A-A (ICTR Appeals Chamber, May 23, 2005) (decreasing the defendant's original multiple sentences (two life sentences and fifteen years) to a single sentence of forty-five years, less time served in detention, owing to Appeals Chamber's *proprio motu* finding of "serious" violations of Kajelijeli's fundamental rights during his arrest and detention).

98. A joint criminal enterprise is an understanding or arrangement amounting to an agreement between two or more persons that they will commit a crime; the understanding or arrangement need not be express, and its existence may be inferred from all the circumstances; it need not have been reached at any time before the crime is committed. *Prosecutor v. Krnojelac*, IT-97-25-T, ¶ 80 (ICTY Trial Chamber, March 15, 2002); *Prosecutor v. Babić*, Case No. IT-03-72-A, ¶ 27 (ICTY Appeals Chamber, July 18, 2005) (describing the third prong of JCE ("extended prong")). For another ICTY JCE conviction *see Prosecutor v. Stakić*, Case No. IT-97-24-A, ¶ 402 (ICTY Appeals Chamber, March 22, 2006). The Rome Statute "common purpose" provision opens the door for the ICC to entertain a theory of vicarious liability. *See* Rome Statute, *op. cit.*, art. 25. The East Timor Special Panels have availed themselves of both joint criminal enterprise and common purpose liability. *See, e.g., Prosecutor v. Barros and Mendonca*, Case No. 01/2004 (Dili Dist. Ct. Serious Crimes Spec. Panel, May 12, 2005, *aff'd* East Timor Ct. App.); *Prosecutor v. De Deus*, Case No. 2A/2004 (Dili Dist. Ct. Serious Crimes Spec. Panel, April 12, 2005). For discussion of joint criminal enterprise generally, *see* Allison Marston Danner & Jenny Martinez, *Guilty Associations, Joint Criminal Enterprise, Command Responsibility, and the Development of International Criminal Law*, 93 CALIF. L. REV. 75 (2005).

99. Statute of the ICTY, S.C. Res. 827, U.N. SCOR, 48th Sess., 3217th mtg. at 29, art. 7(3) (1993); Statute of the ICTR, U.N. SCOR, 49th Sess., 3453d mtg. at 15, U.N. Doc. S/Res/955, art. 6(3) (1994); Rome Statute, *op. cit.*, art. 28(a)(i) (basing command responsibility on, *inter alia*, a finding that the "military commander or person either knew or, owing to the circumstances at the time, should have known that the forces were committing or about

to commit such crimes"), art. 28(b)(i) (envisioning a higher threshold for superior–subordinate relationships outside the military context, according to which responsibility ensues where the superior either knew or consciously disregarded information that clearly indicated that the subordinate was committing or about to commit the crimes); *Prosecutor v. Musema*, Case No. ICTR-96-13-T, ¶ 396 (ICTR Appeals Chamber, Nov. 16, 2001) (convicting director of a tea factory of genocide). The Charles Taylor indictment incorporates theories of command responsibility and joint criminal enterprise.

100. *Prosecutor v. Krstić*, Case No. IT-98-33-A (ICTY Appeals Chamber, Apr. 19, 2004) (distinguishing between joint criminal enterprise and aiding and abetting and substituting on the facts a conviction for aiding and abetting for one based on perpetration of a joint criminal enterprise); *Prosecutor v. Blaškić*, Case No. IT-95-14-A, ¶ 48 (ICTY Appeals Chamber, July 29, 2004) ("[O]ne of the requirements of the *actus reus* of aiding and abetting is that the support of the aider and abettor has a substantial effect upon the perpetration of the crime."); *Prosecutor v. Ndindabahizi*, Case No. ICTR-2001-71-I (ICTR Trial Chamber, July 15, 2004); *Prosecutor v. Rutaganira*, Case No. ICTR-96-3 (ICTR Trial Chamber, March 14, 2005) (convicting as part of a plea agreement for extermination as a crime against humanity based on aiding and abetting by omission); *Prosecutor v. Blagojević and Jokić*, Case No. IT-02-60-T (ICTY Trial Chamber, January 17, 2005) (convicting first defendant for aiding and abetting complicity to commit genocide, crimes against humanity, and war crimes and second defendant for aiding and abetting extermination and persecution as a crime against humanity).

101. Statute of the ICTR, *op. cit.*, art. 2(3)(b); Statute of the ICTY, *op. cit.*, art. 4(3)(b); *Prosecutor v. Niyitegeka*, Case No. ICTR-96-14-A (ICTR Appeals Chamber, July 9, 2004) (convicting defendant on a number of charges, including conspiracy to commit genocide, and sentencing him to life imprisonment); *Prosecutor v. Nahimana*, Case No. ICTR-99-52-T, ¶¶ 1043–1048 (ICTR Trial Chamber, Dec. 3, 2003) (concluding that conspiracy to commit genocide requires the existence of an agreement, but this need not be formal or express and can be inferred from circumstantial evidence; a conspiracy to commit genocide could be comprised of individuals acting in an institutional capacity even in the absence of personal links with each other). The Rome Statute does not clearly grant the ICC authority to prosecute conspiracy or make use of conspiracy as an alternate theory to aiding or abetting to link a particular actor to the substantive offense, but does contemplate "common purpose" liability. Conspiracy played a controversial and largely ineffective role in the Nuremberg trials. Richard Overy, *The Nuremberg Trials: International Law in the Making*, in FROM NUREMBERG TO THE HAGUE 28 (Sands ed., 2003). The IMT ruled that only conspiracy to commit acts of aggressive war could be prosecuted as an independent crime; conspiracy to commit war crimes and crimes against humanity could not be independently prosecuted. Moreover, the IMT refused to embrace the U.S. *Pinkerton* doctrine. In contemporary settings, there is considerable doubt whether conspiracy to commit war crimes is an independent crime under the law of war. The debate between Justices Stevens (writing for a plurality) and Thomas on the United States Supreme Court on this point is instructive. *See Hamdan v. Rumsfeld*, 548 U.S. __ (2006) (slip op.), *available at* http://www.supremecourtus.gov/opinions/05pdf/05-184.pdf. (Justice Stevens' slip op. p. 46) (Justice Stevens holding that conspiracy to commit war crimes is not a recognized violation of the law of war prosecutable by a law of war military commission, and Justice Thomas dissenting). One U.S. District Court has since adopted Justice Stevens' reasoning to rule that conspiracy to commit crimes against humanity or war crimes is not actionable under the law of nations as understood for the purposes of the Alien Tort Claims Act. *See Presbyterian Church v. Talisman*, 01 Civ. 9882 (S.D.N.Y, 2006) (also holding also that international law does not recognize a doctrine of conspiratorial liability that would extend to activity encompassed by the U.S. *Pinkerton* principle).

102. *Association de malfaiteurs* originates in regular domestic law (e.g., Articles 282 and 283 of the Rwandan Penal Code), but has been applied to extraordinary international crimes

with some regularity in Rwanda. It embodies a lower threshold than complicity (which requires that the act be indispensable to the commission of the crime). An example of individual criminal responsibility for *association de malfaiteurs* involves a conviction of a perpetrator who was present and exercised some supervisory functions at a roadblock in Rwanda where criminal attacks allegedly occurred and who was unable to prove that his presence was coerced. *Ministère Public v. Twizeyimana* (June 20, 2000, ch. sp. 1 ière instance Kigali), RMP 8020/S12/RE/MAITRE, RP 060/CS/KIG, p. 10. To convict for genocide based on this theory, it must be shown that the group was created for eliminationist purposes. A group that arose spontaneously without a common intention (*attroupement spontané sans organisation et sans intention commune*) – including a group, in which some members wanted to kill and others did not, that assembled out of curiosity to observe what was occurring after hearing a clamor – does not meet this standard. *Ministère Public v. Sendakiza et al.* (Nov. 11, 1999, ch. sp. 1 ière instance Rushashi), RMP 110.498/S1/NK.A/NT.M/N.G., RP 032/S1/99/CH.SP/Rshi. The *association de malfaiteurs* standard runs below that of accomplice. For a definition of accomplice in domestic Rwandan law applicable to genocide prosecutions, *see* Organic Law No. 8/96 on the organization of prosecutions for offenses constituting the crime of genocide or crimes against humanity committed since 1 October 1990 (Journal Officiel No. 17 du Sept. 1, 1996), art. 53 (defining accomplice as "the person who has, by any means, provided assistance to commit offenses [. . .]").

103. *See, e.g.,* William A. Schabas, *Mens Rea and the International Criminal Tribunal for the Former Yugoslavia,* 37 New England L. Rev. 1019 (2003); Danner & Martinez, *op. cit.*

104. *Prosecutor v. Blaškić,* Case No. IT-95-14-A (ICTY Appeals Chamber, July 29, 2004).

105. *Id.* ¶¶ 41, 42, 62, 166.

106. *Prosecutor v. Brđanin,* Case No. IT-99-36-T (ICTY Trial Chamber, Sept. 1, 2004).

107. Trial of Ulrich Greifelt and Others (United States Military Tribunal, Nuremberg, 1947–1948), reprinted at 8 Law Reports of Trials of War Criminals 1, 50 (1949) (notes on the case, citing judgment of IMT).

108. *Id.* at 52. No such formal amendment to Control Council Law No. 10 was made, because it was believed that judges would exercise their sentencing discretion in light of the IMT recommendation. *Id.* at 53.

109. *Id.* at 50.

110. *Id.* at 58, 62.

111. Makau Mutua, *Savages, Victims, and Saviors: the Metaphor of Human Rights,* 42 Harv. Int'l L. J. 201 (2001).

112. Waller, *op. cit.,* at 244.

113. Translated: He who killed did not see that he was killing a man; in light of the lessons given by the former authorities, he thought he was killing an animal. Rapport d'observation, Les Juridictions Gacaca 3 (6 juillet 2003), Cellule de Karukamba, ASF-Belgium. In this session, a list of accused was drawn up.

114. Cherif Bassiouni, *The Protection of "Collective Victims" in International Law,* in International Protection of Victims 181, 183 (Bassiouni ed., 1988) (describing victims of mass atrocity as groups or groupings of individuals linked by special bonds, considerations, factors or circumstances that, for these very reasons, make them the target of victimization).

115. Ernesto Kiza, Corene Rathgeber, & Holger-C. Rohne, Victims of War: War-Victimization and Victims' Attitudes towards Addressing Atrocities (2005) (draft on file with the author, cited with permission of Holger-C. Rohne); report published as Victims of War – An Empirical Study on War-Victimization and Victims' Attitudes towards Addressing Atrocities (Hamburger Institut für Sozialforschung, 2006). The draft report I discuss includes data from Darfur (Sudan) as a case study that did not appear in the final report.

116. Afghanistan, Bosnia and Herzegovina, Cambodia, Croatia, Democratic Republic of Congo, Israel, Kosovo, Macedonia, Palestine, Philippines, and the Sudan. *Id.* at 60.

117. The research does not exclude ordinary crimes committed during periods of conflict. This suggests a limitation to the utility of this study to the discussion of a victimology of extraordinary international criminality, although this limitation certainly does not dismiss the value of the insights that can be gleaned from this important research.

118. Kiza et al., *op. cit.*, at 90. A 2005 study conducted by the International Center for Transitional Justice and the Human Rights Center (Berkeley) in Uganda found that respondents (mostly victims) supported integrated transitional justice mechanisms that included trials, a truth commission and reparations, and also sanctions that included imprisonment, confessions, and compensation. *See* FORGOTTEN VOICES: A POPULATION-BASED SURVEY ON ATTITUDES ABOUT PEACE AND JUSTICE IN NORTHERN UGANDA (2005).

119. Kiza et al., *op. cit.*, at 154–155.

120. *Id.* at 89, 158. *See also id.* at 41 (corroborating International Committee of the Red Cross research for Afghanistan that showed a striking preference in favor of domestic, even customary, law over international law, with only a small minority favoring prosecution based on international law).

121. *Id.* at 89.

122. *Id.* at 91.

123. *Id.* at 102–103.

124. *Id.* at 103.

125. Fletcher, *From Indifference to Engagement, op. cit.*, at 1022–1023.

126. Kiza et al., *op. cit.*, at 104, 158. It also suggests that victims may have different responses depending on the nature of the involvement of the accused. The research suggests, preliminarily, a stratification of responses, diverse in nature, in which modality of accountability is connected to category of offender. *Id* at 107.

127. *Id.* at 113.

128. *Id.* at 113–114.

129. *Id.* at 91.

130. A CALL FOR JUSTICE (2005), *available at* http://www.aihrc.org.af/rep_detail.htm. Once again, criminal trials formed only part of a broad understanding of justice, with considerable support for lustration, truth-seeking, institutional reform, and reparations. Whereas 90 percent of the six thousand respondents favored lustration/vetting of perpetrators from governmental positions, only 40 percent favored the prosecution of notorious perpetrators.

131. *See* Mark Osiel, *Modes of Participation in Mass Atrocity*, 38 CORNELL INT'L L. J. 793, 805 (2005) (discussing examples of Guatemala, Austria, South Africa, and Israeli persecutions of Jewish collaborators).

132. The ICC subjects victim input to judicial direction and contingent upon being "conducted 'in a manner which is not prejudicial or inconsistent with the rights of the accused and a fair and impartial trial.'" *See* International Criminal Court, *Victims and Witnesses, available at* http://www.icc-cpi.int/victimsissues.html.

133. Ralph Henham, *Some Issues for Sentencing in the International Criminal Court*, 52 INT'L & COMP. L.Q. 81, 85 (2003); Rolf Einar Fife, *Article 77: Applicable Penalties*, in COMMENTARY ON THE ROME STATUTE OF THE INTERNATIONAL CRIMINAL COURT 985, 991 (Triffterer ed., 1999). Minimum sentences ultimately were disfavored.

3. PUNISHMENT OF INTERNATIONAL CRIMES IN INTERNATIONAL CRIMINAL TRIBUNALS

1. *Prosecutor v. Erdemović*, Case No. IT-96-22, ¶ 59 (ICTY Trial Chamber, Nov. 29, 1996).

2. Charter of the International Military Tribunal, 59 Stat. 1544, 82 U.N.T.S. 279, art. 27 (1945).

3. 15 LAW REPORTS OF TRIALS OF WAR CRIMINALS 1, 200–202 (1949). In addition, the discussion of defense pleas briefly mentions facts to consider in mitigation.

4. *See, e.g.*, Vol. 22, TRIAL OF THE MAJOR WAR CRIMINALS BEFORE THE INTERNATIONAL MILITARY TRIBUNAL 524, 527 (1946).

5. Obedience to superior orders explicitly was recognized in Article 8 of the Charter of the International Military Tribunal (IMT) as a mitigating circumstance and not as a defense to the charges. The IMT took into account other mitigating factors. For example, in the case of Funk, the following appears in relation to the war crimes and crimes against humanity charges: "In spite of the fact that he occupied important official positions, Funk was never a dominant figure in the various programmes in which he participated. This is a mitigating fact [...]." Funk was sentenced to life imprisonment. Similarly, proof that "British naval prisoners of war in camps under Doenitz's jurisdiction were treated strictly according to the [Geneva] Convention" was a "fact" the IMT took "into consideration, regarding it as a mitigating circumstance." Doenitz was sentenced to ten years' imprisonment. For Speer, it was recognized in mitigation that he opposed Hitler's scorched earth program, "deliberately sabotage[ed] it at considerable personal risk," and that "he was one of the few men who had the courage to tell Hitler that the war was lost and to take steps to prevent the senseless destruction of production facilities." Speer received twenty years. With regard to von Neurath, it was emphasized in mitigation that he had intervened to release arrested Czechoslovaks, had resigned, and refused to act in certain capacities. He received a term sentence of fifteen years.

6. Charter of the International Military Tribunal, *op. cit.*, art. 6.

7. *Accord*, Robert Cryer, PROSECUTING INTERNATIONAL CRIMES: SELECTIVITY AND THE INTERNATIONAL CRIMINAL LAW REGIME 38–39 (2005).

8. Official Gazette of the Control Council for Germany, No. 3 (January 31, 1946). Article II(4b) of Control Council Law No. 10 provided that "[t]he fact that any person acted pursuant to the order of his government or of a superior does not free him from responsibility for a crime, but may be considered in mitigation."

9. Rt. Hon. The Lord Wright of Durley, *Foreword*, 6 LAW REPORTS OF TRIALS OF WAR CRIMINALS v, v (1948).

10. *Id.* at vi.

11. Trial of Josef Altstötter and Others (United States Military Tribunal, Nuremberg, 1947), reprinted at 6 LAW REPORTS OF TRIALS OF WAR CRIMINALS 1, 28 (1948). Control Council Law No. 10 expressly incorporated the London Agreement, which created the IMT. *Id.* at 27–28.

12. *Id.* at 28; *see also* The Flick Trial (United States Military Tribunal, Nuremberg, 1947), reprinted at 9 LAW REPORTS OF TRIALS OF WAR CRIMINALS 1, 57 (1949) (notes on the case).

13. James Waller, BECOMING EVIL: HOW ORDINARY PEOPLE COMMIT GENOCIDE AND MASS KILLING 92 (2002).

14. The forfeiture of property as a sentence was unusual in the "subsequent proceedings." Article II(3) of Control Council Law No. 10, although giving the judges discretion to punish, provided as examples of punishment: death, imprisonment for life or for a term of years (with or without hard labor), fines, forfeiture of property, restitution, and deprivation of some or all civil rights. Virtually all the sentences involved death (at times subsequently commuted) or imprisonment, with imprisonment dominating as the preferred form of punishment.

15. Trial of Josef Altstötter and Others (United States Military Tribunal, Nuremberg, 1947), reprinted at 6 LAW REPORTS OF TRIALS OF WAR CRIMINALS 1 (1948).

16. *Id.* at 75. Although the military tribunal recognized that abiding by German law was not a defense, it indicated that if this were a defense, many of Lautz's acts would be excusable. *Id.*

17. The Hostages Trial (Wilhelm List and Others) (United States Military Tribunal, Nuremberg, 1948), reprinted at 8 LAW REPORTS OF TRIALS OF WAR CRIMINALS 34, 74 (1949). That said, despite this discussion, for the Tribunal mitigation "is more a matter of grace [...]." *Id.*

18. *Id.* at 92.

19. The Flick Trial (United States Military Tribunal, Nuremberg, 1947), reprinted at 9 LAW REPORTS OF TRIALS OF WAR CRIMINALS 1, 30 (1949).

20. Trial of Weiss and Thirty-Nine Others (General Military Government Court of the United States Zone, Dachau, Germany, 1945), reprinted at 11 LAW REPORTS OF TRIALS OF WAR CRIMINALS 5 (1949).
21. Carlos Santiago Nino, RADICAL EVIL ON TRIAL 9 (1996).
22. Cryer, *op. cit.*, at 46.
23. *Prosecutor v. Blaškić*, Case No. IT-95-14-A, ¶ 680 (ICTY Appeals Chamber, July 29, 2004) (noting that the Appeals Chamber has stated that a revision of a sentence on appeal can be justified due to discernible error in sentencing discretion or if the Appeals Chamber has overturned convictions); *Prosecutor v. Semanza*, Case No. ICTR-97-20-A (ICTR Appeals Chamber, May 20, 2005) (increasing sentence to 35 years from 24.5 years owing to Appeals Chamber's decision to enter additional convictions); *Prosecutor v. Kajelijeli*, Case No. ICTR-98-44A-A, ¶ 291 (ICTR Appeals Chamber, May 23, 2005) (Appeals Chamber review is to be of a "corrective nature"); *Prosecutor v. Kordić and Čerkez*, Case No. IT-95-14/2-A (ICTY Appeals Chamber, Dec. 17, 2004).
24. *Prosecutor v. Kordić and Čerkez*, Case No. IT-95-14/2-A, ¶¶ 1070–1071 (ICTY Appeals Chamber, Dec. 17, 2004) (reducing Čerkez's initial sentence of fifteen years to six years because of the Appeals Chamber's decision to reverse "most of the convictions," thereby entitling it to "itself find the adequate sentence for the remaining convictions").
25. Stuart Beresford, *Unshackling the Paper Tiger – the Sentencing Practices of the Ad Hoc International Criminal Tribunals for the Former Yugoslavia and Rwanda*, 1 INT'L CRIM. L. REV. 33, 51 (2001). *See also Prosecutor v. Brđanin*, Case No. IT-99-36-T (ICTY Trial Chamber, Sept. 1, 2004) (discussing rule change requiring sentencing to be addressed in closing arguments instead of a separate sentencing hearing).
26. ICTY R.P. & EVID., Rule 100(A), *available at* http://www.un.org/icty/legaldoc-e/index.htm. *See also On Transitional Rules of Criminal Procedure*, UNTAET Reg. 2000/30 ss. 29A, (Sept. 25, 2000), *as amended by* UNTAET Regulation 2001/25 (Sept. 14, 2001) [hereinafter UNTAET Regulation 30 as amended]; SPEC. CT. SIERRA LEONE R.P. & EVID., Rule 100, *available at* http://www.sc-sl.org/scsl-procedure.html.
27. Rome Statute of the International Criminal Court, U.N. Doc. A/CONF.183/9, art. 76 [hereinafter Rome Statute]; SPEC. CT. SIERRA LEONE R.P. & EVID., *op. cit.*, Rule 100(B).
28. *Prosecutor v. Semanza*, Case No. ICTR-97-20-A, ¶¶ 345, 377 (ICTR Appeals Chamber, May 20, 2005).
29. *Prosecutor v. Dragan Nikolić*, Case No. IT-94-2-A, ¶ 84 (ICTY Appeals Chamber, Feb. 4, 2005).
30. Statute of the ICTY, S.C. Res. 827, U.N. SCOR, 48th Sess., 3217th mtg. at 29, U.N. Doc. S/Res/827, art. 24(2) (1993); Statute of the ICTR, U.N. SCOR, 49th Sess., 3453d mtg. at 15, U.N. Doc. S/Res/955, art. 23(2) (1994).
31. ICTY R.P. & EVID., *op. cit.*, Rule 87(C); *see also Prosecutor v. Delalić*, Case No. IT-96-21, ¶ 771 (ICTY Appeals Chamber, Feb. 20, 2001) (discussing the discretion of the Trial Chambers to impose consecutive or concurrent sentences). The recent practice has been to pass a single composite sentence. This has given rise to some controversy regarding what types of convictions are impermissibly cumulative. *Prosecutor v. Blaškić*, Case No. IT-95-14-A, ¶¶ 721–22 (ICTY Appeals Chamber, July 29, 2004). The ICTR Rules mandate the Trial Chambers to specify whether multiple sentences are to be served consecutively or concurrently. ICTR R.P. & EVID., Rule 101(C), *available at* http://69.94.11.53/ENGLISH/rules/070605/070605.pdf.
32. *Prosecutor v. Kambanda*, Case No. ICTR-97-23-S, ¶ 30 (ICTR Trial Chamber, Sept. 4, 1998). *See also* ICTY R.P. & EVID., *op. cit.*, Rule 85(A)(vi) (providing that the parties are permitted to produce any relevant information that may assist the Trial Chamber in determining an appropriate sentence); *Prosecutor v. Kvočka et al.*, Case No. IT-98-30/1-A, ¶¶ 668–9, 715 (ICTY Appeals Chamber, February 28, 2005) (recognizing there is "no definitive list of sentencing guidelines," that "sentencing is essentially a discretionary process on the part of a Trial Chamber," and concluding that "the Trial Chamber has discretion as regards the factors it considers in mitigation, the weight it

attaches to a particular mitigating factor, and the discounting of a particular mitigating factor").

33. Rome Statute, *op. cit.*, art. 77(1); *see also id.* art. 78(3).

34. *Id.* art. 78(1) ("In determining the sentence, the Court shall, in accordance with the Rules of Procedure and Evidence, take into account such factors as the gravity of the crime and the individual circumstances of the convicted person.").

35. ICC R.P. & Evid. Rule 145, *available at* http://www.icc-cpi.int/library/basicdocuments/rules(e).pdf.

36. *Id.* Rule 145(3).

37. The following factors come to mind: "degree of intent," *id.*, Rule 145(1)(c), and "commission of the crime for any motive involving discrimination," *id.*, Rule 145(2)(b)(v).

38. Ralph Henham, *Theorising the Penality of Sentencing of International Criminal Trials*, 8(4) THEORETICAL CRIMINOLOGY 429 (2004).

39. Statute of the Special Court for Sierra Leone, S.C. Res. 1315, U.N. SCOR, 55th Sess., 4186th mtg. at 1, arts. 17, 19(1), *available at* http://www.sc-sl.org/scsl-statute.html [hereinafter Sierra Leone Statute]; SPEC. CT. SIERRA LEONE R.P. & EVID., *op. cit.*, Rule 101.

40. Sierra Leone Statute, *op. cit.*, art. 19(1). The Rules of Procedure and Evidence of the ICTR apply *mutatis mutandis* to the conduct of proceedings before the Special Court for Sierra Leone. *Id.* art. 14(1).

41. Spec. Ct. SIERRA LEONE R.P. & EVID., *op. cit.*, Rule 101.

42. *Khmer Rouge Trials, Annex Draft Agreement Between the United Nations and the Royal Government of Cambodia*, G.A. Res. 57/228, U.N. Doc. A/RES/57/228, art. 10 (May 22, 2003); Law on the Establishment of Extraordinary Chambers in the Courts of Cambodia for the Prosecution of Crimes Committed During the Period of Democratic Kampuchea, arts. 38–39, *available at* http://www.derechos.org/human-rights/seasia/doc/krlaw.html. *See also generally*, Ernestine E. Meijer, *The Extraordinary Chambers in the Courts of Cambodia for Prosecuting Crimes Committed by the Khmer Rouge: Jurisdiction, Organization, and Procedure of an Internationalized National Tribunal*, in INTERNATIONALIZED CRIMINAL COURTS 207, 229 (Romano, Nollkaemper, & Kleffner eds., 2004).

43. *On the Establishment of Panels with Exclusive Jurisdiction over Serious Criminal Offences*, U.N. Transnational Administration in East Timor, § 10.1, U.N. Doc. UNTAET/REG/2000/15 (June 6, 2000), *available at* http://www.un.org/peace/etimor/untaetR/Reg0015E.pdf [hereinafter UNTAET Regulation 15]. In one case, three total sentences of thirty-three years and four months were awarded on a theory of conjunction of various convictions. *Prosecutor v. Marqués et al.*, Case No. 09/2000, ¶¶ 1117, 1126 (Dili Dist. Ct. Serious Crimes Spec. Panel, Dec. 11, 2001).

44. UNTAET Regulation 15, *op. cit.*, § 10.2. "With a few minor exceptions, Regulation 2000/15 adopted the law of the International Criminal Court." Suzanne Katzenstein, *Hybrid Tribunals: Searching for Justice in East Timor*, 16 HARV. HUM. RTS. J. 245, 251 (2003).

45. The Rules of the East Timor Special Panels provided a cursory overview of sentencing, permitting imprisonment or fines and allowing for conditional release after conviction. UNTAET Regulation 30 as amended, *op. cit.*, §§ 42–43; *see also id.* § 45 (permitting differentiated treatment of minors).

46. *Id.* § 29A.

47. Statute of the ICTR, *op. cit.*, art. 23(3); Statute of the ICTY, *op. cit.*, art. 24(3) ("In addition to imprisonment, the Trial Chambers may order the return of any property and proceeds acquired by criminal conduct, including by means of duress, to their rightful owners."); Rome Statute, *op. cit.*, arts. 75 (providing for reparations to victims), 77(2) (empowering the ICC to order a fine, and providing details thereof, and to order forfeiture of assets derived directly or indirectly from the crime, in addition to ordering imprisonment); ICC R.P. & EVID., *op. cit.*, Rules 94, 146–147 (providing details regarding request for reparations, the imposition of a fine, and orders of forfeiture); ICTR R.P. & EVID., *op. cit.*, Rules 105–106 (discussing restitution, and also referring to the national legal system of Rwanda as the

vehicle through which a victim may bring an action for compensation); SPEC. CT. SIERRA LEONE R.P. & EVID., *op. cit.*, Rules 104–105 (referencing possibility of forfeiture of property of those convicted and of compensation to victims); UNTAET Regulation 30 as amended, *op. cit.*, §§ 42.3, 50 (permitting confiscation and return of objects seized during the proceeding and creating a civil cause of action for alleged victims to claim compensation); UNTAET Regulation 15, *op. cit.*, § 10.1(c) (permitting as a penalty a forfeiture of proceeds, property, and assets derived directly or indirectly from the crime); Charter of the International Military Tribunal, *op. cit.*, art. 28 (allowing the Tribunal to deprive any convicted person of any stolen property).

48. Stef Vandeginste, *Victims of Genocide, Crimes against Humanity, and War Crimes in Rwanda: The Legal and Institutional Framework of Their Right to Reparation, in* POLITICS AND THE PAST: ON REPAIRING HISTORICAL INJUSTICES 249, 250 (Torpey ed., 2003) (noting that, in practice, these methods face a "rather uncertain future").

49. *See also* Beresford, *op. cit.*, at 36 n.11 (noting that the Nuremberg Tribunal did not avail itself of its authority to return stolen property).

50. Rome Statute, *op. cit.*, art. 79; ICC R.P. & EVID., *op. cit.*, Rule 98. For more information on the Trust Fund, *see International Criminal Court: Trust Fund for Victims, available at* http://www.icc-cpi.int/vtf.html. The Rome Statute also references a Victims and Witnesses Unit, which is geared to those individuals who testify before the ICC. Rome Statute, *op. cit.*, art. 43(6); ICC R.P. & EVID., *op. cit.*, Rules 16–19. Victims also have some opportunities to present their views and observations before the ICC (including to the Pre-Trial Chamber when the Prosecutor requests its authorization to investigate). Tensions are emerging between victims and the ICC Prosecutor. *See infra* Chapter 5.

51. UNTAET Regulation 15, *op. cit.*, § 25.

52. Statute of the ICTR, *op. cit.*, art. 27; Statute of the ICTY, *op. cit.*, art. 28; Sierra Leone Statute, *op. cit.*, art. 23; Rome Statute, *op. cit.*, art. 110; UNTAET Regulation 30 as amended, *op. cit.*, § 43.1.

53. *Prosecutor v. Mau*, 08/C.G/2003/TD.DIL (Dili Dist. Ct. Serious Crimes Spec. Panel, February 23, 2004); *Prosecutor v. Gusmão*, 07/C.G./2003 (Dili Dist. Ct. Serious Crimes Spec. Panel, February 28, 2003); UNTAET Regulation 30 as amended, *op. cit.*, § 43.1. Unconditional release also can be requested.

54. President of the ICTY, Decision of the President on the Application for Pardon or Commutation of Sentence of Miroslav Tadić, Case No. IT-95-9, ¶ 4 (June 24, 2004) (noting that "eligibility for pardon or commutation of sentence in the enforcing states generally 'starts at two-thirds of the sentence served'"). The ordinary domestic laws of the states emergent from the former Yugoslavia also provide for early and conditional release.

55. ICTY R.P. & EVID., *op. cit.*, Rules 123, 124, 125; ICTR R.P. & EVID., *op. cit.*, Rules 124, 125, 126; ICTY PRACTICE DIRECTION IT/146, *Practice Direction on the Procedure for the Determination of Applications for Pardon, Commutation of Sentence and Early Release of Persons Convicted by the International Tribunal* § 7 (April 7, 1999).

56. Nancy Amoury Combs, *Procuring Guilty Pleas for International Crimes: The Limited Influence of Sentencing Discounts*, 59 VAND. L. REV. 69, 116 (2006).

57. Those benefiting from early release at the ICTY include: Dragan Kolundžija (shift commander of the Keraterm camp, who pled guilty to persecution as a crime against humanity and received a three-year sentence); Miroslav Tadić (a member of the Serb Crisis Staff, who was convicted of persecution as a crime against humanity and received an eight-year sentence); Simo Zarić (a Bosnian Serb military supervisor, convicted of persecution as a crime against humanity and received a six-year sentence); Milan Simić (President of the Executive Board of the Bosanski Samac Assembly, who pled guilty to two counts of torture as crimes against humanity and sentenced to five years' imprisonment); Tihomir Blaškić (Colonel in the Croatian Defense Council, whose convictions largely were reversed by the Appeals Chamber resulting in a final sentence of nine years' imprisonment); Anto Furundžija (local commander of a special unit of the military police force of the Croatian

Defense Council known as the Jokers, convicted of two counts of war crimes and sentenced to ten years' imprisonment); Zdravko Mucić (commander of Čelebići camp, sentenced to nine years' imprisonment for war crimes); Milojica Kos (shift commander of guards at the Omarska camp, convicted of crimes against humanity and war crimes and sentenced to six years' imprisonment).

58. Order of the President on the Application for the Early Release of Anto Furundžija, ICTY Case No. IT-95-17/1 (July 29, 2004).

59. *Id.*

60. *Prosecutor v. Dragan Nikolić*, Case No. IT-94-2-A, ¶¶ 97 (ICTY Appeals Chamber, Feb. 4, 2005) (Appeals Chamber reducing sentence from twenty-three years to twenty years because, in fixing a sentence of twenty-three years, the Trial Chamber had erred in attaching too much weight to the possibility of early release).

61. Three individuals had been acquitted at the time the Special Panels ceased operations.

62. William W. Burke-White, *A Community of Courts: Toward a System of International Criminal Law Enforcement*, 24 MICH. J. INT'L L. 1, 67 (2002).

63. *See, e.g., Prosecutor v. Marqués et al.*, Case No. 09/2000, ¶ 28 (Dili Dist. Ct. Serious Crimes Spec. Panel, Dec. 11, 2001) ("The Elements of the Crime provided by the Preparatory Committee [for the International Criminal Court] need to be considered along with the jurisprudence of the ad hoc tribunals.").

64. Organization for Security and Cooperation in Europe Mission in Kosovo, KOSOVO'S WAR CRIMES TRIALS: A REVIEW 46–47, 52 (Sept. 2002). These data are current only to the end of June 2002, at which point seventeen cases had been initiated. *Id.* at 12. The 2002 data from the Kosovo courts indicate an average sentence of 13 years for ordinary crimes and 15.8 years for proscribed international crimes. In this calculation, I excluded one case involving a minor convicted of an ordinary domestic crime; the minor was diverted to a juvenile correctional facility for reeducation for a term of one to five years. The average for international crimes would be slightly lowered by four sentences (seventeen, thirteen, ten, and five years) issued by an international judge in November 2003 against four Kosovo Albanians upon convictions for war crimes and a sentence of twelve years (two years less than the initial sentence in 2001 of fourteen years) issued on a war crimes conviction to a Kosovo Serb on October 25, 2002. OSCE Case Report, *Prosecutor v. Gashi* (Nov. 11, 2003) (*Llapi* case) (document on file with author); Humanitarian Law Center, *Trials Before Kosovo Internationalized Courts, Analysis, Just Sentence For War Crime Against Kosovo Albanian Civilians* (October 25, 2002). Many of the cases are subject to appeal: in fact, a number of sentences have been quashed and some cases currently are being reheard. Many acquittals have been entered. This is mostly due to a practice by international prosecutors of overcharging international crimes. Overall, the operation of the Kosovo hybrid courts is subject to delay, disarray, ethnic bias, and weak reasoning. KOSOVO'S WAR CRIMES TRIALS, *op. cit.*, at 12–28 (data current to June 2002); OSCE Mission in Kosovo, Dep't of Human Rights & Rule of Law, KOSOVO: A REVIEW OF THE CRIMINAL JUSTICE SYSTEM 31–41 (Sept. 1, 2000–Feb. 28, 2001); Rosa Ehrenreich Brooks, *The New Imperialism: Violence, Norms, and the "Rule of Law,"* 101 MICH. L. REV. 2275, 2281 (2003) (concluding that the Kosovo panels are unable to offer consistent and independent rulings); Cryer, *op. cit.*, at 70. A number of detainees have escaped during or pending trial. Beginning in 2004, though, the administration of justice in Kosovo started down a path of increasing regularization, although shortcomings persist with regard to the predictability and professionalism of judges (both domestic and international), competence of defense counsel, and corruption. Organization for Security and Co-operation in Europe Department of Human Rights and Rule of Law Legal System Monitoring Section, KOSOVO: REVIEW OF THE CRIMINAL JUSTICE SYSTEM (APRIL 2003–OCTOBER 2004) CRIME, DETENTION, AND PUNISHMENT 13 (2004). In 2006, a hybrid court in Kosovo convicted, for the first time, senior Kosovo Liberation Army officers of war crimes. Notwithstanding this increased regularization, at the

present time the overall set of data from Kosovo is not terribly probative. Consequently, I do not include it in my analysis.

65. Data compiled from The United Nations, *ICTR Detainees, available at* http://69.94.11.53/ENGLISH/factsheets/detainee.htm (current through to website visit on May 25, 2006). The Appeals Chamber may alter some sentences that currently are under appeal.

66. *Prosecutor v. Kajelijeli*, Case No. ICTR-98-44A-A (ICTR Appeals Chamber, May 23, 2005).

67. *Prosecutor v. Semanza*, Case No. ICTR-97-20-A (ICTR Appeals Chamber, May 20, 2005).

68. Data compiled from ICTY website, http://www.un.org/icty (current through to website visit on May 26, 2006).

69. *Prosecutor v. Stakić*, Case No. IT-97-24-A (ICTY Appeals Chamber, March 22, 2006). As this book went to press, the Appeals Chamber, overturning the twenty-year term sentence issued by an ICTY Trial Chamber, sentenced Stanislav Galić to life imprisonment – thereby resulting in the first actual life sentence at the ICTY.

70. Mark A. Drumbl & Kenneth S. Gallant, *Sentencing Policies and Practices in the International Criminal Tribunals,* 15 FED. SENTENCING REP. 140, 142 (2002).

71. *Prosecutor v. Krstić*, Case No. IT-98-33-A (ICTY Appeals Chamber, Apr. 19, 2004) (reducing sentence on the grounds that Krstić's responsibility for the Srebrenica genocide was more properly characterized as aiding and abetting rather than a co-perpetrator in a joint criminal enterprise); *Prosecutor v. Blaškić*, Case No. IT-95-14-A (ICTY Appeals Chamber, July 29, 2004) (reducing sentence and granting Blaškić early release in light of its quashing most of the convictions owing to its finding that liability-based command responsibility had not been established).

72. By 2006.

73. Data compiled from yearly case information provided by the Judicial System Monitoring Programme (JSMP) and *available at* http://www.jsmp.minihub.org (current through to website visit on May 28, 2006). I included in the data a one-year suspended sentence issued for destruction of property. JSMP constitutes the best source of information regarding justice initiatives in East Timor, in particular the activities of the Special Panels. Overall, there is a lack of informational transparency with regard to the work of the Special Panels.

74. The first conviction involved crimes against humanity connected to the 1999 atrocity. Fernandes then was conditionally released, only to be rearrested for another crime committed in 1999 (a property crime) for which he was sentenced to 1.5 years' imprisonment. I include both sentences in the calculations.

75. *Prosecutor v. Rutaganda*, Case No. ICTR-96-3, ¶ 458 (ICTR Trial Chamber, Dec. 6, 1999), *aff'd* on appeal, *Prosecutor v. Rutaganda*, Case No. ICTR-96-3-A (ICTR Appeals Chamber, May 26, 2003).

76. *Prosecutor v. Kayishema*, Case No. ICTR-95 1 T, ¶ 4 (ICTR Trial Chamber, May 21, 1999) (sentencing order).

77. *Prosecutor v. Krstić*, Case No. IT-98-33-A, ¶ 242 (ICTY Appeals Chamber, Apr. 19, 2004). For an exhortation for the development of guidelines to standardize the sentences meted out by international tribunals, *see* Beresford, *op. cit.*, at 82. To be sure, sentencers in domestic jurisdictions also have discretion to sentence. Certain positive law instruments, however, narrow this discretion. In the case of the United States, the Supreme Court has declared that the Federal Sentencing Guidelines (initially introduced in 1984 and which establish maximum and minimum penalties for offenses) only play an advisory role in the allocation of punishment. *See United States v. Booker*, 125 S. Ct. 738 (2005) (Stevens, J., substantive opinion) (Breyer J., remedial opinion).

78. *Prosecutor v. Delalić*, Case No. IT-96-21-A, ¶¶ 717–718 (ICTY Appeals Chamber, Feb. 20, 2001) (*see also* ¶ 758 (noting that a pattern of sentences does not exist as yet)). *See also Prosecutor v. Kamuhanda*, Case No. ICTR-95-54A-T, ¶ 765 (ICTR Trial Chamber, Jan. 22, 2004); *Prosecutor v. Krstić*, Case No. IT-98-33-A, ¶ 242 (ICTY Appeals Chamber, Apr. 19, 2004) (" . . . the imposition of a sentence is a discretionary decision"); *Prosecutor v. Momir*

Nikolić, Case No. IT-02-60/1-A, ¶ 8 (ICTY Appeals Chamber, March 8, 2006) ("Trial Chambers are vested with a broad discretion in determining an appropriate sentence.").

79. Combs, *Procuring Guilty Pleas, op. cit.*, at 77.

80. *Prosecutor v. Stakić*, Case No. IT-97-24-A, ¶ 405 (ICTY Appeals Chamber, March 22, 2006); *Prosecutor v. Kambanda*, Case No. ICTR-97-23-T, ¶ 124 (ICTR Appeals Chamber, Oct. 19, 2000) (holding that the weight to be attached to mitigating circumstances is a matter of discretion to be reviewable only in cases of abuse of discretion, namely where a sentence is issued that lies outside the discretionary framework provided by the Statute and the Rules).

81. *Prosecutor v. Dragan Nikolić*, IT-94-2-A, ¶¶ 18–19 (ICTY Appeals Chamber, Feb. 4, 2005). *See also Prosecutor v. Kordić and Čerkez*, IT-95-14/2-A, ¶ 1064 (ICTY Appeals Chamber, Dec. 17, 2004); Geert-Jan Alexander Knoops, AN INTRODUCTION TO THE LAW OF INTER-NATIONAL CRIMINAL TRIBUNALS 117 (2003) (citing ICTY pronouncements that it is "not bound to impose the same sentence merely because the facts of two or more cases are comparable").

82. *Prosecutor v. Semanza*, Case No. ICTR-97-20-A, ¶ 394 (ICTR Appeals Chamber, May 20, 2005).

83. *Prosecutor v. Babić*, Case No. IT-03-72-A, ¶ 33 (ICTY Appeals Chamber, July 18, 2005). *See also id.* ¶ 32.

84. *Prosecutor v. Stakić*, Case No. IT-97-24-A, ¶ 382 (ICTY Appeals Chamber, March 22, 2006).

85. Domestic law in the United States, for example, invokes retribution, incapacitation, deterrence, and positive prevention as goals of punishing ordinary common crime. *See, e.g.*, 18 U.S.C. § 3553. For England, *see* Andrew Ashworth, SENTENCING AND CRIMINAL JUSTICE 74 (4th ed., 2005).

86. *Prosecutor v. Stakić*, Case No. IT-97-24-A, ¶ 402 (ICTY Appeals Chamber, March 22, 2006) (stating that "the Appeals Chamber notes that the jurisprudence of the Tribunal and the ICTR consistently points out that the two main purposes of sentencing are deterrence and retribution"); *Prosecutor v. Rutaganda*, Case No. ICTR-96-3, ¶ 456 (ICTR Trial Chamber, Dec. 6, 1999); *Prosecutor v. Marqués et al.*, Case No. 09/2000, ¶ 979 (Dili Dist. Ct. Serious Crimes Spec. Panel, Dec. 11, 2001) ("The penalties imposed on accused persons found guilty by the Panel are intended, on the one hand, as retribution against the said accused, whose crimes must be seen to be punished (*punitur quia peccatur*). They are also intended to act as deterrence; namely, to dissuade forever, others who may be tempted in the future to perpetrate such atrocities by showing them that the international community shall not tolerate such serious violations of law and human rights (*punitur ne peccetur.*)"). For further treatment of deterrence and retribution as the two major motivations behind sentencing perpetrators of mass atrocity, *see Prosecutor v. Serushago*, Case No. ICTR-98-39-S, ¶ 20 (ICTR Trial Chamber, Feb. 5, 1999); *Prosecutor v. Kambanda*, Case No. ICTR-97-23-S, ¶ 28 (ICTR Trial Chamber, Sept. 4, 1998); *Prosecutor v. Brđanin*, Case No. IT-99-36-T, ¶¶ 1090–92 (ICTY Trial Chamber, Sept 1, 2004); *Prosecutor v. Simić*, Case No. IT-95-9, ¶ 1059 (ICTY Trial Chamber, Oct. 17, 2003); *Prosecutor v. Furundžija*, Case No. IT-95-17/1-T, ¶ 288 (ICTY Trial Chamber, Dec. 10, 1998); *Prosecutor v. Todorović*, Case No. IT-95-9/1-S, ¶¶ 28–29 (ICTY Trial Chamber, July 31, 2001); *Prosecutor v. Krnojelac*, Case No. IT-97-25, ¶ 508 (ICTY Trial Chamber, Mar. 15, 2002); *Prosecutor v. Lao*, Case No. 10/2003, ¶ D.2 c) (Dili Dist. Ct. Serious Crimes Spec. Panel, Dec. 3, 2004, *aff'd* East Timor Ct. App., April 12, 2005).

87. Beresford, *op. cit.*, at 41. Unlike the Nuremberg Tribunal, no extant international criminal law institution can issue a death sentence.

88. Jan Klabbers, *Just Revenge? The Deterrence Argument in International Criminal Law*, XII FINNISH Y.B. INT'L L. 249, 251 (2001) (citing the deterrence argument as perhaps the main reason underlying the creation of the ICC).

89. *Prosecutor v. Stakić*, Case No. IT-97-24-T, ¶ 900 (ICTY Trial Chamber, July 31, 2003).

90. *Prosecutor v. Momir Nikolić*, Case No. IT-02-60/1-S, ¶¶ 59, 90 (ICTY Trial Chamber, Dec. 2, 2003). On appeal, the Appeals Chamber in this case emphasized that "[t]he gravity of the offence is the primary consideration when imposing a sentence and is the 'litmus test' for determining an appropriate sentence." *Prosecutor v. Momir Nikolić*, Case No. IT-02-60/1-A, ¶ 11 (ICTY Appeals Chamber, March 8, 2006).

91. *Prosecutor v. Delalić*, Case No. IT-96-21-T, ¶ 1234 (ICTY Trial Chamber, Nov. 16, 1998).

92. M. Cherif Bassiouni, INTRODUCTION TO INTERNATIONAL CRIMINAL LAW 681, 689 (2003); Ralph Henham, *The Philosophical Foundations of International Sentencing*, 1 J. INT'L CRIM. JUSTICE 64, 69, 72 (2003); Beresford, *op. cit.*, at 33; *Prosecutor v. Stakić*, Case No. IT-97-24-A, ¶ 375 (ICTY Appeals Chamber, March 22, 2006) (stating that "[t]he concrete gravity of the crime remains 'the litmus test' in the imposition of an appropriate sentence").

93. *See, e.g., Prosecutor v. Barros and Mendonca*, Case No. 01/2004, ¶ 165 (Dili Dist. Ct. Serious Crimes Spec. Panel, May 12, 2005, *aff'd* East Timor Ct. App.) (listing "just retribution" as a "first" purpose of imposing a penalty).

94. *Prosecutor v. Akayesu*, Case No. ICTR-96-4-S, ¶ 40 (ICTR Trial Chamber, Oct. 2, 1998) ("[A] sentence must reflect the predominant standard of proportionality between the gravity of the offence and the degree of responsibility of the offender.").

95. *Prosecutor v. Kordić and Čerkez*, Case No. IT-95-14/2-A, ¶ 1075 (ICTY Appeals Chamber, Dec. 17, 2004).

96. *Prosecutor v. Momir Nikolić*, Case No. IT-02-60/1-S, ¶ 86 (ICTY Trial Chamber, Dec. 2, 2003). *See also Prosecutor v. Simić*, Case No. IT-95-9, ¶ 1059 (ICTY Trial Chamber, Oct. 17, 2003).

97. *Prosecutor v. Kordić and Čerkez*, IT-95-14/2-A, ¶ 1082 (ICTY Appeals Chamber, Dec. 17, 2004) ("The unfortunate legacy of wars shows that until today many perpetrators believe that violations of binding international norms can be lawfully committed, because they are fighting for a 'just cause'. Those people have to understand that international law is applicable to everybody, in particular during times of war.").

98. *See, e.g., Prosecutor v. Kunarac*, Case No. IT-96-23-T, ¶ 840 (ICTY Trial Chamber, Feb. 22, 2001) (holding that "the likelihood of persons convicted here ever again being faced with an opportunity to commit war crimes, crimes against humanity, genocide or grave breaches is so remote as to render its consideration in this way unreasonable and unfair"); *Prosecutor v. Niyitegeka*, Case No. ICTR-96-14-T, ¶ 484 (ICTR Trial Chamber, May 16, 2003) ("[S]pecific emphasis is placed on general deterrence . . ."), *aff'd Prosecutor v. Niyitegeka*, Case No. ICTR-96-14-A (ICTR Appeals Chamber, July 9, 2004).

99. *See, e.g., Prosecutor v. Mrdja*, Case No. IT-02-59-S, ¶ 16 (ICTY Trial Chamber, Mar. 31, 2004) (holding that the main deterrent effect sought is to turn the perpetrator away from future wrongdoing); *Prosecutor v. Kordić and Čerkez*, Case No. IT-95-14/2-A, ¶¶ 1076–1077 (ICTY Appeals Chamber, Dec. 17, 2004) (although "both individual and general deterrence serve as important goals of sentencing," a sentence should be "adequate to dishearten [the defendant] from re-offending").

100. *Prosecutor v. Beno*, Case No. 4b/2003, ¶ 22 (Dili Dist. Ct. Serious Crimes Spec. Panel, November 16, 2004).

101. *See Prosecutor v. Delalić*, Case No. IT-96-21-A (ICTY Appeals Chamber, Feb. 20, 2001); *Prosecutor v. Deronjić*, Case No. IT-02-61-A (ICTY Appeals Chamber, July 20, 2005); William Schabas, *Sentencing by International Tribunals: A Human Rights Approach*, 7 DUKE J. COMP. & INT'L L. 461, 504 (1997). *But see Prosecutor v. Momir Nikolić*, Case No. IT-02-60/1-S, ¶¶ 85, 93 (ICTY Trial Chamber, Dec. 2, 2003) (rehabilitation mentioned as a "third" goal of sentencing but did not figure in the Trial Chamber's quantification of sentence); *Prosecutor v. Rutaganira*, Case No. ICTR-96-3 (ICTR Trial Chamber, March 14, 2005) (considering as mitigating factors circumstances indicative of convict's prospects for rehabilitation). The judgment of the ICTY Appeals Chamber in *Prosecutor v. Kordić and Čerkez* evidences a confusing treatment of the admittedly complex phenomenon of rehabilitation. The judgment begins by concluding that: "In light of the gravity of many

of the crimes under the International Tribunal's jurisdiction, the weight of rehabilitative considerations may be limited in some cases. […] It would violate the principle of proportionality and endanger the pursuit of other sentencing purposes if rehabilitative considerations were given undue prominence in the sentencing process." *Prosecutor v. Kordić and Čerkez*, IT-95-14/2-A, ¶ 1079 (ICTY Appeals Chamber, Dec. 17, 2004). However, in the same judgment the judges consider the convict's "good rehabilitative prospects" within the context of mitigating factors. *Id.* ¶¶ 1090–91. It could be that international criminal law institutions are inclined to give rehabilitation limited effectivity insofar as it receives little importance in many influential ordinary justice systems.

102. For incapacitation, *see* Anthony Ellis, *What Should We Do With War Criminals?*, in WAR CRIMES AND COLLECTIVE WRONGDOING 97, 103 (Jokić ed., 2001) ("Incapacitation was not much mentioned as an aim of the Nuremberg and Tokyo trials.").

103. *Prosecutor v. Babić*, Case No. IT-03-72-A (ICTY Appeals Chamber, July 18, 2005).

104. *Id.* ¶¶ 59, 60.

105. *Id.* ¶ 3 dissenting judgment.

106. *See, e.g.*, Plavšić plea bargain (discussed *infra* Chapter 6).

107. *See, e.g.*, Marc Lacey, *Victims of Uganda Atrocities Choose a Path of Forgiveness*, N.Y. TIMES (April 18, 2005) at A1 (discussing traditional dispute resolution methods used by the Acholi people in northern Uganda). It is unclear whether the Trust Fund will operate in Uganda or the DRC and, even if so, whether it – or ICC interventions generally – actually will serve restorative goals.

108. *See generally* Mark Osiel, *Modes of Participation in Mass Atrocity*, 39 CORNELL INT'L L. J. 793, 805 (2005). This is not to say that even in places where restorative approaches have gained currency, for example South Africa, that all members of the public, in particular victim communities, are free from retributive impulses nor are conceptually attracted to retributivism.

109. Security Council Res. 1593, ¶ 5 (March 31, 2005).

110. *Prosecutor v. Dragan Nikolić*, IT-94-2-A, ¶ 27 (ICTY Appeals Chamber, Feb. 4, 2005); *Prosecutor v. Musema*, Case No. ICTR-96-13-T, ¶ 396 (ICTR Appeals Chamber, Nov. 16, 2001).

111. *Prosecutor v. Kunarac*, Case No. IT 96-23/1-A, ¶ 385 (ICTY Appeals Chamber, June 12, 2002).

112. *Id.*

113. ICTY R.P. & EVID., *op. cit.*, Rules 101(B)(i), (ii) (identifying "substantial cooperation with the Prosecutor by the convicted person before or after conviction" as a mitigating factor).

114. *See, e.g., Prosecutor v. Simić*, Case No. IT-95-9, ¶ 1062 (ICTY Trial Chamber, Oct. 17, 2003) (stating that the gravity of the crimes is the primary consideration in imposing sentence); *Prosecutor v. Nahimana*, Case No. ICTR-99-52-T, ¶ 1102 (ICTR Trial Chamber, Dec. 3, 2003) (suggesting that the Trial Chamber was motivated by the cruelty of the crimes); *Prosecutor v. Obrenović*, Case No. IT-02-60/2-S, ¶ 62 (ICTY Trial Chamber, Dec. 10, 2003) (" … the gravity of the offense is the 'litmus test' in the determination of an appropriate sentence"); *Prosecutor v. Kayishema*, Case No. ICTR-95-1-T, ¶ 18 (ICTR Trial Chamber, May 21, 1999) (acknowledging the influence of the vicious nature of the murders on sentencing decisions); *Prosecutor v. Jelisić*, Case No. IT-95-10-T, ¶ 130 (ICTY Trial Chamber, Dec. 14, 1999) (acknowledging the influence of the repugnant, bestial, and sadistic nature of the offender's behavior on the tribunal's decision); *Prosecutor v. Muhimana*, Case No. ICTR-95-1B-T, ¶ 599 (ICTR Trial Chamber, April 28, 2005) (citing the zeal of the perpetrator and the sheer number of rapes as aggravating factors).

115. *Prosecutor v. Semanza*, ICTR-97-20-A, ¶ 338 (ICTR Appeals Chamber, May 20, 2005).

116. *Prosecutor v. Erdemović*, Case No. IT-96-22-T, ¶ 85 (ICTY Trial Chamber Nov. 29, 1996); *Prosecutor v. Muhimana*, Case No. ICTR-95-1B-T, ¶¶ 612, 614 (ICTR Trial Chamber, April 28, 2005).

117. *Prosecutor v. Kunarac*, Case No. IT-96-23/1-A, ¶ 381 (ICTY Appeals Chamber, June 12, 2002).
118. *Prosecutor v. Rajić*, Case No. IT-95-12-S, ¶ 117 (ICTY Trial Chamber, May 8, 2006).
119. *Prosecutor v. Stakić*, Case No. IT-97-24-T, ¶ 906 (ICTY Trial Chamber, July 31, 2003) (discussing the accused's "unique pivotal role in co-ordinating the persecutory campaign"); *Prosecutor v. Rutaganda*, Case No. ICTR-96-3, ¶ 470 (ICTR Trial Chamber, Dec. 6, 1999), *aff'd Prosecutor v. Rutaganda*, Case No. ICTR-96-3-A (ICTR Appeals Chamber, May 26, 2003) (affirming sentence of life imprisonment); *Prosecutor v. Ntagerura*, Case No. ICTR-99-46-T, ¶ 813 (ICTR Trial Chamber, Feb. 25, 2004) (systematizing ICTR sentencing patterns of fifteen years to life for principal perpetrators, and lower sentences for secondary or indirect forms of participation); *Prosecutor v. Krstić*, Case No. IT-98-33-A, ¶¶ 266–68 (ICTY Appeals Chamber, Apr. 19, 2004); *Prosecutor v. Vasiljević*, Case No. IT-98-32-A, ¶ 182 (ICTY Appeals Chamber, Feb. 25, 2004) ("[A]iding and abetting is a form of responsibility which generally warrants a lower sentence than is appropriate to responsibility as a co-perpetrator.").
120. *See generally Prosecutor v. Simić*, Case No. IT-95-9, ¶ 1063 (ICTY Trial Chamber, Oct. 17, 2003); *Prosecutor v. Vasiljević*, Case No. IT-98-32-A, ¶¶ 171–172 (ICTY Appeals Chamber, Feb. 25, 2004); *Prosecutor v. Blaškić*, Case No. IT-95-14-A, ¶ 683 (ICTY Appeals Chamber, July 29, 2004).
121. *Prosecutor v. Kamuhanda*, Case No. ICTR-95-54A-T, ¶ 764 (ICTR Trial Chamber, Jan. 22, 2004); *Prosecutor v. Serushago*, Case No. ICTR-98-39-S, ¶ 29 (ICTR Trial Chamber, Feb. 5, 1999).
122. *Prosecutor v. Kayishema*, Case No. ICTR-95-1-T, ¶ 17 (ICTR Trial Chamber, May 21, 1999) (sentence influenced by the fact one of the defendants repeatedly smiled and laughed as genocide survivors testified against him).
123. *Prosecutor v. Simić*, Case No. IT-95-9, ¶ 1064 (ICTY Trial Chamber, Oct. 17, 2003); *Prosecutor v. Stakić*, Case No. IT-97-24-T, ¶ 912 (ICTY Trial Chamber, July 31, 2003).
124. *Prosecutor v. Blaškić*, Case No. IT-95-14-A, ¶ 693 (ICTY Appeals Chamber, July 29, 2004); *Prosecutor v. Deronjić*, Case No. IT-02-61-A, ¶¶ 106, 107, 127 (ICTY Appeals Chamber, July 20, 2005); *Prosecutor v. Obrenović*, Case No. IT-02-60/2-S, ¶ 99 (ICTY Trial Chamber, Dec. 10, 2003).
125. *Prosecutor v. Deronjić*, Case No. IT-02-61-A, ¶ 67 (ICTY Appeals Chamber, July 20, 2005); *see also Prosecutor v. Brđanin*, Case No. IT-99-36-T, ¶ 1099 (ICTY Trial Chamber, Sept. 1, 2004). There appears to be some conflict between the ICTY and ICTR regarding the role of command responsibility as an aggravating factor in sentencing in a case where a conviction has been procured on the basis of command responsibility. The ICC Rules require "abuse of power or official capacity" as an aggravating factor. ICC R.P. & EVID. *op. cit.*, Rule 145(2)((b)(ii).
126. *Prosecutor v. Simić*, Case No. IT-95-9-T, ¶ 1065 (ICTY Trial Chamber, Oct. 17, 2003); *Prosecutor v. Sikirica*, Case No. IT-95-8-S, ¶ 110 (ICTY Trial Chamber, Nov. 13, 2001). It is unclear whether any burden as to mitigating factors can be placed on the accused under the ICC. *See* Rome Statute, *op. cit.*, art. 67(1)(i).
127. *Prosecutor v. Kambanda*, Case No. ICTR-97-23-S, ¶ 54 (ICTR Trial Chamber, Sept. 4, 1998) (noting that a guilty plea should trigger a reduced sentence because victims no longer have to undergo the trauma of trial); *Prosecutor v. Ruggiu*, Case No. ICTR-97-32-I, ¶ 53 (ICTR Trial Chamber, June 1, 2000) (noting that guilty pleas expedite proceedings and save resources); *Prosecutor v. Sikirica*, Case No. IT-95-8-S, ¶ 148 (ICTY Trial Chamber, Nov. 13, 2001) (citing a guilty plea as the "primary factor" to be considered in mitigation of the defendant's sentence); *Prosecutor v. Plavšić*, Case No. IT-00-39 & 40/1-S, ¶ 110 (ICTY Trial Chamber, Feb. 27, 2003).
128. ICTY R.P. & EVID., *op. cit.*, Rule 101(B)(ii); *Prosecutor v. Todorović*, Case No. IT-95-9/1-S, ¶¶ 83–88 (ICTY Trial Chamber, July 31, 2001). Voluntary surrender also has been held to

constitute a mitigating factor. *Prosecutor v. Kupreškić*, Case No. IT-95-16-A, ¶ 430 (ICTY Appeals Chamber, Oct. 23, 2001).

129. *Prosecutor v. Ruggiu*, Case No. ICTR-97-32-I, ¶ 69 (ICTR Trial Chamber, June 1, 2000); *Prosecutor v. Sikirica*, Case No. IT-95-8-S, ¶¶ 152, 194, 230 (ICTY Trial Chamber, Nov. 13, 2001); *Prosecutor v. Todorović*, Case No. IT-95-9/1-S, ¶¶ 89–92 (ICTY Trial Chamber, July 31, 2001); *Prosecutor v. Blaškić*, Case No. IT-95-14-A, ¶ 705 (ICTY Appeals Chamber, July 29, 2004); *Prosecutor v. Milan Simić*, Case No. IT-95-9/2-S, ¶ 94 (ICTY Trial Chamber, Oct. 17, 2002).

130. *Prosecutor v. Jelisić*, Case No. IT-95-10-A, ¶¶ 129–131 (ICTY Appeals Chamber, July 5, 2001).

131. *Prosecutor v. Plavšić*, Case No. IT-00-39 & 40/1-S, ¶¶ 10, 110 (ICTY Trial Chamber, Feb. 27, 2003).

132. *Prosecution v. Strugar*, Case No. IT-01-42-T, ¶ 469 (ICTY Trial Chamber, January 31, 2005) (referring to personal and family circumstances in mitigation, including: age of seventy-one years; poor health; married for forty-seven years and two sons; wife, in poor health, who stays with her two unemployed sons); *Prosecutor v. Bisengimana*, Case No. ICTR-00-60-T, ¶ 143 (ICTR Trial Chamber, April 13, 2006).

133. *Prosecutor v. Krstić*, Case No. IT-98-33-T, ¶ 711 (ICTY Trial Chamber, Aug. 2, 2001) ("[R]eluctant participation in the crimes may in some instances be considered as a mitigating circumstance....."); *Prosecutor v. Erdemović*, Case No. IT-96-22-T*bis*, ¶ 17 (ICTY Trial Chamber, Mar. 5, 1998). "Diminished mental responsibility" also has been considered in this regard as a mitigating factor. *Prosecutor v. Delalić*, Case No. IT-96-21-A, ¶¶ 590, 841 (ICTY Appeals Chamber, Feb. 20, 2001).

134. *Prosecutor v. Krnojelac*, Case No. IT-97-25-T, ¶ 519 (ICTY Trial Chamber, Mar. 15, 2002); *see also id.* ¶ 518 (citing acts of assistance to victims as a mitigating factor); *Prosecutor v. Semanza*, Case No. ICTR-97-20-A, ¶¶ 397–398 (ICTR Appeals Chamber, May 20, 2005) (citing as mitigating factors "an accused's previous good character [...] as well as accomplishments in functions previously held," although also noting that "in most cases the accused's previous good character is accorded little weight in the final determination"). The ICTY Appeals Chamber has ruled that the gravity of the crimes precluded evidence of good character from having significant impact on sentencing. *Prosecutor v. Stakić*, Case No. IT-97-24-A, ¶ 406 (ICTY Appeals Chamber, March 22, 2006).

135. *Prosecutor v. Delalić*, Case No. IT-96-21-T, ¶¶ 1283–1284 (ICTY Trial Chamber, Nov. 16, 1998).

136. *Prosecutor v. Bisengimana*, Case No. ICTR-00-60-T, ¶ 165 (ICTR Trial Chamber, April 13, 2006).

137. *Prosecutor v. Kajelijeli*, Case No. ICTR-98-44A-A, (ICTR Appeals Chamber, May 23, 2005) (the original multiple sentences (two life sentences and fifteen years) were decreased to a single sentence of a fixed term of forty-five years, less time served in detention, owing to Appeals Chamber *proprio motu* finding of "serious" violations of Kajelijeli's fundamental rights during his arrest and detention in Benin). *See also Prosecutor v. Nahimana*, Case No. ICTR-99-52-T, ¶¶ 1106–07 (ICTR Trial Chamber, Dec. 3, 2003).

138. Michael Scharf, BALKAN JUSTICE 67 (1997).

139. *See* ICTY R.P. & EVID., *op. cit.*, Rules 62, 62bis, 62ter (permitting both guilty pleas and plea agreements, although plea agreements have been preferred in practice); ICTR R.P. & EVID., *op. cit.*, Rules 62, 62bis.

140. Marlise Simons, *Plea Deals Being Used to Clear Balkans War Tribunal's Docket*, N.Y. TIMES (Nov. 18, 2003). ICTR defendants are more reticent about pleading guilty; East Timorese defendants tend to plead guilty due to cultural factors that have nothing to do with the enticement of a shorter sentence. Combs, *Procuring Guilty Pleas, op. cit.*, at 73.

141. *Prosecutor v. Momir Nikolić*, Case No. IT-02-60/1 S (ICTY Trial Chamber, Dec. 2, 2003) (Trial Chamber issued a sentence of twenty-seven years, which exceeded the recommendation of the plea agreement where the Prosecutor had agreed to recommend a fifteen- to

twenty-year sentence and the defense a ten-year sentence). The Trial Chamber had expressed a number of reservations with regard to plea bargains for cases of extraordinary international criminality. *Id.* ¶ 73. Despite these reservations, and the fact it did not follow the plea agreement recommendations, the Trial Chamber still found the guilty plea to be significant and to constitute an important factor in mitigation. *Id.* ¶¶ 145, 149. The Appeals Chamber did not quarrel with the Trial Chamber's seemingly contradictory approach to the guilty plea. However, for other reasons, it reduced the sentence to twenty years. *Prosecutor v. Momir Nikolić*, Case No. IT-02-60/1-A (ICTY Appeals Chamber, March 8, 2006).

142. Rome Statute, *op. cit.*, arts. 65–66.

143. *Prosecutor v. Franca da Silva*, Case No. 04a/2001, ¶ 144 (Dili Dist. Ct. Serious Crimes Spec. Panel, Dec. 5, 2002); *Prosecutor v. Atolan*, Case No. 3/2003, ¶ 33 (Dili Dist. Ct. Serious Crimes Spec. Panel, June 9, 2003); *Prosecutor v. De Carvalho*, Case No. 10/2001, ¶¶ 66–69 (Dili Dist. Ct. Serious Crimes Spec. Panel, March 18, 2004); *Prosecutor v. Sufa*, Case. No. 4a/2003, ¶ 33 (Dili Dist. Ct. Serious Crimes Spec. Panel, November 25, 2004) (noting that a guilty plea issued after overwhelming testimony had been adduced against the defendant only triggered minor mitigating effects).

144. *Prosecutor v. Marqués et al.*, Case No. 09/2000, ¶¶ 985–86 (Dili Dist. Ct. Serious Crimes Spec. Panel, Dec. 11, 2001) (identifying the "horrifying manner" of the violence against a "defenseless person" as an aggravating factor in a case involving crimes against humanity).

145. *Id.* ¶ 986.

146. *Id.* ¶ 987; *Prosecutor v. Franca da Silva*, Case No. 04a/2001, ¶ 152 (Dili Dist. Ct. Serious Crimes Spec. Panel, Dec. 5, 2002).

147. *Prosecutor v. Beno*, Case No. 4b/2003, ¶ 20 (Dili Dist. Ct. Serious Crimes Spec. Panel, November 16, 2004) (noting that "particularly despicable [...] is that the accused [...] committed these crimes against his fellow-countrymen in the interest of a foreign power that was illegally occupying his home country").

148. *Prosecutor v. Franca da Silva*, Case No. 04a/2001, ¶ 147 (Dili Dist. Ct. Serious Crimes Spec. Panel, Dec. 5, 2002).

149. *Id.*; *Prosecutor v. De Deus*, Case No. 2A/2004, page 14 (Dili Dist. Ct. Serious Crimes Spec. Panel, April 12, 2005) (noting no previous conviction).

150. *See Prosecutor v. Franca da Silva*, Case No. 04a/2001, ¶ 145 (Dili Dist. Ct. Serious Crimes Spec. Panel, Dec. 5, 2002); *Prosecutor v. Sufa*, Case No. 4a/2003, ¶ 34 (Dili Dist. Ct. Serious Crimes Spec. Panel, November 25, 2004) (citing as a mitigating factor that the defendant "had joined the militia only after he had been severely beaten up himself"); *Prosecutor v. Ena*, Case No. 5/2002, ¶ 99 (Dili Dist. Ct. Serious Crimes Spec. Panel, March 23, 2004) (noting as a mitigating factor that the defendant was living in a very coercive environment and had been forced by threats to join the militia); *Prosecutor v. De Carvalho*, Case No. 10/2001, ¶ 70 (Dili Dist. Ct. Serious Crimes Spec. Panel, March 18, 2004); *Prosecutor v. Maubere*, Case. No 23/2003, page 18 (Dili Dist. Ct. Serious Crimes Spec. Panel, July 5, 2004, sentence increased to eight years, East Timor Ct. App., March 18, 2005) (District Court noting in mitigation "[t]he evolving ambient during the time of the events, which was extremely violent and favourable to the commitment of all types of cruelties, insolences and abuses with major impunity, intensely allowed by the very civil and military authorities during that time").

151. *See, e.g., Prosecutor v. dos Santos*, Case No. 16/2001, ¶ 75 (East Timor Ct. App., July 15, 2003) (holding that the criteria for determining a sentence for genocide derive from the ordinary sentencing provisions of the Portuguese Penal Code); *Prosecutor v. Ena*, Case No. 5/2002, ¶¶ 108, 110 (Dili Dist. Ct. Serious Crimes Spec. Panel, March 23, 2004) (considering aggravating and mitigating factors in the Indonesian Penal Code as applied by East Timorese courts and applying Indonesian law in determining terms of imprisonment).

152. *Prosecutor v. Beno*, Case No. 4b/2003 (Dili Dist. Ct. Serious Crimes Spec. Panel, November 16, 2004) (deferring the start of a five-year sentence by four weeks from the time sentence was issued so that the defendant may prepare his farm and noting that the risk of flight was "comparatively small due to the strong Timorese tradition, rooted in 'Adat', of taking responsibility and paying respect to authority"). In this case, as with others, the convict also had to pay the costs of the proceedings.

153. *Prosecutor v. Franca da Silva*, Case No. 04a/2001, ¶ 146 (Dili Dist. Ct. Serious Crimes Spec. Panel, Dec. 5, 2002).

154. Beresford, *op. cit.*, at 79.

155. *Prosecutor v. Blaškić*, Case No. IT-95-14-A, ¶ 711 (ICTY Appeals Chamber, July 29, 2004). The reasoning of the ICTY Appeals Chamber is worth reproducing in full:

> [A] finding that a "chaotic" context might be considered as a mitigating factor in circumstances of combat operations risks mitigating the criminal conduct of all personnel in a war zone. Conflict is by its nature chaotic, and it is incumbent on the participants to reduce that chaos and to respect international humanitarian law. While the circumstances in Central Bosnia in 1993 were chaotic, the Appeals chamber sees neither merit nor logic in recognising the mere context of war itself as a factor to be considered in the mitigation of the criminal conduct of its participants.

156. *See, e.g., Prosecutor v. Da Costa and Punef*, Case No. 22/2003, page 17 (Dili Dist. Ct. Serious Crimes Spec. Panel, April 25, 2005) ("[G]iven the conditions in which the murders happened and in particular the presence of a multitude of militia members and leaders, it is possible to give some weigh[t] to the idea that a loss of inhibitors took place, accompanied by a loss of individuality. It's common knowledge that a crowd does not think as an individual and does not act as such.").

157. Allison Marston Danner & Jenny Martinez, *Guilty Associations, Joint Criminal Enterprise, Command Responsibility, and the Development of International Criminal Law*, 93 CALIF. L. REV. 75, 142 (2005).

158. I take as a definition of coherence that developed by Thomas Franck: "A rule is coherent when its application treats like cases alike and when the rule relates in a principled fashion to other rules of the same system." Thomas M. Franck, FAIRNESS IN INTERNATIONAL LAW AND INSTITUTIONS 38 (1995).

159. H.L.A. Hart, PUNISHMENT AND RESPONSIBILITY: ESSAYS IN THE PHILOSOPHY OF LAW 25 (1968). For a discussion specific to the ICTY, *see* Pierre Hazan, JUSTICE IN A TIME OF WAR: THE TRUE STORY BEHIND THE INTERNATIONAL CRIMINAL TRIBUNAL FOR THE FORMER YUGOSLAVIA (2004).

4. PUNISHMENT OF INTERNATIONAL CRIMES IN NATIONAL AND LOCAL CRIMINAL JUSTICE INSTITUTIONS

1. Ulrich Sieber, THE PUNISHMENT OF SERIOUS CRIMES: A COMPARATIVE ANALYSIS OF SENTENCING LAW AND PRACTICE (Volume 1: Expert Report) 122 (2004) [hereinafter Sieber Report]. The ICTY commissioned the Sieber Report in 2003 to provide it guidance with regard to domestic legal frameworks in the former Yugoslavia, so that it could clarify its instruction under article 24(1) of the Statute of the ICTY. The Sieber Report also researched the punishment of serious crimes in numerous other countries. It focused on national positive law and legislative enactments and not actual judgments of national or local courts.

2. *Prosecutor v. Dragan Nikolić*, Case No. IT-94-2-S, ¶ 172 (ICTY Trial Chamber, Dec. 18, 2003).

3. *See, e.g.*, Alexandra Barahona de Brito, Carmen González-Enríquez, & Paloma Aguilar, *Introduction, in* THE POLITICS OF MEMORY: TRANSITIONAL JUSTICE IN DEMOCRATIZING SOCIETIES 1, 4 (Barahona de Brito, González-Enríquez, & Aguilar eds., 2001).

4. This differentiation was not without controversy among many South Africans.

5. *See, e.g., United States v. Calley,* 46 C.M.R. 1131 (U.S. Army Court of Military Review, 1973) (twenty years' confinement at hard labor for murder of not less than thirty people and assault, reduced from the initial sentence of life imprisonment, owing to mitigating factors such as the unconventional nature of the war in Vietnam and factors personal to Calley such as deficiencies in his judgment, perception, and stability). Also of note are the various sentences issued by courts-martial regarding the abuse of prisoners at the Abu Ghraib prison in Iraq (these proceedings did not accuse the defendants of torture as an extraordinary international crime, nor of war crimes, but rather of infringements of the Uniform Code of Military Justice).

6. *See generally,* Barahona de Brito et al., *op. cit.,* at 3–10; Susan Kemp, *The Inter-Relationship Between the Guatemalan Commission for Historical Clarification and the Search for Justice in National Courts,* 15 CRIM. L. F. 67, 99 (2004) (commenting on trials of paramilitaries in Guatemala that resulted in lengthy periods of imprisonment). In Argentina's "Trial of the Century" in 1985, five individuals prominent in the military *junta* were convicted of human rights crimes and sentenced to terms ranging from life imprisonment to 4.5 years. Alexandra Barahona de Brito, *Truth, Justice, Memory, and Democratization in the Southern Cone,* in THE POLITICS OF MEMORY: TRANSITIONAL JUSTICE IN DEMOCRATIZING SOCIETIES 119, 122 (Barahona de Brito, González-Enríquez, & Aguilar eds., 2001). These convictions subsequently were pardoned by presidential decree, only to give rise to a new series of prosecutions for illegal abduction and adoption of children. *Id.* at 137. This back-and-forth tussle continues on a variety of cases in many national jurisdictions, including Argentina, thereby further complicating their utility as case studies for the exploration of penological rationales. In 2005, a Spanish court convicted a former Argentine naval captain, Adolfo Scilingo, of crimes against humanity and torture (committed from 1976 to 1983 against Spanish citizens during the *junta*) and sentenced him to 640 years' imprisonment. Looking ahead, a number of cases involving extraordinary international crimes committed in Guatemala, Argentina, Chile, and Rwanda are moving forward within the Spanish judicial system, suggesting that at a certain point a sufficiently developed jurisprudence may arise to assess sentencing patterns. In Ethiopia, thousands of prisoners detained in regard to extraordinary international crimes committed during the "Red Terror" rule of Mengistu Haile Mariam await trial, often for years already, although some have been sentenced to fixed terms of imprisonment or death. Mengistu, exiled in Zimbabwe, himself faces legal process in Ethiopia. In the event the Ethiopian courts are able to move forward with these cases in a transparent manner, this might offer some data to assess sentencing patterns. Cases of war crimes and torture committed in Afghanistan have been adjudicated in Dutch and Afghan courts. On October 14, 2005, the Hague District Court in the Netherlands sentenced two former Afghan generals serving in military security to nine and twelve years in prison for war crimes and torture committed in Afghanistan from the late 1970s to the early 1990s under Afghanistan's then Communist regime.

7. Alain Destexhe, RWANDA AND GENOCIDE IN THE TWENTIETH CENTURY 21–35 (1995) (noting that Rwanda, the former Yugoslavia, and the Holocaust are the only three cases of full genocide in the twentieth century, although there may have been lesser genocidal crimes).

8. Mark Osiel, *The Banality of Good: Aligning Incentives Against Mass Atrocity,* 105 COLUM. L. REV. 1751, 1809–1810 n.270 (2005) (arguing that domestic prosecutors have an incentive to prosecute few persons in the interests of social reconciliation but then noting that "Rwanda does not come within the terms of the model presented in this Article, in that prosecution is not limited to top echelons and does not aim to overcome intergroup conflict on mutually agreeable terms").

9. Actually, the total number of victims remains contested, with the Rwandan government placing it at over one million. The 500,000 to 800,000 range, however, is the most commonly cited range in the general literature.

10. DÉNOMBREMENT DES VICTIMES DU GÉNOCIDE: RAPPORT FINAL, Ministère de l'Administration locale, de l'Information, et des Affaires Sociales 26 (2002).

11. Also called the Rwandese Patriotic Army. In this book, I use the term Rwandan, although Rwandese also is found in general usage to describe a citizen of Rwanda or as an adjective. In 2002, the RPA was renamed the Rwandan Defense Forces (RDF).

12. Organic Law No. 8/96 on the organization of prosecutions for offenses constituting the crime of genocide or crimes against humanity committed since 1 October, 1990 (Journal Officiel No. 17 du 1er sept., 1996) (establishing categories of offenders, punishments, a trial and appellate structure, and limiting jurisdiction to events occurring from October 1, 1990, to December 31, 1994).

13. Organic Law establishing the organization, competence and functioning of Gacaca Courts charged with prosecuting and trying the perpetrators of the crime of genocide and other crimes against humanity, committed between October 1, 1990, and December 31, 1994, Nos. 40/2000 (January 26, 2001) and 33/2001 (June 22, 2001).

14. *18 Sentenced to Death in Rwanda in 2003 – Amnesty*, Hirondelle News Agency (Lausanne) (May 31, 2004).

15. William A. Schabas, *Genocide Trials and Gacaca Courts*, 3 J. Int'l Crim. Just. 879, 888 (2005).

16. *Cited in id.* at 880 (data from January 2005).

17. BBC, *Rwanda starts prisoner releases*, *available at* http://news.bbc.co.uk/2/hi/africa/4726969.stm. On May 5, 2003, twenty thousand confessed genocide perpetrators were released to their home communities after spending nearly a decade in jail. Owing to complaints from genocide survivors, some of those released subsequently were redetained.

18. The Organic Law stipulates that a perpetrator sentenced for multiple crimes shall serve the most severe sentence. 1996 Organic Law, *op. cit.*, art. 18. Sentences are therefore not cumulative.

19. Restitution has not been ordered and, accordingly, falls outside the ICTR's law-in-practice.

20. *See, e.g., Ministère Public v. Buregeya and Uwitonza* (March 22, 1998, 1 ière instance, Kibuye), RMP 56.886/S4/BA/KRE/KBY/2000, RP 002/01/2000 (defendant #2 convicted of Category 4 property offenses – eating pillaged meats – by association with a group of pillagers and sentenced to five years' imprisonment, suspended for four years); *Ministère Public v. Ndererehe and Rwakibibi* (October 21, 1999, ch. sp. 1 ière instance Nyamata), RP 066/97/C.S./Nmata/GDe, RMP 101825/S1/BAZ/Nmta/K.A. (convicting defendant of a Category 4 crime and sentencing him to a suspended sentence of three years' imprisonment – so he was freed immediately – plus restitution, for his pillage of seven goats).

21. Punishments taken from Mark A. Drumbl, *Rule of Law Amid Lawlessness: Counseling the Accused in Rwanda's Domestic Genocide Trials*, 29 Colum. H. R. L. Rev. 545, 588 n.175 (1998).

22. Jens David Ohlin, *Applying the Death Penalty to Crimes of Genocide*, 99 Am. J. Int'l L. 747, 754 (2005).

23. *See, e.g., Auditorat Militaire v. Rwahama* (Nov. 24, 1998, ch. sp. Conseil de Guerre, Kigali); 1996 Organic Law, *op. cit.*, art. 7.

24. *See, e.g., Ministère Public v. Bugirimfura et al.* (Apr. 2, 1999, 1 ière instance, Gitarama), RMP 21.102/S4/K.C., RP 70/GIT/CH.S/2/99 (aff'd on appeal, March 11, 2001, Cour d'appel de Nyabinsindu).

25. *Ministère Public v. Kabirigi et al.* (Dec. 10, 1998, 1 ière instance, Kibuye), RMP 51.498/S4/C.M./KBY/97, RP Ch. Sp.005/01/97; *see also* 1996 Organic Law, *op. cit.*, art. 11.

26. *Ministère Public v. Bizimungu* (March 11, 1999, 1 ière instance, Kibungo), RMP 82282/S4/ND/NSE, RP 0084/EX/R2/98/KGO.

27. 1996 Organic Law, *op. cit.*, arts. 5(3), 9. However, my discussions with the prosecution suggested that, at the time, there was a willingness to go beyond the statutory framework to occasionally allow Category 1 defendants to benefit from the reduced sentences if they entered a confession and guilty plea. Drumbl, *Rule of Law, op. cit.*, at 588.

28. Proceedings from previous trials may be admissible. *Ministère Public v. Nteziryayo (Emmanuel) et al.* (November 30, 2001, 1 ière instance, Butare), RMP 44223/S8/KA, RP 84/2/2001, p. 21.

29. *Ministère Public v. Kabirigi et al.* (Dec 10, 1998, 1 ière instance, Kibuye), RMP 51.498/S4/C.M./KBY/97, RP Ch. Sp.005/01/97, pp. 29–30. Article 66 of the Rwandan Code of Criminal Procedure defines *dégradation civique* and this definition is incorporated by the 1996 Organic Law.

30. *See, e.g., Auditorat Militaire v. Barayagwiza* (Nov. 26, 1998, ch. sp. Conseil de Guerre, Kigali), RMP 1663/AM/KGL/NZF/97, RP 0012/CG-CS/98; *Auditorat Militaire v. Dusabeyezu* (Dec. 22, 1998, ch. sp. Conseil de Guerre, Gisenyi).

31. Amnesty International, GACACA: A QUESTION OF JUSTICE 17 (December 2002) (AI Index: AFR 47/007/2002) (referencing Liprodhor statistics). The 2002 statistics reflect only the first six months of that year.

32. *Report on the situation of human rights in Rwanda submitted by the Special Representative, Mr. Michel Moussalli, pursuant to Commission resolution 1999/20*, U.N. Doc. E/CN.4/2000/41, ¶ 136.

33. GACACA: A QUESTION OF JUSTICE, *op. cit.*

34. *See* http://www.asf.be/FR/Frameset.htm.

35. *See, e.g., Ministère Public v. Sibomana* (Sept. 17, 1997, 1 ière instance Butare), RMP 43.715/S7/K.C., RP 09/01/97 (in addition to other sanctions, the court ordered legal fees against offender and the seizure of all his assets wherever these may be plus interest).

36. *Ministère Public v. Minani* (Sept. 23, 1997, 1 ière instance, Gitarama), RP 007/GIT/CH.S/97 (sentencing defendant to five years plus a fine of 5,000 Rwandan francs and *dégradation civique limitée* for five years following the serving of his sentence).

37. *Ministère Public v. Mukakayijuka* (January 15, 1999, ch sp. 1 ière instance Kigali), RMP 7049/S1/MB, RP 034/CS/KGO (sentencing a Category 3 defendant to two years' imprisonment and noting that she must be punished with the most severe punishment available for the crimes for which she was convicted, but providing no explanation as to why this was the case).

38. International Centre for the Study and the Promotion of Human Rights and Information, THE GENOCIDE AND THE CRIMES AGAINST HUMANITY IN RWANDAN LAW, COMMENTARY 42 (1997).

39. *See, e.g., Drumbl, Rule of Law, op. cit.*, at 585, 587–590, 629–630.

40. William A. Schabas & Martin Imbleau, INTRODUCTION TO RWANDAN LAW 59 (1997).

41. Drumbl, *Rule of Law, op. cit.*, at 626–627. *See also* Jeremy Sarkin, *The Tension Between Justice and Reconciliation in Rwanda: Politics, Human Rights, Due Process and the Role of the Gacaca Courts in Dealing with the Genocide*, 45(2) J. AFRICAN L. 143, 146 (2001); Erin Daly, *Between Punitive and Reconstructive Justice: The Gacaca Courts in Rwanda*, 34 N.Y.U. J. INT'L L. & POL. 355, 367 (2002) ("[T]he transitional Rwandan government of national unity has been committed to principles of retributive justice.").

42. Drumbl, *Rule of Law, op. cit.*, at 577 n.138.

43. *Ministère Public v. Kabirigi et al.* (Dec. 10, 1998, 1 ière instance, Kibuye), RMP 51.498/S4/C.M./KBY/97, RP Ch. Sp.005/01/97, p. 23 (with regard to defendant #8).

44. *See, e.g., Ministère Public v. Sibomana* (Sept. 17, 1997, 1 ière instance Butare), RMP 43.715/S7/K.C. and RP 09/01/97, p. 7 (convicting defendant of genocide as member of Category 2 and sentencing him to life imprisonment, *dégradation civique*, ordering legal fees against him, and noting that the premeditated nature of his crime deserved the most severe sanction).

45. *See, e.g., Ministère Public v. Nteziryayo (Emmanuel) et al.* (November 30, 2001, 1 ière instance Butare), RMP 44223/S8/KA, RP 84/2/2001 (referring to seemingly aggravating factors such as defendant's authority ("*il disposait du droit de vie ou de mort dans son secteur*"), his personal participation in the attacks, zeal, and excessive evil (killing of an

old lady with an axe), to sentence him to life imprisonment in spite of defense counsel's recommendation of a sentence of seven to eleven years and other stated mitigating factors such as pleading guilty, that the defendant was dragged into the massacres by the authorities, and that the defendant spoke the truth thereby easing the court's work).

46. This is why the court spared Anastase Nkinamubanzi, the bulldozer driver, a death sentence. For an example where no weight was given, *see Ministère Public v. Nduwumwami* (Oct. 6, 1997, 1 ière instance Cyangugu), RMP 79119/S2/BA, RP 006/97/CSC (sentencing defendant for raping a minor under sixteen years of age to life imprisonment (Category 2), *dégradation civique*, 5 million Rwandan francs for material and moral damages, and 18,700 Rwandan francs for legal fees; the court remained unmoved by the fact that, after the trial had begun, the defendant admitted the facts, expressed vivid regrets, and dispensed with the witnesses that he himself wanted to call). For an example where weight was given, *see Ministère Public v. Gakuru et al.* (February 12, 1999, 1 ière instance Gisenyi), RMP 61.312/S5/ML/N.K.T.-91/01/99 (appeal pending, Cour d'appel de Ruhengeri), p. 8 (guilty pleas formally were rejected because the accused delivered them for the first time during the proceedings, but the court accepted them as mitigating factors to reduce some defendants' sentences to twenty years (Category 2 convictions, for life) and other defendants' to sixteen years (Category 2 convictions, for life) insofar as the latter defendants' partial guilty pleas were more complete and sincere).

47. *Ministère Public v. Nzirasanaho et Munyakazi*, (September 9, 1998, ch. sp. 1 ière instance Nyamata); *Ministère Public v. Gakuru et al.* (February 12, 1999, 1 ière instance Gisenyi), RMP 61.312/S5/ML/N.K.T.-91/01/99 (appeal pending, Cour d'appel de Ruhengeri).

48. *Ministère Public v. Nzabonimpa* (Dec. 28, 1998, 1 ière instance, Gisenyi), RMP 69.430/S4/KD, RP/R1/98. *See also Ministère Public v. Bizimungu* (March 11, 1999, 1 ière instance, Kibungo), RMP 82282/S4/ND/NSE, RP 0084/EX/R2/98/KGO (court cumulated the guilty plea plus minor status and set sentence at six years' imprisonment for a Category 2 offender); *see also Ministère Public v. Nsabamungu* (Nov. 16, 1999, 1 ière instance, Kibungo), RMP 82641/S4~D/NSE 0124EX/R2/99/KGO (accused minor who pled guilty received an additional discount reducing sentence to 3.5 years plus legal fees for a Category 2 offense); *Ministère Public v. Nsabimana et al.* (Feb. 3, 2000, 1 ière instance, Kibungo), RMP 82515/S4/ND/NSE, RP 0115/EX/R2/99/KGO (in a case involving complete and sincere guilty pleas, an additional discount was made for the minor status of the defendants, reducing their sentences for a Category 2 conviction to four years, four years, and six years, respectively).

49. *See, e.g., Ministère Public v. Rwagakiga et al.* (March 25, 1999, ch. sp. 1 ière instance Ruhengeri), RMP 39509/S4/MB.F, RP 027/R1/98, judgment against this defendant aff'd Cour d'appel de Ruhengeri (January 24, 2001) (sentencing a Category 2 sixteen-year-old defendant who pled tardily to nine years' imprisonment for a Category 2 offense); *Ministère Public v. Karangwa et al.* (April 11, 2000, ch. sp. 1 ière instance Ruhengeri), RMP 35072/S4/SMJ, R.P. 037/R1/99 (sentencing a minor defendant who made a partial guilty plea to fifteen years' imprisonment for a Category 1 offense), modified on appeal where the Cour d'appel de Ruhengeri (June 27, 2002) affirmed the conviction but moved this defendant from Category 1 to Category 2.

50. *Ministère Public v. Kanyabugande et al.* (May 2, 1997, 1 ière instance Byumba), request for appeal denied Cour d'appel de Kigali (Dec. 9, 1997) (with regard to defendant #18).

51. *Ministère Public v. Minani* (Sept. 23, 1997, 1 ière instance, Gitarama), RP 007/GIT/CH.S/97.

52. *Id.*

53. *Ministère Public v. Munyangabo et al.* (June 10, 1998, 1 ière instance, Gikongoro), RMP 98809/S2/MP/97, R.P. 0017/1/GIRO (*"habituellement elle est d'un esprit compatissant comme en témoigne le fait d'avoir caché trois enfants Tutsis jusqu'à l'arrêt de la guerre"*).

54. *Ministère Public v. Siboruginwa et al.* (Oct. 22, 1999, 1 ière instance, Gitarama) (citing as a mitigating factor the Twa ethnicity of the defendants, insofar as *"l'ethnie minoritaire Twa*

qui n'est pas traitée sur le même pied d'égalité que les autres dans le pays et qui est sans droits").

55. *Id.*

56. *Ministère Public v. Sibomana et al.* (Dec. 3, 1998, ch. sp. 1 ière instance Rushashi), RMP 110 502/NK.A/J.T., RP 017/S1/98. This suggests a conflation of factors in mitigation with those factors that attenuate individual criminal responsibility.

57. *Id.* at pp. 14, 16.

58. *Ministère Public v. Munyangabo et al.* (June 10, 1998, 1 ière instance, Gikongoro), RMP 98809/S2/MP/97, R.P. 0017/1/GIRO, p. 13 (*"[il] n'a pas fait parti des personnes qui ont preparé l'attaque"*); *Ministère Public v. Rukeribuga et al.* (Dec. 17, 2001, 1 ière instance, Kibuye), RMP 51336/S4/G.M./NSE/97, RP Ch.Sp. 19/01/00 (*"diminution de peine car responsibilité moindre par rapport à ses coauteurs"*).

59. 1996 Organic Law, *op. cit.*, Chapter VII. Victims also may institute criminal proceedings through private prosecutions in situations where the Rwandan prosecutor has not done so but has been requested to do so. *Id.* arts. 29(2), (4).

60. *Rwanda: Court sentences five to death for genocide*, IRIN News (October 16, 2001) (on file with the author, *available at* http://www.irinnews.org).

61. *Ministère Public v. Sahinkuye (Albert)* (Feb. 19, 1998, 1 ière instance, Cyangugu), RMP 78.777/S2/BMG/KRL, R.P. 008/97. Category 1 offenders are held jointly and severally liable for all damages caused in the country by their criminal acts, regardless of where the offenses were committed. 1996 Organic Law, *op. cit.*, art. 30(1).

62. *Ministère Public v. Bizimana alias Mabuye* (February 20, 2002, 1 ière instance, Gikongoro), RMP 42.031/S8/NKM/NRA, R.P. 0098/3/GIRO.

63. *Ministère Public v. Twahirwa* (June 16, 1999, 1 ière instance, Kibungo). *See also Ministère Public v. Karamira* (February 14, 1997, ch. sp. 1 ière instance Kigali), R.P. 006/KIG/CS, RMP433/S12/CT/KP (awarding 1,137,650,000 Rwandan francs).

64. *Ministère Public v. Higiro (Célestin) et al.* (March 14, 2003, 1 ière instance, Butare), RMP 49932/S7, RP 35/1/99.

65. *Ministère Public v. Nteziryayo (Emmanuel) et al.* (November 30, 2001, 1 ière instance, Butare), RMP 44223/S8/KA, RP 84/2/2001.

66. *Id.* at p. 26.

67. *Ministère Public v. Rwanteli et al.* (Oct. 8, 1997, 1 ière instance Cyangugu), RMP 78 003/S2/NY.U/BMG, RP 003/97/CS, pp. 23–24.

68. *Auditorat Militaire v. Ukurikiyimfura et al.* (April 17, 2001, Conseil de Guerre), RMP 1507/AM/KGL/NZF/97, RP 0003/Cg CS/98), p. 26.

69. *See, e.g., Ministère Public v. Karamira* (February 14, 1997, ch. sp. 1 ière instance Kigali), R.P. 006/KIG/CS, RMP433/S12/CT/KP (awarding 1 million Rwandan francs to a victim who lost a spouse, 850,000 for a parent, and 750,000 for a sibling); *Ministère Public v. Murindangabo et al.* (Sept. 27, 2002, Cour d'appel de Nyabisindu), RP 76/02/2000, RPA 145/1/001/NZA (awarding 2 million Rwandan francs for the loss of a spouse and 1.5 million for the loss of a child, and also adjusting the moral damages in light of the number of years before the victims' respective retirements).

70. It remains unclear whether those convicted by the ICTR would escape *partie civile* claims in the domestic courts through the operation of *ne bis in idem* or, more practically, because they are in Arusha or in a foreign country in many cases serving life sentences.

71. Swiss Military Court of Appeal 1A (May 26, 2000), discussed in Luc Reydams, *International Decision*, 96 AM. J. INT'L L. 231 (2002). The Military Court of Appeal decision was partially dismissed by the Cour de cassation on April 27, 2001, but solely in regard to the deferred expulsion of the defendant from Switzerland ordered by the Military Court of Appeal, not the sentence.

72. *Kigali Wants Catholic Priest Extradited from France*, Hirondelle News Agency (January 13, 2006) (on file with the author).

73. *Jugement, Ntezimana, Higaniro, Mukangango, et Mukabutera*, Cour d'assises de l'arrondissement administrative de Bruxelles-Capitale, *available at* http://www.asf.be/AssisesRwanda2/fr/fr_VERDICT_verdict.htm.

74. *Id.* at p. 14.

75. *See generally* Naomi Roht-Arriaza, THE PINOCHET EFFECT: TRANSITIONAL JUSTICE IN THE AGE OF HUMAN RIGHTS (2005).

76. Adrien Katherine Wing & Mark Richard Johnson, *The Promise of a Post-Genocide Constitution: Healing Rwandan Spirit Injuries*, 7 MICH. J. RACE & L. 247, 280 n.321 (2002).

77. Some judges are accused of having taken part in the 1994 genocide. These individuals have been asked to resign (some have been arrested).

78. Sarkin, *Tension, op. cit.*, at 152–153; Stef Vandeginste, *Rwanda: Dealing with Genocide and Crimes against Humanity in the Context of Armed Conflict and Failed Political Transition*, in BURYING THE PAST: MAKING PEACE AND DOING JUSTICE AFTER CIVIL CONFLICT 223, 240 (Biggar ed., 2001).

79. James Munyaneza, 56,500 *Suspects Face Gacaca*, THE NEW TIMES (KIGALI) (March 11, 2005). According to officials, 60,000 files are ready for adjudication, 3,500 of which fall outside *gacaca* jurisdiction owing to their involving Category 1 accused. *Id.*

80. *Over 4,000 Suspects Judged in 2005 by Gacaca, Close to 500 Acquitted*, Hirondelle News Agency (Lausanne) (January 10, 2006).

81. Organic Law establishing the organization, competence and functioning of Gacaca Courts charged with prosecuting and trying the perpetrators of the crime of genocide and other crimes against humanity, committed between October 1st, 1990 and December 31, 1994, No. 16/2004 (June 19, 2004), pmbl ("*Considérant qu'il importe de prévoir des peines permettant aux condamnés de s'amender et de favoriser leur réinsération dans la société rwandaise sans entrave à la vie normale de la population*"). *See also Tribunaux gacaca et travail d'intérêt general*, 13–14 REFORME PÉNALE ET PÉNITENTIAIRE EN AFRIQUE 1–2 (mai 2001) (on file with author).

82. 2004 Organic Law, *op. cit.*, pmbl.

83. *Id.*

84. 2001 Organic Law, *op. cit.*, art. 96.

85. 2004 Organic Law, *op. cit.*

86. *Id.* art. 2(2).

87. *Id.* art. 2(1).

88. *Id.* art. 41.

89. Lars Waldorf, *Mass Justice for Mass Atrocity: Rethinking Local Justice as Transitional Justice*, 79 TEMP. L. REV. 1, 55 (2006) ("international donors and international NGOs successfully pressed the government for assurances that gacaca courts would not impose the death penalty").

90. 2004 Organic Law, *op. cit.*, art. 73.

91. *Id.* art. 75.

92. *See, e.g.*, Jane Ciabattari, *Rwanda Gambles on Renewal, Not Revenge*, Women's E-news (October 9, 2000) (on file with the author).

93. 2004 Organic Law, *op. cit.*, art. 80.

94. Waldorf, *op. cit.*, at 54 n.296.

95. 2004 Organic Law, *op. cit.*, art. 68, Chapter VII.

96. *See* Gabriel Gabiro, *Rwanda Genocide: Paying for Reconciliation*, Hirondelle News Agency (Dec. 19, 2002) (on file with author).

97. Category 1 minors who refuse to confess, or whose confessions have been rejected, incur a sentence ranging from ten to twenty years. Minors in this Category who confess as stipulated incur a prison sentence ranging from eight to ten years. Category 2 minors who either kill or commit serious attacks with the intent to kill who refuse to confess, or whose confessions have been rejected, incur a sentence ranging from eight to ten years. Those who confess after their names have appeared on the list established by the *gacaca* court

of the *cellule* incur a sentence from 6 to 7.5 years, but out of this sentence they serve half of their time in custody and the remainder is commuted into community service. Those who confess before the list is drawn up incur a prison sentence ranging from 3.5 to 6 years' imprisonment, again out of this sentence they serve half in custody and the remainder is commuted into community service. Category 2 minors who commit offenses against the person without intention to kill are sentenced to ranges of 2.5 to 3.5 years (refusal to confess/confession rejected); 1.5 to 2.5 years (confess after list drawn up); and 6 months to 1.5 years (confess before list drawn up). In each of these permutations, the minor is to serve half of the sentence in community service.

98. République Rwandaise, MANUEL EXPLICATIF SUR LA LOI ORGANIQUE PORTANT CRÉATION DES JURIDICTIONS *GACACA*, COUR SUPRÊME (Départment des Juridictions Gacaca).

99. This largely replicates the Organic Law, although the *Manuel explicatif* provides a concrete example. *Id.* at 99.

100. *Id.*

101. *Id.*

102. 2004 Organic Law, *op. cit.*, art. 67.

103. Republic of Rwanda, *National Service of Gacaca Jurisdictions, The Situation of Trials from Gacaca Courts as per 06/10/2005* (on file with the author). Unless otherwise indicated, the statistics in this paragraph derive from this source.

104. Certain high-profile accused remain within the *gacaca* process. For example, the head of the Catholic Church in Rwanda, Archbishop Thaddée Ntihinyurwa, faces *gacaca* proceedings in Cyangugu in order to determine whether or not he should be named as a suspect. The former Rwandan Defense Minister came before a *gacaca* court in April 2005, where he denied charges of failing to stop troops under his command from carrying out killings.

105. *Over 4,000 Suspects Judged in 2005, op. cit.*

106. Avocats sans frontières, MONITORING DES JURIDICTIONS *GACACA:* PHASE DE JUGEMENT, RAPPORT ANALYTIQUE 24 (mars–septembre 2005) (on file with the author).

107. *Id.*

108. Human Rights Watch, WORLD REPORT (EVENTS OF 2005) 124 (2006).

109. *Rwandan general arrested on genocide charges*, THE GLOBE AND MAIL (Sept. 6, 2005); Schabas, *op. cit.*, at 881–882; A. Meldrum, *1 million Rwandans to face killing charges in village courts*, THE GUARDIAN (January 15, 2005). *See also* Jacques Fierens, Gacaca *Courts: Between Fantasy and Reality*, 3(4) J. INT'L CRIM. JUST. 896, 900 (2005).

110. *See* Mark A. Drumbl, *Punishment, Postgenocide: From Guilt to Shame to Civis in Rwanda*, 75 N.Y.U. L. REV. 1221, 1245–1252 (2000); Christian Scherrer, GENOCIDE AND CRISIS IN CENTRAL AFRICA 126 (2002) (claiming that from 40 to 66 percent of male Hutu farmers, 60 to 80 percent of professionals, and nearly all civil servants participated in the genocide; and describing millions of others as "indirectly responsible"); Philip Gourevitch, WE WISH TO INFORM YOU THAT TOMORROW WE WILL BE KILLED WITH OUR FAMILIES: STORIES FROM RWANDA 244 (1998) (citing statement by Paul Kagame, currently President of Rwanda, that as many as one million people had participated directly or indirectly in the genocide). But the numbers are contested, depending on the definition of perpetrator. *See, e.g.*, Osiel, *op. cit.*, at 1752–1753 n.4 (citing an estimate of well over 200,000 "immediate participants" in the Rwandan genocide, but noting that this "figure does not include those who identified Tutsi neighbors to militias or were present in mobs whose other members committed murderous acts"). In the case of *gacaca* proceedings, the spike in the number of potential defendants is also in small part due to new proceedings initiated to prosecute witness tampering and assault of witnesses.

111. Schabas, *op. cit.*, at 881–882.

112. *See generally* PRISCILLA HAYNER, UNSPEAKABLE TRUTHS: CONFRONTING STATE TERROR AND ATROCITY 192–195 (2001); *see also* Jennifer Widner, *Courts and Democracy in Postconflict Transitions: A Social Scientist's Perspective on the African Case*, 95 AM.

J. Int'l L. 64, 65–66 (2001) (discussing cases of Uganda and Somalia in addition to Rwanda).

113. Fierens, *op. cit.*, at 913, n.58 (citing C. Ntampaka, "Le retour à la tradition dans le jugement du génocide rwandais: le *gacaca*, justice participative," 48 *Bulletin de l'Académie royale des sciences d'Outre-mer* (2002) 419–455; C. Ntampaka, "Le *gacaca* rwandais, une justice répressive participative," 6 *Actualité du droit international humanitaire. Les dossiers de la Revue de droit pénal et de criminologie* (2001) 211–225).

114. 2004 Organic Law, *op. cit.*, art. 93 (explicitly permitting sentence appeals when "the person was given a sentence contradictory to the legal provisions on offenses").

115. *Id.* art. 29(2).

116. Fierens, *op. cit.*, at 916. *See also* Phil Clark, *Justice without Lawyers: The Gacaca Courts and Post-Genocide Justice and Reconciliation in Rwanda* (Ph.D. dissertation, politics, University of Oxford, September 2005, version on file with the author and cited with permission), ch. 3, pp. 5–6 (describing the *gacaca* law as a complex synthesis of Western law and historical Rwandan practices).

117. *See generally* Drumbl, *Punishment, Postgenocide, op. cit.* (discussing initial enthusiasm for *gacaca*). *Gacaca's* reintegrative shaming potential, as well as its ability to trigger constructive civil dissensus, has become underachieved in practice.

118. *See, e.g.*, Amnesty International, Rwanda: The Troubled Course of Justice, Report AFR 47/015/2000 (April 26, 2000); Amnesty International, Rwanda: The Enduring Legacy of the Genocide and War (April 6, 2004).

119. Fierens, *op. cit.*, at 903 (referring to Constitution of June 4, 2003).

120. *Id.* at 903–904.

121. Munyaneza, *op. cit.*

122. *See, e.g.*, Swisspeace, *Rwanda: Semi-annual Risk Assessment (May to October 2005)* 5–6 (2005), *available at* http://www.swisspeace.org/fast.

123. Vandeginste, *op. cit.*, at 239.

124. American RadioWorks, *Rwanda's Revolutionary Justice* (July 2002), *available at* http://www.americanradioworks.com/features/justiceontrial/rwanda_print.html; Naomi Roht-Arriaza, *Reparations Decisions and Dilemmas*, 27 Hastings Int'l & Comp. L. Rev. 157, 193 (2004).

125. Scott Straus, *Letter from Rwanda*, 29 Newsletter of the Institute for the Study of Genocide 9 (2002).

126. Clark, *op. cit.*, at ch. 6, p. 24.

127. A French magistrate has issued arrest warrants against RPF officials for alleged crimes committed in 1994, specifically the shooting down on April 6, 1994, of the airplane carrying the leaders of Rwanda and Burundi that was the trigger event for the genocide. These warrants have caused a rupture in diplomatic relations between France and Rwanda.

128. S.C. Res. 1503, U.N. SCOR, 58th Sess., 4817th mtg., U.N. Doc. S/Res/1503 (2003). Del Ponte remains as ICTY Chief Prosecutor.

129. Clark, *op. cit.*, at ch. 6, p. 12.

130. General surveys among the overall population, including Hutu prisoners, are favorable to *gacaca*. *See, e.g.*, Timothy Longman, Phuong Pham, & Harvey M. Weinstein, *Connecting justice to human experience: attitudes toward accountability and reconciliation in Rwanda*, in My Neighbor, My Enemy: Justice and Community in the Aftermath of Mass Atrocity 206, 215–217, 222 (Stover & Weinstein eds., 2004) (noting that overall attitudes toward *gacaca* were quite positive and demonstrated stronger support than for ICTR and domestic trials); Luis Salas, *Reconstruction of Public Security and Justice in Post Conflict Societies: The Rwandan Experience*, 26 Int'l J. Comp. & Applied Crim. J. 165, 187 (2002) (citing national surveys showing that Rwandans feel *gacaca* will help in reunification and peace); Peter Uvin & Charles Mironko, *Western and Local Approaches to Justice in Rwanda*, 9 Global Governance 219, 227 (2003) (reporting that a great majority of Rwandans as

well as a majority of the prison population were ready to participate in *gacaca* in 2001); *Rwanda – About 92 percent of population supports traditional courts – survey*, BBC News (March 6, 2003) (reporting that 92 percent of the Rwandan population finds *gacaca* a viable remedy, a mediation and reconciliation tool, and as key to a new phase in countrywide development); Gabriel Gabiro, *Gacaca Courts Edge On* (June 5, 2003) (on file with author) ("[A]mong many Rwandans, Gacaca also seems to be the most acceptable of all other local and international efforts to bring perpetrators of the 1994 genocide to justice.").

131. The Rwandan government has rejected the implementation of the prototypical restorative justice mechanism, namely a truth and reconciliation commission along the lines of the South African model. A National Unity and Reconciliation Commission has been established, whose work is geared to civic and peace education, the monitoring of policies and programs, and community reconciliation activities with a view to emphasizing shared culture. Its focus, however, is not directed toward individual perpetrators, bystanders, or historiographies.

132. *See* Drumbl, *Punishment, Postgenocide, op. cit.*, at 1241–1263.

133. Drumbl, *Rule of Law, op. cit.*, at 604–609 (1998). Other observers report similar findings. *See, e.g.*, Gourevitch, *op. cit.*, at 244; Neil Boisen, Focus Group Study Report: Knowledge, Attitudes and Practices Among Inmates of Rwandan Detention Facilities Accused of Crimes of Genocide 25 (U.S. Institute of Peace, 1997); Jeremy Sarkin, *The Necessity and Challenges of Establishing a Truth and Reconciliation Commission in Rwanda*, 21 Hum. Rts. Q. 767, 772 (1999).

134. Gabriel Gabiro, *Running Away from the Genocide*, Hirondelle News Agency (Oct. 8, 2003) (on file with author); Widner, *op. cit.*, at 69 (reporting that high-level organizers of the genocide construct this solidarity after they reestablish authority in prison). Phil Clark, in his recently conducted longitudinal interviews with a select number of parolees, reports that one parolee did not feel guilty about what he had done and another affirmed that his fellow detainees had become akin to his family. Clark, *op. cit.*, at ch. 4, pp. 14, 17, 19.

135. The Organization for African Unity found that "denial of the one-sided genocide of April to July 1994 remains an unshakable article of [radical Hutu] faith. Accordingly, there is no need for collective atonement or for individual acknowledgment of culpability." Organization for African Unity Report, ch. 23.61 (July 7, 2000), *available at* http://www.internetdiscovery.org/forthetruth/Rwanda-e/EN-III-T.htm. Stef Vandeginste concludes that "[i]t is a widely shared perception [. . .] among Hutu [. . .] that victor's justice is being done." Vandeginste, *op. cit.*, at 236. Jeremy Sarkin observes that the use of the legal system has "led to increased human rights violations, anger, and distrust of the system among both victims and accused." Sarkin, *The Necessity and Challenges, op. cit.*, at 771.

136. *Genocide Suspects Rush to Confess Ahead of Deadline*, Hirondelle News Agency (Feb. 20, 2004) (on file with author).

137. Some individuals who promptly confessed were lower-level offenders slated for immediate release because they already had spent about a decade in prison and, thereby, have been imprisoned awaiting trial longer than they would have been imprisoned were they to have been found guilty through *gacaca* of the crimes with which they were charged. In January 2003, Rwandan President Paul Kagame issued a decree for the release of suspects "that had been (or risked spending) in detention without trial longer than they would serve should they be convicted, as well as confessed criminals that had served most of their time in jail." Gabriel Gabiro, *Clamping Killers and Survivors Together*, Hirondelle News Agency (Feb. 24, 2004) (on file with author). Some of the confessions lack authenticity. Gabriel Gabiro, *Gacaca Courts Edge On* (June 5, 2003) (on file with author).

138. Drumbl, *Punishment, Postgenocide, op. cit.*, at 1237–1239.

139. On lenity, *see* article 4 Bosnia and Herzegovina Criminal Code. *See also generally* Rome Statute of the International Criminal Court, U.N. Doc. A/CONF.183/9, art. 24(2) ("In

the event of a change in the law applicable to a given case prior to a final judgment, the law more favourable to the person being investigated, prosecuted or convicted shall apply.").

140. *Prosecutor v. Dragan Nikolić*, Case No. IT-94-2-A, ¶ 84 (ICTY Appeals Chamber, Feb. 4, 2005) (discussing principle of *lex mitior*, namely whether changes in law should inure to the benefit of the accused).

141. Sieber Report, *op. cit.*, at 26–27.

142. *Id.* at 30.

143. *Id.* at 35.

144. *Accord, Prosecutor v. Dragan Nikolić*, Case No. IT-94-2-S, ¶¶ 155–156 (ICTY Trial Chamber, Dec. 18, 2003).

145. *Prosecutor v. Rašević and Todović*, Case No. IT-97-25/1-PT, ¶ 44 (ICTY Referral Bench, July 8, 2005).

146. Sieber Report, *op. cit.*, at 31.

147. *Id.* at 52.

148. The Montenegran electoral result might encourage a similar outcome in Kosovo which, from the Serbian perspective, would be much more controversial.

149. Sieber Report, *op. cit.*, at 53–54.

150. *Id.* at 56–57.

151. Bosnia and Herzegovina Criminal Code, art. 48.

152. *Id.* art. 39.

153. Sieber Report, *op. cit.*, at 37.

154. *Id.* at 37–38.

155. *Prosecutor v. Mejakić et al.*, Case No. IT-02-65-T, ¶ 59 (ICTY Referral Bench, July 20, 2005).

156. Sieber Report, *op. cit.*, at 47–48.

157. Organization for Security and Co-operation in Europe, Department of Human Rights and Rule of Law Legal System Monitoring Section, Kosovo: Review of the Criminal Justice System (April 2003–October 2004) Crime, Detention, and Punishment 47 n.187 (2004) [hereinafter Kosovo: Review (2004)].

158. *Id.* at 11.

159. *Id.* at 6, 34, 44.

160. *Id.* at 34 n.115.

161. *Id.* (calling the Kanun "vengeful").

162. Organization for Security and Cooperation in Europe, Human Rights Department, War Crimes Trials Before the Domestic Courts of Bosnia and Herzegovina: Progress and Obstacles 12 (March 2005) (document on file with the author) [hereinafter War Crimes Trials 2005]; Kosovo: Review (2004), *op. cit.*, at 13; Organization for Security and Cooperation in Europe, Plea Agreements in Bosnia and Herzegovina 1 (2005) [hereinafter Plea Agreements] (noting that plea agreements, a "common law based mechanism," have become "one of the core mechanisms within the criminal procedure of Bosnia and Herzegovina since its introduction in 2003" in a broad variety of cases ranging from minor trespassing offenses to crimes against humanity).

163. Plea Agreements, *op. cit.*, at 5.

164. *Id.* at 20, 26, 28 (reporting on the use of plea bargains for both ordinary and extraordinary offenses, but noting that in Bosnia and Herzegovina plea agreements have been used in four war crimes cases and that these generally did not require cooperation on the part of the defendant).

165. Sieber Report, *op. cit.*, at 68.

166. *Id.*

167. *Id.* at 66, 69, 76.

168. *Id.* at 75.

169. War Crimes Trials 2005, *op. cit.*

170. *Id.* at 11. Information on the War Crimes Chamber is online, *available at* http://www. sudbih.gov.ba.

171. BBC, *War crimes court opens in Bosnia, available at* http://news.bbc.co.uk/2/hi/europe/ 4331887.stm.

172. WAR CRIMES TRIALS 2005, *op. cit.*, at ii.

173. *Id.* at i.

174. *Id.* at 6.

175. *Id.* at i. Courts in Bosnia and Herzegovina continue to issue judgments for extraordinary international crimes that postdate the 2005 OSCE Report. In January 2006, a Bosnian court sentenced a former Muslim soldier to fourteen years' imprisonment for killing Croat civilians during the Bosnian Wars. Late in 2005, a Bosnian Serb court sentenced three former Serb police officers to up to twenty years' imprisonment for the murders of Muslim civilians in 1994. On February 11, 2005, a Bosnian Serb court acquitted eleven Bosnian Serb police officers on war crimes charges, leading to criticism by a number of human rights groups. Humanitarian Law Center, Press Release, War Crimes Trials Before National Courts, *First war crimes trial in Republika Srpska* (March 20, 2005).

176. WAR CRIMES TRIALS 2005, *op. cit.*, at ii.

177. *Id.*

178. Compiled from case information *id.* at 52–56.

179. E-mail from Ernesto Kiza, Max-Planck Institut, to Mark Drumbl, August 23, 2005 (on file with the author and cited with permission).

180. *Id.*

181. *Id.*

182. *Id.*

183. *See, e.g.*, Associated Press, *Prosecutors welcome Canada's ruling to extradite Kosovo war crimes suspect* (September 23, 2005) (reporting that a decision by Canadian authorities to extradite a Serb paramilitary soldier to Serbia to face trial is a "show of confidence" in the Serb judicial system).

184. BBC News, *Serbs jailed for Vukovar massacre* (December 12, 2005), *available at* http://news. bbc.co.uk/2/hi/europe/4521520.stm.

185. BBC, *Serb video 'executioners' charged* (October 7, 2005), *available at* http://news.bbc. co.uk/2/hi/europe/4320504.stm (reporting that five former Serbian policemen from the notorious Scorpions unit have been charged with murder in the 1995 Srebrenica massacre).

186. Nicholas Wood, *Video of Serbs in Srebrenica Massacre Leads to Arrests*, N.Y. TIMES (June 3, 2005) (citing an opinion poll that showed that over 50 percent of respondents did not know about war crimes in Bosnia or did not believe they had taken place).

187. Humanitarian Law Center, Press Release, *Serbia Is Not Doing Enough To Fulfil Its Obligations Towards The Victims Of Armed Conflicts In The Former Yugoslavia* (December 10, 2005).

188. Organization for Security and Cooperation in Europe Mission to Croatia, BACKGROUND REPORT: DOMESTIC WAR CRIMES TRIALS 2004 3, 10–11 (April 26, 2005) [hereinafter BACKGROUND REPORT 2005].

189. Organization for Security and Cooperation in Europe Mission to Croatia, SUPPLEMENTARY REPORT: WAR CRIME PROCEEDINGS IN CROATIA AND FINDINGS FROM TRIAL MONITORING (June 22, 2004) [hereinafter SUPPLEMENTARY REPORT].

190. *See, e.g.*, BACKGROUND REPORT 2005, *op. cit.*

191. *Id.* at 3.

192. *Id.* at 4.

193. *Id.* at 18.

194. *Id.* at 17, 31.

195. OSCE Mission to Croatia, *Domestic War Crimes Trials, available at* http://www.osce.org/ croatia/13402.html.

196. BACKGROUND REPORT 2005, *op. cit.*, at 4.
197. *Id.* at 11, 14. Some trials proceeded *in absentia*. *Id.* at 40.
198. *Id.* at 14.
199. *Id.* at 36 (citing article 38 of the 1993 Criminal Code).
200. *Id.* at 15, 36. In 2005 Croatian courts issued higher sentences. For example, in December 2005 a Croatian court sentenced an ethnic Serb paramilitary member to fifteen years for participating in the killings of six Bosnian men at Srebrenica.
201. *Id.* at 48.
202. SUPPLEMENTARY REPORT, *op. cit.*, at 11.
203. Organization for Security and Cooperation in Europe Mission to Croatia, BACKGROUND REPORT: DOMESTIC WAR CRIMES TRIALS 2003 24 (2004).
204. *Id.*
205. Organization for Security and Cooperation in Europe Mission to Croatia, BACKGROUND REPORT: DOMESTIC WAR CRIMES TRIALS 2002 19 (2003).
206. BACKGROUND REPORT 2005, *op. cit.*, at 36.
207. *Id.* at 36–37, 39 (all mitigating factors discussed).
208. *Id.* at 37.
209. *Id.* at 37–38.
210. *Prosecutor v. Branko Stanković*, Osijek County Court K 50/02, September 9, 2002, confirmed by the Supreme Court, I Kz 878/02–5 (February 4, 2003).
211. *Prosecutor v. Milos Loncar*, K-18/02–110, conviction confirmed by the Supreme Court, I Kz 791/02–6, (May 6, 2005).
212. BACKGROUND REPORT 2005, *op. cit.*, at 38–39.
213. *Id.* at 39.
214. Press Release, OSCE *Mission Says Domestic War Crimes Trials Have Improved in Croatia but More Progress Needed, available at* http://www.osce.org/item/14055.html?print = 1 (noting particular improvements regarding whether a Serb war crime defendant will receive a fair trial before the Croatian judiciary, but also expressing concerns over unsubstantiated proceedings against Serbs, *in absentia* trials, unwarranted arrests, and the continuing high error rate in trial court verdicts triggering reversals from the Supreme Court). *See also* Associated Press, *Croatian Court Acquits Serb Prison Guard of War Crimes* (October 31, 2005) (on file with the author) (discussing case of Jovan Petković, a former Serb prison guard accused of raping and subjecting a female inmate to psychological torture during her incarceration; Petković had been sentenced *in absentia* to twelve years, then was extradited from Switzerland in 2005; on October 31, 2005, he was acquitted by a Croatian court of war crimes charges because the key witness retracted parts of her allegations in the retrial held in Croatia).
215. Re J, IV-26/96, Higher Regional Court at Düsseldorf (September 26, 1997); judgment subsequently confirmed by the German Federal Constitutional Court, BverfG, December 12, 2000, 2BvR 1290/99 (confirming the constitutionality of sentencing by German courts of individuals convicted of genocide in Bosnia). Jorgić was found guilty of eleven cases of genocide, in conjunction with several cases of dangerous bodily harm, deprivation of liberty and/or murder, but in all cases as acting as an accessory to these crimes.
216. BayObLG, Judgment, December 15, 1999, 6 St 1/99.
217. BayObLG, Judgment, May 23, 1997, 3 St 20/06, NJW 1998 392. For commentary on the *Djajić* case, *see* Christoph J. Safferling, *International Decision, Prosecutor v. Djajić, No. 20/96, Supreme Court of Bavaria, 3d Strafsenat, May 23, 1997*, 92 AM. J. INT'L L. 528 (1998).
218. Higher Regional Court at Düsseldorf (Nov. 29, 1999), 2 StE 6/97.
219. Re J, IV-26/96, Higher Regional Court at Düsseldorf (September 26, 1997).
220. *Id.*
221. *Prosecution v. Sarić*, Eastern Division of High Court (Third Chamber) (November 25, 1994) (judgment confirmed by the Danish Supreme Court on August 15, 1995, and a subsequent

application to the European Court of Human Rights was declared inadmissible on February 2, 1999).

222. The judgment reports that the "jury were in agreement on an additional question relating to the possibility of increasing the sentence." *Id.* at 5. Sarić was also permanently extradited from Denmark and, owing to a mental condition that developed following the commission of the crimes, ordered to be hospitalized until the sentence could be served. *Id.* at 5–6.

223. Carlos Santiago Nino, Radical Evil on Trial 13 (1996).

224. *Id.* at 12. Collaboration and national indignity were created as new offenses following the liberation of France and were not categorized as extraordinary international crimes.

225. *Id.* at 11.

226. *Id.* at 12.

227. Mauthausen Trial (March 29–May 13, 1946), information *available at* http://www.jewish-virtuallibrary.org/jsource/Holocaust/WarCrime42.html. The Mauthausen trial was held by the American Military Tribunal sitting in the former Dachau concentration camp.

228. Nino, *op. cit.*, at 9 (reporting, with regard to severity of sentence, research by John H. Herz that "in the more than 1,000 cases tried between 1959 and 1969, fewer than 100 of the convicted Nazi criminals received life sentences and less than 300 received limited terms" and that "[i]n the following twelve years, there were 6,000 convictions, but only 157 were for life imprisonment").

229. *Id.* at 10.

230. *Yamashita v. Styer* (In re Yamashita), 327 U.S. 1 (1946) (U.S. Supreme Court affirming death sentence issued by a military commission in the Philippines against Japanese General Yamashita for war crimes, but not commenting on the penological purpose or rationale of the sentence).

231. Trial of Hans Albin Rauter (Netherlands Special Court in The Hague, May 4, 1948, and Netherlands Special Court of Cassation, January 12, 1949), reprinted at 14 Law Reports of Trials of War Criminals 89, 109 (1949).

232. *Id.* at 110.

233. *See, e.g.*, Trial of Hauptsturmführer Amon Leopold Goeth (Supreme National Tribunal of Poland, Cracow, 1946), reprinted at 7 Law Reports of Trials of War Criminals 1, 4 (1948).

234. 7 Law Reports of Trials of War Criminals 84, 86, 88 (1948).

235. 11 Law Reports of Trials of War Criminals 103 (1949).

236. 14 Law Reports of Trials of War Criminals 158–159 (1949).

237. The Peleus Trial (British Military Court for the Trial of War Criminals (Hamburg), 17–20 October, 1945), reprinted at 1 Law Reports of Trials of War Criminals 1, 20 (1947) (notes on the case); *see also* 1 Law Reports of Trials of War Criminals 109 (1947).

238. 11 Law Reports of Trials of War Criminals 103 (1949).

239. 3 Law Reports of Trials of War Criminals 88–89 (1948). The Norwegian lawmakers also noted that war criminals "increased their guilt by systematically committing whole series of the most appalling crimes." *Id.* at 89.

240. 3 Law Reports of Trials of War Criminals 96–97 (1948).

241. *See, e.g.*, Trial of General von Mackensen and General Maelzer (British Military Court (Rome), 18–30 November, 1945) reprinted at 8 Law Reports of Trials of War Criminals 1, 2 (1949) (case report stating that "[b]oth accused were found guilty and sentenced to death by being shot. The Confirming Officer confirmed the findings on both accused but commuted both sentences to imprisonment for life."); Trial of Albert Kesselring (British Military Court (Venice), 17 February–6 May, 1947), reprinted at 8 Law Reports of Trials of War Criminals 9, 12 (1949) (confirming officer commuting death sentence to life imprisonment); Trial of Helmuth von Ruchteschell (British Military Court (Hamburg), 5 to 21 May, 1947), reprinted at 9 Law Reports of Trials of War Criminals 82, 86 (1949) (confirming officer not confirming guilt on one of the convictions and reducing sentence

from ten to seven years' imprisonment); The Peleus Trial (British Military Court for the Trial of War Criminals (Hamburg), 17–20 October, 1945), reprinted at 1 Law Reports of Trials of War Criminals 1, 13 (1947) (all sentences confirmed by Commander-in-Chief, British Army of the Rhine); The Almelo Trial (British Military Court for the Trial of War Criminals (Almelo), 24–26 November, 1945), reprinted at 1 Law Reports of Trials of War Criminals 35, 41 (1947) (all sentences confirmed by Commander-in-Chief, British Army of the Rhine).

242. Trial of Sergeant-Major Shigeru Ohashi and Six Others (Australian Military Court (Rabaul), 20–23 March, 1946), reprinted at 5 Law Reports of Trials of War Criminals 25, 26 (1948).

243. Trial of Lieutenant General Kurt Maelzer (United States Military Commission (Florence, Italy), 9–14 September, 1946), reprinted at 11 Law Reports of Trials of War Criminals 53, 53 (1949).

244. The Dachau Concentration Camp Trial (General Military Government Court of the United States Zone, Dachau, 15 November–13 December, 1945), reprinted at 11 Law Reports of Trials of War Criminals 5, 8 (1949). See also The Abbaye Ardenne Case (Canadian Military Court (Aurich), 10–28 December, 1945), reprinted at 4 Law Reports of Trials of War Criminals 97, 109 (1948) ("The Convening Authority, however, commuted the death sentence to one of life imprisonment, on the grounds that Meyer's degree of responsibility did not warrant the extreme penalty.").

245. See, e.g., Trial of Carl Bauer et al. (Permanent Military Tribunal at Dijon, October 18, 1945), reprinted at 8 Law Reports of Trials of War Criminals 15, 16 (1949) (recognizing that two defendants had acted on Bauer's orders, admitting this as an extenuating circumstance, and sentencing them to five years' imprisonment each). In some cases, treatment of superior orders as going to mitigation and not to exculpation was recognized in the positive law instruments that enabled the military or civilian proceedings. Trial of Hans Szabados (Permanent Military Tribunal at Clermont-Ferrand, June 23, 1946), reprinted at 9 Law Reports of Trials of War Criminals 59, 61 (1949) (notes on the case); United States Law and Practice Concerning Trials of War Criminals by Military Commissions and Military Government Courts, 1 Law Reports of Trials of War Criminals 120 (1947).

246. Trial of Lieutenant-General Shigeru Sawada and Three Others (United States Military Commission (Shanghai), 27 February, 1946–15 April, 1946), reprinted at 5 Law Reports of Trials of War Criminals 1, 7 (1948).

247. See, e.g., The Peleus Trial (British Military Court for the Trial of War Criminals (Hamburg), 17–20 October, 1945), reprinted at 1 Law Reports of Trials of War Criminals 1, 20–21 (1947) (notes on the case) (U-boat commander and medical officer sentenced to death by shooting in spite of their plea of superior orders, but mitigation found on the basis of superior orders for another defendant sentenced to fifteen years' imprisonment). In this case, the U-boat engineer was sentenced to life imprisonment "probably" because he opposed the order given by the commander to another accused. Id. at 21. See also Trial of Bruns and Two Others (Eidsivating Lagmannsrett and the Supreme Court of Norway, 20 March and 3 July, 1946), reprinted at 3 Law Reports of Trials of War Criminals 15, 18 (1948).

248. The Belsen Trial (British Military Court, Luneberg, 17 September–17 November, 1945), reprinted at 2 Law Reports of Trials of War Criminals 1, 122–125 (1947).

249. Trial of Wilhelm Gerbsch (Special Court in Amsterdam, First Chamber, April 28, 1948), reprinted at 13 Law Reports of Trials of War Criminals 131, 132 (1949).

250. Trial of Alois and Anna Bommer and their Daughters (Permanent Military Tribunal at Metz, February 19, 1947), reprinted at 9 Law Reports of Trials of War Criminals 62, 66 (1949) (citing provisions of the French Penal Code).

251. Trial of Willy Zuehlke (Netherlands Special Court in Amsterdam, August 3, 1948, and the Netherlands Special Court of Cassation, December 6, 1948), reprinted at 14 Law Reports of Trials of War Criminals 139, 141 (1949) (also noting in mitigation that the

illegal arrests "did not originate with the accused"). Zuehlke initially was sentenced to seven years' imprisonment and the Netherlands Special Court of Cassation reduced that sentence to five years on account of its treatment of the mitigating circumstances.

252. The Jaluit Atoll Case (United States Military Commission (Marshall Islands), 7–13 December, 1945), reprinted at 1 LAW REPORTS OF TRIALS OF WAR CRIMINALS 71, 76 (1947) (reducing sentence of one defendant to ten years' imprisonment on this basis). This is an interesting factor insofar as it can extend to the automaticity of mass atrocity in contexts of bureaucratized violence.

253. The Dreierwalde Case (British Military Court (Wuppertal), 11–14 March, 1946), reprinted at 1 LAW REPORTS OF TRIALS OF WAR CRIMINALS 81, 84 (1947).

254. The Zyklon B Case (British Military Court (Hamburg), 1–8 March 1946), reprinted at 1 LAW REPORTS OF TRIALS OF WAR CRIMINALS 93, 102 (1947).

255. Id.

256. Trial of Wilhelm Gerbsch (Special Court in Amsterdam, First Chamber, April 28, 1948), reprinted at 13 LAW REPORTS OF TRIALS OF WAR CRIMINALS 131, 132 (1949).

257. Trial of Tanabe Koshiro (Netherlands Temporary Court-Martial (Macassar), 5 February, 1947), reprinted at 11 LAW REPORTS OF TRIALS OF WAR CRIMINALS 1, 2–4 (1949) (citing also the notes on the case).

258. Trial of Willi Mackensen (British Military Court, Hannover, January 28, 1946), reprinted at 11 LAW REPORTS OF TRIALS OF WAR CRIMINALS 81, 81 (1949).

259. Trial of Hans Albin Rauter (Netherlands Special Court in The Hague, May 4, 1948, and Netherlands Special Court of Cassation, January 12, 1949), reprinted at 14 LAW REPORTS OF TRIALS OF WAR CRIMINALS 89, 110 (1949).

260. Id. As I noted in the previous section, some national courts in the former Yugoslavia that have sentenced perpetrators of ethnic cleansing in the 1990s may part company with these rationales.

261. Trial of Shigeki Motomura and 15 Others (Netherlands Temporary Court-Martial at Macassar, July 18, 1947), reprinted at 13 LAW REPORTS OF TRIALS OF WAR CRIMINALS 138, 145 (1949).

262. Trial of Washio Awochi (Netherlands Temporary Court-Martial at Batavia, October 25, 1946), reprinted at 13 LAW REPORTS OF TRIALS OF WAR CRIMINALS 122, 125 (1949) (notes on the case).

263. Rebecca Wittmann, BEYOND JUSTICE: THE AUSCHWITZ TRIAL (2005).

264. Id.

265. Personal visit, November 19, 2006.

266. Id.

267. Trial of Adolf Eichmann, Criminal Case No. 40/61, in the District Court of Jerusalem.

268. Id. ¶¶ 221–222. The applicable Israeli legislation excluded superior orders as a defense to liability. In this regard it tracked Nuremberg. The court explicitly noted that the rejection of the defense of superior orders was justified in that: "Perhaps it is not a vain hope that the more this recognition [of the rejection of the defense] takes root in the minds of men, the more they will refrain from following captive after criminal leaders, and then the rule of law and order in the relations between nations will be reinforced." Id. ¶ 220.

269. Id. ¶¶ 222, 226–228.

270. Id. ¶ 231.

271. Id. ¶ 235.

272. Id. ¶ 231.

273. Id. ¶¶ 241–242.

274. Trial of Adolf Eichmann in Jerusalem: Judgment Part 26/Sentence, available at http://www.ess.uwe.ac.uk/genocide/Eichmannza.htm.

275. The State of Israel v. Adolf Eichmann (S. Ct. Israel, May 29, 1962), 36 INT'L L. REP. 277 (1968).

276. Id. at 313.

277. Id. at 339.

278. R. v. Sawoniuk, [2000] 2 Cr. App. Rep. 220, [2000] Crim L.R. 506 (LEXIS printout on file with the author).
279. *Id.* at p. 3 of LEXIS printout (on file with the author).
280. Sue Clough, *Killer, 78, Gets Life For War Crimes*, THE TELEGRAPH (U.K.) (April 2, 1999); BBC News, *Life for War Criminal* (April 1, 1999), *available at* http://news.bbc.co.uk/1/hi/uk/307921.stm.
281. On the Barbie trial, *see generally* Leila Sadat Wexler, *The Interpretation of the Nuremberg Principles by the French Court of Cassation: From Touvier to Barbie and Back Again*, 32 COLUM. J. TRANSNAT'L. L. 289 (1994).
282. David Stout, *Paul Touvier, 81, French War Criminal*, N.Y. TIMES (July 18, 1996).
283. Leila Sadat Wexler, *Reflections on the Trial of Vichy Collaborator Paul Touvier for Crimes against Humanity in France*, 20 L. & SOC. INQUIRY 191, 209 (1995).
284. For more information regarding *l'affaire Papon*, *see* THE PAPON AFFAIR: MEMORY AND JUSTICE ON TRIAL (Golan ed., 2000).
285. Touvier, in fact, was "a relatively minor figure." Sadat, *Reflections on the Trial of Vichy Collaborator Paul Touvier, op. cit.*, at 199.
286. The ten-year sentence was confirmed by the Cour de Cassation in 2004, which thereby rejected Papon's final appeal.
287. BBC News, *Killer Nazi Prison Guard Jailed*, *available at* http://news.bbc.co.uk/1/hi/world/europe/1359526.stm.
288. Associated Press, *Joseph Schwammberger, 92, Nazi Labor Camp Commander, Dies*, N.Y. TIMES (December 4, 2004).
289. Franz-Norbert Piontek, *Germany Jails Ex-Nazi In "Last War Crimes Trial,"* Reuters Wire Service (on file with the author).
290. Sadat, *Reflections on the Trial of Vichy Collaborator Paul Touvier, op. cit.*, at 211.
291. BBC News, *Killer Nazi Prison Guard Jailed, op. cit.*

5. LEGAL MIMICRY

1. They do so for a variety of reasons. National agents may learn from the transnational judicial dialogue they engage in with their international counterparts. *See, e.g.*, Anne-Marie Slaughter, A NEW WORLD ORDER (2004). They may hold a good faith belief that criminal trials constitute an effective accountability mechanism. Additionally, as discussed in Chapter 4, certain state officials may prefer centralized frameworks to consolidate power and, hence, be attracted to prosecutorial models attached to the state or an international organization, instead of anchored in local communities or local leaders.
2. Rama Mani, BEYOND RETRIBUTION: SEEKING JUSTICE IN THE SHADOWS OF WAR 47–48 (2002).
3. *Id.* at 48, 81. It is important not to essentialize. There are instances of overlap between the values promulgated by Western and non-Western legal systems; moreover, conflicts among systems are not necessarily unbridgeable. However, when the replication of Western systems becomes a *grundnorm* for institutional design, any meaningful process of bridging and integrating diffuse values may become jeopardized.
4. I do not discuss the principles that should govern the concurrent application of authority exclusively among national institutions. That said, I recognize the possibility that modalities such as extradition, and the potential assertion of jurisdiction over a suspect based on universality (in cases when such an assertion trumps one based on territoriality or nationality), also may have a homogenizing effect in terms of process and punishment. Universal jurisdiction permits any court anywhere to prosecute and punish extraordinary international criminals.
5. And, in some cases, physically distant, in that institutions are sited away from the conflict or postconflict society. Although referrals and complementarity are designed to mitigate

the negative effects of physical externalization of justice, they by definition do not dissipate methodological externalization and, in fact, may contribute to it.

6. There is a vast scholarly literature on legal transplants. *See, e.g.*, Alan Watson, LEGAL TRANSPLANTS: AN APPROACH TO COMPARATIVE LAW (2d ed., 1993); Pierre Legrand, *The Impossibility of "Legal Transplants,"* 4 MAASTRICHT J. EUROPEAN & COMP. L. (2000); William Twining, *Diffusion of Law: A Global Perspective,* 49 J. LEGAL PLURALISM 1 (2004).

7. North American Free Trade Agreement, U.S.-Canada-Mexico, 32 I.L.M. 605 (1993) [hereinafter NAFTA]; Ari Afilalo, *Meaning, Ambiguity and Legitimacy: Judicial (Re-) Construction of NAFTA Chapter 11,* 25 Nw. J. INT'L L. & BUS. 279 (2005).

8. Chapter 11 provides five specific kinds of protection: national treatment, most favored nation, minimum standard of treatment, preclusion of performance requirements, and against expropriation. *See, e.g.*, NAFTA, *op. cit.*, arts. 1102, 1103, 1105, 1110.

9. *See, e.g.*, International Centre for Settlement of Investor Disputes, Case No. ARB(AF)/98/3, *The Loewen Group, Inc. v. United States,* Final Award (June 26, 2003), *available at* http://www.state.gov/documents/organization/22094.pdf.

10. Afilalo, *op. cit.* Referencing the *Loewen* case, Afilalo concludes that the legitimacy of the NAFTA would be jeopardized were the arbitral panel to have found for the complainants, inasmuch as this would too quickly have threatened the normal course of operation of the U.S. legal system.

11. David A. Westbrook, *Theorizing the Diffusion of Law: Conceptual Difficulties, Unstable Imaginations, and the Effort to Think Gracefully Nonetheless,* 47 HARV. INT'L L.J. 489, 490 (2006).

12. *Prosecutor v. Norman,* Case No. SCSL-2003-08-PT, Decision on the Request by the Truth and Reconciliation Commission of Sierra Leone to Conduct a Public Hearing with Samuel Hinga Norman, ¶ 33 (Oct. 29, 2003).

13. René David & John E.C. Brierley, MAJOR LEGAL SYSTEMS IN THE WORLD TODAY (1985).

14. Antonio Cassese, INTERNATIONAL CRIMINAL LAW 365–88 (2003). There are also a number of mixed national jurisdictions.

15. For example, some national common law systems permit prosecutorial appeal of acquittals in criminal cases, while others (such as the United States) do not. International criminal process permits prosecutorial appeal. In fact, the Appeals Chamber of the ICTY and ICTR can substitute (and has, upon appeal, substituted), entirely new convictions or more serious convictions (for example, as a primary perpetrator instead of a secondary perpetrator) than what had initially been imposed at trial. *See, e.g., Prosecutor v. Semanza,* Case No. ICTR-97-20-A (ICTR Appeals Chamber, May 20, 2005). In these situations, the Appeals Chamber affixes sentence, instead of merely remitting a matter to the Trial Chamber for redetermination of sentence.

16. Basil S. Markesinis, *A Matter of Style,* 110 LAW Q. REV. 607 (1994).

17. Cassese, *op. cit.*, at 384; Geert-Jan Alexander Knoops, AN INTRODUCTION TO THE LAW OF INTERNATIONAL CRIMINAL TRIBUNALS 6 (2003).

18. Daryl A. Mundis, *Book Review,* 97 AM. J. INT'L L. 1012, 1013 (2003) (reviewing Richard May & Marieke Wierda, INTERNATIONAL CRIMINAL EVIDENCE (2002)).

19. Admittedly, there also are examples in U.S. criminal procedure where separate sentencing hearings are not provided for, so – as is the case throughout this discussion – these are not watertight conclusions, but general tendencies.

20. Rome Statute of the International Criminal Court, U.N. Doc. A/CONF.183/9, art. 76 [hereinafter Rome Statute].

21. For example, on the topic of admissibility, the ICTR Trial Chamber in the *Akayesu* judgment held that "any relevant evidence having probative value may be admitted into evidence, provided that it is being in accordance with the requisites of a fair trial. [. . .] [H]earsay evidence is not inadmissible *per se* and [the Trial Chamber] has considered such evidence, with caution[.]" *Prosecutor v. Akayesu,* Case No. ICTR-96-4-T, ¶ 136 (ICTR

Trial Chamber, Sept. 2, 1998). *See also* discussion *supra* Chapter 2; ICC R.P. & Evid. Rule 63(5) ("The Chambers shall not apply national laws governing evidence [...]"), *available at* http://www.icc-cpi.int/library/basicdocuments/rules(e).pdf. However, the internationalized law of evidence for mass atrocity prosecutions remains the output of a process of tweaking the familiar to make it more permissive rather than formulating something new tailored specifically for collective system criminality. M. Cherif Bassiouni, Introduction to International Criminal Law 626–627 (2003). *See also* Mark Drumbl, *Case-Note, Prosecutor v. Krstić, ICTY Authenticates Genocide at Srebrenica and Convicts for Aiding and Abetting*, 5 Melbourne J. of Int'l Law 434 (2004).

22. Håkan Friman, *Procedural Law of Internationalized Criminal Courts*, in International- ized Criminal Courts 325, 356 (Romano, Nollkaemper, & Kleffner eds., 2004) (" ... the international courts provide examples of *sui generis* procedural regimes with elements of the different legal traditions ... with components from both the common law and civil law tradition"). These very modest innovations in international procedure, however, are absent from the punishment schemes of extant international institutions.

23. *See generally* Ralph Henham, *Some Issues for Sentencing in the International Criminal Court*, 52 Int'l & Comp. L. Q. 81 (2003). I recognize that, among Western powers, there are deep divisions between the United States, on the one hand, and other Western countries, on the other, when it comes to supporting the ICC. These differences, however, are attributable to power politics, not divergent jurisprudential approaches to methodologies of prosecuting and punishing extraordinary international criminals, which the United States has strongly supported in ad hoc legalist institutions that it can influence. Many Western common law countries are staunch supporters of the ICC, such as Canada, New Zealand, the United Kingdom, and Australia.

24. For Koskenniemi, "individualism" is a "recent aspect of Western thinking that may under- mine forms of experience or ways of life that cannot be articulated in the individualist terms familiar to the (developed) West." Martti Koskenniemi, *Hersch Lauterpacht and the Development of International Criminal Law*, 2 J. Int'l Crim. Just. 810, 824 (2004).

25. George Fletcher, *Liberals and Romantics at War: The Problem of Collective Guilt*, 111 Yale L. J. 1499, 1511 (2002).

26. Boaventura de Sousa Santos, *The Heterogeneous State and Legal Pluralism in Mozambique*, 40 Law & Soc. Rev. 39, 51 (2006).

27. Ralph Henham, *Conceptualizing Access to Justice and Victims' Rights in International Sentencing*, 13(1) Social & Legal Studies 27, 36 (2004).

28. For general treatment of the phenomenon of externalization of justice, *see* Chandra Lekha Sriram & Brad R. Roth, *Externalization of Justice: What Does It Mean and What Is at Stake?*, XII Finnish Yearbook of International Law 3 (2001).

29. This constraint can affect internationalized national tribunals and hybrid institutions. In Sierra Leone, for example, officials in the region and the Special Court for Sierra Leone recommended that former Liberian President Charles Taylor, the Court's most prominent indictee, be moved to ICC facilities in The Hague for trial out of fears that prosecuting him in Sierra Leone might destabilize the region. Taylor was eventually transferred to ICC facilities to face eleven counts of war crimes and crimes against humanity that, looking ahead, will be adjudged in proceedings conducted entirely by the Special Court for Sierra Leone.

30. Nancy Amoury Combs, *Procuring Guilty Pleas for International Crimes: The Limited Influ- ence of Sentencing Discounts*, 59 Vand. L. Rev. 69, 131 (2006).

31. *See, e.g.*, Bassiouni, *op. cit.*, at 554 (discussing profound public distrust for the judicial system in Kosovo owing to Serbian-sanctioned discrimination).

32. David Chuter, War Crimes: Confronting Atrocity in the Modern World 231 (2003).

33. *Search for Speed and Reconciliation*, The Economist 48 (October 6, 2001).

34. *Rwanda Says UN Lawyer on Most Wanted Genocide List*, Hirondelle News Agency (Lausanne) (Feb. 28, 2006) (on file with the author).

35. Samantha Power, "A PROBLEM FROM HELL": AMERICA AND THE AGE OF GENOCIDE 364–385 (2002).
36. John Torpey, *Introduction*, in POLITICS AND THE PAST 22 (Torpey ed., 2003).
37. *Prosecutor v. Furundžija*, Case No. IT-95-17/1-T, ¶ 290 (ICTY Trial Chamber, Dec. 10, 1998).
38. Mark Osiel, *The Banality of Good: Aligning Incentives Against Mass Atrocity*, 105 COLUM. L. REV. 1751, 1754 n.10 (2005).
39. Sanja Kutnjak Ivković & John Hagan, *The Politics of Punishment and the Siege of Sarajevo: Toward a Conflict Theory of Perceived International (In)justice*, 40 L. & SOC'Y. REV. 369, 385 (2006).
40. Chandra Lekha Sriram, *Globalising Justice: From Universal Jurisdiction to Mixed Tribunals*, 22 NETH. Q. HUM. RTS. 7, 22 (2004) (reporting calls among certain East Timorese for international tribunals to take over prosecutions in East Timor); Press Release, *available at* http://www.jsmp.minihub.org/Press%20Release/2005/May/050524%20End%20SPSC.pdf (in light of the Special Panels' ceasing operation, issuing a call for an international tribunal to take over). *But see* Colum Lynch & Ellen Makashima, *E. Timor Atrocities Detailed*, WASHINGTON POST (Jan. 21, 2006) at A12 (East Timorese government officials firmly expressing their opposition to an international tribunal for East Timor owing *inter alia* to concerns about the impact of prosecutions on democratic transition).
41. Peter Uvin & Charles Mironko, *Western and Local Approaches to Justice in Rwanda*, 9 GLOBAL GOVERNANCE 219, 223 (2003); *see also* Timothy Longman, *The Domestic Impact of the International Criminal Tribunal for Rwanda*, in INTERNATIONAL WAR CRIMES TRIALS: MAKING A DIFFERENCE? 33–41 (Ratner & Bischoff eds., 2004) (noting widespread ignorance of the work of the ICTR among Rwandans but finding that those aware of the ICTR's work had a more positive perception of the ICTR than did those unaware of its work).
42. Many Tutsi believe that, although ICTR trials place considerable emphasis on the rights of the accused, they disregard the rights of victims and witnesses. Kingsley Chiedu Moghalu, *Image and Reality of War Crimes Justice: External Perceptions of the International Criminal Tribunal for Rwanda*, 26 FLETCHER F. WORLD AFFAIRS 21, 29 (2002). Some Rwandan Hutu see the ICTR as political and designed to pursue victors' justice, regardless of its emphasis on due process. Others, however, see it as less political than the Rwandan national courts, particularly in high-profile cases.
43. Longman, *The Domestic Impact of the International Criminal Tribunal for Rwanda, op. cit.*
44. Luis Salas, *Reconstruction of Public Security and Justice in Post Conflict Societies: The Rwandan Experience*, 26 INT'L J. COMP. & APPLIED CRIM. JUST. 165, 191 (2002).
45. Alison Des Forges & Timothy Longman, *Legal Responses to Genocide in Rwanda*, in MY NEIGHBOR, MY ENEMY: JUSTICE AND COMMUNITY IN THE AFTERMATH OF MASS ATROCITY 49, 56 (Stover & Weinstein eds., 2004).
46. *Id.*
47. Laura Fraser, *Coffee, and Hope, Grow in Rwanda*, N.Y. TIMES (August 6, 2006). The budget for the East Timor panels was U.S. $6.3 million in 2001. Suzanne Katzenstein, *Hybrid Tribunals: Searching for Justice in East Timor*, 16 HARV. HUM. RTS. J. 245, 258 (2003). The ICTY has cost U.S. $630 million since its inception in 1993. Daryl A. Mundis, *The Judicial Effects of the "Completion Strategies" on the Ad Hoc International Tribunals*, 99 AM. J. INT'L L. 142, 142 n.2 (2005).
48. I do not say that, in the absence of the ICTR, all of these funds would have gone to reconstruction. In fact, but for the ICTR, none of this money ever may have been raised. The fact that the ICTR was able to attract such funding demonstrates the pull that liberal legalist interventions have upon the sensibilities of donor organizations and nations.
49. Helena Cobban, *Think Again: International Courts*, FOREIGN POLICY, No. 153, 22, 24 (March/April 2006). State accountability mechanisms deliberately were eschewed in

Mozambique's transition from systemic conflict. Instead, local communities turned to traditional healers who conducted ceremonies to reintegrate fighters.

50. William W. Burke-White, *A Community of Courts: Toward a System of International Criminal Law Enforcement*, 24 MICH. J. INT'L L. 1, 45 (2002).

51. *Prosecutor v. Akayesu*, Case No. ICTR-96-4 (ICTR Appeals Chamber, June 1, 2001).

52. *Prosecutor v. Musema*, Case No. ICTR-96-13-T (ICTR Appeals Chamber, Nov. 16, 2001).

53. *Prosecutor v. Nahimana, Barayagwiza, and Ngeze*, Case No. ICTR-99-52-T (ICTR Trial Chamber, Dec. 3, 2003).

54. The discussion that follows distills an argument presented in much greater detail in Mark A. Drumbl, *Judging the 11 September Terrorist Attack*, 24 HUM. RTS. Q. 323 (2002) and in Mark A. Drumbl, *Victimhood in Our Neighborhood: Terrorist Crime, Taliban Guilt, and the Asymmetries of the International Legal Order*, 81 N.C. L. REV. 1, 92–105 (2002).

55. Letter sent by Ambassador John Negroponte to Richard Ryan, President of the Security Council, reprinted in *United States officially informs United Nations of strikes*, WASHINGTON TIMES (Oct. 9, 2001) at A14.

56. Roy Gutman, Christopher Dickey, & Sami Yousafzai, *Guantanamo Justice?*, NEWSWEEK 34, 35 (July 8, 2002).

57. *See generally* Human Rights Watch, *Rwanda*, in PLAYING THE "COMMUNAL CARD": COMMUNAL VIOLENCE AND HUMAN RIGHTS (1995).

58. THE NATIONAL SECURITY STRATEGY OF THE UNITED STATES OF AMERICA 12 (March 2006).

59. In *Hamdan v. Rumsfeld*, the U.S. Supreme Court ruled *inter alia* that Common Article 3 of the Geneva Conventions applies to the conflict against Al-Qaeda. *Hamdan v. Rumsfeld*, 548 U.S. ___ (2006) (slip op.), *available at* http://www.supremecourtus.gov/opinions/05pdf/05-184.pdf. The Court invalidated the military commissions the United States had set up to prosecute a handful of Guantánamo detainees (in Hamdan's case, the charges involved conspiracy to commit war crimes). The Court held that these commissions fell short of minimal Common Article 3 requirements, in particular the preclusion of "the passing of sentences and the carrying out of executions without previous judgment pronounced by a regularly constituted court, affording all the judicial guarantees which are recognized as indispensable by civilized peoples." The Court, however, did not specify exactly what would be required for military commissions to meet these requirements, noting that there was considerable flexibility ("Common Article 3 obviously tolerates a great degree of flexibility in trying individuals captured during armed conflict [. . .]"). *Id.* opinion of the Court at p. 72. Only a plurality of the Court ruled that Common Article 3 requirements incorporated at least the barest of trial protections recognized by customary international law. It appears that, for the majority of the Court, conformity with U.S. courts-martial practice would satisfy minimal Common Article 3 requirements; in fact, the Court even left the door open for military commissions to depart from U.S. courts-martial practice if a practical need could explain the departure. U.S. courts-martial practice is less respectful of liberal due process than procedure at the ICC or ad hoc tribunals. The 2006 Military Commissions Act was passed by Congress, and signed by the President, in response to the *Hamdan* judgment. For a discussion of this legislation, *see* Mark A. Drumbl, *The Expressive Value of Prosecuting and Punishing Terrorists: Hamdan, the Geneva Conventions, and International Criminal Law*, 75 GEO. WASH. L. REV. (forthcoming 2007).

60. *See generally* José E. Alvarez, *Torturing the Law*, 37 CASE W. RES. J. INT'L L. 175 (2006).

61. Statute of the ICTR, U.N. SCOR, 49th Sess., 3453d mtg. at 15, art. 8(2) (1994); Statute of the ICTY, S.C. Res. 827, U.N. SCOR, 48th Sess., 3217th mtg. at 29, art. 9(2) (1993). *See also* Robert Cryer, PROSECUTING INTERNATIONAL CRIMES: SELECTIVITY AND THE INTERNATIONAL CRIMINAL LAW REGIME 132, 136 (2005) (citing, as further examples of primacy, ICTY Statute art. 29 and ICTR Statute art. 28 (on cooperation) and ICTY Statute art. 18(2) and ICTR Statute art. 17(2) (empowering the ad hoc Prosecutor to investigate on a state's territory without the consent of the state)).

62. In the case of *gacaca* for genocide, there is an attempt to democratize the accountability process by having judges elected from and by local communities.

63. This increased willingness also is evident in the Security Council's referral of the Darfur violence to the ICC, insofar as the Security Council noted the "possibility of conducting proceedings in the region." Security Council Res. 1593 (March 31, 2005). *See also* ICC R.P. & EVID., *op. cit.*, Rule 100 (permitting ICC to sit in a state other than the host state). On a broader policy basis, the UN Secretary-General has expressed a desire for transitional justice initiatives to "eschew one-size-fits-all formulas and the importation of foreign models" but then in the same document paradoxically urges the ratification of the ICC, which risks, albeit less blatantly than the ad hocs, these very results. *Rule of Law, Transitional Justice, Conflict and Post-Conflict Societies, Report by the Secretary-General*, UN Doc. S/2004/616 (Aug. 3, 2004) (on file with author).

64. *See* Statute of the Special Court for Sierra Leone, S.C. Res. 1315, U.N. SCOR, 55th Sess., 4186th mtg. at 1, art. 8(2) (2000), *available at* http://www.sc-sl.org/scsl-statute.html.

65. Chandra Lekha Sriram, *Wrong-Sizing International Justice? The Hybrid Tribunal in Sierra Leone*, 29 FORD. INT'L L. J. 472 (2006).

66. For a discussion of difficulties faced by hybrid institutions, *see* Rosa Ehrenreich Brooks, *The New Imperialism: Violence, Norms, and the "Rule of Law,"* 101 MICH. L. REV. 2275, 2296 (2003) (discussing obstacles for the Kosovo hybrid panels); Katzenstein, *op. cit.*, at 246, 253 (noting that some of the initial problems at the hybrid tribunals include inefficiency, incorrect application of international law, failure to apply international law, minimization of local participation, insufficient building of capacity, and failure to uphold due process standards); Suzannah Linton, *Rising from the Ashes: The Creation of a Viable Criminal Justice System in East Timor*, 25 MELB. U. L. REV. 122, 176 (2001) (reporting shortcomings in the management of the hybrid tribunals).

67. Rome Statute, *op. cit.*, art. 1 (providing that the ICC "shall be complementary to national criminal jurisdictions").

68. Within the context of signing onto and ratifying the Rome Statute, another wrinkle is the divergent attitudes of European countries, on the one hand, and the United States, on the other hand, toward the ICC as an institution. As I set out in Chapter 1, U.S. disquiet with the ICC flows not from the ICC's model of prosecution and punishment but, rather, from the possibility that it might exercise jurisdiction over U.S. nationals. To this end, other countries have been subject to political pressure by the U.S. and European countries to join or not join the Rome Statute, and in many cases states that have joined have also concluded agreements at the behest of the United States to limit jurisdiction in certain cases. That said, two researchers "elicited very little statistical evidence that the ICC represents a proxy war in a global battle for moral, legal, or political dominance between Europe and the United States." *See generally* Allison Marston Danner & Beth Simmons, *Why States Join the International Criminal Court* 34 (manuscript on file with the author, 2006).

69. *See generally id.* at 32.

70. Cassese, *op. cit.*, at 158.

71. Allen Buchanan, JUSTICE, LEGITIMACY, AND SELF-DETERMINATION 323 (2004). *See also* Richard H. Pildes, *The Dark Side of Legalism*, 44 VA. J. INT'L L. 145, 159–161 (2003).

72. Jed Rubenfeld, *The Two World Orders*, WILSON Q. 22 (Autumn 2003).

73. *Id.* at 26–27.

74. *Id.* at 27.

75. *Id.*

76. *See, e.g.*, ICC R.P. & EVID., *op. cit.*, Rules 86, 89, 93 (Rule 86 states the ICC Trial Chamber and other organs of the ICC "shall take into account the needs of all victims and witnesses [. . .] in particular, children, elderly persons, persons with disabilities and victims of sexual or gender violence"). For more information on victims and the ICC, *see Participation of victims in proceedings and reparation, available at* http://www.icc-cpi.int/victimsissues/victimsparticipation.html.

77. Decision of January 17, 2006, on Participation of Victims, ICC Pre-Trial Chamber, *available at* http://www.icc-cpi.int/library/cases/ICC-01-04-101_tEnglish-Corr.pdf.

78. Jeffrey Gettleman, *Uganda Peace Hinges on Amnesty for Brutality*, N.Y. Times (Sept. 15, 2006).
79. *See* José E. Alvarez, *Crimes of States/Crimes of Hate: Lessons from Rwanda*, 24 Yale J. Int'l L. 365 (1999).
80. For example, in order to conform to expectations of impartiality and neutrality, the Special Court for Sierra Leone has prosecuted the activities of both rebels and government forces even though both groups may not share equal moral responsibility for the pervasiveness of crimes against humanity in the country. On a more general note, referencing an interlocutory decision by the ICTY in the *Tadić* case, Ruti Teitel argues that the legalist argument that the use of the criminal law can depoliticize ethnicity is flawed "insofar as the offenses that are often at issue, such as massive persecution, tend to involve systemic policy [and] a mix of individual and collective responsibility." Ruti Teitel, *Humanity's Law: Rule of Law for the New Global Politics*, 35 Cornell Int'l L. J. 355, 379 (2002).
81. Alan J. Kuperman, *Rwanda in Retrospect*, 79 Foreign Affairs 94 (2000); Alison Des Forges & Human Rights Watch, Leave None to Tell the Story: Genocide in Rwanda (1999).
82. On hate propaganda in Rwanda generally, *see* William A. Schabas, *Hate Speech in Rwanda: The Road to Genocide*, 46 McGill L. J. 141 (2000).
83. Dallaire also reported on poor training and bad behavior on the part of some peacekeepers, although a minority.
84. *See generally*, Roméo Dallaire, Shake Hands with the Devil: The Failure of Humanity in Rwanda (2003).
85. Both of these completion strategies were well received by the Security Council. *See* S.C. Res. 1503 (August 28, 2003); S.C. Res. 1534 (March 26, 2004). Several factors motivate these completion strategies: financial pressure from donor states; a desire to wind down the work of the tribunals; the integration of national actors; and the modernization of national sociolegal structures.
86. Institute for War and Peace Reporting, Tribunal Update (Sept. 9, 2004), *available at* http://www.iwpr.net/index.pl?tribunal_index.html; *Completion Strategy of the International Criminal Tribunal for Rwanda*, ¶ 7, U.N. Doc. S/2004/341 (2004); *Report on the Judicial Status of the International Criminal Tribunal for the Former Yugoslavia and the Prospects for Referring Certain Cases to National Courts*, U.N. Doc. S/2002/678 (2002).
87. There appears to be greater largesse with regard to what happens to nonindicted individuals insofar as "[i]t will be up to the local judiciaries to decide whether to complete the investigations and prosecute the cases." *Carla del Ponte Addresses the Security Council*, ICTY Press Release (December 15, 2005), *available at* http://www.un.org/icty/pressreal/2005/speech/delponte-sc-051215.htm.
88. *ICTY President Pocar Addresses the Security Council*, ICTY Press Release (December 15, 2005), *available at* http://www.un.org/icty/pressreal/2005/speech/pocar-sc-051215.htm.
89. In its form applicable to proceedings pending in December 2005.
90. ICTY Rules of Procedure and Evidence, Rule 11*bis*(A), *available at* http://www.un.org/icty/legaldoc-e/index.htm.
91. *Id.* arts. 11*bis*(B), (C).
92. *ICTY President Pocar Addresses the Security Council*, *op. cit.*
93. For an enumeration of the content of a "fair trial," *see Prosecutor v. Mejakić et al.*, Case No. IT-02-65-T, ¶ 68 (ICTY Referral Bench, July 20, 2005) (representative of the adversarial common law model of adjudication); *see also* Statute of the ICTY, *op. cit.*, art. 21; Statute of the ICTR, *op. cit.*, art. 20.
94. A case in which referral was denied is *Prosecutor v. Dragomir Milošević*, Case No. IT-98-29/1-PT, ¶ 24 (ICTY Referral Bench, July 8, 2005) (referral denied owing to the gravity of the crimes, number of civilians affected, and the senior military position of the accused).
95. *Prosecutor v. Mejakić et al.*, Case No. IT-02-65-AR11bis.1, ¶ 44 (ICTY Appeals Chamber, April 7, 2006).
96. *ICTY President Pocar Addresses the Security Council*, *op. cit.*

97. Although not a situation of a referral, the relationship between the Iraqi High Tribunal (IHT) and the general courts in Iraq also speaks to this tension. Whereas the IHT, a specialized entity tasked with processing a dozen (or so) notorious defendants associated with the Ba'ath regime, is comparatively well funded, the general court system in Iraq – which is completely deluged with defendants suspected of gruesome, and freshly committed, sectarian violence – is perilously underfunded and dysfunctional.

98. *Prosecutor v. Mejakić et al.*, Case No. IT-02-65-T, ¶¶ 28–30 (ICTY Referral Bench, July 20, 2005).

99. *See, e.g., Prosecutor v. Janković*, Case No. IT-96-23/2-AR11bis.2 (Decision on Rule 11*bis* Referral) ¶¶ 13–14, 16 (ICTY Appeals Chamber, November 15, 2005).

100. *Prosecutor v. Rašević and Todović*, Case No. IT-97-25/1-PT, ¶ 19 (ICTY Referral Bench, July 8, 2005).

101. BBC News, *Rwandan anger at suspect transfer*, available at http://news.bbc.co.uk/1/hi/world/africa/4717828.stm (reporting that Rwanda wishes to receive referred cases but that this option has been rejected by the ICTR because Rwanda will not repeal the death penalty).

102. *ICTR Prosecutor Requests Transfer of Bagaragaza Case to Norway for Trial*, ICTR Press Release, ICTR/INFO-9-2-471.EN (February 15, 2006). For the purposes of this case, ICTR Rule 11*bis* did not read exactly the same as ICTY Rule 11*bis*.

103. *Id.*

104. *Transfer of Bagaragaza case to the Kingdom of Norway denied*, ICTR Press Release, ICTR/INFO-9-2-477.EN (May 22, 2006).

105. Alhagi Marong, *The ICTR Appeals Chamber Dismisses the Prosecutor's Appeal to Transfer Michel Bagaragaza for Trial to Norway*, ASIL INSIGHT (Vol. 10, Issue 25, October 3, 2006). The Appeals Chamber underscored how approaching the accusations against Bagaragaza as ordinary substantive crimes triable under domestic substantive criminal law runs the risk of trivializing their nature and the significance of the Rwandan atrocity.

106. Rome Statute, *op. cit.*, art. 17(1)(a) (limiting the jurisdiction of the ICC only to situations where a state with jurisdiction is unable or unwilling genuinely to investigate or prosecute); art. 17(1)(b) (making a matter admissible at the ICC if the state has investigated and the state has decided not to prosecute the person concerned if the decision reflects an unwillingness or inability genuinely to prosecute).

107. The ICC Rules of Procedure and Evidence allow a state to present evidence whether "its courts meet internationally recognized . . . standards for [. . .] independent and impartial prosecution" in order to satisfy the complementarity test. ICC R.P. & EVID., *op. cit.*, Rule 51. For a discussion of how the complementarity principle may dissuade states from deploying restorative justice mechanisms such as truth commissions, *see* Jennifer Llewelyn, *A Comment on the Complementary Jurisdiction of the International Criminal Court: Adding Insult to Injury in Transitional Contexts*, 24 DALHOUSIE L.J. 192 (2001).

108. Mahnoush H. Arsanjani & W. Michael Reisman, *The Law-in-Action of the International Criminal Court*, 99 AM. J. INT'L L. 385, 391 (2005) (citing, however, a policy paper that regularly refers to the domestic initiatives for these lower-ranking perpetrators as "prosecutions").

109. *See, e.g.,* Carsten Stahn, *Complementarity, Amnesties, and Alternative Forms of Justice: Some Interpretive Guidelines for the International Criminal Court*, 3 J. INT'L CRIM. J. 695, 713 (2005) ("even alternative forms of justice must guarantee basic fair trial rights to the accused" under the complementarity test). *But see contra* Kevin Jon Heller, *The Shadow Side of Complementarity: The Effect of Article 17 on National Due Process* (2006) (unpublished manuscript on file with the author, cited wth permission) (arguing that ICC jurisdiction only is triggered when due process at the national level makes it more difficult to convict an accused).

110. Rome Statute, *op. cit.*, art. 53(1)(c).

111. Arsanjani & Reisman, *op. cit.*, at 399 n.56.

112. Rome Statute, *op. cit.*, art. 53(3)(b). Furthermore, investigations and prosecutions that continue following due consideration under article 53 can be deferred by the Security Council by virtue of article 16 of the Rome Statute. The wording of article 16, which requires a majority of the Security Council and all five permanent members to vote to defer, makes it politically improbable that the Security Council would so act. That said, the possibility of deferral does represent, on the one hand, some putatively public control over the ICC's decisionmaking but, on the other, weakens the ICC's deterrent value by adding another layer of selectivity and indeterminacy to the exercise of jurisdiction.

113. *See, e.g.*, Alain Pellet, *Internationalized Courts: Better Than Nothing...*, in INTERNATIONALIZED CRIMINAL COURTS 439 (Romano, Nollkaemper, & Kleffner eds., 2004).

114. Article 14 of the International Covenant on Civil and Political Rights can serve as an example of these guarantees. International Covenant on Civil and Political Rights, G.A. Res. 2200A, U.N. GAOR, 21st Sess., Supp. No. 16, U.N. Doc A/6316 (1966).

115. Cryer, *op. cit.*, at 143, 164.

116. *Accord, id.* at 164. In terms of substantive law, although not formally required, many parties have enacted implementing legislation that amends or modifies domestic criminal law to incorporate the substantive crimes proscribed by the Rome Statute.

117. Mohamed M. El Zeidy, *The Ugandan Government Triggers the First Test of the Complementarity Principle: An Assessment of the First State's Party Referral to the ICC*, 5 INT'L CRIM. L. REV. 83, 99 (2005). A number of other African states have referred matters as well. The Ugandan violence has cross-border effects in the DRC and in southern Sudan; the Lord's Resistance Army, in fact, has benefited in the past from the support of the Sudanese government.

118. Eric Blumenson, *The Challenge of a Global Standard of Justice: Peace, Pluralism, and Punishment at the International Criminal Court*, 44 COLUM. J. TRANSNAT'L L. 801, 808 n.23 (2006); *see also* Cryer, *op. cit.*, at 225.

119. Case Concerning Armed Activities on the Territory of the Congo (*Democratic Republic of the Congo v. Uganda*), International Court of Justice (ICJ General List, No. 116, Dec. 19, 2005) (final judgment).

120. Similarly, there is evidence that the decision by the DRC to refer appalling domestic atrocity to the ICC served a number of purposes, including offering "a politically expedient solution for the Congolese president to deal with potential electoral rivals." William W. Burke-White, *Complementarity in Practice: The International Criminal Court as Part of a System of Multi-level Global Governance in the Democratic Republic of Congo*, 18 LEIDEN J. INT'L L. 557, 559 (2005). In his work on the Extraordinary Chambers in the Courts of Cambodia, Burke-White observes how Cambodian leader Hun Sen "has been able to use the threat of prosecution as a political tool against his enemies. In so doing he has externalized the political costs onto the U.N." Burke-White, *A Community of Courts*, *op. cit.*, at 39.

121. Blumenson, *op. cit.*, at 810 (citing a survey by Uganda's Refugee Law Project that reported antagonism toward ICC intervention among the victim community).

122. *Id.* at 809 n.24. I would note that there is certainly no guarantee that Acholi leaders or interlocutors speak for all members of their communities.

123. Joanna R. Quinn, *Sophisticated Discourse: Why and How the Acholi of Northern Uganda are Talking about International Criminal Law* 16 (2006) (unpublished manuscript on file with the author, cited with permission).

124. Marc Lacey, *Victims of Uganda Atrocities Choose a Path of Forgiveness*, N.Y. TIMES (April 18, 2005) at A1; BBC News, *LRA Victims Seek Peace with Past*, *available at* http://news.bbc.co.uk/2/hi/africa/5341474.stm; Joanna R. Quinn, *Comparing Formal and Informal Mechanisms of Acknowledgement in Uganda* 8 (2006) (unpublished manuscript on file with the author, cited with permission) (noting that, in many parts of Uganda,

customary mechanisms "have more *de facto* authority than comparative Western models"). Helena Cobban reports that Acholi leaders seek Kony's reintegration into Acholi society through traditional rituals, which they believe is the best guard against future violence. Helena Cobban, *Forgiveness: More Important Than Prosecuting War Criminals*, CHRISTIAN SCIENCE MONITOR (Aug. 17, 2006).

125. Children compose 80 percent of the membership of the Lord's Resistance Army.

126. Blumenson, *op. cit.*, at 816 n.46. Quinn notes that that the Ugandan government also has to some extent formalized these customary practices. Quinn, *Sophisticated Discourse, op. cit.*, at 26–27. This is a similar phenomenon to that evident in Rwanda.

127. Burke-White, *Complementarity in Practice, op. cit.*, at 569–570, 572. A number of trials for crimes against humanity and war crimes have in fact concluded at the military level in the DRC. Avocats sans frontières, *Premier jugement pour crimes de guerre en RDC* (March 27, 2006) (on file with the author); Avocats sans frontières, *Nouvelle condemnation pour crimes contre l'humanité par le tribunal de garnison de Mbandaka* (June 21, 2006) (on file with the author). These trials invoked the language of the Rome Statute, were conducted through processes that Avocats sans frontières deemed met international due process standards, and resulted in the conviction, fining, and incarceration of over forty defendants.

128. Burke-White, *Complementarity in Practice, op. cit.*, at 574 ("[T]here are strong indications that the ICC, as a supranational layer of governance authority, is altering incentives at the national level and catalyzing reform efforts.").

129. *World this Week*, THE ECONOMIST 8 (March 19, 2005); Lacey, *op. cit.* The Ugandan government instituted an amnesty plan for many lower-level rebels in 2000. As of January 2005, nearly 15,000 applications for amnesty had been received. *See* Quinn, *Sophisticated Discourse, op. cit.*, at 16. Quinn observes that the ICC referral "put[s] into doubt" the future of the amnesty process. *Id.* at 20.

130. Mark Osiel, *Modes of Participation in Mass Atrocity*, 39 CORNELL INT'L L. J. 793, 817–820 (2005).

131. Gettleman, op. cit.

132. As of the summer of 2006, the Ugandan Parliament has expressed an intention to incorporate traditional rituals into national law as part of the peace process with the Lord's Resistance Army. Along with standardizing these rituals, this initiative would seemingly place them in methodological conflict with ICC trials for those rebel leaders the ICC has indicted, assuming the ICC obtains custody over these indictees.

133. Rome Statute, *op. cit.*, art. 5.

134. Dapo Akande, *International Law Immunities and the International Criminal Court*, 98 AM. J. INT'L L. 407, 408 (2004).

135. Helena Cobban reports: "In late 1998, when leaders of the three ethnic groups in Bosnia were discussing creating a joint truth commission to establish a common record of the past decade, they were told bluntly by ICTY's Chief Prosecutor, Louise Arbour, that such an effort would contaminate her evidence. Arbour also told aid donors not to support the Bosnian initiative, which set back its plans considerably." Helena Cobban, *The Legacies of Collective Violence*, BOSTON REVIEW (April/May 2002), *available at* http://bostonreview.net/BR27.2/cobban.html.

136. *See* Leopold von Carlowitz, *Crossing the Boundary from the International to the Domestic Legal Realm: UNMIK Lawmaking and Property Rights in Kosovo*, 10 GLOBAL GOVERNANCE 307, 319 (2004).

137. William J. Long & Peter Brecke, WAR AND RECONCILIATION 3 (2003) (offering case studies on Colombia, North Yemen, Chad, Argentina, Uruguay, Chile, El Salvador, Mozambique, South Africa, and Honduras).

138. *Id.* at 71.

139. *See supra* Chapter 2.

6. QUEST FOR PURPOSE

1. Joshua Dressler, UNDERSTANDING CRIMINAL LAW 6–8 (1987).
2. David Mendeloff, *Truth-Seeking, Truth-Telling, and Postconflict Peacebuilding: Curb the Enthusiasm?*, 9 INTERNATIONAL STUDIES REVIEW 355, 368 (2004).
3. *See, e.g., Prosecutor v. Delalić*, Case No. IT-96-21, ¶ 806 (ICTY Appeals Chamber, Feb. 20, 2001) (holding that offender rehabilitation should be considered as a relevant factor but not one that should be given undue weight); *Prosecutor v. Kunarac*, Case No. IT-96-23, ¶ 843 (ICTY Trial Chamber, Feb. 22, 2001) (holding that the use of preventive detention as a general sentencing factor is not fair or reasonable). In the *Stakić* case, the ICTY Trial Chamber, citing German developments in "modern criminal law," suggested that general deterrence could be linked to "reintegrating potential perpetrators into the global society." *Prosecutor v. Stakić*, Case No. IT-97-24-T, ¶ 902 (ICTY Trial Chamber, July 31, 2003). This somewhat novel link did not, however, receive play in the Appeals Chamber judgment in *Stakić*, in which the sentence of life imprisonment was reduced to a forty-year term. *Prosecutor v. Stakić*, Case No. IT-97-24-A (ICTY Appeals Chamber, March 22, 2006).
4. For example, "[i]n the East Timorese world view, offenders must reconcile with their victims if balance is to be restored following a crime." Nancy Amoury Combs, *Procuring Guilty Pleas for International Crimes: The Limited Influence of Sentencing Discounts*, 59 VAND. L. REV. 69, 136 (2006).
5. *See supra* Chapter 4. For commentary that predates my experiences, *see* Mahmood Mamdani, *Reconciliation Without Justice*, 46 S. AFRICAN R. BOOKS 3–5 (Nov.–Dec. 1996) (observing that "Rwanda exemplifies . . . the pursuit of justice without reconciliation. . . . ").
6. Laurel E. Fletcher, *From Indifference to Engagement: Bystanders and International Criminal Justice*, 26 MICH. J. INT'L L. 1013, 1022–1023 (2005). Commentators have opined that demands to extradite suspects to the ICTY may have prolonged the conflict in the Balkans, aggravated political instability within successor states in the region, and prematurely weakened local courts. *See, e.g.,* Nils Christie, *Answers to Atrocities: Restorative Justice as an Answer to Extreme Situations*, in VICTIM POLICIES AND CRIMINAL JUSTICE ON THE ROAD TO RESTORATIVE JUSTICE 379, 387 (Fattah & Parmentier eds., 2001); Jack Snyder & Leslie Vinjamuri, *Trials and Errors: Principles and Pragmatism in Strategies of International Justice*, INT'L SECURITY 5, 12, 23 (Winter 2003/2004); Steven Erlanger, *Did Serbia's Leader Do the West's Bidding Too Well?*, N.Y. TIMES § 4, p. 4 (Mar. 16, 2003).
7. Immanuel Kant, THE METAPHYSICAL ELEMENTS OF JUSTICE (Ladd trans., 2d ed., 1999); Immanuel Kant, THE PHILOSOPHY OF LAW: AN EXPOSITION OF THE FUNDAMENTAL PRINCIPLES OF JURISPRUDENCE AS A SCIENCE OF RIGHT (1796) (Hastie trans. 1887). *See also* Michael Moore, *The Moral Worth of Retribution*, in PRINCIPLED SENTENCING: READINGS ON THEORY & POLICY 150, 150 (von Hirsch & Ashworth eds., 1998) ("[W]e are justified in punishing because and only because offenders deserve it"); Joshua Dressler, *Hating Criminals: How Can Something that Feels So Good Be Wrong?*, 88 MICH. L. REV. 1448 (1990) (review essay); Jean Hampton, *Correcting Harms versus Righting Wrongs: The Goal of Retribution*, 39 UCLA L. REV. 1659, 1686 (1992).
8. G.W.F. Hegel, PHILOSOPHY OF RIGHT ¶ 101, p. 71 (1821) (Knox trans., 1952).
9. *Accord,* Ralph Henham, *Conceptualizing Access to Justice and Victims' Rights in International Sentencing*, 13(1) SOCIAL & LEGAL STUDIES 27, 36 (2004).
10. Robert Cryer, PROSECUTING INTERNATIONAL CRIMES: SELECTIVITY AND THE INTERNATIONAL CRIMINAL LAW REGIME 198 (2005).
11. Diane Marie Amann, *Group Mentality, Expressivism, and Genocide*, 2:2 INT'L CRIM. L. REV. 93, 116 (2002). *See also* Antoine Garapon, *Three Challenges for International Criminal Justice*, 2 J. INT'L CRIM. JUST. 716 (2004).
12. Press Release, International Criminal Tribunal for the Former Yugoslavia, *Address by Carla Del Ponte, Prosecutor of the International Criminal Tribunal for the Former Yugoslavia to the United Nations Security Council* (Nov. 27, 2001).

13. The ICTY and ICTR Prosecutors have considerable discretion to investigate and prosecute. Hector Olásolo, *The Prosecutor of the ICC Before the Initiation of Investigations: A Quasi-Judicial or a Political Body?*, 3 INT'L CRIM. L. REV. 87, 125, 130 (2003).

14. Suzanne Katzenstein, *Hybrid Tribunals: Searching for Justice in East Timor*, 16 HARV. HUM. RTS. J. 245, 274 (2003).

15. *But see* Rome Statute of the International Criminal Court, U.N. Doc. A/CONF.183/9, art. 16 [hereinafter Rome Statute] (giving the Security Council a right to demand by resolution postponement of Prosecutorial action). Cryer underscores this provision as an example of selectivity in the ICC's operation. Cryer, *op. cit.*, at 226.

16. Allison Marston Danner, *Enhancing the Legitimacy and Accountability of Prosecutorial Discretion at the International Criminal Court*, 97 AM. J. INT'L L. 510, 510 (2003).

17. *Id.* at 521. *See also* Olásolo, *op. cit.*, at 105.

18. Olásolo reports that even when there is judicial review by the ICC of Prosecutorial discretion, this "simply passes to these judicial bodies the political discretion originally conferred upon the Prosecutor." Olásolo, *op. cit.*, at 142.

19. Mégret estimates that the ICC will be able to prosecute a dozen cases a year. Frédéric Mégret, *Three Dangers for the International Criminal Court: A Critical Look at a Consensual Project*, XII FINNISH Y.B. INT'L L. 193, 213 (2001).

20. Olásolo, *op. cit.*, at 107–108.

21. Rome Statute, *op. cit.*, art. 53(2)(c); *see also* Olásolo, *op. cit.*, at 111, 141 (arguing that the lack of a definition of "interests of justice" gives the Prosecutor the broadest possible scope of political discretion to decide whether or not to prosecute).

22. David Chuter, WAR CRIMES: CONFRONTING ATROCITY IN THE MODERN WORLD 94, 96–97 (2003).

23. In the context of ordinary common crime, in particular in common law jurisdictions, immunities, dropped charges, and sentence reductions are often exchanged for guilty pleas or testimony. Similar arrangements also are commonly found in the practice of international and internationalized criminal tribunals.

24. Miriam J. Aukerman, *Extraordinary Evil, Ordinary Crime: A Framework for Understanding Transitional Justice*, 15 HARV. HUM. RTS. J. 39, 62 (2002).

25. Comparisons among the sentences of common courts in Iraq punishing serious ordinary crimes and the sentences of the Iraqi High Tribunal (IHT) in matters of crimes against humanity and war crimes reveal a similar overall equivalence in terms of severity of sanction. *See generally* Michael Moss, *Legal System in Iraq Staggers Beneath the Weight of War*, N.Y. TIMES (Dec. 17, 2006). There are a large number of acquittals in the beleaguered ordinary court system, although trials are much more perfunctory than the reasonably long proceedings thus far at the IHT.

26. Jens David Ohlin, *Applying the Death Penalty to Crimes of Genocide*, 99 AM. J. INT'L L. 767 (2005) (observing that "[a]rguably, the moral severity of genocide indicates that traditional methods of punishment might be inadequate to the retributive task"); Aukerman, *op. cit.*, at 59 (observing that "[r]adical evil involves horrific acts that even ordinary criminals would find appalling").

27. Taken from trial transcript, *available at* http://www.ceausescu.org/ceausescu_texts/revolution/trial-eng.htm.

28. *The State of Israel v. Adolf Eichmann* (S. Ct. Israel, May 29, 1962), 36 INT'L L. REP. 277, 341 (1968).

29. Hannah Arendt, *Letter to Karl Jaspers of 17 August 1946*, in Hannah Arendt & Karl Jaspers, HANNAH ARENDT, KARL JASPERS: CORRESPONDENCE, 1926–1969 54 (1992).

30. Immanuel Kant, THE PHILOSOPHY OF LAW 198 (trans., 1974).

31. *Prosecutor v. Deronjić*, Case No. IT-02-61-S, ¶ 177 (ICTY Trial Chamber, Mar. 30, 2004) (noting that "in most countries a single act of aggravated murder [*n.b.* murder committed by participation in shooting and/or motivated by ethnic bias] attracts life imprisonment or the death penalty"); *Prosecutor v. Dragan Nikolić*, Case No. IT-94-2-S, ¶ 172 (ICTY Trial

Chamber, Dec. 18, 2003); Stuart Beresford, *Unshackling the Paper Tiger – the Sentencing Practices of the Ad Hoc International Criminal Tribunals for the Former Yugoslavia and Rwanda,* 1 INT'L CRIM. L. REV. 33, 90 (2001).

32. *Prosecutor v. Furundžija,* Case No. IT-95-17/1-T, ¶ 290 (ICTY Trial Chamber, Dec. 10, 1998) ("It is the infallibility of punishment . . . which is the tool for retribution, stigmatization and deterrence. This is particularly the case for the International Tribunal: penalties are made more onerous by its international stature, moral authority and impact. . . .").

33. An additional wrinkle is the operation of the *nulla poena sine lege* principle that, in some contexts, may preclude the punishment imposed by an international institution to exceed that ordinarily available at the national level within the relevant jurisdiction.

34. *Prosecutor v. Kordić and Čerkez,* IT-95-14/2-A, ¶ 1086 (ICTY Appeals Chamber, Dec. 17, 2004) (genocide and war crimes against civilians under the SFRY Criminal Code were punishable with imprisonment of a minimum of five years or the death penalty [the latter could be substituted with imprisonment for a term of twenty years]).

35. *Prosecutor v. Mrdja,* Case No. IT-02-59-S, ¶¶ 121, 122, 129 (ICTY Trial Chamber, March 31, 2004) (sentencing defendant to seventeen years' imprisonment when a national court would have been able to impose a term of twenty years); *Prosecutor v. Obrenović,* Case No. IT-02-60/2-S, ¶¶ 58, 60, 156 (ICTY Trial Chamber, Dec. 10, 2003); *Prosecutor v. Kunarac et al.,* Case No. IT-96-23/1-A, ¶ 349 (ICTY Appeals Chamber, June 12, 2002) (affirming Kunarac's sentence of twenty-eight years); *Prosecution v. Strugar,* Case No.IT-01-42-T, ¶ 473 (ICTY Trial Chamber, January 31, 2005) (affirming as a matter of law that the ICTY Trial Chamber can impose a sentence greater than that which would have been imposed by SFRY courts).

36. *See, e.g.,* Sanja Kutnjak Ivković & John Hagan, *The Politics of Punishment and the Siege of Sarajevo: Toward a Conflict Theory of Perceived International (In)justice,* 40 L. & Soc'Y. REV. 369, 379 (2006).

37. *See, e.g., Prosecutor v. Rajić,* Case No. IT-95-12-S, ¶¶ 7–8 (ICTY Trial Chamber, May 8, 2006).

38. *Prosecutor v. Muhimana,* Case No. ICTR-95-1B-T, ¶ 592 (ICTR Trial Chamber, April 25, 2005).

39. Ohlin, *op. cit.,* at 755 n.59.

40. *Prosecutor v. Semanza,* Case No. ICTR-97-20-A, ¶ 380 (ICTR Appeals Chamber, May 20, 2005). *See also id.* ¶ 393.

41. *Prosecutor v. Bisengimana,* Case No. ICTR-00-60-T, ¶ 194 (ICTR Trial Chamber, April 13, 2006).

42. *Cf* Rome Statute, *op. cit.,* art. 110 (providing that when the convict has served two-thirds of the sentence, or twenty-five years in the case of life imprisonment, the ICC shall review the sentence to determine whether or not it should be reduced based on the convict's willingness to cooperate with the court, assistance in locating assets, or other factors establishing a clear and significant change of circumstances); ICC R.P. & EVID. Rules 211, 223–224, *available at* http://www.icc-cpi.int/library/basicdocuments/rules(e).pdf.

43. Chuter, *op. cit.,* at 222. The health care available to ICTR convicts imprisoned in Mali is not as comprehensive as that available in the ICTR detention unit. But it is superior to what is available to those imprisoned in Rwandan prisons. Moreover, should ICTR convicts begin to serve sentence in Western prisons, then their level of health care would well surpass that available in Rwanda.

44. HIV-positive ICTR witnesses, who often travel from Rwanda to Arusha to testify on behalf of the Prosecution, reportedly do not receive equivalent medication to defendants (although the ICTR Witness and Victims Support Unit has made this need a priority). *See generally* Samantha Power, *Rwanda: The Two Faces of Justice,* 50 NEW YORK REVIEW OF BOOKS (January 16, 2003).

45. Nancy Amoury Combs, *International Decisions,* 97 AM. J. INT'L L. 923, 936 (2003).

46. Combs, *Procuring Guilty Pleas, op. cit.*, at 93 n.106.

47. *Id.* at 132.

48. This is an area in which retribution brushes up with expressivism.

49. For example, in Rwanda the state is entitled to pursue *dégradation civique*.

50. Differences among the national frameworks become more ambiguous in cases of lower-level offenders.

51. William Schabas, GENOCIDE IN INTERNATIONAL LAW 9 (2000).

52. *Prosecutor v. Mrdja*, Case No. IT-02-59-S, ¶¶ 121, 122, 129 (ICTY Trial Chamber, March 31, 2004). *See also Prosecutor v. Kordić and Čerkez*, IT-95-14/2-A, ¶ 1085 (ICTY Appeals Chamber, Dec. 17, 2004); *Prosecutor v. Stakić*, Case No. IT-97-24-T, ¶ 887 (ICTY Trial Chamber, July 31, 2003) (noting that national sentencing practice "will . . . be considered, although in itself is not binding").

53. *Prosecutor v. Ruggiu*, Case No. ICTR-97-32-I, ¶ 31 (ICTR Trial Chamber, June 1, 2000) ("While the Chamber will refer as much as practicable to the sentencing provisions under the law [of Rwanda], it will also exercise its unfettered discretion to determine sentences."). In cases where a departure from national practices is occasioned, reasons for the departure must be provided and the divergence explained. *Prosecutor v. Semanza*, Case No. ICTR-97-20-A, ¶¶ 345, 377 (ICTR Appeals Chamber, May 20, 2005). In the case of the ICTR, the judges' guarded approach to including national sentencing practice persists notwithstanding exhortations by ICTR Prosecutors that the existence of the death penalty and life imprisonment in the domestic Rwandan penal law justify a harsher sentence at the ICTR. William A. Schabas, *Genocide Trials and Gacaca Courts*, 3 J. INT'L CRIM. J. 879, 888 (2005). Schabas posits that the reference to national sentencing practice in the ICTR Statute was included to protect the defendant, not justify severe punishment. *Id.* at n.22. This is another indication that the distinction between national sentencing practices in Rwanda and the former Yugoslavia does not suffice as explanation for the divergent severity of sentences issued by the ICTY and ICTR.

54. *Prosecutor v. Marqués et al.*, Case No. 09/2000, ¶ 1116 (Dili Dist. Ct. Serious Crimes Spec. Panel Dec. 11, 2001) (holding, in a manner similar to the ICTY, that "the sentencing practices in the courts of East Timor may be used for guidance, but [are] not binding").

55. *Prosecutor v. Blagojević and Jokić*, Case No. IT-02-60-T (ICTY Trial Chamber, January 17, 2005).

56. *Prosecutor v. Krstić*, Case No. IT-98-33-A, ¶¶ 248, 250 (ICTY Appeals Chamber, April 19, 2004).

57. *Prosecutor v. Stakić*, Case No. IT-97-24-A, ¶ 375 (ICTY Appeals Chamber, March 22, 2006) ("The Appeals Chamber stresses that there is no hierarchy of the crimes within the jurisdiction of the Tribunal [. . .]"). Some ICTR judgments suggest that genocide and crimes against humanity are more serious than war crimes; genocide also has been referred to as the "crime of crimes." *See, e.g., Prosecutor v. Kambanda*, Case No. ICTR-97-23-S, ¶ 14 (ICTR Trial Chamber, Sept. 4, 1998).

58. *See, e.g., Prosecutor v. Erdemović*, Case No. IT-96-22-T (ICTY Trial Chamber, Nov. 29, 1996).

59. *Prosecutor v. Bisengimana*, Case No. ICTR-00-60-T, ¶¶ 136–137 (ICTR Trial Chamber, April 13, 2006).

60. *Prosecutor v. Bralo*, Case No. IT-95-17-S (ICTY Trial Chamber, December 7, 2005).

61. *Prosecutor v. Sikirica*, Case No. IT-95-8-S, ¶ 149 (ICTY Trial Chamber, November 13, 2001) (noting that a guilty plea saves the international tribunal the time and effort of a lengthy investigation and trial); Michael P. Scharf, *Trading Justice for Efficiency: Plea-Bargaining and International Tribunals*, 2 J. INT'L CRIM. JUST. 1070, 1076 (2004) ("It is noteworthy that the international Tribunals have primarily justified plea-bargaining in terms of conserving scarce judicial resources . . .").

62. *Prosecutor v. Todorović*, Case No. IT-95-9/1-S, ¶ 80 (ICTY Trial Chamber, July 31, 2001).

63. *See generally* Combs, *Procuring Guilty Pleas, op. cit.*
64. Ralph Henham & Mark Drumbl, *Plea Bargaining at the International Criminal Tribunal for the Former Yugoslavia*, 16 CRIM. L. F. 49, 54 (2005). Segments of the comparative discussion of the situation of plea-bargained convicts that follows draw from *id.* at 57–58.
65. *Prosecutor v. Babić*, Case No. IT-03-72-A (ICTY Appeals Chamber, July 18, 2005) (Appeals Chamber confirmed a sentence that exceeded the Prosecutor's recommendation owing to the gravity of the crime and held that the Trial Chamber acted correctly when it departed from the Prosecutor's recommendation). For an example from the ICTR, *see Prosecutor v. Bisengimana*, Case No. ICTR-00-60-T (ICTR Trial Chamber, April 13, 2006) (issuing a sentence of fifteen years while the plea agreement recommended a sentence between twelve and fourteen years). In the *Dragan Nikolić* case, an ICTY Trial Chamber issued a sentence of twenty-three years to a defendant who had concluded a plea agreement in which the Prosecutor recommended a sentence of fifteen years. *Prosecutor v. Dragan Nikolić*, Case No. IT-94-2-S (ICTY Trial Chamber, Dec. 18, 2003). The Trial Chamber in imposing a higher sentence had focused on retributive concerns such as brutality, the number of crimes committed, and the underlying intention to humiliate and degrade. The Appeals Chamber reduced the sentence to twenty years. *Prosecutor v. Dragan Nikolić*, Case No. IT-94-2-A (ICTY Appeals Chamber, Feb. 4, 2005). The Appeals Chamber held that the defendant understood that the recommendation was just a recommendation and that exceeding it constituted an appropriate exercise of the Trial Chamber's discretion.
66. Combs, *Procuring Guilty Pleas, op. cit.*, at 87.
67. *Prosecutor v. Momir Nikolić*, Case No. IT-02-60/1-S, ¶ 183 (ICTY Trial Chamber, Dec. 2, 2003).
68. *Prosecutor v. Momir Nikolić*, Case No. IT-02-60/1-A (ICTY Appeals Chamber, March 8, 2006). The Appeals Chamber found that the Trial Chamber had committed a number of errors: (1) the Trial Chamber doubly counted the role the defendant played in the commission of the crime; (2) the Trial Chamber relied on a translation error as evidence of the gravity of the offense (the error involved comments by defense counsel in closing, imputed to the defendant, that "only" seven thousand individuals had been murdered at Srebrenica, which the Trial Chamber had found "shameful," when defense counsel actually had stated that "around" seven thousand individuals had been murdered); and (3) the Trial Chamber did not provide a reasoned opinion regarding how it relied upon the evasiveness, untruthfulness, and confusion of the defendant's testimony tendered in his cooperation with the Prosecutor to reduce the value of cooperation as a mitigating factor. *Id.* at ¶¶ 61–62, 70–73, 114.
69. *Prosecutor v. Plavšić*, Case No. IT-00-39 & 40/1-S, ¶¶ 16, 42 (ICTY Trial Chamber, Feb. 27, 2003).
70. *Prosecutor v. Babić*, Case No. IT-03-72-S, ¶ 102 (ICTY Trial Chamber, June 29, 2004), *aff'd* on appeal, *Prosecutor v. Babić*, Case No. IT-03-72-A (ICTY Appeals Chamber, July 18, 2005).
71. *Prosecutor v. Jokić*, Case No. IT-01-42/1-S, ¶ 8 (ICTY Trial Chamber, March 18, 2004), *aff'd* on appeal, *Prosecutor v. Jokić*, Case No. IT-01-42/1-A (ICTY Appeals Chamber, August 30, 2005) (sentence of seven years affirmed even though Appeals Chamber vacated many of the convictions initially entered on the basis of superior responsibility).
72. *Prosecution v. Strugar*, Case No. IT-01-42-T (ICTY Trial Chamber, January 31, 2005).
73. On the subject of age as a mitigating factor, in December 2005 an ICTR Trial Chamber sentenced Aloys Simba, a sixty-seven-year-old senior Rwandan army officer, to twenty-five years in prison following a trial. Although Simba's sentence did not involve a plea bargain, the negligible practical effect of age in mitigation indicates retributive gaps between ICTY and ICTR sentencing practice. In another case, though, the ICTR did turn to the defendant's advanced age and weak health to mitigate sentence. *Prosecutor v. Ntakirutimana et al.*, Case No. ICTR-96-10, ¶ 898 (ICTR Trial Chamber, Feb. 21, 2003).
74. *Prosecutor v. Mrdja*, Case No. IT-02-59-S, ¶ 129 (ICTY Trial Chamber, March. 31, 2004).

75. *Prosecutor v. Češić*, Case No. IT-95-10/1-S, ¶¶ 3, 13, 111 (ICTY Trial Chamber, March 11, 2004).
76. *Prosecutor v. Jelisić*, Case No. IT-95-10-T (ICTY Trial Chamber, December 14, 1999).
77. *Prosecutor v. Deronjić*, Case No. IT-02-61-S, ¶¶ 44, 97–98, 277, 280 (ICTY Trial Chamber, March 30, 2004).
78. *Id.*, ¶¶ 135, 230, 280.
79. *Prosecutor v. Deronjić*, Case No. IT-02-61-A, ¶ 151 (ICTY Appeals Chamber, July 20, 2005).
80. *Accord*, Julian A. Cook, III, *Plea Bargaining at The Hague*, 30 YALE J. INT'L L. 473, 477 (2005) (noting "a plea hearing process that varies considerably from courtroom to courtroom due, in large part, to the illimitable discretion that the Tribunal rules afford ICTY judges").
81. Combs, *Procuring Guilty Pleas, op. cit.*, at 127.
82. *See, e.g., Prosecutor v. Franca da Silva*, Case No. 04a/2001, ¶ 145 (Dili Dist. Ct. Serious Crimes Spec. Panel, Dec. 5, 2002).
83. *Prosecutor v. Atolan*, Case No. 3/2003, ¶ 29 (Dili Dist. Ct. Serious Crimes Spec. Panel, June 9, 2003). For this panel, remorse "is . . . of minor importance[,] . . . what matters is the practical . . . cooperation with the Prosecution." *Id.* ¶ 32.
84. Combs, *Procuring Guilty Pleas, op. cit.*, at 73.
85. *Id.* at 74. *See also id.* at 145 (noting the Special Panels' "somewhat arbitrary sentencing practices" in plea-bargained cases).
86. *See, e.g., Prosecutor v. Rutaganira*, Case No. ICTR-95-1C-T (ICTR Trial Chamber, March 14, 2005) (plea agreement involving not just the withdrawal of charges, but also the Prosecutor's requesting that acquittals be entered on the charges to which the defendant did not plead guilty). Rutaganira was sentenced to six years' imprisonment – the ICTR's shortest sentence to date.
87. *Prosecutor v. Bisengimana*, Case No. ICTR-00-60-T (ICTR Trial Chamber, April 13, 2006).
88. Combs, *Procuring Guilty Pleas, op. cit.*, at 103–104.
89. *Id.* at 73, 117–118.
90. Cesare Beccaria, ON CRIMES AND PUNISHMENT (1764) (Young trans., 1986).
91. *Prosecutor v. Kordić and Čerkez*, IT-95-14/2-A, ¶ 1076 (ICTY Appeals Chamber, Dec. 17, 2004) (noting that "both individual [*n.b.* specific] and general deterrence serve as important goals of sentencing;" also discussing reintegrative deterrence).
92. Aukerman, *op. cit.*, at 65, n.148 ("in the transitional justice context 'deterrence' almost always refers to 'general deterrence'").
93. *Prosecutor v. Rutaganda*, Case No. ICTR-96-3-T, ¶ 456 (ICTR Trial Chamber, December 6, 1999), *aff'd* on appeal, *Prosecutor v. Rutaganda*, Case No. ICTR-96-3-A (ICTR Appeals Chamber, May 26, 2003).
94. Report of the Secretary-General, IN LARGER FREEDOM – TOWARDS DEVELOPMENT, HUMAN RIGHTS, AND SECURITY FOR ALL, UN Doc. A/59/2005, ¶ 138 (March 21, 2005).
95. *See, e.g.,* William W. Burke-White, *Complementarity in Practice: The International Criminal Court as Part of a System of Multi-level Global Governance in the Democratic Republic of Congo*, 18 LEIDEN J. INT'L L. 557, 587 (2005) (noting also the methodological limitations to his research and the impossibility of turning these data to provide statistically meaningful evidence that the ICC has had direct deterrent effect).
96. Jerry Fowler, *A New Chapter of Irony: The Legal Implications of the Darfur Genocide Determination*, 1:1 GENOCIDE STUDIES AND PREVENTION 29, 36 (2006). There also is vivid debate regarding the suitability of deterrence as a justification for punishment under ordinary common criminal law. *See, e.g.,* James Gilligan, VIOLENCE 94–96 (1996) (arguing that rational self-interest models that underlie deterrence theory are based on ignorance of what violent people really are like); H.L.A. Hart, *Prolegomenon to the Principles of Punishment*, in H.L.A. Hart, PUNISHMENT AND RESPONSIBILITY: ESSAYS IN THE PHILOSOPHY OF LAW 1–27 (1968) (doubting the validity of deterrence in domestic contexts to ordinary common criminals).

97. John Braithwaite, CRIME, SHAME AND REINTEGRATION 69 (1989); Chuter, *op. cit.*, at 271; Michael Tonry, *The Functions of Sentencing and Sentencing Reform*, 58 STAN. L. REV. 37, 52 (2005).

98. ICTY Press Release, *ICTY President Pocar Addresses the Security Council* (December 15, 2005).

99. Martha Minow, BETWEEN VENGEANCE AND FORGIVENESS 50 (1998) ("Individuals who commit atrocities on the scale of genocide are unlikely to behave as 'rational actors,' deterred by the risk of punishment."); Judith Shklar, LEGALISM: LAW, MORALS, AND POLITICAL TRIALS 187 (rev. ed., 1986) (wondering "whether international criminal law can fulfill in any degree the great function of criminal law – the deterrence of potential criminals"). *See also* Beresford, *op. cit.*, at 43; Christopher Rudolph, *Constructing an Atrocities Regime: The Politics of War Crimes Tribunals*, 55 INT'L ORG. 655, 683–684 (2001); Immi Tallgren, *The Sensibility and Sense of International Criminal Law*, 13 EUR. J. INT'L L. 561, 561 (2002); David Wippmann, *Atrocities, Deterrence, and the Limits of International Justice*, 23 FORDHAM INT'L L.J. 473, 474 (1999).

100. Mégret, *op. cit.*, at 203.

101. *Id.*

102. Robert D. Kaplan, THE COMING ANARCHY 44–45 (2000).

103. Jaime Malamud-Goti, *Transitional Governments in the Breach: Why Punish State Criminals?*, 12 HUM. RTS. Q. 1 (1990).

104. Michael Ignatieff, THE LESSER EVIL 121 (2004).

105. Alette Smeulers, *What Transforms Ordinary People into Gross Human Rights Violators?*, in UNDERSTANDING HUMAN RIGHTS VIOLATIONS – NEW SYSTEMATIC STUDIES 239, 247 (Carey & Poe eds., 2004) (citations omitted).

106. *See, e.g.*, Krijn Peters & Paul Richards, *Fighting with Open Eyes: Youth Combatants Talking About War in Sierra Leone*, in RETHINKING THE TRAUMA OF WAR 76, 109 (Bracken & Petty eds., 1998) (noting that child soldiers "seek to stay alive using their strength and ingenuity as best they can"); Kimberly Lanegran, *Developments in International Law Regarding Recruitment of Child Combatants from the Special Court for Sierra Leone* 4 (2006) (unpublished manuscript on file with the author, cited with permission).

107. Mark J. Osiel, MASS ATROCITY, ORDINARY EVIL, AND HANNAH ARENDT 157 (2001); *see also* Amy Chua, WORLD ON FIRE 9, 124 (2004) (arguing that the simultaneous global spread of democracy and markets is a major aggravating cause of ethnic violence, in particular in countries with a market-dominant ethnic minority and a poor majority of a different ethnic group).

108. Klabbers notes a similar phenomenon at the national level: "[i]n *Barbie*, the French *Cour de Cassation* ended up exempting France (and, by extension, democratic states generally), from any possible complicity in crimes against humanity by linking such crimes to states practicing 'a hegemonic political ideology.'" Jan Klabbers, *Book Review*, 15 EUR. J. INT'L L. 1055, 1056 (2004).

109. In *Rajić*, an ICTY Trial Chamber held that "punishment aims at reinforcing the validity and the effectiveness of the breached rules of international humanitarian law vis-à-vis the perpetrator, the victims and the public." *Prosecutor v. Rajić*, Case No. IT-95-12-S, ¶ 69 (ICTY Trial Chamber, May 8, 2006). In the *Rauter* case, expressivism was explicitly cited by the Netherlands Special Court of Cassation as an important purpose of punishment. Trial of Hans Albin Rauter (Netherlands Special Court in The Hague, May 4, 1948, and Netherlands Special Court of Cassation, January 12, 1949), reprinted at 14 LAW REPORTS OF TRIALS OF WAR CRIMINALS 89, 109 (1949).

110. Patricia Wald, *Book Review*, 99 AM. J. INT'L L. 720, 725 (2005).

111. David Garland, PUNISHMENT AND MODERN SOCIETY: A STUDY IN SOCIAL THEORY 252 (1990).

112. As the Nuremberg judges insisted, "only by punishing individuals who commit [crimes against international law] can the provisions of international law be enforced." International

Military Tribunal (Nuremberg), Judgment and Sentences (Oct. 1, 1946), *reprinted in* 41 AM. J. INT'L L. 172, 221 (1947).

113. Emile Durkheim, THE DIVISION OF LABOR IN SOCIETY (1933).

114. For further writing on punishment as moral education, *see* H.L.A. Hart, PUNISHMENT AND RESPONSIBILITY 255 (1968); Andrew von Hirsch, CENSURE AND SANCTIONS 10 (1993).

115. Antonio Cassese, *Reflections on International Criminal Justice*, 61 MOD. L. REV. 1, 1 (1998).

116. Molly Moore, *Trial of Milošević Holds Lessons for Iraqi Prosecutors*, WASHINGTON POST (October 18, 2005) at A19.

117. *See generally* David Luban, *Beyond Moral Minimalism*, 20 ETHICS & INTERNATIONAL AFFAIRS 353 (2006).

118. Lawrence Douglas, THE MEMORY OF JUDGMENT (2001) (writing within the context of the Holocaust).

119. *Prosecutor v. Krstić*, Case No. IT-98-33-A, ¶ 34 (ICTY Appeals Chamber, April 19, 2004).

120. Telford Taylor, THE ANATOMY OF THE NUREMBERG TRIALS 54 (1992).

121. Robert Hariman, POPULAR TRIALS: RHETORIC, MASS MEDIA, AND THE LAW 2, 18 (ed. 1990).

122. Proceedings conducted locally also can be broadcast to a global audience. The process of diffusion, however, can be more complex.

123. There are important differences between the proceedings held in Nuremberg and Adolf Eichmann's trial in Jerusalem. Whereas Nuremberg principally involved documentary evidence, *Eichmann* turned on victim testimony; whereas Nuremberg focused on Nazi aggression, *Eichmann* focused on crimes against the Jewish people.

124. Nuremberg required a nexus between the existence of an aggressive war and crimes against humanity. This was so, according to William Schabas, owing to unease on the part of the Allies that the independent criminalization of crimes against humanity might restrict Allied governments with regard to their own national minorities or in the colonies. William A. Schabas, AN INTRODUCTION TO THE INTERNATIONAL CRIMINAL COURT 42 (2d ed., 2004). The requirement of a nexus between aggressive war (or any armed conflict at all) and crimes against humanity has since departed international criminal law.

125. *See, e.g.*, Tristram Hunt, *Whose Truth? Objective Truth and a Challenge for History*, 15 CRIM. L. F. 193, 197 (2004) (discussing the work of historian Richard Evans, who argues that phenomena such as the "judicialization of history" that arise from retrospective criminal law bring a crass categorization among perpetrators, bystanders, and victims that actually presents obstacles to understanding the past, appreciating the diffuseness of historical synthesis, and educating for the future); Eric Stover, *Witnesses and the promise of justice in The Hague*, in MY NEIGHBOR, MY ENEMY: JUSTICE AND COMMUNITY IN THE AFTERMATH OF MASS ATROCITY 104, 116 (Stover & Weinstein eds., 2004) (noting that, although the ICTY has convened four trials based on attacks by Bosnian Croats on the ethnically mixed village of Ahmici, a study reveals that there is "absolutely no indication that these trials have in any way transformed the way in which Croats in the village interpret what happened"). David Mendeloff questions the instrumental usefulness of obtaining "truth." He notes that "we actually know very little about the impact of truth-telling or truth-seeking on peace." Mendeloff, *op. cit.*, at 356. *See also id.* at 365: "[T]he truth-telling literature relies heavily on anecdotal evidence." Mendeloff observes situations where "collective forgetting" might have proven "conducive to harmony and cooperation," such as postFranco Spain and Mozambique. *Id.* at 367.

126. According to South African Justice Albie Sachs, microscopic and logical truths are exacted on a "beyond a reasonable doubt" standard derived from a sequential proof of facts. Albie Sachs, Lecture at Columbia University School of Law (Apr. 13, 1999), cited and discussed in Mark A. Drumbl, *Punishment, Postgenocide: From Guilt to Shame to Civis in Rwanda*, 75 N.Y.U. L. REV. 1221, 1283 (2000) (notes on file with author). For Sachs, experiential and dialogic truths are different. They emerge phenomenologically when people come forward and tell their stories. Restorative mechanisms – whether in the form of truth commissions

or traditional dispute resolution – may constitute comfortable sites for such storytelling. Through a process of accretion over time, these expressions of experience create an overarching historical narrative that can displace preexisting narratives that normalized or legitimized violence. For Sachs, courts do not encourage experiential or dialogic truths.

127. Aukerman, *op. cit.*, at 73.

128. Martti Koskenniemi, *Between Impunity and Show Trials*, 6 Max Planck Yearbook of U.N. Law 1, 33 (2002) (discussing Milošević proceedings).

129. Elizabeth Neuffer, The Key to My Neighbor's House 298 (2002).

130. The IHT's Dujail judgment was announced in November 2006. Written reasons were issued in December 2006. The trial attracted considerable concern regarding its apparent departure from internationalized due process standards and the fact that three defense lawyers and a witness had been assassinated. Sentences for convicted defendants ranged from death to term imprisonment (15 years). An appeals court affirmed most of the IHT sentences, including Saddam Hussein's, in December 2006. Hussein was executed. In the IHT judgment, only 4 (of 283) pages dealt with sentence (in addition, there was a brief discussion in Part 2 of the judgment regarding the legality of punishment). The IHT offered no explanation as to the purposes of sentencing. In addition to being brief, the sentencing discussion was rote and repetitive. The IHT listed the convicts and their convictions, ordered as to type of conviction, and then stipulated a penalty. The IHT did not explain, for the public, exactly why some of the defendants received lesser sentences than others. To be sure, a discerning reader could total the numbers of convictions, and the crimes for which convictions were issued, and come to some conclusion that the gravity of certain convictions exceeded that of others or that an accumulation of convictions mechanically led to a harsher sentence. However, such inferences never were explicated. The IHT did not mention aggravating or mitigating factors. It remains unclear whether what the IHT took as aggravating factors in sentencing were identical to factors it considered in finding liability (the Nuremberg judges did this, but the ICTY, which sentences less severely than the IHT, has repudiated such double-dipping).

131. For example, Plavšić refused to involve anyone else in the violence or testify in any other cases. She took responsibility for her own actions, but stated that this responsibility was hers "alone" and was not to be "extend[ed] to other leaders who have a right to defend themselves." Combs, *International Decisions, op. cit.*, at 934 (citing reports). The bargained-for testimony of another defendant who pled guilty was subsequently found to be evasive and even false. *See, e.g., Prosecutor v. Momir Nikolić*, Case No. IT-02-60/1-A, ¶ 106 (ICTY Appeals Chamber, March 8, 2006) ("[T]he mere fact that the Deronjić Trial Chamber gave significant weight to the accused's co-operation notwithstanding certain false statements does not illustrate that the Trial Chamber in this case abused its discretion in reaching a different result."); *see also Prosecutor v. Krstić*, Case No. IT-98-33-A, ¶ 94 (ICTY Appeals Chamber, April 19, 2004) (hesitating to rely independently on Deronjić's plea-bargained testimony in the proceedings against Krstić owing to discrepancies in Deronjić's testimony and the ambiguity surrounding some of the statements he had made).

132. *See, e.g., Prosecutor v. Sikirica*, Case No. IT-95-8-S, ¶ 149 (ICTY Trial Chamber, Nov. 13, 2001) ("... a guilty plea contributes directly to one of the fundamental objectives of the international tribunal: namely, its truth-finding function"); *Prosecutor v. Todorović*, Case No. IT-95-9/1-S, ¶ 81 (ICTY Trial Chamber, July 31, 2001) (stating that "a guilty plea is always important for the purpose of establishing the truth in relation to a crime").

133. *Prosecutor v. Deronjić*, Case No. IT-02-61-S, ¶ 4 (ICTY Trial Chamber, March 30, 2004) (Schomburg, J., dissenting).

134. Combs, *International Decisions, op. cit.*, at 931. Other cases where charges were dropped include *Prosecutor v. Bisengimana*, Case No. ICTR-00-60-T, ¶¶ 136–137 (ICTR Trial Chamber, April 13, 2006); *Prosecutor v. Mrdja*, Case No. IT-02-59-S, ¶¶ 4–5 (ICTY Trial Chamber, March 31, 2004) (dropping charge of crime against humanity as part

of the plea bargain). Babić also pled guilty to one count of persecution as a crime against humanity in exchange for agreement by the ICTY Prosecutor to drop four other charges. *Babic Admits Persecuting Croats*, BBC News (Jan. 27, 2004), *available at* http://news.bbc.co.uk/2/hi/europe/3433721.stm.

135. Combs, *Procuring Guilty Pleas, op. cit.*, at 91.

136. *Id.* at 91–92.

7. FROM LAW TO JUSTICE

1. Paul Roberts, *Restoration and Retribution in International Criminal Justice: An Exploratory Analysis*, in Restorative Justice and Criminal Justice 115, 119 (von Hirsch et al., eds. 2002).

2. Martti Koskenniemi, *International Law in Europe: Between Tradition and Renewal*, 16 Eur. J. Int'l L. 113, 114 (2005); Martti Koskenniemi, The Gentle Civilizer of Nations: The Rise and Fall of International Law 1870–1960 (2001).

3. Koskenniemi, *International Law in Europe, op. cit.*, at 115. It is important to differentiate universality from universalism. "[U]niversalism is the attempt to eliminate particularity and achieve uniformity at [the] global level; 'universality' is the attempt to bring out and develop the global resonance of particular ideas." Susan Marks & Andrew Clapham, International Human Rights Lexicon 398 (2005).

4. Stuart Hampshire, Innocence and Experience 90 (1989). Hampshire describes these "great evils" as follows: "murder and the destruction of life, imprisonment, enslavement, starvation, poverty, physical pain and torture, homelessness, friendlessness." *Id.* He thus writes well beyond the proscriptions of international criminal law.

5. David Luban, *Intervention and Civilization: Some Unhappy Lessons of the Kosovo War*, in Global Justice and Transnational Politics 79, 103 (De Greiff & Cronin eds., 2002). The unique moral gravity of genocide is set out in Richard J. Bernstein, Radical Evil: A Philosophical Interrogation (2002). *See also* David Hirsch, The Law Against Genocide: Cosmopolitan Trials 156 (2003) (observing that "there is no one who argues that genocide is traditional in a particular 'culture' [. . .] there is universal agreement that a social formation, a group of people, must not be allowed to murder entire populations").

6. Larry May, Crimes Against Humanity 22 (2005) (finding such a justification by reference "to the security principle, the international harm principle, *jus cogens* norms, and the international rule of law").

7. *The State of Israel v. Adolf Eichmann* (Sup. Ct. Israel, May 29, 1962), 36 Int'l L. Rep. 277, 287, 291 (1968).

8. To be sure, not all scholarly communities adopt the *legal* definition of these crimes (at least this has been my experience). Historians, political scientists, and anthropologists may define genocide somewhat differently. Also, in some cases (for example, crimes against humanity), these definitions have evolved over time.

9. The line between procedure and substance is not watertight. Procedure can affect substance; substance can affect procedure.

10. May, Crimes, *op. cit.*, at 252.

11. I use the term path dependence crudely. For a sophisticated treatment of path dependence, *see* Oona Hathaway, *Path Dependence in the Law: The Course and Pattern of Change in a Common Law Legal System*, 86 Iowa L. Rev. 601 (2001). Path dependence has considerable potential as an analytic tool. One possible direction for future research is to explore whether other areas of international law, for example economic relations or environmental protection, derive from dominant national practices and, if so, to contrast this process of diffusion with that of international criminal law.

12. May, Crimes, *op. cit.*, at 175.

13. *Id. See also* David Chuter, WAR CRIMES: CONFRONTING ATROCITY IN THE MODERN WORLD 94, 96–97 (2003).

14. Radhika Coomaraswamy, *Identity Within: Cultural Relativism, Minority Rights and the Empowerment of Women*, 34 GEO. WASH. INT'L L. REV. 483, 513 (2002).

15. Kant revisited cosmopolitanism as taught by the Cynics and Stoics. He invoked their teachings in his elucidation of the concept of cosmopolitan law. Immanuel Kant, POLITICAL WRITINGS (ed. Reiss, trans. Nisbet, 2d ed., 1991).

16. Summarizing the Stoic approach, Nussbaum writes that "[w]e need not give up our special affections and identifications, whether ethnic or gender-based or religious. We need not think of them as superficial, and we may think of our identity as constituted partly by them." Martha C. Nussbaum, *Patriotism and Cosmopolitanism, in* FOR LOVE OF COUNTRY? 9 (Nussbaum, 2002).

17. Nussbaum, *Patriotism and Cosmopolitanism, op. cit.*; Martha C. Nussbaum, *Reply, in* FOR LOVE OF COUNTRY? 131 (Nussbaum, 2002); Martha C. Nussbaum, *Kant and Cosmopolitanism, in* PERPETUAL PEACE: ESSAYS ON KANT'S COSMOPOLITAN IDEAL 25–57 (Bohman & Lutz-Bachmann eds., 1997); Martha C. Nussbaum, FRONTIERS OF JUSTICE: DISABILITY, NATIONALITY, SPECIES MEMBERSHIP (2006).

18. David Hollinger, POSTETHNIC AMERICA 84–85 (1995) (positing that cosmopolitans are receptive to "recognition, acceptance, and eager exploration of diversity" and, unlike universalists, do not view diversity as a problem).

19. David Held, DEMOCRACY AND THE GLOBAL ORDER: FROM THE MODERN STATE TO COSMOPOLITAN GOVERNANCE (1995).

20. Kok-Chor Tan, JUSTICE WITHOUT BORDERS: COSMOPOLITANISM, NATIONALISM, AND PATRIOTISM 102–105 (2004) (writing largely within the context of economic justice). *See also* Hirsch, *op. cit.* (constructing international criminal law as an incipient form of cosmopolitan law).

21. Kwame Anthony Appiah, COSMOPOLITANISM: ETHICS IN A WORLD OF STRANGERS xviii (2006) ("A creed that disdains the partialities of kinfolk and community may have a past, but it has no future.").

22. Paul Schiff Berman, *Seeing Beyond the Limits of International Law*, 84 TEX. L. REV. 1265 (2006).

23. Nussbaum, *Patriotism and Cosmopolitanism, op. cit.*, at 4.

24. *Id.* at 14.

25. Nussbaum, *Reply, op. cit.*, at 141.

26. *Id.* at 135.

27. Kwame Anthony Appiah, *Cosmopolitan Patriots, in* FOR LOVE OF COUNTRY? 22 (Nussbaum, 2002) (describing "rooted cosmopolitanism" and "cosmopolitan patriotism").

28. Appiah, COSMOPOLITANISM, *op. cit.*, at xxi. By moving international law from its focus on states to include a vision of individuals as independent moral actors, and then bestowing international legal personality upon individuals, the ICC propounds a cosmopolitan conception of international law.

29. Berman, *Seeing Beyond, op. cit.*, at 1303–1304. *See also* Paul Schiff Berman, *Towards a Cosmopolitan Vision of Conflict of Laws: Redefining Government Interests in a Global Era*, 153 U. PA. L. REV. 1819, 1821–1823 (2005) (considering cosmopolitanism in choice of law and civil procedure).

30. Berman, *Seeing Beyond, op. cit.*, at 1304–1305. For a general discussion, *see also* Jeremy Waldron, *Minority Cultures and the Cosmopolitan Alternative*, 25 U. MICH. J. L. REFORM 751 (1992).

31. This term is from Anthony Giddens, THE THIRD WAY: THE RENEWAL OF SOCIAL DEMOCRACY 66 (1998). Giddens writes within the starkly different context of reforming social democracy, specifically in Great Britain. He does include a chapter on the cosmopolitan nation and cultural pluralism, in which the term cosmopolitan pluralism is not developed.

32. For more detailed treatment of this argument, *see* Mark A. Drumbl, *Punishment, Postgenocide: From Guilt to Shame to Civis in Rwanda*, 75 N.Y.U. L. REV. 1221, 1224–1225 (2000). *See also* Jeremy Sarkin & Erin Daly, *Too Many Questions, Too Few Answers: Reconciliation in Transitional Societies*, 35 COLUM. HUM. RTS. L. REV. 661, 665–666 (2004) (positing that the meaning of reconciliation will be different in each society).

33. I personally do not see a convincing empirical or experiential basis for such a conclusion.

34. Mattias Kumm, *The Legitimacy of International Law: A Constitutionalist Framework of Analysis*, 15 EUR. J. INT'L L. 907, 921 (2004).

35. Yuval Shany, *Toward a General Margin of Appreciation Doctrine in International Law?*, 16 EUR. J. INT'L L. 907, 907 (2005).

36. *Id.* at 910, 939.

37. Mark A. Drumbl, *Collective Violence and Individual Punishment: The Criminality of Mass Atrocity*, 99 Nw. U. L. REV. 539, 610 (2005), my use of this term reprised in Harvey M. Weinstein & Eric Stover, *Introduction: conflict, justice, and reclamation*, in MY NEIGHBOR, MY ENEMY: JUSTICE AND COMMUNITY IN THE AFTERMATH OF MASS ATROCITY 1, 12 (Stover & Weinstein eds., 2004).

38. For example, the Eichmann trial was widely televised.

39. Michael Slote explores virtue ethics through the writings of Hutcheson, Hume, and Martineau. *See* Michael Slote, *War Crimes and Virtue Ethics*, in WAR CRIMES AND COLLECTIVE WRONGDOING 77 (Jokić ed., 2001).

40. Anthony Ellis, *Introduction*, in WAR CRIMES AND COLLECTIVE WRONGDOING 1, 14 (Jokić ed., 2001). *See also* Slote, *op. cit.*, at 81 (noting that a morality of war crimes based on sentimentalist virtue ethics will, in determining what is just, "look to what people (notably but not exclusively legislators) are trying to do with a nation's future" [emphasis omitted]).

41. "[A] basic tenet of social reconstruction or reclamation is the need for post-war communities to define and take ownership of the processes of justice and reconciliation." Weinstein & Stover, *Introduction: conflict, justice and reclamation, op. cit.*, at 18. Moreover, as I have argued should be the case in Afghanistan, international criminal law interventions would do well to encourage the inclusion of all community members in the processes by which community norms are edified. Mark A. Drumbl, *Rights, Culture, and Crime: The Role of Rule of Law for the Women of Afghanistan*, 42 COLUM. J. TRANSNAT'L L. 349 (2004). Many local customs to which international law understandably expresses considerable reticence are in fact promulgated by elites unrepresentative of local populations or religious leaders unrepresentative of the members of religious communities. By fostering access to the construction of representative local norms instead of binarily opposing extant local norms to international standards and then imposing those international standards, international legal intercessions can help overcome the democratic deficit. Instead of encouraging mimicry by national institutions that may pursue ulterior motives, perhaps international criminal law intercessions can empower locally.

42. The XVIIth International Congress of Penal Law (Beijing, China, September 2004), Resolutions, Section IV, Concurrent National and International Criminal Jurisdiction and the Principle "Ne bis in idem," Part I, General Principles 1, 2 (on file with the author).

43. *Id.*

44. For additional background information on the atrocities in the Sudan, *see* Beth Van Schaack, *Darfur and the Rhetoric of Genocide*, 26 WHITTIER L. REV. 1101 (2005); Rosanna Lipscomb, *Restructuring the ICC Framework to Advance Transitional Justice: A Search for a Permanent Solution in Sudan*, 106 COLUM. L. REV. 182 (2006).

45. *Janjaweed* literally means devils on horses.

46. United Nations, International Commission of Inquiry on Darfur, *Report to the United Nations Secretary-General*, pursuant to Security Council Resolution 1564 (January 25, 2005).

47. S.C. Res. 1593 (March 31, 2005) (United States, China, Algeria, and Brazil abstaining). Sudan is not a party to the Rome Statute. The Sudan referral is therefore an example of how the ICC can act like an ad hoc tribunal in situations where the Security Council finds a breach of the peace, threat to the peace, or an act of aggression. Resolution 1593 did consider "the possibility of conducting proceedings in the region." *Id.* ¶ 3.

48. *Sudanese President Vows to Defy U.N. Vote*, WASHINGTON POST (April 3, 2005) at A30.

49. Elizabeth Rubin, *If Not Peace, Then Justice*, NEW YORK TIMES MAGAZINE 43, 44–45 (April 2, 2006).

50. On August 13, 2005, a Sudanese court convicted three low-level members of the Sudanese Army of "waging war" in Darfur. *Show Trials are Not Substitutes for International Criminal Courts*, Damanga Statement, SUDAN TRIBUNE (August 23, 2005) (on file with the author). This court, referred to as the Darfur Special Criminal Court, was specially established by decree of the Sudanese government to prosecute individuals for crimes committed in Darfur. *Id.* On November 18, 2005, this court sentenced two soldiers to death for torturing and killing civilians. High-level defendants have not yet been implicated. Victims' rights groups are concerned that trials conducted in the Sudan do not do justice to victims nor prevent the government from continuing to perpetrate atrocities against its own population.

51. For a much broader discussion of the *Pashtunwali, see* Drumbl, *Rights, Culture, and Crime, op. cit.*

52. For example, in 2006, Afghanistan's National Security Court convicted a former head of intelligence and deputy prime minister of war crimes and sentenced him to death by shooting for killing hundreds of people during communist rule. Yousuf Azimy, *Afghan Court Sentences Former Spy Chief to Death* (Reuters, Feb. 25, 2006) (on file with the author). Afghans generally view state courts as corrupt.

53. The use of young girls as chits to settle feuds is practiced elsewhere, even where officially illegal. In November 2005, a village council in Pakistan decreed that five young women should be "abducted, raped or killed" for refusing to honor marriages that "were part of a compensation agreement ordered by the village council and reached at gunpoint after the father of one of the girls shot dead a family rival." Isambard Wilkinson, *Blood Debt Women Offered Up for Rape*, THE TELEGRAPH (UK) (November 22, 2005). At the time of the agreement, the girls ranged in age from six to thirteen years old. Compensatory arrangements that involve handing over women to resolve disputes are called *vani* in this region of Pakistan. *Vani* has been banned by the Pakistani Parliament, but this ban "has been widely ignored." *Id.*

54. Drumbl, *Rights, Culture, and Crime, op. cit.*, at 386–88. *See also generally* Isobel Coleman, *Women, Islam, and the New Iraq*, 85:1 FOREIGN AFFAIRS 24, 25–26 (January/February 2006) (discussing the views of scholars that the content of certain Islamic laws emerged from "selective interpretation by patriarchal leaders and a mingling of Islamic teachings with tribal customs and traditions" undertaken historically for purposes of consolidating the control exercised by such leaders).

55. June 2006.

56. John F. Burns, *Hussein Lawyer Seized and Slain in Baghdad Raid*, N.Y. TIMES (June 22, 2006); Joshua Partlow & Bassam Sebti, *Hussein Defense Lawyer Kidnapped, Killed*, WASHINGTON POST (June 21, 2006); Sabrina Tavernise & Christine Hauser, *Another Lawyer in Hussein's Trial Is Slain by Gunmen*, N.Y. TIMES (Nov. 8, 2005).

57. John F. Burns, *Hussein's Trial Resumes in Baghdad*, N.Y. TIMES (Nov. 28, 2005).

58. Another example involves the United Nations Security Council's unanimous resolution to transfer Charles Taylor to The Hague to be tried by the Special Court for Sierra Leone sitting in the ICC's courtroom facilities. *See* Security Council Resolution 1688 (June 16, 2006). Sweden and the U.K. have promised to jail Taylor if he is ultimately convicted. Sierra Leonean officials fear that the prosecution of Charles Taylor in Freetown would destabilize the region.

59. Rwanda has fairly tranquilly conducted ten thousand prosecutions in the Specialized Chambers of the national courts.

60. *See generally* Donald Francis Donovan & Anthea Roberts, *The Emerging Recognition of Universal Civil Jurisdiction*, 100 Am. J. Int'l L. 142, 153 (2006).

61. *Id.* at 142.

62. There is limited coordination between the ICJ and the various international criminal courts with regard to the consistent development of substantive law.

63. Whether through private law or extrajudicial mechanisms.

64. Just because a justice initiative is restorative in nature does not necessarily equate it with collective sanction. Restorative justice can narrowly focus on individuals with the level of proven guilt that a liberal criminal trial would require.

65. In its 1993 judgment in *Aloeboetoe et al. Case (Reparations)*, the InterAmerican Court of Human Rights awarded monetary damages to victims of a massacre in a tribal village in Suriname. Suriname had admitted its liability, so the dispute proceeded to issues of compensation and reparation. One of the points of dispute was whether customary tribal law or Suriname's civil law applied. The InterAmerican Commission on Human Rights asserted that tribal law applied and that the application of tribal law would permit group recovery for the tribe as a whole. *Aloeboetoe et al. Case (Reparations)*, Judgment (September 10, 1993), ¶¶ 55, 81, 83. The InterAmerican Court, however, refused to award damages to the tribe as a whole and, instead, awarded damages individually where claims were proved to be causally related to the harms. I thank Diane Marie Amann for this reference. The ICC Rules are responsive to this issue, in that they permit reparations to be awarded on an "individualized basis" or, where the ICC "deems it appropriate, on a collective basis or both." ICC R.P. & Evid. Rule 97(1), *available at* http://www.icc-cpi.int/library/basicdocuments/rules(e).pdf.

66. *See supra* Chapter 2.

67. Such state criminal responsibility is not accepted by publicists (for example, the International Law Commission). James Crawford, *The drafting of the Rome Statute*, in From Nuremberg to The Hague 109, 116 (Sands ed., 2003).

68. Mark A. Drumbl *Pluralizing International Criminal Justice*, 103 Mich. L. Rev. 1295 (2005) (spooling out the differences among collective guilt, collective responsibility, and collective liability); Hannah Arendt, *Collective Responsibility*, in Responsibility and Judgment (Kohn ed., 2003). For further discussion of collective responsibility, *see* Joel Feinberg, *Collective Responsibility*, 65 Journal of Phil. 674 (1968); Larry May, Sharing Responsibility (1992).

69. With one exception: where every member of the group actually contributed equally to the wrongdoing, and did so through pertinent positive action. "There is nothing wrong in principle with the idea of assigning guilt to an entire population, assuming that everyone has indeed engaged in the same transgression. As Arendt points out, that is the situation in the Biblical story of the towns of Sodom and Gomorrah...." May, Crimes, *op. cit.*, at 161.

70. As a criminal law doctrine, joint criminal enterprise obviously involves culpability, not responsibility.

71. *See* Application of the Convention on the Prevention and Punishment of the Crime of Genocide (*Bosn. & Herz. v. Yugo.*), 1993 I.C.J. 3 (Apr. 8). The (former) FRY had filed a counterclaim in 1997 (which it withdrew on September 10, 2001), in which it requested the ICJ adjudge that Bosnia and Herzegovina was responsible for the genocide of Serbs. *See* Order, Case Concerning Application of the Convention on the Prevention and Punishment of the Crime of Genocide (*Bosn. & Herz. v. Yugo.*), 2001 I.C.J. 91 (Sept. 13).

72. The Confederation of Serbia and Montenegro was dissolved in May 2006 when, following a plebiscite, Montenegro narrowly voted for independence. Serbia now is the successor state to Serbia and Montenegro.

73. *See* Application of the Convention on the Prevention and Punishment of the Crime of Genocide (*Croat. v. Yugo.*), 1999 I.C.J. 118 (July 2) (alleging that Serbia and Montenegro remains liable for infringements of the Genocide Convention by virtue of the activities of

FRY armed forces and paramilitary detachments on the territory of Croatia from 1991 to 1995).

74. Case Concerning Application of the Convention on the Prevention and Punishment of the Crime of Genocide (*Bosn. & Herz. v. Yugo.*), I.C.J. General List No. 91 (July 11, 1996) (preliminary objections).

75. *Id.* ¶ 32.

76. *Id.*, joint declaration of Judge Shi and Judge Vereshchetin (emphasis in original).

77. *Id.*

78. Marko Milanović, *State Responsibility for Genocide*, 17 EUR. J. INT'L L. 553, 589 (2006).

79. The ICJ may rule in favor of Serbia and Montenegro. It may do so by concluding that there was no genocide in Bosnia as a whole (which is the thrust of Bosnia and Herzegovina's claim) or at Srebrenica specifically (the latter finding would entail disagreement with the ICTY's finding that genocide occurred at Srebrenica). Obversely, if the ICJ were to rule that genocide occurred in Bosnia as a whole, this, too, would diverge from the ICTY's approach. The ICJ is not bound to follow the ICTY although, formally, ICTY judgments are "judicial decisions" and, hence, constitute a subsidiary source of international law. *See* Statute of the International Court of Justice, 59 Stat. 1055, art. 38(1)(d) (June 26, 1945). Alternately, the ICJ may dismiss the Bosnian claim on the basis that genocidal intent cannot be attributed to the state of Serbia and Montenegro, or that the state had no control over perpetrators found to have genocidal intent. The ICJ may even avoid these difficult questions entirely and dismiss based on other grounds, possibly including – in a maneuver that smacks of avoidance doctrine – revisiting jurisdiction. The groundwork for such a maneuver already may have been laid in 2004 by virtue of how a majority of the ICJ disposed of Serbia and Montenegro's claims against certain NATO states. Case Concerning the Legality of Use of Force (*Serb. & Mont. v. Belgium et al.*), ICJ General List No. 105 et al. (December 14, 2004). Serbia and Montenegro had filed suit regarding alleged violations of international law triggered by what it argued was an unlawful use of force by a number of NATO countries involved in the "humanitarian armed intervention" bombings of the FRY in 1999. Although all ICJ judges agreed that the preliminary objections as to jurisdiction should be granted (and the claim dismissed), a number of judges disagreed with the reasoning of the majority insofar as it related to the Genocide Convention. Seven judges noted in a joint declaration that the majority's approach "appears to leave some doubt as to whether Yugoslavia was a party, between 1992 and 2000, to the United Nations Genocide Convention. Such an approach could call into question the solutions adopted by the Court with respect to its jurisdiction in the case brought by Bosnia-Herzegovina against Serbia and Montenegro for the application of the Genocide Convention." Joint Declaration of Vice-President Ranjeva, Judges Guillaume, Higgins, Kooijmans, Al-Khasawneh, Buergenthal, and Elaraby, ¶ 13. *See also* Separate Opinion of Judge Higgins, ¶ 18; Separate Opinion of Judge Elaraby, Part V.

80. Thomas Franck, *State Responsibility in the Era of Individual Criminal Culpability*, Butterworth Lecture, Queen Mary, University of London, Department of Law (October 10, 2005) pp. 19–20 (earlier draft manuscript on file with the author). Franck considers that acts attributed to the state "are the acts of the society as a whole unless it can be shown that the conditions of governance in that state, at the critical time when genocide was being planned and executed, were such that the people, by asserting their power, could not have resisted." *Id.* at p. 18. Mark Osiel is similarly minded. "When state-sponsored mass atrocity enjoys the substantial support of a country's population, its citizens should share the costs of redressing it. This is especially true when the regime perpetrating the atrocities was relatively democratic, responsive to popular will, like Serbia during the Balkan wars." Mark Osiel, *The Banality of Good: Aligning Incentives Against Mass Atrocity*, 105 COLUM. L. REV. 1751, 1841 (2005).

81. Examples include: corporate law, including litigation against corporations under the Alien Tort Claims Act (affecting shareholders not responsible for and generally with no influence

over corporate action); law of agency; insurance law; social host liability; and professional responsibility. *See also* George Fletcher, *Liberals and Romantics at War: The Problem of Collective Guilt*, 111 YALE L. J. 1499, 1536 (2002).

82. *See, e.g.*, Daryl J. Levinson, *Collective Sanctions*, 56 STAN. L. REV. 345 (2003) (discussing collective legal sanctions against groups in nonWestern societies). The United Nations Security Council has invoked some of the harshest kinds of collective sanctions, for example the imposition of economic sanctions on a state and monitoring of a state's activities.

83. *See, e.g.*, Case Concerning Armed Activities on the Territory of the Congo (*Democratic Republic of the Congo v. Uganda*), International Court of Justice (ICJ General List, No. 116, December 19, 2005) (final judgment).

84. *Id.* ¶ 345. The ICJ did engage in a form of avoidance doctrine when it came to ignoring the DRC's claim that Uganda committed aggression and should be responsible therefore. On February 3, 2006, the ICJ dismissed upon jurisdictional grounds a claim brought to it by the DRC against Rwanda regarding violence on Congolese territory that might have overlapped with the ICC's investigations. International Court of Justice, Press Release 2006/4, Armed Activities on the Territory of the Congo (*Democratic Republic of the Congo v. Rwanda*, 2002) (February 3, 2006).

85. Drumbl, *Pluralizing International Criminal Justice, op. cit.*, at 1315–1319, 1322. For an example of one author's difficulties in distinguishing guilt from responsibility, and resultant essentialization of my work, *see* Lars Waldorf, *Mass Justice for Mass Atrocity: Rethinking Local Justice as Transitional Justice*, 79 TEMP. L. REV. 1, 83 (2006).

86. Fletcher actually develops his analysis within the context of collective guilt instead of collective responsibility. Fletcher, *Liberals and Romantics at War, op. cit.* (arguing that collective guilt actually has a sound grounding in Western culture); George P. Fletcher, *Collective Guilt and Collective Punishment*, 5 THEORETICAL INQUIRIES IN LAW 163, 168, 169, 173–174 (2004) (assuming that collective guilt is a "plausible [. . .] and sometimes healthy response to collective wrongdoing" and discussing the biblical reference in Genesis in which ten of Joseph's brothers come to the collective conclusion that they are guilty for having ignored their brother's cries of pain).

87. "[C]ollective responsibility can sometimes be more productive of societal healing and harmony than is the accusation and counter-accusation of the criminal trial's attempt to establish individual responsibility." May, CRIMES, *op. cit.*, at 246.

88. Osiel, *The Banality of Good, op. cit.*, at 1839–1840. Osiel is one of the few scholars to explore the role of incentives, monitoring, and policing in contexts of mass atrocity. His ultimate proposal – the imposition of monetary sanctions on the military officer corps – is fairly modest.

89. James Waller, BECOMING EVIL: HOW ORDINARY PEOPLE COMMIT GENOCIDE AND MASS KILLING 205 (2002).

90. Matthew Krain, *International Intervention and the Severity of Genocides and Politicides*, 49 INT'L STUD. Q. 363, 383 (2005).

8. CONCLUSION: SOME IMMEDIATE IMPLICATIONS

1. The expression is from Frank O. Bowman III, *The Failure of the Federal Sentencing Guidelines: A Structural Analysis*, 105 COLUM. L. REV. 1315, 1327 (2005).

2. Laurel E. Fletcher, *From Indifference to Engagement: Bystanders and International Criminal Justice*, 26 MICH. J. INT'L L. 1013 (2005).

3. M. Cherif Bassiouni, INTRODUCTION TO INTERNATIONAL CRIMINAL LAW 703 (2003).

Index

CPSIA information can be obtained at www.ICGtesting.com
Printed in the USA
BVOW03s1714050115

381834BV00001B/1/P

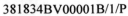